Russian Culture, Property Rights, and the Market Economy

The Russian Federation is struggling, since Perestroika and the Glasnost, in a futile attempt to become a "normal" member in the occidental family of market economies. The attempt largely fails because corporations do not live up to Western standards of behavior, and private contracts are often not respected. What is the cause of Russia's observed difficulties? It is commonly believed that these difficulties are an expected outcome of a rocky transition from a Marxist centrally planned system to a market-based economy. This book challenges the accepted wisdom. In tracing the history of contract and corporation in the West, it shows that the cultural infrastructure that gave rise to these patterns of economic behavior have never taken root in Russian soil. This deep divide between Russian and Western cultures is hundreds of years old and has little, if anything, to do with the brief seventy-year-long experimentation with overtly Marxist ideology. The transformation of Russia into a veritable market economy requires much more than an expensive and difficult transition period: It mandates a radical change in Russia's cultural underpinnings. The book's main thesis is supported by an in-depth comparison of Western and Russian theology, philosophy, literary and artistic achievements, musical and architectural idioms, and folk culture.

Uriel Procaccia is a professor of law at the Interdisciplinary Center in Israel. He is also a long-term visiting professor of law at the Benjamin N. Cardozo Law School in New York City and a member of the Rationality Center at the Hebrew University of Jerusalem. He previously acted as Dean of the Law School at the Hebrew University of Jerusalem. He has written numerous books in Hebrew, including a major work on the theory of corporate law and a major text on the law of bankruptcy.

The publisher gratefully acknowledges the support of the Jacob Burns Institute of Advanced Legal Studies of the Benjamin N. Cardozo School of Law for the publication of this book.

Russian Culture, Property Rights, and the Market Economy

URIEL PROCACCIA
The Interdisciplinary Center Herzliya

 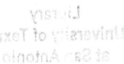

CAMBRIDGE
UNIVERSITY PRESS

CAMBRIDGE UNIVERSITY PRESS
Cambridge, New York, Melbourne, Madrid, Cape Town, Singapore, São Paulo

Cambridge University Press
32 Avenue of the Americas, New York, NY 10013-2473, USA

www.cambridge.org
Information on this title: www.cambridge.org/9780521835060

First published 2007

Printed in the United States of America

A catalog record for this publication is available from the British Library.

Library of Congress Cataloging in Publication Data

Procaccia, Uriel.
Russian culture, property rights, and the market economy / Uriel Procaccia.
    p.   cm.
Includes bibliographical references and index.
ISBN-13: 978-0-521-83506-0
ISBN-10: 0-521-83506-2
1. Capitalism – Russia (Federation)   2. Contracts – Russia (Federation)   3. Right of property –
Russia (Federation)   4. Russia (Federation) – Economic conditions – 1991–   5. Russia
(Federation) – Social conditions – 1991–   6. Post-communism – Russia (Federation)   I. Title.
HC340.12.P7692   2007
330.947–dc22   2006019641

ISBN   978-0-521-83506-0 hardback

For Anat, Orren, Yuval, Gail, and Ronni

Contents

Preface

The last three decades of the twentieth century and the first few years of our own witnessed a profound change in the face of legal scholarship. A largely scholastic, rule-oriented discipline was transformed almost overnight into an inductive, policy-oriented science informed by a variety of insights liberally borrowed from other disciplines. This transformation was occasioned by a sudden realization that *legal* rules are designed to regulate *nonlegal* aspects of life (commerce and industry, family relationships, morals, or the public domain). This perennial interplay between the regulating discipline (law) and the various regulated states of the world (everything else) imposed a new challenge for lawyers, especially academic lawyers. To be proficient in their job, they had to thoroughly familiarize themselves not only with the crafting of rules or with technical skills of interpretation, but also with the various aspects of human existence that are regulated by law but are, by the same token, largely informed by a variety of other forces (love or envy, economic incentives, social pressures, religious convictions, age, prejudice, fear, or scientific discovery).

Perhaps the most sweeping of these reformist movements was an enormous tide of scholarship in the interface of law and economics. Broadly speaking, this new branch of learning seeks to apply economic insights to patterns of behavior regulated by law. It is designed to guide legislators, judges, and interpreters of the law to seek solutions that take into account not only the initial formal injunctions of the legal system, but also their final incidence, given the expected economic behavior of the affected players. Side by side with the law and economics movement, a variety of other interdisciplinary methods came to the fore including, *inter alia*, law and psychology, law and the humanities (literature, theater, music), law and sociology, law and linguistics, and in short, as this plethora of new learning is often referred to, "Law and."

The "Law and" revolution liberated the legal system from its puerile dream of self-sufficiency, of the once canonic illusion that optimal rules could be generated by their own internal manipulation, by "pure" law or lawyering, or by the system's own "principled" consistency. Now we all know better. We realize, for example, that antitrust laws are about imperfect competition, or that the sentencing of offenders is about the sociology of deviant behavior or about some formulation of moral philosophy. This is, without a doubt, a gigantic step forward. Nonetheless, a truly radical transformation of the concept of law is still in the embryonic stage. The world is a complex nexus of phenomena. The regulated extra-legal sphere cannot easily be pigeonholed; law rarely interacts "only" with economic behavior, or exclusively with deviant or criminal impulses, or with the internal governance of civic institutions to the exclusion of everything else. It often concerns all of these and many other things to boot. The "Law and" movement still falls short of fulfilling its mission because most of its practitioners are normally content to see the law through the prism of a single nonlegal discipline (e.g., economics, psychology, music), rather than in a multidisciplinary configuration that brings into focus insights from as many relevant bodies of knowledge as possible. There is a clear need to move in that direction. This book is a humble attempt to rise to that challenge.

I am painfully aware that any attempt to combine numerous disciplines in a single academic thrust is a very tall order. Nevertheless, daring attempts must be contemplated on occasion and insisted on when they are crucial for the validity of the results. This volume was crafted with this objective in mind, because I sensed that a single-pronged interdisciplinary inquiry of contract, its history, and the numerous formative factors that fashion its ultimate configuration within any given culture would almost surely miss the mark. The practical question that quickened the whole project was whether an appropriate set of incentives (and a large monetary investment) could transform Russia from a centrally planned society to a "Western" market economy with privatized industry, civic institutions of a Western democratic ilk, secure property rights, and routinely enforceable contracts. Since the question thus formulated has to do with "incentives," it was often considered from a Western economic perspective by a formidable army of (Western) theoreticians. The Russian government, in turn, was eager to hire them for advice and assistance. Large amounts of money were then invested to ease existing budgetary constraints, and enormous payoffs were made available to lure enterprise and entrepreneurship. Policy makers were content to delegate to the relevant players the role of maximizing their utility. They trusted the "invisible hand" to transform their individual self-regarding strategies into an aggregate Social Good. Superficially, the players did what was expected of them, but the final outcome turned out to be a far cry from the anticipated result. More than a decade after *Perestroika* and *Glasnost*, the Russian economy is still faltering; democracy is shaky; the securities markets are still a farce; privatization turned itself into a kleptocracy; and contract, the major foundation of all private law and all capitalistic institutions, is still unfathomable to the large bulk of the Russian nation. To understand what went wrong one need not try to find fault with the principles of Western neo-classical economics as such that were posited at the base of the reform. Rather, one should inquire why it was difficult to implement these principles on Russian soil. Clearly, the reaction of the Russian people to "Western" incentives was heavily conditioned by the history, culture, and life experiences of the relevant players, which were radically different from the history, culture, and life experiences of Westerners.

In some important sense, then, this book is about law. It tries to explain why law in Russia is different from law in the West. Due to the huge economic effort that was invested in transforming Russia into a market economy, the book focuses on the choice of incentives that were designed to accomplish that goal. In that sense, the book is also about law and economics. But the main thrust of the book's thesis is to demonstrate the inadequacy of these incentives, given the very different social norms that animate Russian men and women in their quest to fulfill their deeper aspirations. In that respect, the book is about law *and* economics *and* culture, with a strong emphasis on the third and last element of this inseparable *troika*. I am firmly convinced that there is no other way.

I am deeply indebted to a large number of individuals who read some or all of my former drafts and generously offered their comments and observations. Special thanks are due to Maya Bar-Hillel, Lior Barshack, Peter Bouteneff, Lester Brickman, Hanna Caine-Braunschvig, Paul Cantor, David Carlson, Ellen Chirelstein, Marvin Chirelstein, Peter Goodrich, Zohar Goshen, David Heyd, Milly Heyd, Anat Horovitz, Arthur Jacobson, Yaacov Kariv, Hanna Kedar, Father Leonid Kishkovsky, Michael Kubovy, Nomi Levitsky, Stephen Morse, Yuval Procaccia, Anat Rosenberg, Michel Rosenfeld, Jeanne Schroeder, Uzi Segal, Paul Shupack, Richard Weisberg, Charles Yablon, and Dirk Zetzche. Iris Argaman provided invaluable service in handling the complex matter of the copyright permissions for the numerous images in this book. The Benjamin N. Cardozo School of Law and the Faculty of Law at the Hebrew University provided financial support, which made the research and eventual publication of this volume possible.

Introduction

The General Outline of the Book

In the bleak, dreary December of 1995, well after the introduction of *Perestroika* and *Glasnost*, I was invited to teach a short course in Moscow on what was loosely termed "capitalist law." My job was to initiate my young disciples into such Western ideas as the corporate form, commercial paper, and the other main subjects of *lex mercatoria*, broadly defined. Having detected many a blank expression among their young, eager faces, I quickly discerned the reason for their consternation: No one ever took the trouble to familiarize them with the fountainhead of all private law – contract. The law school curriculum was saturated, it turned out, with courses about such subjects as public law and criminal law. Private law in general, and contract law in particular, were conspicuously left out. Although the Russian Federation has a new civil code, which includes a hefty section on contract,[1] it does not appear to fare very well within the

---

[1] Vladimir Toumanov, "Freedom of Contract and Constitutional Law in Russia," in A. M. Rabello and P. Sarcevic (eds.), *Freedom of Contract and Constitutional Law*, Jerusalem: Harry Sacher Institute, 241 (1998). Toumanov speaks about present-day freedom of contract in Russia as a foregone conclusion. His own documentary evidence for this claim, however, leaves much room for doubt. Although Article 8 of the Constitution of the Russian Federation guarantees the freedom of *economic activity* (an inherently ambiguous term), the Constitution does not appear to refer directly to freedom of *contract*. The new Civil Code has (only) one telling reference to this term. It now reads: "Citizens and legal entities shall freely conclude contracts. Compulsory conclusion of contract is not allowed, except in particular cases where the responsibility to conclude a contract is stipulated by the present Code, law or an obligation that was voluntarily undertaken." The message of this section can be easily understood if examined against the backdrop of the former Soviet legal regime. Under Soviet law, "citizens and legal entities" were indeed forced to enter into legal obligations, farcically called "contracts," e.g., for the provision of certain production quotas. For a clear account of this "contractual" period, see Allan Farnsworth and Viktor Mozolin, *Contract Law in the USSR and the United States*, Lanham, MD: University Press of America, Volume 1, pp. 12ff (1987). The new Code frees all Russians of this coerced relationship, which is a significant step forward, but hardly an internalization of the ethos of contractual freedom.

Russian academic circles. Several of my Russian colleagues (law professors, as it were) had only a very fleeting notion of what contract law might be all about, and an astounding lack of curiosity to find out. One could simply not engage them in a meaningful conversation about such a lackluster topic. I then took to the frosty, snow-covered streets of the capital, where a lively, although, by Western standards, primitive private economy was then shaping up. I could not fail to notice that all the transactions that were visible to the naked eye were either barter transactions or "real" (spot) contracts, that is, involving instantaneous exchanges of goods for cash. All cash payments were closely scrutinized for fear of counterfeit. No personal checks were ever accepted as means of payment. Russian banks, it turned out, did not issue checkbooks to their customers. No one, not even luxurious (and immensely pricey) hotels in downtown Moscow would accept travelers' checks as a means of payment, although both Moscow and St. Petersburg boasted one location each where travelers' checks could be cashed out by the American Express Company. It then occurred to me that Russian law schools were not interested in coaching their students in the intricacies of contract law, because Russians were not keen to engage in contractual behavior. The state did not encourage contractual behavior by generating tools of commerce (checks, letters of credit, a credible securities market), nor did it establish a good record as an enforcer of broken promises. As I observed the ordinary Russian people in their shops and farms, in their humble sidewalk booths, and in their plush modern establishments, these folks simply did not contract.[2]

---

[2] One immediately apparent reason for shunning contracts as a means of alienating rights within Russian society has to do with the widespread corruption of the bureaucracy and the court system. If to win a case one has to be more efficient than one's adversary in either bribing the judge or intimidating her, there seems to be very little significance to nominal promises. This insight, of a potentially unbridgeable gap between promise and performance, led some thoughtful reformers to suggest that Russia adopt private and commercial laws that are "self-enforcing," i.e., that do not have to rely on the court system for assistance in cases of repudiation and breach. See Bernard Black and Reinier Kraakman, "A Self-Enforcing Model of Corporate Law," *Harvard Law Review* 109:1912 (1996). This "self-enforcing" model that was suggested by Black and Kraakman (for more on "self enforcing" norms, see the next footnote) was actually acted on by the Russian authorities, and a new corporate code was especially crafted to accommodate its insights. But, like so many other well-intentioned Western-propelled blueprints for reform, it failed, as was readily conceded by its own authors: See Bernard Black, Reinier Kraakman, and Anna Tarassova, "Russian Privatization and Corporate Governance: What Went Wrong?" *Stanford Law Review* 52:1731 (2000). In this newer piece of scholarship, the authors suggested that no privatization of the Russian economy would ever materialize until the system is "cleansed" of the corrupt elements in its infrastructure; when the system is rotten to the core, even self-enforcement cannot resuscitate its failing spirit. In this book I wish to reach beyond this corruption-based explanation. How could one explain that Russian promisees were left at the mercy of corrupt officials with little or no hope of vindicating their just expectations? And why didn't the same corrupt system impede other advances of the human spirit, like art and the *belles lettres* or scientific achievement? It is submitted that bare promises, unlike science or literature, were not perceived as a subject worth fighting for; they fell prey to corruption due to their own intrinsic feebleness, rather than as a consequence of the contaminated nature of the enforcement system itself.

This does not imply, of course, that *some* contracts were not being negotiated, signed, and even kept on Russian soil. The country does have some
futures markets, where sellers get current consideration in exchange for post-
poned promises. Trading in oil futures is a good illustration of this necessity.
Many *commercial* enterprises (as distinguished from private individuals) must
trade promises to stay afloat the tide. Some major consumer transactions (e.g.,
buying an apartment or a house) cannot depend on instantaneous delivery of
the finished product. Most of these necessary transactions, however, take place
either among repeat players or among commercial enterprises. *Repeat players*
are economic actors who repeatedly offer the same kind of goods or services in
the same market and depend on their reputation for their long-term survival.
Repeat players are constrained to keep their promises regardless of the law's
command, and independently of the willingness of the state to come to the
rescue of disappointed promisees. Even in a state of absolute anarchy – "the
state of nature" in Hobbesian terms – repeat players would have an incentive
to keep their promises and to guarantee customer satisfaction.[3] Unsurprisingly,
Russian repeat players are commonly engaged in contractual relationships.[4]
Contracts among enterprises, also very common, are of great interest to the
outside observer. Following the demise of the socialist regime, it became apparent that the default rate of interenterprise debt was staggeringly high.[5] The
government tried to address this problem by allowing victims of contractual
breaches to obtain punitive damages at a *daily* rate of 0.5% of the value of their
claims. When the initial post-Communist hyperinflation was partially arrested,

[3] Contracts among repeat players are actually the prime example of "self-enforcing" legal norms,
i.e., of norms whose enforcement does not depend on the coercive effort of organized society. If
more than a single merchant offers the same kind of merchandise in a given community, none can
afford to deliver less than the stipulated bargain, because potential customers might move their
business elsewhere. This basic insight is well documented in the theoretical contract literature;
see, for example, Anthony Kronman, "Contract Law and the State of Nature," *Journal Law,
Economics and Organization* 1:5 (1985).

[4] In a famous article written in 1974, Marc Galanter offered a different view of the behavior of
repeat players, which he differentiated from "one shotters." Galanter suggested that the most
obvious characteristic of repeat players lies in their interest to maximize gains in the long run
(rather than in each individual transaction). Their main strategy is to adapt to new rules, legal
and otherwise, that can be used for the attainment of this goal, including a judicious use of the
legal system and the development of alternative dispute resolution techniques. See Marc Galanter,
"Why the 'Haves' Come Out Ahead: Speculations on the Limits of the Legal System," *Law and
Society Review* 9:95 (1974). In a recent article, it was suggested that Russian repeat players do not
conform to Galanter's model. They do not use restraint in suing defaulting debtors and are less
innovative in adapting to the changing legal environment than their Western counterparts. See
Kathryn Hendley, Peter Murrell, and Randi Ryterman, "Do 'Repeat Players' Behave Differently
in Russia? An Evaluation of Contractual and Litigation Behavior of Russian Enterprises," *Law
and Society Review* 33:833 (1999). It goes without saying that these empirical results do not
contradict the tautological assertion that repeat players engage in contractual behavior more
often than "one shotters."

[5] Kathryn Hendley, "Growing Pains: Balancing Justice and Efficiency in the Russian Economic
Courts," *Temple International and Comparative Law Journal* 12:303 (1998).

this rate assumed draconian proportions. Everybody, promisors and promisees alike, immediately responded impulsively and lawlessly to this effort to ensure contractual compliance. Promisees delayed their lawsuits to the last day of the statute of limitations, in order to obtain the largest possible penalty, although it was quite unrelated to their actual losses. Promisors simply did not pay the penalties (and, quite often, they did not pay the principal amount of their obligations, either). To force them to comply, the state promulgated a rule that penalties could be levied directly against the bank account of the defaulting enterprise. Numerous enterprises immediately responded by conducting their respective money transactions outside of the banking system. In the end, the state gave up and repealed its *imprimatur* of punitive damages.[6] In spite, then, of the numerous contracts that are negotiated, relied on, and even fulfilled in Russia today, Russian contracts, and Russian contract law, still rest on uniquely shaky foundations.

It is crucial to understand that to opt out of contract is not a trifling matter. The entire market economy is based on contracts. So is the process of privatization, and, indeed, in the Russian context, the hope for a prosperous future, freed from the yoke of a heavy-handed central planner. Obviously, there has never been a conscious decision to opt out of contract, certainly not on the national level.[7] This stark reality "forced itself," as it were, on Russian policy makers against their better judgment. As long as this reality lingers on,[8] however, it is hard to imagine how the Russian Federation can hope to get under way toward its much hoped-for economic recovery.[9]

[6] The different stages of this ongoing saga are narrated in detail in Kathryn Hendley, Peter Murrell, and Randi Ryterman, "Punitive Damages for Contractual Breaches in Comparative Perspective: The Use of Penalties by Russian Enterprises," *Wisconsin Law Review* 639 (2001). See also, David Campbell, "Breach and Penalty as Contractual Norm and Contractual Anomie," *Wisconsin Law Review* 681 (2001).

[7] Even the Soviet regime, during the reforms introduced by the Gorbachev administration, was painfully aware of the necessity to introduce market economy thinking, including contracts, to the Soviet Union as a means of revitalizing the economy. A new concept – a "law-based state" (*pravovoe gosudarstvo*) – was coined in preparation of a limited transition to the family of market economies. See, in general, Donald Barry (ed.), *Toward the "Rule of Law" in Russia? Political and Legal Reform in the Transition Period*, Armonk, NY: M. E. Sharpe (1992).

[8] Some commentators, the more optimistic, point to the possibility of enforcing some obligations in court (although conceding that most litigants prefer, based on their experience, extrajudicial forms of dispute resolution). The most insistent among them are Kathlyn Hendley, Peter Murrell, and Randi Ryterman. See their joint article, "A Regional Analysis of Transactional Strategies of Russian Enterprises," *McGill Law Journal* 44:434 (1999). Most commentators do not agree.

[9] The broad issue of where Russia is heading, from an economic point of view, is far from being settled. The first years of "transition" were not very good, and the entire economy approached a total state of collapse in August 1998, when Russia defaulted on its foreign debt. In the last months of 1998, and much more so during 1999, important macroeconomic steps were taken that resuscitated the Russian economy in many important respects. For a few years the economy grew at the robust annual rate of up to 6%, the external public debt declined, the stock market was revived, the fiscal balance turned around from a large deficit to a small surplus, and inflation was meaningfully curbed. Many of these positive developments, however, were probably linked to temporary causes such as the rise in the prices of oil worldwide and the

But is the Russian aversion to the idea of contract really a permanent feature of the country's legal culture? Many starry-eyed observers routinely claim that this may not be the case. They point to the fact that during the seventy-odd years of Socialist dictatorship, the ruling Soviet ideology repudiated private property, and the snubbing of contracts could be expected as an offshoot of the broader proposition. According to this point of view, it is only a matter of time until the old lore vanishes, making room, in its retreat, for the revival of secure property rights and of contracts.

The central theme of this book, however, is that this interpretation of history is both short-sighted and misleading. In my view, the Russian antipathy to contracts is much more deeply ingrained. It reflects a set of values that are as ancient as Christian Russia itself[10] and has its roots way back in the tenth

---

sharp devaluation of the ruble. Structural changes of the economy, including meaningful deregulation and a revival of the small business sector, have not been seriously attempted and most of the country's riches are accumulated in the hands of a few oligarchs, whose good fortunes are viewed with hostility by the general population. In more recent times, the economy has slumped again and many observers are concerned that the short revival of 1999–2002 is not a sustainable phenomenon, especially if the oil bonanza reverses itself and oil prices start to decline. See, generally, David Owen and David Robinson (eds.), *Russia Rebounds*, New York: International Monetary Fund (2003). As this manuscript goes to press there has been another revival of the Russian economy, mainly attributable to the unprecedented prices of oil in the world markets. But even this temporary improvement on the macroeconomic level has only marginal, if any effect on the observed data regarding the keeping of contractual promises. Surprisingly, some commentators do not share this view. According to at least one paper, the overall current record of contract enforcement in Russia roughly corresponds to the record of all but the most advanced legal systems. See Simeon Djankov, Rafael La Porta, Florencio Lopez-de-Salinas, and Andrei Sheleifer, *Courts*, World Bank publications online, http://www.doingbusiness.org/ExploreTopics/EnforcingContracts/Details.aspx?economyid=159. The authors' methodology seems to have left, however, a lot to be desired, as they relied completely on responses they solicited from local attorneys. In fact, the authors looked for evidence concerning the efficiency of enforcement of just two kinds of contracts, bounced checks and eviction of nonpaying tenants, and neglected to pay attention to the fact that Russian banks do not issue checks to their customers. Nor have they noticed the means of enforcement (in the case of tenant evictions) that hardly conform, on many occasions, to some of the basic tenets of the Rule of Law. A much more careful recent study has revealed that, "while problems with contract enforcement can occur in any economy, in the transitional Russian economy they have reached epidemic proportions." See Elena Vinogradova, "Working Around the State: Contract Enforcement in the Russian Context," *Socio-Economic Review* 4:447 (2006). An absorbing theoretical explanation for the Russian economy's difficulties to rise to the challenge of free markets is offered in Mancur Olson's posthumous work, *Power and Prosperity, Outgrowing Communism and Capitalist Dictatorships*, New York: Basic Books (2000). Olson's observations commonly assume, however, that the missing link between the Russian economy (and other unsuccessful economies) and prosperity is to be found in the structure of these economies, rather than in the deeper cultural reasons for the existing structure.

[10] This does not mean, of course, that Russia has never experienced brisk commercial periods in its history. Both Kiev in the south and some urban centers in the north, notably the ancient republic of Novgorod, dominated important trade routes to Scandinavia, Germany, Byzantium, and the Asiatic markets. Moreover, as late as the sixteenth century, travelers' accounts narrate village prosperity and construction boom in the cities to an extent unrivaled in the West. One

century. While history may teach us that no historical processes are ever irreversible, the transformation of this particular pattern of path dependency may involve a rather radical transformation of the Russian collective psyche and is not likely to transpire anytime soon. The benevolent Western world, which holds its breath in anticipation of the Russian integration into the larger family of contracting nations, with privatized institutions and a vibrant market economy, might have to continue to hold its breath for a long, long time.

It is not an easy task to identify a set of values or cultural tenets that uniquely characterizes a whole nation. They emerge out of its history, theology, art, and letters. They leave their mark on the spiritual achievements of the nation in science, politics, and war; in this volume I examine a large number of these cultural manifestations; a special emphasis is put on one glaring expression of the Russian spirit, the Orthodox Icon. As will become readily apparent, Russian Orthodox iconography far transcends its own (significant) artistic value. It is, in fact, a window into the Russian soul. Nor is it limited to a theological method of interpreting the world. It contains, in its own microcosmic form, an entire social order. This social order is designed to be immutable and to hold its ground against the changing *mores* and the ever-frivolous tides of time.

The normative justification of Western idea of contract is also based on an identifiable set of cultural assumptions. Contracts and icons can be pitted, then, one against the other, with our eyes set for discerning similarities on the one hand and inconsistencies on the other. My point is not that these two cultural constructs are merely *different*. Different entities can be united in marriage and thrive. The point is that icons and contracts are based on *incompatible* sets of values. Put differently, I maintain that an "icon society" cannot be, at the same time, a "contract society." As long as Russia is going to preserve its ancient affinity to the values represented by the Orthodox Icon, the market economy, privatization, and a host of other occidental manifestations of the human spirit will be kept at bay.

Here is my game plan, which I strive to keep as simple as possible. This introductory chapter contains a short essay on the centrality of the Orthodox

sixteenth-century traveler wrote that the whole territory between Moscow and Yaroslavl "abounds with little villages which are so full of people that it is surprising to look at them. The earth is all well-sown with grain, which the inhabitants bring to Moscow in such enormous quantities that it seems surprising." Another wrote: "Furs and wax are taken from there to Germany . . . and saddles, clothing, and leather from there to Tataria; weapons and iron are exported only by stealth or with special permission. . . . However, they export broadcloth and linen garments, axes, needles, mirrors, saddlebags, and other such goods." See Alexander Yanov, *The Origins of Autocracy*, pp. 2–3 (1981). The author is quick to comment, however, that this temporary wealth did not survive for more than a few decades and was quickly dissipated; without ever regaining its momentum, not later than 1571, when, as a result of the unfortunate Livonian War, Moscow was sacked by the Tatars. Many other cities were ravaged as well; their young warriors were slaughtered and many were imprisoned and enslaved. Nor is there any evidence that, even during the brief periods of commercial prosperity, were commercial contracts, involving future promises, executed between Russian traders and their domestic or foreign counterparts.

Icon in Russian culture.[11] It is an essential part of this exploration for at least two reasons. First, I wish to substantiate my claim that icons may be used as credible proxies for Russian culture in general. This claim is certainly not trivial, given the enormous contribution of the Russian genius to world culture in such diverse (and seemingly "Western," or universal) fields as literature, music, and dance, to name just a few examples. Second, I counter the possible contention that Russian icons are pan-Orthodox in nature as much as they reflect uniquely Russian cultural traits. True, the first icons were originally imported to Russia from ancient Byzantium. Similar icons were either imported to, or crafted in, the other vast territories of the Byzantine cultural sphere of influence, in such regions as Greece, Serbia, Bulgaria, and the Middle East. However, Russia developed, and brought to perfection, a wholly original iconographic style that sets it apart from its Byzantine origin. Serb icons, for instance, or those that remained in the Sinai Peninsula, with all their striking beauty and great spirituality, are decidedly un-Russian. The Russian icon appears to be a uniquely Russian phenomenon.

In all the ensuing chapters, I pursue a pairwise comparison between the ideas that gave rise to the concept of contract in the West and the cultural substratum – literary, theological, historical, and otherwise – that shines through the Russian icon. I try to detect the intellectual pedigree of each important contractual notion, and then consider its mode of acceptance, or lack thereof, within the Russian culture. The second chapter deals with Western *humanism*, its impact on the development of contract, and its conspicuous neglect in Russian culture and iconography. The third chapter repeats the same pattern by exploring Western *individualism*. The fourth chapter stresses the historical submissiveness of the Russian people to a strong central *authority*, and its relative absence in the West, also an important reason for the observed contractual behavior in the two cultures. The West developed, as is shown in the fifth chapter, a strong inclination to interpret *wealth* as a value. The Russians have always been of two minds in this matter, as is self-evident in their culture and iconography. This too contributed to the contractual disparities between Russia and the West. Chapter 6 characterizes Western culture, as well as Western law, as based on *reason* and *experience*, on man's rationally motivated inquisitiveness with regard to the phenomenal world. This method of validating propositions left a clear mark on the ascent of contract in the West, but it made only a tardy and faint entry into the Russian scene. The seventh and last chapter characterizes Russian society as an icon society, one that perceives the world through *images* and through its unique *theology of presence*. The West, by counterdistinction, has forsaken the predominance of images in its commitment to accommodate the *printed word*, again a powerful tool in the development of occidental contract doctrine. The book ends with a brief set of concluding remarks. None of the chapters, viewed in isolation, can carry

---

[11] A fuller cultural discussion of the meaning of icons in Russian culture is deferred to Chapter 7, *infra*.

the weight of the entire argument, but the *cumulative* effect of this comparison yields, it seems to me, an overwhelming landscape of incongruity, inconsistency, and conflict. When the whole evidence is weighed and considered, the argument transforms itself from speculation to certainty. Obviously, the evidence is gleaned from many different disciplines. It rips apart, as it were, the traditional boundaries between law, art, theology, history, economics, and sociology. It is a tall order, I know, but quite necessary, I submit, for understanding the otherwise inexplicable puzzle leading to the failure of contract in modern Russian society.

A Terminological Note About Contract

I wish to clarify on the threshold what I mean by a "contract." The notion of exchange is almost as ancient as human civilization. Abraham bought a piece of real estate from Heth, which later became his (and the other patriarchs') site of entombment. The biblical Divinity itself was quite keen on striking agreements, and was notably firm in exacting a harsh price for their eventual breaches. I do not refer to these forms of exchange as "contracts." As used in this study, the term must include at least the following two attributes. First, the parties must be free to forge their agreement as they wish, without regard to pre-existing forms. For example, a contractual agreement need not correspond to any particular preset prototype (e.g., sale of goods, a real estate lease agreement, or a contract of employment). It can be completely idiosyncratic (a promise to manufacture a five-wheeled car). I refer to this feature of modern contract law as "the freedom to deviate from contractual prototypes."[12] Second, it need not depend for its validity on simultaneous exchange. This means that "bare" promises should be enforceable, even if the parties intend to fulfill them in the remote future, and even if they are not supported by present consideration. I refer to this feature of modern contract law as the "binding power of bare promises."[13]

For the modern Western mind, both of these properties, the freedom to deviate from contractual prototypes and the binding power of bare promises, are

---

[12] Although modern, the freedom to depart from contractual prototypes has it roots in ancient Roman Law, which recognized, at least in principle, the notion of the *contractus innominatus*, or the contract without a name. The closest paradigm of the *contractus innominatus* was obtainable by a rather simple method of contracting called *stipulatio*.

[13] The distinction between instantaneous exchange and executory promises and the binding effect of the latter came into being in the Renaissance. Chapter 2, infra, develops this legal theme within its historical perspective. Thomas Hobbes, in his *Leviathan* (1651) noted (in Chapter 14) that "one of the contractors may deliver the thing contracted for on his part, and leave the other to perform his part at some determinate time after, and in the meantime be trusted; and then the contract on his part is called a pact, or covenant: or both parts may contract now to perform hereafter, in which cases he that is to perform in time to come, being trusted, his performance is called keeping of promise, or faith, and the failing of performance, if it be voluntary, violation of faith."

more or less taken for granted. But this need not necessarily be the case. Come to think of it, it is not immediately apparent why the state should commit its coercive power to enforce some idiosyncratic private preferences, idly committed by one individual to another.[14] This puzzle is further aggravated when we consider that rather than finish off with their highly personalized set of preferences by an instantaneous exchange, the parties choose to procrastinate, and then to burden the keepers of the peace with the task of enforcing them at great public expense. But these are the vagaries that modern Western contract law goes by,[15] and it is in this sense that contractual behavior is notoriously lacking in Russia today.

Icons, Art, and Ideas

Many Russian (and non-Russian) icons are great works of art. They often radiate a soft translucent air of spirituality that illuminates the object from within and furnishes it with a great sense of serenity and beauty. Nevertheless, icons have never been produced, venerated, or valued for their mere artistic value. In that respect they differ greatly from most other artistic manifestations, whose value is largely attributable to their aesthetic characteristics. A Monet or a Velásquez, for instance, is valued precisely because it stimulates in its viewers an agreeable aesthetic sensation, while the "story" that it tells (say, water lilies resting in a pond, or a young *infanta* choked in her intricate girdles) is of a decidedly secondary interest.

This is hardly the case with icons. Icons send messages. These messages encrypt literary missives. They always seem to be making some sort of a statement, to which the viewers are expected to respond in kind. Thus, icons are admitted to the communion of the faithful as active participants with whom the faithful interact. They are valued for what they say and what they do, and for what the people who venerate them say and do to, and with them, rather than for what they simply look like. Icons have always raised a great deal of controversy. Some of these controversies have led to war, want, and misery. None of these wars were waged on aesthetic[16] grounds, for none of the warring factions paid the slightest attention to the beauty (or lack thereof) of the subject of dispute.[17] They were all waged for what the icons were imagined to

---

[14] See Arthur Leff, "Injury, Ignorance and Spite: The Dynamics of Coercive Collection," *Yale Law Review* 80:1 (1970).

[15] I make no claim here that the "basis of contract" in Western jurisprudence is necessarily promise, rather than something else (e.g., reliance or unjust enrichment). I do, however, make the more modest claim that in Western jurisprudence bare promises are commonly enforceable.

[16] The term "aesthetics" in this passage and throughout these pages is used in the narrower, Benedetto Croce–inspired meaning, which relates to artistic excellence, and not in the broader sense, which admits aesthetic considerations into other fields of human endeavor.

[17] Moshe Barasch, *Icon, Studies in the History of an Idea*, New York: New York University Press (1992). Barasch writes: "Now, it is important to remember in our context that in the various great debates concerning the icon's status, the aesthetic attitude never even came up for discussion.

have said or done, or for what their venerators seemed to have said or done to, or with them. Obviously, the best-known historical example (but by no means the only one) is associated with the so-called iconoclastic wars of the early Middle Ages, which did not terminate until the so-called "Triumph of Orthodoxy" in 843 A.D.[18] The enemies of icons, the iconoclasts, interpreted the material rendering of saintly images as a blatant violation of the Second Commandment. According to their rhetoric, the practice of iconography was in fact heretical and had to be forcibly eradicated as a form of idolatry. True to their doctrine, they actually went ahead and destroyed all the existing icons throughout the Byzantine Empire. The only early icons that were saved from their wrath were the inaccessible ones, notably the large collection in the Saint Catherine Monastery on Mount Sinai. The defenders of icons, the iconodules, far from invoking the redeeming *aesthetic* value of their objects of veneration, developed an alternative doctrine of their own, proclaiming the saintliness of the images and their redeeming *theological* value.[19] To be sure, the debate was much energized by hidden political undercurrents. Those secret agendas had very little to do with the theological hair-splitting debates that were raging on the surface. Rather, they concerned an agitated power struggle between the secular rulers of the Empire and the insurgent forces of the Church, who used icon veneration as a means of gathering influence and clout.[20] But whether the

> For both the breakers of images and their defenders, the iconoclasts and the iconodules from late Antiquity to the Reformation, an aesthetic attitude was utterly beyond consideration. However dramatically opposed their views of icons may have been, they held the common conviction that the image does not exist for itself, that it is not autonomous, and that it should bring the spectator beyond mere contemplation" (ibid., 4).

[18] The doctrinal vindication of the sanctity of icons was ordained in the Seventh (and last) Ecumenical Council, which convened at Nicaea in 787 A.D. The proclamation of the Seventh Council was briefly overruled by the Emperor Leo V the Armenian in 815, but the veneration of icons was finally reinstated in 843 A.D. by the Empress Theodora, whose name was forever linked, following that event, with the Triumph of Orthodoxy.

[19] With some simplification, the theological argument holds that interpreting saintly images as an idolatrous violation of the Second Commandment ignores the dual nature of Christ and its crystallization in the Doctrine of Incarnation. By choosing to appear in the flesh, Christ himself perfected an icon of his own divine Self; thus, by rejecting Christ's own choice as a form of idolatry, the iconoclasts themselves are performing an act of heresy. They also fail to understand that icons are mere reflections of the human side of the represented entity, while its divine nature remains safely encased in the mystery of the invisible. See St. John of Damascus, *On the Divine Images: Three Apologies Against Those Who Attack the Divine Images*, translated by David Anderson (2000). St. John's classic work itself was completed at the height of the iconoclastic period, in the first half of the eighth century; his main arguments are still used in Orthodox services today in defense of the holy icons and the very essence of the Orthodox faith itself.

[20] See Jaroslav Pelikan, *The Christian Tradition*, Chicago: University of Chicago Press, Volume 2, Chapter 3 (1974) (which shows how this doctrinal dispute was used as a veil to hide the realities of an essentially political struggle). See also Arnold Hauser, *The Social History of Art*, London: Routledge, Volume 2, pp. 145ff (1951) (attributing Emperor Leo III's iconoclastic decrees to his interest in curbing the political power of the Church and his desire to align himself with certain social elites who were opposed to the veneration of images).

iconoclastic wars were about theology or about politics, one thing is certain, they were not about art or about aesthetics.

Icons and Other Forms of Pictorial Expression in Russia

Consider the gradual development of artistic expression in the West during these last thousand years. It spun a rich mosaic of styles and modes of expression. It moved from the early medieval style to the Romanesque, from the Gothic to the early, high, and late Renaissance styles, and from thence to the Baroque and to the Rococo. It then started its slow ascent to Romanticism, to Neo-Realism, and then to the early and late phases of Impressionism, Expressionism, Surrealism, Cubism, and Abstraction, and then, once again to Conceptualism and to a whole range of neo-figurative renditions of real-life objects. It was, and still is, in a constant state of flux, forming new modes of expression and tossing them back into the large repository of the past.

By sharp counterdistinction, Russia had one, and only one, *authentic* style of artistic expression, the Russian Icon. For many centuries, from the formative years of the Russian nation in the tenth century to the sixteenth-century Muscovite School of painting, Russia's art remained transfixed in this sole medium, while other forms of artistic expression were almost imperceptible. When Michelangelo was painting the Sistine Chapel in the Vatican and European artists started to explore Mannerism and the Baroque, Russian artists were still bent on producing their ancient craft, obeying a rigid code of execution that remained largely unaltered, and unadulterated, throughout the centuries.[21] As will become apparent later on, this canonic list of painting injunctions, rigid as it may have seemed on the surface, could not arrest the natural craving of Russian artists to innovate and break new paths. But these innovations were necessarily constrained to half tones and nuances while occidental contemporaries were moving by leaps and bounds. The seventeenth century saw a rapid decline in the artistic quality of Russian icons, along with the emergence of new forms of artistic expression, which were largely borrowed from the West.[22] This Western influence marshaled onto center stage the full array of Western styles, from Realism to Impressionism to the Abstract. It is an influence that dominates Russian "high culture" painting to this day, while the craft of icon painting was relegated to the domain of popular art and to the folklore. From a purely artistic point of view, it certainly did not regain its former splendor, a fact that is well appreciated by art connoisseurs the world over, and is fully reflected in the

---

[21] In many ways, the strict observation of traditional principles is a distinct feature of the Orthodox faith in general. See, for instance, Timothy Ware, *The Orthodox Church*, London: Penguin Books, pp. 195ff (revised ed., 1997). In this authoritative treatise, the author testifies that, "when Orthodox are asked at contemporary inter-Church gatherings to sum up what they see as the distinctive characteristic of their Church, they often point precisely to its changelessness, its determination to remain loyal to the past, its sense of *living continuity* with the Church of ancient times."

[22] James Billington, *The Icon and the Axe*, New York: Vintage Books, p. 36 (1970).

marketplace. In spite of the unquestionable *artistic* decline in post-sixteenth-century Russian icons, I maintain that the icon still retains its former dominant role as the sole truly authentic art form of the Russian people throughout the centuries.

My argument rests on four related notions. My first point emerges from what I have already stated: The cardinal importance that people attach to icons far transcends their artistic value.[23] Consequently, the indisputable decline in the artistic excellence of post-sixteenth-century icons does not necessarily imply any paring down of their overall significance in the life of the Russian people. Russian craftsmen have never ceased to produce sacred images for personal and liturgical consumption, and most Russian homes still boast a very special place, usually called "the beautiful corner," where heirlooms and newly acquired icons are constantly on display and are routinely used for comfort and veneration. Nor are those icons within the exclusive domain of God-fearing people. They are venerated by saints and sinners alike, by the holy and by the profane.[24] They are, in a way, religious objects, to be sure; but much more importantly, they are cultural statements, part and parcel of being a Russian Christian.

Second, it is impossible to miss the perception that Western-inspired Russian artists did not represent in their collective output an "authentic sentiment" of the Russian people itself.[25] They practiced a highly exclusionary form of self-expression, which gave vent to the often-pathetic ambition of a thin elitist class to single itself out of the vast multitudes of a largely illiterate and definitely

[23] It appears that the popular Russian word for "holy" or "saintly" – *prepodobny* – means, simply, "very like," a clear allusion to the holy icons. See ibid., p. 8.

[24] Even the great sinner Fyodor Pavlovitch Karamazov, steeped as he may have been in corruption and debauchery, appears to have had icons in his home as well, although he may have spat on them to give vent to his disapproval of mystical feeling. See Fyodor Dostoyevsky, *The Brothers Karamazov*, translated by Constance Garnett, New York: Modern Library, p. 143 (1937). In his brief snapshot, *Akulka's Husband*, being a scene from *The House of the Dead* (1859–1861), Dostoyevsky describes the practice of selling oneself to military service in lieu of reluctant well-to-do conscripts. Pending the actual enlistment of the seller to the army, the latter was permitted absolute tyranny in the house of his "employers." "He can make them put up with so much that they're better off taking the icons out, so the saints don't see what goes on," he comments (translation by Andrew MacAndrew). Interestingly, most of the caricatured protagonists depicted in Nicholas Gogol's ghastly "poem" (as he called it), "Dead Souls," decorated their mansions in Western or Westernized art, with absolutely no icons to be seen anywhere. I interpret this omission as a salient feature of Gogol's social disapproval of the petty landed aristocracy and ascending bourgeoisie of his time. As is well known, Gogol himself ended his life as a fundamentalist religious recluse and repented his attempt to engage in literary experiments, which he came to consider as sacrilegious.

[25] Even more modern writers such as Dostoyevsky shared the view that the Western ways of representing Christian themes in art were outright heretical. For his attack on Holbein's *Christ in the Tomb* and other non-Orthodox forms of iconography, see Z. Malenko and J. Gebhard, "The Artistic Use of Portraits in Dostoyevsky's *Idiot*," *Slavic and East European Journal* 243 (1961).

xenophobic peasant society. It fell in line with the inclination of the boyar society to converse in French or to display an Italianate taste for architecture, much ridiculed by some of the great Russian writers of the nineteenth century.[26] It never had a fighting chance to penetrate into the countryside, to the wooded provincial landmass of the North, or to the endless Steppes stretching from the Ukraine to the Pacific, or, for that matter, to the vast masses of the urban poor. For the Russian people, it was icons all the way down to the present day.[27]

My third point is that the conscious effort to substitute a foreign lore for the homemade stuff was often doomed to failure. One prime example comes to mind. The greatest jeopardy to the Russian iconographic tradition came about during the seventy years of Communist dictatorship. Religion was dismissed as an "opiate of the masses" and its practice was severely restricted, on pain of cruel punishment. Churches were stripped of their icons, which were used, in turn, as firewood.[28] The creation of new icons was strictly forbidden. But the Communist regime itself was also struggling in its eternal campaign to "reach" the people and to be accepted as its alternative form of veneration.[29] The Communist regime found out, however, much to its chagrin, that it was not easy to be accepted as an object of veneration without the intermediation of iconographic symbols. In the end, the question was not whether the regime could "make it" without icons, but, rather, what kind of icons did it have to use in order to bridge the gap between the new religion and its intended beneficiaries.[30] The Communist regime chose to use the canonical language of the despised Christian images. Figure 1, *We Swear to You, Comrade Lenin*, is a typical Communist icon, cast in plaster during the darkest days of Stalin's murderous dictatorship.

---

[26] *See* the Appendix (St. Petersburg) to Chapter 4, infra.

[27] This view is strongly held by a number of recent Russian philosophers and theologians. For example, the early twentieth-century essayist, Evgenii Trubetskoi, made the point that Russian icons capture everything that is authentic, pure, and indigenous in the Russian soul, and thus there is an amazingly close approximation between Russian history and Russian iconography. For a graciously written account of Trubetskoi's essays by his own American-born grandson, see Peter Bouteneff, "The Timeless Steps into Time: The Icon in the Vision of E. N. Trubetskoi," *Modern Greek Studies Yearbook* 10/11:675 (1994–95).

[28] The touching story of Rublev's famous icon *Spas* (the Savior), and how it was saved from the fire during the Stalinist regime, is told by James Billington in *The Face of Russia*, New York: TV Books, pp. 31ff (1999).

[29] For a psychoanalytic interpretation of legal systems as objects of veneration, and of their lack of sustained viability without such veneration, see Sylviane Colombo, "Parricide and the Search for Legality," *Sri Lanka Journal of International Law* 5:3 (1993).

[30] In a recent book, Oleg Kharkhordin brilliantly drew attention to the many parallels between Soviet public practices and their Eastern Orthodox antecedents. For example, each good Communist was required to reflect repeatedly on his or her character and role in society in a manner highly reminiscent of the Orthodox practice of doing penance in the public domain. See Oleg Kharkhordin, *The Collective and the Individual in Russia: A Study of Practices*, Berkeley: University of California Press (1999).

FIGURE 1. Evgeni Vuchetich, Pavel Fridman, Grigori Postnikov, and Pyotr Yatsyno, *We Swear to You, Comrade Lenin* (detail), 1949.

Joseph Stalin is clearly visible as the central figure in a long line of flanking dignitaries. The dignitaries' position in this representation, relative to Stalin, is not coincidental. The most senior figures are those who enjoy a greater physical proximity to the central figure, while the ones at the extreme ends are the lesser luminaries. A faint likeness of Vladimir Lenin is clearly visible in the background, beyond the dominant figure and his imposing entourage. The human figures are located in front of the Kremlin walls, separating the visible dignitaries and the invisible sacred space behind them, which is protected from the onlookers' reach (visual and otherwise) by an impenetrable fortified barrier. Where did this iconographic idea originate? Orthodox practitioners should not find it difficult to discern. As it turns out, every Russian Orthodox church has an elongated screen that stretches all the way across the structure and separates the nave from the altar.[31] This partition creates a physical barrier that enables the congregation to watch the clergy during the liturgy, but not to observe the actual devotional labor at the altar. This work is executed within the hidden sacred space behind the partition. This perennial screen, termed an *iconostasis*, is in reality a board on which individual icons are permanently on display.[32] Individual icons are not placed on the iconostasis for decorative purposes, and each icon has a fixed place, which is quite immutable. In many Russian churches a central place of honor is reserved for Christ *Pantocrator* (Lord of the universe; and not otherwise, for instance, not as part of a crucifixion icon). The other saintly figures are arranged around the central figure with a descending order of seniority, according to the relative distance between them and the Redeemer.[33] The *Pantocrator*'s authority is further enhanced by scriptural texts, such as "Come unto me, all ye that travail and are heavy laden, and I will refresh you." It is implied, although not figuratively represented, that the *Pantocrator* is "an image of Christ seated at the right hand of the Father."[34] Figure 2 illustrates a typical Orthodox iconostasis, of a type prevalent across Eastern Christianity.

The resemblance between these two groups of images, the *Pantocrator* amidst His saints in the Christian version and Stalin surrounded by the Party stalwarts in the anti-Christian version, is striking but not surprising. This is not only because a student of Christianity learns to expect Christ and Antichrist to mirror image each other in a rather symmetrical fashion.[35] It is also because new religions (in this case, the Marxist lore) often utilize the sacred symbols of the discarded faith as a deliberate method to win the confidence and the

---

[31] Michel Quenot, *The Icon*, Crestwood, NY: St. Vladimir Seminary Press, pp. 47ff (1996). The architectural positioning of this screen implies a deeper subtextual meaning. As it separates the altar from the nave, it makes the actual performance of the religious rites that take place behind it invisible to the faithful. This opaqueness of the ritual bestows, without a doubt, a greater air of authority on the priests and maneuvers the faithful into a mode of submission. Quenot, a devout practitioner himself, offers the following apologetic explanation: "Often misunderstood today, the iconostasis should be reevaluated in terms of the theology of the icon. By no means a barrier, the iconostasis is, positively speaking, the maximal expression of all that the icon can reveal to us visually. Behind it there is nothing to be seen. Why? Simply because the wondrous mystery that is celebrated there could never be situated on our human, visual level" (ibid.). There is little wonder that the idea of an iconostasis (in its corrupted form) was found attractive to the authorities during the Stalinist regime in the Soviet Union.

[32] The iconostasis is, in reality, a pan-Orthodox creation. However, until fully developed in the golden age of Russian iconography (mainly in the fifteenth century), the iconostasis has mainly been a low partition separating the choir from the nave, rather than what it is today, the main site for hanging icons within the church. As the number of icons on the iconostasis gradually increased, it also rose in height, as well as in its spiritual role in the architecture of the church. See Mahmoud Zibawi, *The Icon, Its Meaning and History*, Collegeville, MN: Liturgical Press, p. 138 (1993).

[33] James Billington, *The Icon and the Axe*, pp. 33–35 (1970).

[34] Michel Quenot, *The Icon*, p. 130 (1996).

[35] Bernard McGinn, *Antichrist, Two Thousand Years of Human Fascination with Evil*, New York: Columbia University Press (2000).

FIGURE 2. Modern iconostasis, Greek Catholic Melkite Church of the Annunciation, Jerusalem, early twentieth century.

veneration of the faithful.[36] This pattern of invoking Orthodox icons in the service of the Socialist State repeats itself over and over again.[37] There can be very little doubt both that the practice was deliberate and that it was wisely banking on an extremely deep-rooted sentiment of the Russian people. It was designed to transform its otherwise threatening subject matter, in this case the Socialist Cause, to take (the propagandist) appearance of the familiar and

[36] The Catholic Church in Latin America was quite famous for this strategy. For example, the most devoutly venerated site of Mexican Catholics is the Santa Maria Guadalupe shrine at the outskirts of Mexico City. The shrine was constructed on a sacred site used for centuries by the indigenous population and is adorned by such pre-Columbian religious icons as the flying serpent (*quetzalcoatl*). Maria Guadalupe is a brown Madonna who chose to reveal herself, for the first time, to a local Indian of humble descent. By snubbing the Spanish conqueror and aligning herself with the conquered, she immediately took root as the dominant local saint in the indigenous pantheon.

[37] In the ensuing chapters I illustrate the similarity of Christian and Communist icons on numerous occasions. It is interesting to note that the Marxist concept of art was not very different from the theology of icons. "All art is quite useless," declares the ultimate aesthete, Oscar Wilde, in his preamble to his masterpiece, *The Picture of Dorian Gray*. Such a frivolous attitude could never be embraced by the Marxist approach to artistic expression. Art was held by the Marxists to be inspired by a "higher" social purpose. It is a tool to bond the individual to his or her community and a dialectical move of class struggle leading to a reformed society. See Ernst Fischer, *The Necessity of Art, a Marxist Approach*, translated by Anna Bostock, New York: Penguin Books, (1963).

the homegrown. It is the familiar and the homegrown that has been around Russian households from time immemorial, and carries about it a sense of the inevitable and the absolute. It was a powerful political tool, and it was very cleverly applied.[38]

My fourth and last point is that modern Russian art, with all its path-breaking freshness and innovation,[39] is often unable, or unwilling, to break loose of its own iconographic traditions. This point has already been noted in the literature on numerous occasion, but I would like to succinctly reiterate it in the context of the two best-known abstract artists of the last century, Wassily Kandinsky and Kazimir Malevitch. In what ways might these two innovating artists follow the canons of Orthodox iconography? While icons are made to tell a story, both Kandinsky and Malevitch are the epitome of the abstract. How could Malevitch's famous white on white canvases (Figure 3) be anything but themselves? How could Kandinsky's works, which were designed to be equally balanced from whichever side of the frame someone chose to hang them on the wall, be anything but a combination of forms and blots of color?

Kandinsky's personal biography is intimately connected with the Russian icon. Growing up in Moscow, he studied both law and economics (successfully, it turns out; on completion of his studies he was offered a chair of jurisprudence at a Russian university). In those formative years of his career, however, he was roaming the streets of the capital, drinking in its rich colors and studying in detail its numerous icons. According to his own testimony, the roots of his later professional development as an artist can be traced back to those early artistic impressions.[40] But this is obviously not the deeper connection between the artist's abstract style and the world of icons. Kandinsky happened to be one of those rare artists who do not merely *do* things, but feel an urge to philosophize

[38] A well-known use of the arts for the attainment of political goals was made by the Soviet regime in its attitude to film making. Lenin, the absolute political animal, considered the cinema to be the ultimate artistic art form and started a long and successful tradition of film making in the Soviet Union. See David Robinson, *The History of World Cinema*, New York: Stein and Day Publications, p. 124 (1973). The most renowned Soviet producer, Sergei Eisenstein, employed in his propagandist, yet beautiful first movies, traditional iconic ideas as a means of penetrating the collective psyche of his audience. Thus, both in his very first feature-length movie, *Strike* (1924) and in his signature work, *Battleship Potempkin* (1925), he did not attempt to portray the protagonists as his Western contemporaries did, as real flesh and blood individuals. In fact, neither one of these two masterpieces has any protagonists at all. They both pit "the masses," as an icon of Good, against "the (bourgeois) government," as the embodiment of Evil. Individual human qualities are submerged into their iconic "ideas." The moving frames suggest a reality beyond the visible. Eisenstein movies are meant to be seen through rather than looked at. They appear to have been hugely successful as a political tool, although one surmises that if they were directed at a Western audience their effectiveness would have been greatly reduced.

[39] A recent publication hailing the alleged innovativeness of contemporary (in this case, female) Russian artists is John Bowlt and Matthew Drutt (eds.), *Amazons of the Avant Garde: Alexandra Exeter, Natalia Goncharova, Liubov Popova, Olga Rozanova, Varvara Stepanova, Nadezhda Udaltsova* (A Guggenheim Museum exhibition catalog, 2000).

[40] Kandinsky's life story, complete with his own views of his artistic development and what influenced it, is compiled in Will Grohmann, *Wassily Kandinsky: Life and Work*, New York: H. N. Abrams (1959).

FIGURE 3. Kazimir Malevitch, *White on White*, 1918.

about them as well. His views of what art (in general, not just his own) should be about are summarized in an early publication, *Concerning the Spiritual in Art*, which was published in 1912.[41] In that treatise it becomes abundantly apparent that Kandinsky was not championing the abstract style, of which many consider him as the Founding Father, for purely aesthetic reasons. In fact, aestheticism as such did not interest Kandinsky at all. What motivated him in choosing this medium was his belief that colors and forms have a "language" of their own, which, like any other language, is capable of evoking emotional responses in its viewers. For example, he believed that horizontal lines exude coldness,

[41] References to this work are based on a 1947 English translation authorized by Mme. Nina Kandinsky, for which she supplied the artist's corrections and additions for a new edition of the original German text that never saw the light of day. It is based on a 1914 translation to English by Michael Sadleir, with what is termed "a considerable retranslation" by Francis Golffing, Michael Harrison, and Ferdinand Ostertag.

while vertical lines are "hot." Colors, too, invoke nonvisual associations like moods or musical sounds. I find it of no consequence to offer my personal views whether Kandinsky's blunt assertions are theoretically defensible or just happen to represent figments of his own imagination. What does matter is his personal conviction that it is the role of lines, colors, and compositions to narrate a story and to guide the viewers into nonpictorial planets. This, in essence, is the main mission of icon painters as well. As we have already seen, the aesthetic consideration is definitely secondary in the description of the icon's role in society; icons are judged by the efficacy of their "messages," what they have to "say" to their audiences, and what their venerators say to, and do with, them. The messages of icons are nonpictorial. Painting an icon is the use of lines and colors to trigger a dialogue between the venerated object and its audience. Icons do not exist within their own closed universe. They extend themselves into open discourse and pry open the viewers' minds and hearts.

Kandinsky himself is the most articulate spokesman for this set of ideas. The modern self-proclaimed connoisseur, he complains,

does not search for the internal feeling of a picture directly for himself, he worries himself into looking for "closeness to nature," or "temperament," or "handling," or "tonality," or "perspective" and so on. His eye does not probe the external expression to arrive at the internal significance.

It is entirely futile to mimic natural objects, he proclaims, because

when we assert that external nature is the source of all art, we must remember that, in patterning, natural objects are used as symbols, almost as though they were mere hieroglyphics.

Distancing oneself from mimicking nature does not imply, however, that the artist is relegated to a purely aesthetic domain of color and form:

[I]f we begin at once to break the bonds that bind us to nature and devote ourselves purely to combinations of pure color and independent form, we shall produce works which are mere geometric decoration . . .

Such decorations do not capture the soul of the artistic expression. Beauty of form and color, he says, is not a sufficient aim by itself, despite the assertions of pure aesthetes. The additional element, which endows these icons with artistic significance, is the "idea" behind them:

In a conversation with an interesting person, we endeavor to get at his fundamental ideas and feelings. We do not bother about the words he uses, nor his spelling. . . . The meaning and ideas are what concerns [sic!] us. We should have the same attitude when confronted with a work of art if we are to absorb its abstract effect.[42]

The story of Kazimir Malevitch is even more interesting. During his long and prolific career, Malevitch experimented with a broad spectrum of artistic styles, from Realism to Impressionism, Expressionism, Fauvism, Cubism, Futurism,

---

[42] Ibid., pp. 67–70.

and Neo-Primitivism.[43] But his greatest contribution to painting was formulated in his own personal style, which he called "Suprematism."[44] Malevitch's own account of the exact nature of Suprematism is not always easy to decipher. Not unlike Kandinsky, Malevitch's theoretical writings verge on the poetic, an idiom that is not always compatible with clarity of presentation. Malevitch denounces in his writings the "art of the past" as putting itself at the service of some external, nonartistic goal. "The art of the past which stood, at least ostensibly, in the service of religion and the state," he writes, "will take on a new life in the pure (unapplied) art of Suprematism, which will build up a new world – the world of feeling."[45] Superficially, this declaration may be interpreted as a desire to break with the old iconographic tradition, because it views art as an end unto itself, rather than as a tool to promote social ideas. However, Malevitch aligned himself with the art of the icons in a much more profound way. One of the central tenets of Russian iconography lies in the assumption that the phenomenal world cannot be captured by artistic means and conveyed to the viewer "as is." The artist cannot, and is not allowed to, observe external objects with the eyes of the flesh. He is required to look into his own soul for spiritual communion with God's creation. Realism must be discarded as heretical attempt to revoke this principle, and hence all Russian iconography is two-dimensional, stylized, spiritual, transcendent, and unrealistic.[46] Malevitch displays the greatest allegiance to this iconographic notion, that the "true" world cannot be grasped by our senses. It is too mysterious and complex for the easy task of sensual interpretation, and thus it befalls the artist to represent it symbolically, or to echo it indirectly, by iconographic means.[47] Since the screen separating what there is and what we can sensually perceive of it (i.e., between ontological reality and epistemic observation) is impenetrable, visible icons must be radically divorced from any sensual interpretation of the represented objects. Only by creating this sharp distinction between objects

[43] See, in general, Evgenia Petrova et al. (eds.), *Malevitch, Artiste et Théoricien*, Paris: Toile (1990), which offers a synoptic view of Malevitch's experimentation with those artistic styles.

[44] On Malevitch's progress through the different art styles toward Suprematism, and on the special role of Suprematism in modern art history, see Dmitry Sarabianov, "Kazimir Malevitch and His Art, 1900–1930," in Kazimir Malevitch (an exhibition catalogue issued by the National Art Gallery, Washington, DC; the Armand Hammer Museum of Art and Cultural Center, Los Angeles; and the Metropolitan Museum of Art, New York, 1991), p. 164.

[45] Kazimir Malevitch, *The Nonobjective World*, pp. 67ff (1927; English translation by Howard Dearstyne, 1959), reprinted in Herschel Chipp (ed.), *Theories of Modern Art*, Berkeley: University of California Press, pp. 341ff (1968).

[46] This theme is elaborated in much greater detail in Chapter 6, infra.

[47] For an interesting account of Malevitch's hidden iconographic agenda see, significantly, Bruno Duborgel, *Malevitch, La Question de l'Icone*, St. Etienne, France: Publications de Saint Etienne (1997). According to Duborgel's argument, the painting of icons is, paradoxically, an iconoclastic form of artistic expression. The painting of icons, just like the oeuvre of Kazimir Malevitch, is an attempt to offer a visible rendering of the invisible, by mimicking not physical objects but the prototypes thereof, by suggesting a transfiguration of figures or a transformation of forms. The ultimate rejection of physical objects, the ultimate Platonic idea of the prototype representing them, is the idea of the abstract!

and their representation can the artist fulfill his higher mission. The ultimate negation of sensual reality is, of course, a radically abstract style, and minimalist abstraction is ideally suited to achieve this goal.[48] These ideas must have loomed large in Malevitch's mind. He writes:

To the Suprematist the visual phenomena of the objective world are, in themselves, meaningless; the significant thing is feeling, as such, quite apart from the environment in which it is called forth. The so-called "materialization" of the feeling in the conscious mind really means the materialization of the reflection of feeling through the medium of some realistic conception. Such a realistic conception is without value in Suprematist art.... To the Suprematist, the appropriate means of representation...ignores the familiar appearance of objects.

In referring to his famous early twentieth-century masterpiece, in which a black square can be viewed on a white background (Figure 4), he states: "This was no 'empty square' which I had exhibited but rather the feeling of nonobjectivity." And, in one sentence, "the Suprematist does not observe and does not touch – he feels."[49]

On the Uniquely Russian Element in Orthodox Iconography

Christian religious icons did not originate in Russia. They actually seemed to have made their first appearance in Roman Egypt in the first centuries of the Common Era, especially in the mummy paintings of such burial sites as ancient Fayyoum (see Figure 5). To understand this claim one has to fathom one of the most crucial theological axioms relating to the meaning of icons. In other forms of pictorial expression, images "represent" objects, that is, they are supposed to reflect someone, or something, that is "out there," beyond the limits of the reflecting work of art. Icons, on the other hand, are not supposed to reflect an external object, but to form an extension of the object itself. If the *Theotokos* (Mother of God), for example, is depicted in an icon, she herself exists in the icon, such that the icon extends her presence from the external world to the

---

[48] The idea that absolute nothingness, or the absolutely abstract, has an articulate story of its own is not peculiar only to Orthodox theology. In fact, it is common to many creeds that rejected the (humanistic) iconographic traditions of the Roman Catholic Church, which seek out the "is" and believe both in the artist's capability and in her right to render a fair representation of it. For a learned study of the role of blank spaces in Reformist portraiture, see Peter Goodrich, "The Iconography of Nothing, Blank Spaces and the Representation of Law in Edward VI and the Pope," in Costas Douzinas and Lynda Nead (eds.), *Law and the Image, the Authority of Art and the Aesthetics of Law*, Chicago: University of Chicago Press, p. 89 (1999). Another interesting form of making a statement by representing a void was recently brought to the fore by exploring the art of Evaristo Baschenis, a seventeenth-century local luminary from Bergamo. Baschenis specialized in painting musical instruments in still-life settings. Clearly, these instruments were not producing any music, as they were all covered with a thick layer of dust. See Enrico de Pascale, "In Praise of Silence," in Andrea Bayer (ed.), *The Still Lifes of Evaristo Baschenis: The Music of Silence*, New York: Metropolitan Museum of Art, p. 30 (2000).

[49] Kazimir Malevitch, *The Nonobjective World*, supra, pp. 67–70.

FIGURE 4. Kazimir Malevitch, *Black Square*, circa 1923–30.

piece of wood carrying her image.[50] Now the ancient funerary culture of Egypt has always been fully compatible with this worldview. The whole purpose of its

[50] The theological aspects of the material nature of icons are firmly pedigreed to the great theologian Dionysius Areopagita, who probably lived in Syria in the early sixth century (the biographical outline of Dionysius' life is not clear). Dionysius' main theme was the resolution of the so-called question of theophany, or God's revelation. The question is, how can God, being of a totally transcendent nature, be known to humans who perceive reality through the senses, that is, by the employment of materialistic means? Dionysius seems to have answered this question by suggesting that God chose to reveal Himself to humankind by imprinting Himself on His Image, a concept that is both similar and dissimilar to His transcendent nature. Thus, although the Image is not, in itself, God, it is also not totally devoid of His divine presence, which is mysteriously engrafted upon it by the process of the theophany. The nature of the symbol, and hence of icons, lies, then, in the embodiment of the represented in some material object, which is, at the same time, similar to, and different from, its prototypical source. Its similarity is mandated by the doctrines of the revelation and the incarnation, and its difference is a reflection of the transcendence of the divine. For a general introduction, to these subjects, see Moshe Barasch, *Icon*, New York: New York University Press, pp. 158ff (1992). For further details about this "theology of presence," see Chapter 7, infra. Incidentally, one need not be a mystic

FIGURE 5. *Man with a Mole* (a Fayyoum "portrait"), circa 130–50 A.D.

existence was to preserve the identity of the dead in its physical proxy, whether this proxy, or manifestation, was a sculpture, a painted likeness, a death mask, or any other extension of the self. When early Christianity started to generate its first martyrs, the martyrs too were extended, like everyone else, into their painted images at their gravesites. And when the hostile authorities denied the

to embrace the plausibility of "similar dissimilarities." Any competent portrait painter knows that she is looking for some features that are more revealing than the "accurate" account of photographic representation. For a fascinating story of how Picasso found a way to render a perfect representation of his female sitter employing minimalist means, see Francoise Gilot and Carlton Lake, *Life with Picasso* (1964), as quoted by E. H. Gombrich, "The Mask and the Face: The Perception of Physiognomic Likeness in Life and in Art," in E. H. Gombrich, Julian Hochberg, and Max Black, *Art, Perception and Reality*, Baltimore, MD: Johns Hopkins University Press, p. 28 (1973).

living their privilege of venerating the dead at the site of their entombment, they separated their painting from the mummy (by actually sawing the likeness of the saints off their wooden burial chests) and carried them to their hiding places. The dead traveled with them wherever they went;[51] their presence in their likeness and the saintly martyrdom attached to their memory thus presaged Orthodox iconography by producing icons before the birth of Orthodoxy itself. Once formulated, however, Orthodoxy was quick to catch up.

Given the wide geographical and cultural spread of religious icons across the Orthodox world (and beyond), one may legitimately ask why this book is uniquely concerned with bonds between *Russian* icons and *Russian* law. If icons are actually pan-Orthodox phenomena, the cultural *substratum* lying at their base should give rise to pan-Orthodox legal manifestations, rather than to some characteristic features of the Russian legal system. More specifically, if the underlying cultural underpinnings, which generated the prototypical idea of icons, are incompatible with the reign of Contract, contractual behavior should be absent not only in Russia, but also throughout the domain of the Orthodox icon.

This is a fair question, and it is not easily resolved. Nevertheless, some observations are appropriate at this point. First, it is important to emphasize that no claim is being made that Russian culture is necessarily the *only* one that is incompatible with the flourishing of contractual ideas. Additional examples abound. For example, Jewish Law, much as it has captivated the imagination of ingenious scholars throughout Jewish history, has never embraced the concept of contract as we understand it in the West,[52] and this is in spite of the decidedly iconoclastic principles of the Jewish Faith.[53] What does this mean? It simply means that the absence of contract can be explained in ways other than by the prevalence of icons, hardly a surprising idea. Within the Orthodox world, too, where icons *are* prevalent, one presumably encounters varying degrees of contractual behavior. To the extent that within a given culture icons and contract peacefully coexist, there must be some dominant countervailing circumstance

---

[51] On the Fayyoum portraits and their theology of presence, see Euphrosyne Doxiadis, *The Mysterious Fayum Portraits, Faces from Ancient Egypt*, London: Thames and Hudson (1995). See also, Bénéfice Geoffroy-Schneiter, *Fayum Portraits* (1998).

[52] The great Maimonides stated, in his *Hilchot Mechira* (Law of Sales), 1, that "no sale can be consummated by mere words, even if there are witnesses who verify the transaction" (p. 1). The authoritative *Shulchan Aruch, Choshen Mishpat* 1, states that "no sale can be consummated by mere words. For example, if one person says to another, for how much will you sell me this item and the other gave him a price, and the parties resolved to commit themselves to the deal, they are both free to repudiate their commitment . . . but after the item was transferred from the seller to the purchaser, repudiation is no longer possible" (p. 189) (both texts are freely translated by me). This noncompromising rule was partially modified in some individual circumstances; see, generally, Menachem Elon, *Ha'mishpat Ha'ivri* (Jewish Law), Jerusalem: Magnus, Volume 1, p. 69 (3rd. ed., 1988).

[53] Of the three principal monotheistic religions, Christianity seems to be the only one that found ways to interpret the Second Commandment in a nonliteral fashion. Much more will be said on the cultural significance of this broader interpretation in the following pages.

rendering this coexistence possible. The subject matter of this book is strictly limited to the domain of Russian culture, with an express disclaimer as to the relationship between icons and contract across the globe.

Nor would it be accurate to say that Russian iconography is a mere fraction of a larger, pan-Orthodox, or pan-Byzantine, phenomenon. It has its roots in Byzantine iconography,[54] to be sure, and even beyond. However, much of Russian culture originated in the West and underwent a radical transformation, that is, a totally *original* transformation, on Russian soil. It happened in music and in dance, in literature and in drama, in cinematography and in the visual arts, of which the Russian icon assumes such a prominent position.[55]

There are a variety of factors distinguishing Russian icons from the Byzantine prototypes. The differences were perhaps less accentuated in the early stages, but Russian icons assumed unmistakable local characteristics as the centuries rolled on. The first great Russian resident perfecting this art form was really a Byzantine émigré, Theophanes the Greek, who imported his homeland's artistic grammar and transplanted it onto Russian soil (see Figure 6). Theophanes' style differed, however, from the canons or representation in the "Greek" world of his day. Presaging the Kandinskys and Malevitches of half a millennium later, Theophanes was nothing less than a genius of abstraction. Devoid of any form of embellishment, his starkly beautiful works reduce all representations to their bare symbols, deprive them of any third-dimensional depth, and deny them of any derivation other than the purely prototypical. To use Mahmoud Zibawi's insightful phrase, Theophanes did not really transgress the existing canons of Byzantine art, but he surely "transcended" and "exceeded" them.[56]

---

[54] In the beginning, the art of Kievian Rus' was totally Byzantine. Around the year 1130, a wonderful Virgin *Eléousa* (the prototypical form of the Mother of Tenderness) was imported to Kiev from Constantinople (see Figure 12) It was then transferred to Valdimir, where she was immediately "Russified" and assumed the name of the *Vladimirskaya*, or the Virgin of Vladimir. The *Vladimirskaya* participated in many a Russian war and gave inspiration, as she still does today, to generations of venerating folks, from all walks of life. Her lasting influence on Russian iconography, although modified by later stylistic developments, was never eradicated. The *Vladimirskaya* was not alone in representing pure Byzantine iconography on Russian soil. Early Kievian art, admirably represented by the mosaics in the Church of St. Michael and the Cathedral of Sancta Sophia in Kiev, for example, are unadulterated canonical Byzantine works of art.

[55] James Billington has gone so far as to make it a major thesis of much of his extensive work on Russian culture. In his view, Russian culture always moves in three distinct stages. In the first stage, something, such as an artistic form, is borrowed from the West and mimicked by local artists and craftsmen. In the second stage, the borrowed object assumes a life of its own. In its new, transformed stage, the art form becomes radically original and entirely Russian. More often than not, it far surpasses, in its expressive and artistic qualities, the original Western art form. In the third and final stage, the borrowed – and transformationally perfected – art form is threshed away to make room for the next borrowed form and for new bursts of originality. For an abbreviated, highly readable account of this thesis, see James Billington, *The Face of Russia*, New York (1999).

[56] Mahmoud Zibawi, *The Icon, Its Meaning and History*, Collegeville, MN: Liturgical Press, p. 128 (1993).

FIGURE 6. Theophanes the Greek, *Dormition of the Virgin*, late fourteenth century.

From an art-historical perspective, this alien genius was able to set the tone for a largely indigenous art form. He managed to do this because, by coincidence or design, he struck a note of commitment to the Medieval Byzantine worldview, which exceeded Byzantium's own commitment to itself. In turn, it came to symbolize, on Russian soil, Russia's lack of acceptance of modernity and of the Renaissance. This subject will engross our attention, in nuance and detail, as this story unfolds.

But the great truly Russian masters who followed in his footsteps, notably the greatest of them all, Andrei Rublev, and, following him, Master Dionysii, paved the way for something of a different feather. In their work, design acquired pre-eminence over color, and the abstract was given center stage, at the expense of the concrete. Color itself, while gaining in spiritual luminosity, lost its former

Byzantine splendor.[57] Light replaced brightness because, as I elaborate later, Russian iconography is, even more than its Byzantine progenitor, set upon "painting the soul."[58] It is less concrete and more abstract, as, again, will be shown later, because of its rejection of the material world and its acceptance of an idealized worldview, where symbols and allusions take the place of natural objects and banish them from the eye of the beholder. Compared to its Byzantine origins, Russian iconography from Rublev on was more linear and less substantial in representation,[59] its colors more subdued and luminous, the figures more prototypical and angelic, and the scenery less earthy and more celestial.[60] In short, it enshrined the medieval concept of humankind and of the universe as a whole, while the West was slowly progressing in the opposite direction of a humanist, anthropocentric revolution.[61]

The coming of age of an independent Russian school of iconography is easy to explain. While Southern Rus', like the Serbian and Bulgarian territories that lay to the West, were constantly exposed to the dominant Byzantine influence, the northern centers in Moscow, Novgorod, and Pskov (which constituted the main schools of Russian iconography) were separated from Byzantium by vast territorial expanses, hostile Asiatic warriors, and extremely poor communications. With the final fall of Byzantium in 1453, Russia assumed its new role as the center of the Orthodox world. The old Byzantine iconographic prototypes assumed local characteristics, and new types (e.g., local saints, like the first Russian martyrs, Boris and Gleb; see Figure 7) advanced to center stage.[62]

Traditional types, including, significantly, the all-Russified *Theotokos* and even the various conventional images of the Savior, took their coloration from the black earthen hues of Northern Russia; from the local pagan rites; and from the practical, down-to-earth needs of the local peasantry.[63] Indigenous

---

[57] Ibid., pp. 125ff.

[58] This profound expression is, of course, the title of Robin Cormack's insightful book, *Painting the Soul*, Chicago: University of Chicago Press (1997).

[59] The spirituality and abstraction of the linear, as compared to the earthiness of the substantial, was captured by Paul Klee in his *Théorie de L'Art Moderne*, Geneva: Editions Gonthier, p. 35 (1985). This claim is easy to understand. While the line alludes to the represented object, and thus treats it prototypically, i.e., abstractly, the substantial attempts to mimic reality in all its richness and nuances.

[60] Zibawi, ibid., p. 138.

[61] In his doctrinally correct book, *The Icon*, Crestwood, NY: St. Vladimir Press (1996), Michel Quenot laments (pp. 72ff) the gradual corruption, as he perceives it, of Western iconographic representation as it moved from the (supposedly pure) Romanesque period through the Gothic era, the Renaissance, and the Baroque. By counterdistinction, Orthodox iconography remained untouched (much to Quenot's delight), thus retaining its original purity of expression, its spirituality, and the continued abstract promise inherent in its veneration.

[62] See Viktor Nikitch Lazarev, *The Russian Icon From Its Origins to the Sixteenth Century*, translated from the Italian by Colette Joly Dees, Collegeville MN: Liturgical Press, pp. 21ff (1997).

[63] Many a Russian icon is engulfed in a soft white cloud, reminiscent of the early Slavonic sun-ritualistic customs that are typical of Nordic cultures. Perhaps the same could be said about the prevalent use of ochre, which is reminiscent of a waning sun and a typical Russian iconographic

FIGURE 7. *Boris and Gleb*, mid-fourteenth century.

pagan rites, for example, white horses as emblems of the Nordic Sun god, took root in the local Christian iconography (e.g., in depicting St. George and the dragon – see Figure 8).[64] On the basis of these and similar observations, it can

coloration. The pitch black of the northern forest, especially during the long tormenting winter
months, and the deep brown of the fertile earth are also typical of Russian iconography.
[64] James Billington, *The Face of Russia*, New York: TV Books, pp. 52, 128 (1999).

FIGURE 8. *St. George and the Dragon*, an early fifteenth-century icon of the Novgorod School.

be concluded that "early Russian icons form a totally original artistic world," although one "which is not easy to penetrate."[65]

Russia does not have a separate iconographic theology. This is hardly surprising. By the time the first icons were shipped from Byzantium to Rus' and then produced and reproduced on Russian soil, "the triumph of Orthodoxy," that is, the subjugation of the iconoclasts by the iconodules, was already a fait accompli. Byzantium had a universally accepted doctrinal foundation of iconography, complete with a detailed reasoning for the centrality of icon

[65] Ibid., p. 30.

veneration in the Orthodox Faith.[66] The wholesale importation of this spiritual cargo into Rus' was focused on the cargo itself, rather than on the ideological justification of its existence. "Russian Orthodoxy," writes Billington, "tended to accept unquestioningly Orthodox definitions of truth and Byzantine art; but the complex philosophical traditions and literary conventions of Byzantium (let alone the classical and Hellenic foundations of Byzantine culture) were never properly assimilated. Thus, factually, Russia took over 'the Byzantine achievement ... without the Byzantine inquisitiveness.'"[67] Clearly, the importance of icon veneration in Russia far exceeded, and still exceeds, its importance in other Orthodox societies. While icons were, of course, widespread in Byzantium, it was hardly the main art form in Constantinople; rather, it was mosaic. While it spread throughout the "Greek" world, Greece itself embellished its shrines with murals more than with icons. Only in Russia did it become the principal form of artistic expression.[68] Russian icons far transcend their relatively limited role in houses of worship, but this can hardly be said of other cultures. The glow of their spirituality dominated, for better or for worse, Russian ideas about art and about life as late as the nineteenth century, and arguably far beyond that point.[69] The great Leo Tolstoy's reflections about art are instructive in this respect.[70] According to Tolstoy, artistic creation is not about beauty or aesthetics. Rather, it is about the transmission of feeling from the artist to the spectator. A successful work of art is one that conveys this feeling successfully and causes the spectator to partake in the feeling that was sensed by the artist in the process of creation. The proximity between this vision and the world of icons is striking. The rejection of the role of aesthetics in the viewer's sentiment to the Holy Icons; the perception of art as a set of practical tools in the advancement of morals; the total subordination of the materialistic to the "spiritual in art" à la Kandinsky; the unique taxonomy, again à la Kandinsky, of the "spiritual" in art as belonging to the categories of feeling, not to the cognitive faculties; and the deep religious faith that animates it all – all these ideas and many more of a similar ilk bestow upon the Russian icon its special meaning and significance

---

[66] This ideological foundation dates back particularly to the theological reasoning of John of Damascene and Theodore of Studion. John's ideas are formulated (in English translation) in his *On the Divine Images: Three Apologies Against Those Who Attack the Divine Images*, translated by David Anderson, Crestwood, NY: St. Vladimir Seminary Press (1980). Theodore's ideas were translated in *On the Holy Icons*, translated by Catharine Roth (1981). An orderly interpretation of these apologies is given by Moshe Barasch, *Icon*, New York: New York University Press, pp. 185ff (1992).

[67] James Billington, *The Icon and the Axe*, New York: Vintage, p. 6 (1970).

[68] Tamara Talbot-Rice, *Russian Icons*, London: Spring Books, p. 9 (1963).

[69] Many a modern Russian thinker still believes that the world of icons reflects a set of values that ought to be followed in the moral conduct of modern people. For a poetically beautiful expression of this belief, see Pavel Florensky, *Iconostasis*, translated by Donald Sheehan and Olga Andrejev, Crestwood, NY: St. Vladimir Seminary Press (1996; first published in 1922).

[70] The following lines are based on Tolstoy's celebrated art-critical essay, "What Is Art?," which he published in 1896, after, according to his own testimony, fifteen years of reflection on the subject.

and makes its study a useful tool in understanding Russian culture in more general terms.

We are ready, then, to proceed to the next step, to demonstrate how a contract worldview and an icon worldview, like oil and water, simply do not mix. In each chapter I offer a pairwise comparison that brings to the fore this inevitable conclusion of conflict and incompatibility.

2

Humanism

The rise of contract as a legitimate social instrument is not a trivial proposition. Unlike property, which seems to be endemic to the human race,[1] contract briefly shines[2] and then wanes again in different societies along the course of history. Western contract law has its roots in Aristotelian philosophy. It was baptized on the European continent by the methodical genius of St. Thomas Aquinas and then spread far and wide in this embryonic form from France to Spain to the Low Countries and beyond. Throughout this long journey it had its

[1] Property seems to be evolving whenever its benefits, in a given human environment, exceed its costs, i.e., whenever the utility of holding private entitlements exceeds the concomitant burdens. The costs of property are those associated with defining private entitlements (e.g., the fencing of land or the marking of cattle) and protecting them from rival, unauthorized, claimants (e.g., thieves). When goods are plentiful there is no reason to bear these costs, because the enjoyment of the goods is not conditioned on exclusivity of title. When scarcity replaces plenty, however, not earmarking specific goods for the exclusive use of their owners gives an incentive to all existing players to exhaust them at an accelerated pace, to the common detriment of all (to use a famous example, to catch every single fish in a common pond at a rate that does not allow the fish population in the pond to regenerate itself). Some primitive tribes, then, may not experience the institution of property, but this is only because given the plentiful nature of their consumer and other goods, conferring title on individual people of these goods entails more costs than benefits. Even primitive tribes develop fairly sophisticated forms of ownership with regard to scarce goods. See Harold Demsetz, "Towards a Theory of Property Rights," *American Economic Review* 57:13 (1967). For a more recent contribution see Robert Ellickson, "Property in Land," *Yale Law Journal* 102:1315 (1993). Given these considerations, it is hardly surprising that the concept of property took root on Russian soil. Even Marxist ideology could not eradicate it; the more thoughtful among the Marxist theorists did not even try. See Evgeny Pashukanis, *Law and Marxism, a General Theory*, translated by Barbara Einhorn, London: Pluto Press (1983) (first published in Russian in 1924 and then in German in 1929, from which this translation seems to be derived).

[2] The most striking example of an idea resembling modern contract in antiquity is the form of *stipulatio* in late classical Roman law. The "stipulator" could promise almost anything to the promisee, provided she used a sufficiently solemn language (the promisee had to respond in kind) as a measure of weeding out frivolous utterances. A more detailed analysis of *stipulatio* falls outside the ambit of this book.

peaks and retreats; it moved forward and then it moved back again;[3] but it had not assumed its modern, fully developed form until the late sixteenth or early seventeenth century, as Europe was swept by the tidal wave of the Renaissance.

In the first part of this chapter, I sketch out the development of contract as promise in the main occidental legal systems. A parallel development failed to occur, either contemporaneously or in later centuries, on Russian soil. Both this evolution itself and its conspicuous absence in other cultures requires an explanation. Various explanations for this phenomenon abound.[4] In this chapter I focus on one principal theory, which runs like a red thread throughout this book, namely the centrality of the individual person in a *humanist* society.

On the Evolution of Enforceable Contracts

Once again, it is a common error to believe that enforceable agreements have always been a central underpinning of civic society.[5] Although agreements have presumably been *made* from times immemorial, their content, the contractual stipulation, could not be *enforced*, as a general proposition, until well into the sixteenth and seventeenth centuries.[6]

The Common Law of England

The judges and other practitioners who pieced together over the course of several centuries the Common Law of England have never been famous for their theoretical acumen. They seldom made references to the subtle cultural undercurrents that informed their way of thinking. They impressed upon their audience the illusory sense that the product of their labor nourished itself from its own internal logic.[7] Nevertheless, as the river of life gushed forward, so did the law of the realm, and no other system has proven as resilient to the

---

[3] For a thorough critical historical analysis of the European roots of early contract law, see James Gordley, *The Philosopical Origins of Modern Contract Doctrine*, New York: Oxford University Press (1991).

[4] Many contemporary commentators believe that Russia's current problems with the market economy in general and its struggle to accept contract law in particular result from the surviving ethos of the Bolshevist regime. See, for example, Vladimir Toumanov, "Freedom of Contract and Constitutional Law in Russia," in Alfredo Rabello and Petar Sarcevic (eds.), *Freedom of Contract and Constitutional Law*, Jerusalem: The Harry and Michael Sacher Institute for Legislative and Comparative Law, p. 241 (1998).

[5] For a completely ahistorical understanding of the concept of agreement, whether based on promise or otherwise, see, for example, Margaret Gilbert, "Is an Agreement an Exchange of Promises?," *Journal of Philosophy* 90:627 (1993).

[6] James Ames, "The History of Assumpsit," *Harvard Law Review* 2:252 (1888).

[7] As virtually all post-modern commentators are quick to point out, the practice of concealing the cultural bias of authority makes it seem all the more powerful and less vulnerable to critical skepticism, because hinging authority on its own "intrinsic" logic makes it appear more scientific and "objectively" fitting. This explanation falls in line with the theory that judges, like other market agents, are bent on maximizing their own power within the body politick and would be loath to dilute it by exposing their dependence on extrajudicial *desiderata*.

changing *mores* of time than the Common Law of England.[8] It is the task of the legal historian to interpret these details, unassisted by explicit judicial pronouncements, by portraying the logic of doctrinal developments as part and parcel of their larger cultural ambience. In the following lines I trace the nascent idea of modern contract within the Common Law tradition.

As late as the final decades of the twelfth century, it was possible for a leading English author to declare flatly that, "it is not the custom of the court of the Lord King to protect private agreements."[9] This sweeping statement was not entirely accurate. Some merchants could avail themselves of the jurisdiction of their specialized tribunals.[10] Other private parties could bind themselves contractually if they used a sealed document, a "covenant," which was normally secured by a penal bond. In case of default, the bond could be executed against the person of the debtor, resulting in incarceration, sometimes of indefinite duration. But formal covenants had their problems. A creditor who lost her covenant (or let the wax wear off) was left without a remedy. A debtor who neglected to destroy the covenant upon payment remained liable. The ethereal concept of contract was thus solidified, or condensed, into the material element of the waxed instrument and did not have an independent existence of its own. It is hard to know if this or some other reason accounted for the sparse use of sealed instruments during the Middle Ages; the fact remains, however, that they were never in wide circulation.[11] To effectuate exchange, the parties resorted to informal contracting, and this is where our story begins.

Informal contracting is, or at least has been, the contract law of ordinary people. It is not confined, like the Law Merchant, to a specialized commercial

---

[8] The classical exposition of the Common Law's vitality is given by Roscoe Pound, *The Spirit of the Common Law*, Somerset, NJ: Transaction Publishers (1999).

[9] R. de Glanvill, *Treatise on the Laws and Customs of the Realm of England*, G. Hall, ed., Book 10, Chapter 18, Oxford: Oxford University Press (1965). Glanvill's treatise was written in about 1180.

[10] The historical origins of the Law Merchant go back to the ancient civilizations of the Near East, China, and the Arab traders of the early Middle Ages. It was developed by Italian traders in the central part of the Middle Ages and spread throughout Europe and beyond. It applied only to "merchants," although the exact definition of this term is not entirely clear. It covered international transactions among merchants of different nationalities, as well as transactions made in local fairs, even among merchants belonging to a single nationality. Aggrieved parties could seek justice in specialized tribunals, which were not accessible to the general public. The Law Merchant sanctioned executory promises, especially in sales transactions. Other typical contracts included the finance of commerce, shipping, insurance, and the pooling of risk through contracts of partnership. See the fascinating volume by Wyndham Anstis Bewes, *The Romance of the Law Merchant*, London: Sweet & Maxwell (1923; reprinted 1988). The evolution of the Law Merchant was powered by the merchants themselves, who wished to enforce their commercial customs within the closed circles, organizations, or fraternities to which they belonged. See Leon Trakman, *The Law Merchant: The Evolution of Commercial Law*, Buffalo, NY: William S. Hein (1983).

[11] A short, readable, and entirely reliable source for this and other historical comments contained in this chapter is A. W. B. Simpson, "Historical Introduction to Cheshire," in Fifoot and Furmston's *Law of Contract*, London: Butterworths (13th ed., 1996).

subset of the population. Nor is it restricted, like the law of sealed instruments, to the literate few who, during the Middle Ages, were by and large members of the clergy and, on occasion, of the landed aristocracy.[12] Informal contacting, normally by word of mouth, had to conform to the exigencies of the so-called "writ system." One could only bind oneself in fairly circumscribed circumstances, which were recognized by a writ, or a "form of action." The existing forms of action constituted a *numerus clausus*. None of those forms could be altered to fit the idiosyncratic preferences of the parties. One could safely lend money, for example, because an obligation to return the loan fitted the writ of "debt"; one could safely rent a tangible item, because possession could be regained by using the writ of "detinue." A lot of things could *not* be committed by contractual stipulation, simply because no fitting form of action could be found. Notably and most importantly, one could not commit oneself to do anything (build a house, sing a song) because there was no writ in existence that covered the contingency.[13] To the modern mind, this is a striking state of affairs. If a given writ was found missing, why was it not immediately crafted to enable the parties to do what they wanted to do? Surely there were no observable moral reasons, at least in principle, for this omission, because what the parties wished but could not accomplish was not necessarily devoid of moral merit. For the medieval mind, however, this omission was not striking at all. Medieval jurists did not even consider the possibility of intentionally messing with the existing forms of action, let alone repudiating the whole *modus operandi* altogether and replacing it with a more generalized concept of contract. It is illuminating to trace how, and at what historical period, changes started to creep in.

Contract sneaked its way into the walled city of the writ system by using tort law as its Trojan horse. Tort law recognized the form of "trespass" (and, later, "trespass on the case") to redress certain cases of wrongdoing committed by one individual against another. In 1367, a physician promised to cure a patient from his ailments, but in actual fact he exacerbated the patient's condition. This was really a mixed case of tort (medical malpractice, in modern parlance) and contract (an unfulfilled promise). It was the former element of the case that enabled the court to rule in favor of the plaintiff.[14] An unadulterated case of contract was brought a few years later against a builder who failed to

---

[12] James Thompson (ed.), *The Literacy of the Laity in the Middle Ages*, Berkeley: University of California Press (1939).

[13] It was often suggested to me that medieval law did not actually need a functioning set of contract law. The merchant class, who particularly needed contracts, could get a measure of enforcement in their specialized tribunals and the peasant society in the countryside was content to make do with instantaneous exchange. The fact remains, however, that merchants could not satisfactorily contract with nonmerchants and, more importantly, that nonmerchants needed to strike agreements *inter se* as well. A peasant might wish, for example, to pledge to devote his efforts for a designated purpose, to sell his next year's crop, or to exchange promises with another person. None of these commonplace stipulations could be carried out in the old writ system. The struggle for generalized assumpsit in the Middle Ages was not a futile disputation.

[14] *Skyrne v. Butolf* (1367) YB 2 Ric 2 (Ames Series) 223.

perform but did not otherwise cause any damage or injury. The court rejected the claim on the ground that trespass on the case supported instances of "malfeasance" (tort) but not instances of "nonfeasance" (broken promises).[15] It took more than a century for the Common Law judges to realize that oftentimes there is no real difference between faulty performance of some promise (that is, malfeasance) and simple nonperformance (nonfeasance), as all the economic consequences of both instances may be indistinguishable.[16] And then it took almost one additional century to solidify this realization and to formulate it as a general legal proposition. In the well-known *Slade's Case*[17] of 1602,[18] the court famously ruled that "every contract executory imports in itself an assumpsit," or, more intelligibly, every outstanding promise is, in itself, binding (for having been assumed – or assumpsit – by the promisor).[19] The *Slade* promise was thus pronounced to exist in itself, regardless of the identity of the parties (one need not be a merchant to get a remedy), without corporeal reification (as in the case of covenants), without regard to form (as in the case of trespass), and in spite of its entirely executory nature (as distinguished from the case of instantaneous exchange).

That was indeed an ominous leap forward. But some recent legal historians seem content to elucidate these developments as if the struggle were fought and then won on purely doctrinal grounds. David Ibbetson, for example, strives to show that many Common Law judges wished to introduce a generalized theory about the enforceability of executory contracts (i.e., "assumpsit") for some time prior to *Slade's Case*. They were barred from doing so for two cumulative reasons: From a technical point of view, many people objected to interpreting the writ of debt too broadly, for fear that a sweeping interpretation would violate the delicate boundaries between the distinctive forms of action. From a normative point of view, it was argued that the triumph of assumpsit might impair the defendant's privilege to "wage his law."[20] Not much can be said about the first ground for objection, except, perhaps, the obvious. The forms of action are procedural devices. These are man-made tools crafted for the

---

[15] *Walton v. Brinth* (1400) YB 2 Hen 4, fo 3 pl 9.

[16] It would be awkward, for instance, to draw a distinction between the case of a repairman who promises to fix a television set but fails to show up, and the case of a repairman who does show up but fails to properly repair it. This insight was first grafted into decisional law in 1533, in the case of *Pickering v. Thoroughgood*, 9 YB Sel Soc 4.

[17] John Slade, a farmer in Devon, owned a "close" of land where he grew wheat and rye. He ploughed the land and sowed the field, and the ears of his crop came out plush and full. He sold it to the defendant for an agreed price, but when he harvested his yield the defendant refused to accept delivery or to pay the price.

[18] (1602) 4 Co Rep 91a, Yelv 21, Moore KB 433, 667.

[19] The Court continued: "[F]or when one agrees to pay money, or to deliver any thing, thereby to another . . . and the other in consideration thereof agrees to pay so much money as such a day, in that case both mutual executory agreement of both parties imports in itself reciprocal actions upon the case, as well as actions in debt . . ."

[20] David Ibbetson, "Sixteenth Century Contract Law: Slade's Case in Context," *Oxford Journal of Legal Studies* 4:295 (1984).

attainment of substantive justice. Clearly, then, it seems odd to compromise substantive desirable outcomes for the sake of saving the integrity of their procedural means. The second ground has to do with a certain medieval procedure that allowed the defendant to defeat a claim based on the writ of debt (but not of assumpsit) by swearing to its falsity, if she could bring eleven more witnesses to swear along with her. It was allegedly feared that if assumpsit were allowed to triumph without the safety net of waging one's law, the courts might be flooded with spurious claims. As Ibbetson himself explains, however, this kind of reasoning does not hold much water, since in the sixteenth century the practice of waging one's law fell out of grace anyway (it was considered ungentlemanly to exercise it). It was also appreciated that the required eleven witnesses could easily be recruited for ready cash.[21]

The futility of attempting to understand assumpsit on technical grounds manifests itself even more clearly when one examines the parallel progress that was achieved during approximately the same period on the European Continent. This comparison is interesting, because lawyers in France, Spain, Italy, and Flanders never heard of assumpsit, of the English forms of action, of trespass on the case, of waging one's law, or of the Common Law distinction between malfeasance and nonfeasance. Certainly the niceties of these distinctions could not have played a role in their evolving ideas about the enforceability of contract.

The European Continent

Anyone bold enough to lump together all civil law jurisdictions as if they were made of the same feather must proceed at one's own peril. If reduced to their bare elements, however, many European legal systems share a lot in common, and it is to that kind of sketchy portrayal that I wish to turn at this point. Furthermore, it will be seen that if we use only rough brushstrokes, the evolution of contract law on the Continent and on the British Isles looks strikingly similar as well.[22] All major European systems are based on the august structure of the law of ancient Rome. The ancient Romans themselves, like the Common Law judges, were pragmatists with little taste for theoretical generalizations. As the famous phrase goes, they developed a magnificent structure of contract *laws*, but not a unified theory of Contract *Law*. These contract laws were not altogether dissimilar to the English forms of action, because one had to tailor one's

---

[21] Ibid. The Court in *Slade's Case* specifically addressed this state of affairs. It ruled: "And to the objection which has been made that it would be mischievous to the defendant that he should not wage his law . . . to that it was answered that it should be accounted to his folly that he did not take sufficient witnesses with him to prove the payment he made: but the mischief would be rather on the other party, for now experience proves that men's consciences grow so large that the respect of their private advantage, rather induces men (and chiefly those who have declining estates) to perjury."

[22] This point is repeatedly made by James Gordley, *The Philosophical Origins of Modern Contract Doctrine*, New York: Oxford University Press (1991) and serves as one of the central themes in his erudite manuscript.

claim to fit the rigid boundaries of one or the other of these legal molds. One of these molds, *stipulatio*, was more malleable than the others, because one could promise almost anything and be bound by one's word, if one only conformed to a specified set of formalities.[23] It appears, however, that the widespread use of *stipulatio* declined along the course of history and came into disuse in the Middle Ages.[24] As the original genius of Roman Law itself started to fade away with the decline of the Roman Empire and the weakening of memory, its living image was all in the eye of the beholder. Its formal brokers were the academic interpreters of the Roman tradition, first called the "glossators" and later referred to as the jurists of the "scholastic" tradition.

Different generations of glossatorial and post-glossatorial jurists toiled on different parts of the European Continent in a (not necessarily concerted) effort to find some meaning and a sense of purpose in the old Roman texts. This was obviously not an easy task. Roman law evolved over the course of many centuries, and given its highly pragmatic nature, it was aimed at addressing different kinds of concerns, each pertaining to its own spatial and temporal challenges. There was hardly any "deep structure" of "typically Roman" legal norms that could profitably be identified to address the needs and exigencies of real people over the course of two millennia.[25] Consequently, various generations of jurists chose to highlight within the Roman sources entirely different selections. The first scholars who "discovered" in the Roman sources a set of ideas that led to the recognition of enforceable promises worked in the otherwise obscure town of Salamanca (and established the so-called glorious Salamanca School).

[23] These formalities were aimed at weeding out unintentional commitments. The promisee had to ask the promisor if he undertook to abide by his promise, and the promisor had to confirm that he did. Both promisor and promisee had to use especially designated words ("Spondes? Spondeo!"), or else the entire ritual was void.

[24] The Roman Empire at its heyday resembled in many of its economic and commercial manifestations the emerging market economy that reemerged in post-medieval Europe. There is little wonder that *stipulatio* made its appearance in that glorious period, then all but disappeared for a thousand years, only to be resuscitated, disguised either in assumpsit form or – on the European Continent – under some other name in the sixteenth century. To the best of my knowledge, the first commentator to discover this juridical parallel between classical Rome and the rise of Western capitalism has been Max Weber in his very first works. See Anthony Giddens, *Capitalism and Modern Social Theory, an Analysis of the Writings of Marx, Durkheim and Max Weber*, Cambridge: Cambridge University Press, pp. 119ff (1971).

[25] Early Roman jurisprudence was based on the so-called "Twelve Tables," composed around the middle of the fifth century B.C. "Classical" Roman Law evolved around the second century A.D. (The famous jurist Gaius wrote his "Institutions," the only full surviving comprehensive text from that era, about 161 A.D. The Emperor Justinian oversaw the codification of all pervious legal learning in his "*Corpus Juris Civilis*" (the "*Digesta*") during his reign in the sixth century A.D. The Byzantine Empire itself lingered on, of course, for many centuries after that. Only a naïve theorist could entertain the thought that the diverse social, economic, and spiritual needs of the Roman (and Greek Byzantine) people over the course of such a long era could have a single, unifying legal "deep structure." To compound the difficulty, authentic Roman texts were not freely available before the invention of the printing press. For many centuries there was only one surviving text of the *Digesta*, which was kept behind bars to preserve the treasure from careless handling. See, on this matter, Chapter 7, supra.

Prominent Salamanca jurists included such luminaries as Luis de Molina (1535–1600) and Francisco Suarez (1548–1617), both of the Jesuit Order. Their effort was joined by Leonard Lessius (1554–1623), a fellow Jesuit of Flemish extraction. It was perhaps the latter who formulated, for the first time, the idea that promise *as such* had a binding force.[26] Lessius' ideas were still debated on the Continent, whereto they spread, throughout the seventeenth century,[27] but finally these ideas took root and, having taken root, were taken for granted.[28] Leonard Lessius was not aware of *Slade's Case* and its formal complications (the writ of trespass on the case, the budding writ of assumpsit, waging one's law), but came upon his "discovery" of contract as promise three years, not more, after the *Slade* Court handed down its historic ruling. His reputation as a legal sage spread throughout the Continent. The merchants of his hometown of Antwerp sought him out and consulted him on matters of justice.

Lessius and Slade: Do They Have Anything in Common?

The close proximity of *Slade's Case* and of Lessius' theoretical work, and the universal triumph of their new doctrine across Western Europe, cannot be bypassed without an explanation. James Gordley makes an attempt to trace these developments to their philosophical roots. Unlike Ibbetson, who views the development of assumpsit through the narrower prism of precedent and the intrinsic logic of the Common Law, Gordley offers a broader interpretation. The Jesuits of Salamanca and Antwerp, he maintains, did not simply *interpret* the Roman sources. They *synthesized* them with the old Aristotelian ideas that certain promises had to be kept as an omen of truth and honesty, and with the Thomistic absorption of these ideas on the basis of Christian moral imperatives. European contract occurred, according to Gordley's views, simply because some deep-thinking individuals had the wisdom, erudition, and drive to synthesize all these ideas and to concoct, in their own minds, the final yield. This fruit of their imagination, the enforceable promise, happened to retail so well across Europe, simply because it was smart, well crafted, and convincing. Gordley is not very clear on how those ideas spread so swiftly to Britain and seemingly does not have any evidence to support the proposition.[29] Being a devout follower of these ideas himself, he considers it a paradox that they finally had their moment of triumph exactly at an age, the seventeenth century,

---

[26] Lessius' *magnus opus*, *De Justitia et Jure*, was originally published in Leuven, Lyons, Paris, and Venice in 1605.

[27] Even great jurists of the seventeenth century, including Hugo Grotius (1583–1645) and Samuel Pufendorf (1632–1694) remained, for long periods in their lives, unconvinced. See Gordley, ibid., p. 73.

[28] In the eighteenth century they firmly appear in canonical textbooks (see, for example, the entire oeuvre of the great French jurist Robert Pothier, who, in due course, influenced the doctrinal systematization of the law of England).

[29] Although he does maintain that the British treatise writers were influenced by some leading Continental writers, such as Grotius, Pufendorf, Domat, and Pothier (all of whom, by the way, were preceded by the holding of the Court in the *Slade's Case*). See ibid., pp. 134ff.

when the old Aristotelian authority lost its grip on the contemporary collective mind.[30] It hardly occurs to him that if contract triumphed across Europe and the British Isles exactly when both Aristotle and Aquinas fell out of grace,[31] it stands to reason to look for an explanation elsewhere.

This explanation is not hard to find. People tend to be affected by the culture of their own period and to be imbued with its *Zeitgeist*. Both *Slade* and Lessius appeared on the scene at the same historical period, at the height of the Renaissance. The Renaissance may be interpreted as the sum total of a large and mutually complementary set of ideas that gave rise to an incredibly broad spectrum of historical manifestations – in the letters, in art, in science, and in law. Modern law, like modern science or even modern art, has many of its roots in that set of ideas. In this as well as in the next chapter, I focus on what seems to be the single most important contract-related notion of that epoch, *the humanist interpretation of the universe*.

Why should this notion be so crucial to the development of modern contract law? In a nutshell, the flip side of the freedom to contract is the burden of enforcing contracts. If A has a freedom to commit the fulfillment of a promise to B, this in effect means that if A attempts to repudiate the promise, B has a valid claim not only against A, the promisor, but also against Leviathan, the embodiment of organized society. In her private thrust against A, B may legitimately expect others – the courts, the public enforcement machinery, the *fiscus* – to pull the chestnuts out of the fire for her. By their private agreement, A and B harness the might of Leviathan to the chariot of their individual will. The legitimacy of private contracting reflects a hierarchy whereby the State, as the embodiment of organized authority, makes itself subservient to its own subjects, be their individual order of preferences whimsical as it may. Had this hierarchy been reversed it would have been harder to see how, and for what purpose, organized society should consent to abide by the contractual stipulations of ordinary people.[32]

---

[30] Gordley, ibid., pp. 112ff.

[31] The early glossators of the Roman tradition who toiled in the newly formed University of Bologna at the beginning of the twelfth century were, of course, quite familiar with Aristotelian learning. It would be preposterous to suggest that they lacked the intellectual capacity to grasp his doctrines and to apply it to the subject matter of their scholarship. The fact that they did not apply themselves in that direction is evidence that their time was not ripe for it or, even more plausibly, that when contract was finally "discovered," fully half a millennium later, it had nothing to do with Aristotelian scholarship and everything to do with the surrounding cultural *milieu*.

[32] The modern paradigm of a reversed hierarchy is the Nazi or Fascist State of the twentieth century. The core of fascist ideology is that collective society ought to be perceived as an abstract, independent entity with distinct interests of its own. These interests are not derived from the individual *desiderata* of its members and take priority over those *desiderata*. It is fully consistent with this reversed order of priorities that the entire German economy was based on such coerced concepts as slave labor and its war machine was fed by coerced conscription *usque ad mortem*. These central features of the Nazi State made a mockery of whatever vestiges of the freedom to contract were spared in the formal law books. For a succinct account of the total corruption of

This explanation is not meant to preempt other approaches to the subject. The largely rural, agrarian, and feudal system of the Middle Ages could have maintained its economic viability without much commercial activity. The Renaissance and post-Renaissance centuries witnessed successive processes of commercialization, urbanization, and industrialization, which called for a greater reliance on the exchange of promises. One could argue, therefore, that Occidental contract was born to economic necessity, which was, in itself, a post-medieval apparition. However, this kind of argument is at least partially circuitous, because commercialization in itself is a web of contracts, a huge contractual *nexus* between and among persons of commerce, and neither urbanization nor industrialization can be conceptualized without it. It is the spirit of the Renaissance (not only its humanism but other things as well)[33] that moved masses of people to the urban centers, involved them in intricate systems of exchange, and eventually ushered in the other features of industrialized modernity. Significantly, the failure of the Renaissance spirit to take root on Russian soil is intimately linked, I maintain, to the fatal retardation in that vast and plentiful land of commercial entrepreneurship, of urban growth, of the rise of industry, and, ultimately, of contract.

In the rest of this chapter I document the centrality of Man in Renaissance culture and iconography and its categorical opposite in Eastern Orthodox culture and iconography.

Renaissance Culture and Iconography

The gradual decline of the Middle Ages and the flowering of the Renaissance in Europe witnessed a marked difference in the perceived role of Man in the universe. An enthusiastic supporter of this point of view described this process in the following florid terms:

During the Middle Ages, man had lived enveloped in a cowl. He had not seen the beauty of the world, or had seen it only to cross himself, and turn aside and tell his beads and pray. Like St. Bernard traveling along the shores of the Lake Leman, and noticing neither the azure of the waters, nor the luxuriance of the vines, nor the radiance of the mountains with their robe of sun and snow, but bending a thought-burdened forehead over the neck of his mule; even like this monk, humanity had passed, a careful pilgrim, intent on the terrors of sin, death, and judgment, along the highways of the world, and had scarcely known that they were sightworthy or that life is a blessing. Beauty is a

---

private law in Nazi Germany, see, for instance, Norman Marsh, "Some Aspects of the German Legal System under National Socialism," *Law Quarterly Review* 62:366 (1946). Even given individualism and the so-called "will theory," it is not trivial to show why society must make itself available for the enforcement of private agreements. This point was forcefully made by Gordley, ibid., and constitutes one of the main theses of his book.

[33] In subsequent chapters I examine several of these other features that contributed to the rise of the contract-oriented *homo economicus*. These features include individualism (Chapter 3, infra), the dwindling role of authority (Chapter 4, infra), the importance of wealth (Chapter 5, infra), of reason and experience (Chapter 6, infra), and of the written word (Chapter 7, infra).

snare, pleasure a sin, the world a fleeting show, man fallen and lost, death the only certainty, judgment inevitable, hell everlasting, heaven hard to win.... These were the fixed ideas of the ascetic mediaeval Church. The Renaissance shattered and destroyed them... a new ideal was established, whereby man strove to make himself the monarch of the globe on which it is his privilege as well as destiny to live.[34]

This view of the Renaissance is clearly pedigreed to the great Jacob Burck-hardt, whose principal *oeuvre, Die Kultur der Renaissance in Italien,*[35] first published in 1860, set the tone for all subsequent discussions about the rise of modernity.[36] According to the so-called Burckhardt thesis, the culture of the Renaissance in Italy created a sudden rift in the history of humankind. It jettisoned the idealistic and dogmatic worldview of the Middle Ages and assumed in its stead a brand new understanding of both the universe as a set of objective phenomena and of the centrality of the human race as a criterion for identifying the Social Good. Burckhardt was fully aware, of course, of the many grave social injustices that afflicted Italian society in the fifteenth and sixteenth centuries.[37] His "thesis," though, was not that actual conduct was necessarily more *humane*, but rather that it was more *humanist*, in the sense that humankind as a whole, and the state of being an individual person in particular, were first perceived as the main standard for the appreciation of other phenomena. Though less theatrical than Symonds' perception of the Renaissance, Burckhardt's famous words are well worth citing as well:

In the Middle Ages, both sides of human consciousness – that which was turned within and that which was turned without – lay dreaming, or half awake beneath a common veil. The veil was woven of faith, illusion, and childish prepossession, through which the world and history were seen clad in strange hues. Man was conscious of himself only as a member of a race, people, party, family, or corporation – only through some general category. In Italy this veil first melted into air; an *objective* treatment and consideration of the State and of all the things of this world became possible. The *subjective* side at the same time asserted itself with corresponding emphasis; man became a spiritual *individual*, and recognized himself as such.[38]

Now Burckhardt's thesis fell out of vogue with numerous modern critics, some of whom have driven home a number of valid points. Do these revisionist claims raise any reasonable doubt concerning the centrality of the individual person in the culture of the Renaissance? I do not think so. The main prong of

---

[34] John Symonds, *Renaissance in Italy*, Volume 1, p. 13 (1888).

[35] Jabob Burckhardt, *The Civilization of the Renaissance in Italy* (1860). All references to Burck-hardt's book are to S. G. C. Middlemore's translation (The Phaidon Press and Oxford University Press, 1944).

[36] Phillip Lee Ralph, *The Renaissance in Perspective*, London: G. Bell, especially pp. 2ff (1973).

[37] The great *humanist* revolution of the Renaissance had only an oblique connection to any *human-itarian* values. On the sharp distinction between humanist achievement and moral deterioration in that ominous period, see, e.g. Ralph Roeder, *The Man of the Renaissance*, New York: Viking Press (1933).

[38] *The Civilization of the Renaissance*, p. 81.

attack largely launched by some medievalists is that the process of Man's rise to the center of the Universe, as well as of her scholarly interest in the classics and in the world around her, preceded the Renaissance by at least two centuries.[39] Further arguments along the same lines emphasized the crucial contribution of the Middle Ages to the development of philosophy and the natural sciences and even went so far as to claim that the Renaissance was actually *inferior* to the preceding centuries in some of these respects.[40]

Finally, an articulate post-modern attempt to discredit Burckhardt as a naïve nineteenth-century historian, argued that humanism, like most other social constructs, cannot be perceived as an "objective" exogenous occurrence, one that just happened to transpire during the Renaissance. Rather, it is the result of a "self-fashioning" mechanism that allows its practitioners to deploy themselves in a social role that is advantageous to them, given the power struggle between and among their contemporaries.[41] The contemporary players in this game are, presumably, the members of the ruling classes in the fifteenth to the seventeenth centuries (the "humanists") while the act of taking their self-fashioning seriously is nothing but a figment of the imagination of some upper-class nineteenth-century intellectuals.

It does transcend the scope of my discussion to settle this controversy,[42] but, happily, it is not necessary to do so. For even if we assume, along with the revisionist historians, that the germs of the Burckhardt observations were sown in the centuries preceding the Renaissance, few reasonable observers can possibly deny that they came into full bloom during this period. Nor does it matter much, from my perspective, whether humanism materialized during the Renaissance as an *objective* phenomenon, that is, whether it was just "out there," or was laboriously constructed by self-interested players as their *subjective* idea, trope, mask, or even a form of deception. Even if the latter is the correct interpretation of history (which, incidentally, I doubt), it must be admitted that the players' attempt at fashioning themselves as participants in a humanist society was ingeniously well crafted.

It is to that kind of self-perception (or self-fashioning, for that matter) that I wish to turn at this stage.

---

[39] An influential book written in this vein is Charles Haskins, *The Renaissance of the Twelfth Century*, Cambridge, MA: Harvard University Press (1927).

[40] For some leading authorities, see Philip Lee Ralph, note 36 supra, at pp. 6ff.

[41] A particularly influential work in this vein is Stephen Greenblatt, *Renaissance Self-Fashioning: From More to Shakespeare*, Chicago: University of Chicago Press (1980).

[42] Many have striven to do so. See, for example, John Martin, "Inventing Sincerity, Refashioning Prudence: The Discovery of the Individual in Renaissance Europe," *American Historical Review* 102:1309 (1997). In this essay Martin shows, with admirable erudition, how key concepts that occupied the Renaissance mind, e.g., prudence and sincerity, as virtues to be striven for, reflect a deeply individualistic perception of the self and a total breach from former medieval notions of community and adaptation. Martin shows that this stage of self-consciousness, and the legitimacy of individual claims to uniqueness and a sense of autonomy, developed along parallel lines in Catholic Europe (e.g., in the writings of Montaigne) and in the philosophy of the Reformation.

A common cliché attributes to the people of the Renaissance the inclination to revitalize the spirit of the classical world, which lay dormant for a thousand years. This is certainly true, but, given the great versatility of the classical world, it is a matter of great interest to see exactly what parts of it were chosen as objects of veneration and how the chosen parts were interpreted and used. Not surprisingly, Renaissance people often selected bits and pieces from that inexhaustible source exactly *because* they formed a perfect fit with their preconceived ideas about the world and their own role in it. A famous example relates to the *opus* of the famous first-century B.C. Roman architect, Marcus Vitruvius Pollio. Vitruvius' literary output[43] concerned all the artifices of his craft – from walls to floors, from altars to public baths, theaters, aqueducts, temples, and all modes of construction. Professional architects from Bramante to Michelangelo to Palladio were known to have heeded his advice. However tediously technical his work may seem to some lay readers, he was held in high esteem among painters and draftsmen of the Renaissance, quite regardless of his prowess as a dispenser of architectural advice. The main reason for this aspect of Vitruvius' reputation lies in a few lines in his work, in which he suggests that the standard for all beauty stems from the respective bodies of men and women, and all ideal proportions must imitate their natural example. Here are the lines themselves:

Without symmetry and proportion there can be no principles in the design of any temple; that is, if there is no precise relation between its members, as in the case of those of a well shaped man.[44]

Vitruvius goes on to explain how a well-shaped man is made. His height is equal to the distance between the extremities of his outstretched hands (thus forming a perfect square), and he is encased within a perfect circle if he parts his legs and stretches his arms upwards in a 45 degree angle. Most everyone is familiar with the famous Leonardo drawing of Vitruvian Man (Figure 9).[45]

Vitruvius also praises the ancient Doric architects for selecting the human body as the standard for their aesthetic achievement:

Wishing to set up columns in that temple, but not having rules for their symmetry, and being in search of some way by which they could render them fit to bear a load and also of a satisfactory beauty of appearance, they measured the imprint of a man's foot and compared this with his height. On finding that, in a man, the foot was one sixth of the height, they applied the same principle to the column, and reared the shaft, including the capital, to a height six times its thickness at its base. Thus the Doric column, as used in buildings, began to exhibit the proportions, strength, and beauty of the body of a

---

[43] Vitruvius (Marcus Vitruvius Pollio), *The Ten Books on Architecture*, translated by Morris Hicky Morgan, New York: Dover (1960; being a republication of the Harvard University Press publication of 1914) (first published in the first century B.C).

[44] Ibid., p. 72.

[45] Leonardo's famous work is not the only one that borrowed its inspiration from the Vitruvian ideal. In fact, the subject was quite common. One particularly beautiful Vitruvian figure was drawn by Francesco di Giorgio and is kept in the famous Turin Library.

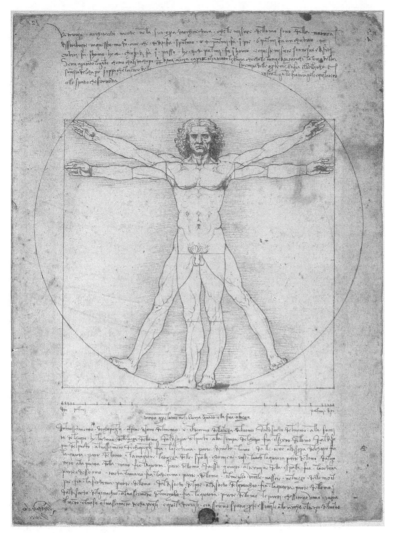

FIGURE 9. Leonardo da Vinci, *Vitruvian Man*, circa 1492.

man. Just so afterwards, whey they desired to construct a temple to Diana in a new style of beauty, they translated these foot-prints into terms characteristic of women, and thus first made a column the thickness of which was only one eighth of its height, so that it might have a taller look. . . . Thus in the invention of the two different kinds of columns, they borrowed manly beauty, naked and unadorned, for the one, and for the other the delicacy, adornment and proportions characteristic of women."[46]

These two passages are Vitruvius' only references to the standard of beauty attributed to him, and they are buried in several hundred pages of architectural

[46] Ibid., p. 103.

shoptalk of the most mundane variety. The Renaissance artists made a telling choice by targeting this isolated reference to the human figure and attaching to it such an ominous significance.

This choice falls in line with the discovery of the people of the Renaissance of their *own* importance, of their own pivotal role in the order of the universe. Their fascination with themselves radiated into their art as well as into anything else they invented. Lorenzo Ghiberti, for instance, the famous *Quattrocento* winner of the baptistery doors competition in Florence, was one of the first ever to theorize about art, and he used this opportunity to write mainly about himself.[47] It is hard to miss Ghiberti's narcissistic fascination with his own artistic achievement and his reading of his own imagined genius as a formative figure in art history.[48] Perhaps there is a silver lining in Ghiberti's approach, since the pivotal position of Man in the universe could not have conceivably come about if one were not to look up to oneself as the role model for this perceived fantasy.

A less self-centered version of Renaissance humanism is amply demonstrated by Ghiberti's associate and a fellow artist and art theoretician, Leon Battista Alberti. His writings, as well as his artistic output, are all imbued with a recurring *leitmotif* – that the purpose of all art, as well as of morality, is to serve the simple needs and thus, indirectly, to cater to the higher aspirations, of ordinary people.[49] His architectural achievement, which culminated in the famous Palazzo Rucellai in the heart of Florence (completed around the middle of the fifteenth century), is the most articulate living memory of his credo. Simple in design and well proportioned, shunning all pretext of excess lavishness, it stands witness to the comfort, spaciousness, and dignified appearance demanded by its bourgeois patrons. This architectural "message" should be considered in conjunction with the much acclaimed certitude of other Quattrocento masters – like, notably, Masaccio and the inimitable Piero della Francesca – that *space spells dignity*, as each *persona* rightfully reigns within the boundaries of her own airy surroundings. Within this space each *persona* is allowed to gracefully interact with her neighboring objects, all sharing in the sweetness of their harmonious *milieu*.[50]

Perhaps the most striking theoretical evidence for the humanism of Renaissance iconography can be found in its greatest conceptual mistake, the doctrine

---

[47] Ghiberti wrote three volumes of "commentaries" (*I Commentarii*). These volumes were published in Italian around 1447. There is no full English translation of this work; even the Italian is hard to come by, although it appears, with an accompanying German text, in Julius von Schlosser, *Lorenzo Ghibertis Denkwurdigkeiten*, Berlin: Julius Bard (1912). The commentaries span both the history and the theory of art and include (in the second volume) a long autobiographical narrative.

[48] Michael Levey, *Early Renaissance*, London: Penguin Books, pp. 24ff (1967).

[49] On this recurring theme in Alberti's life and literary and artistic work, see Joan Kelly-Gadol, *Leon Battista Alberti: Universal Man of the Early Renaissance*, Chicago: University of Chicago Press (1969).

[50] Levey, ibid., pp. 115ff.

of *Ut Pictura Poesis*, or the holding that painting and poetry are sister forms of artistic expression. The followers of this theory may be led to believe, for instance, that Dante or Shakespeare are great poets because they "draw" or "paint" their characters so skillfully, while Botticelli or Van der Weiden paint so well because of the excellence of their narrative. It is entirely beside the point to argue for or against this proposition, for its main significance lies in its widespread acceptance during the Renaissance. Since the main domain of poetic expression is human emotions, the belief in its central role in the world of painted imagery "elevates," as it were, the art of painting into the most intimate spheres of the human soul.[51] Leonardo himself is very explicit about the duty of the artist to portray these emotions:

A good painter has two chief objects to paint, man and the intention of his soul; the former is easy, the latter hard, because he has to represent it by the attitudes and movements of the limbs. . . . The most important consideration in painting is that the movements of each figure expresses its mental state, such as desire, scorn, anger, pity, and the like. In painting, the actions of the figures are in every case expressive of the purpose in their minds.[52]

And how well he executed his own prescription! No one in the whole world described this better than the licentious, yet poetically imaginative Walter Pater. Looking at the alluring Gioconda, this is what Pater saw:

The presence that rose thus so strangely beside the waters, is expressive of what in the ways of a thousand years men had come to desire. . . . It is a beauty wrought out from within upon the flesh, the deposit, little cell by cell, of strange thoughts and fantastic reveries and exquisite passions. Set it for a moment beside one of those white Greek goddesses or beautiful women of antiquity, and how would they be troubled by this beauty, into which the soul with all its maladies has passed! All the thoughts and experience of the world have etched and moulded there, in that which they have of power to refine and make expressive the outward form. . . . She is older than the rocks among which she sits; like the vampire she has been dead many times, and learned the secrets of the grave; and has been a diver in deep seas, and keeps their fallen day about her; and trafficked for strange webs with Eastern merchants. . . . Certainly Lady Lisa might stand as the embodiment of the old fancy, the symbol of the modern idea.[53]

This belief – not only in the centrality of Man in the universe, but also in his importance, dignity, and individuality, or else in her assigned role as a

---

[51] The maxim *ut pictura poesis* was coined in antiquity by Horace, who was certainly not a great art theoretician by modern standards. Horace's own snaring in the pitfall of his maxim is no doubt attributable to the emphasis he placed on human empathy; as he famously said, "si vis me flere, dolendum est primum ipsi tibi," or "if you wish to make me cry, you must be immersed in pain yourself." For a magnificent essay on the subject at hand, see Rensselaer Lee, *Ut Pictura Poesis: A Humanistic Theory of Painting*, New York: Norton (1967).

[52] *The Notebooks of Leonardo da Vinci*, selected and edited by Irma Richter, Oxford: Oxford World's Classics Paperback, p. 176 (1998; first published in 1952).

[53] Walter Pater, *The Renaissance*, edited by Adam Phillips, Oxford: Oxford World's Classics, p. 80 (1986) (Pater's essay on Leonardo was composed in 1869).

standard for other abstract entities, such as Beauty, Grace, Inventiveness, and even Morality – swept across Western Europe. This includes, of course, the British Isles, although one is hard-pressed to identify universally recognizable painted images that convey this message. Contemporary Britons, alas, were not so good with the brush (unless one is inclined to naturalize such transient residents as Hans Holbein).[54] But even a cursory look at the plays of William Shakespeare (remember the maxim _ut pictura poesis_) more than compensates for this void. As Harold Bloom cogently argues,

Shakespeare ... went beyond all precedents (even Chaucer) and invented the human as we continue to know it. A more conservative way of stating this would seem to me a weak misreading of Shakespeare: it might contend that Shakespeare's originality was in the _representation_ of cognition, personality, character. But there is an overflowing element in the plays, an excess beyond representation, that is closer to the metaphor we call "creation." The dominant Shakespearean characters – Falstaff, Hamlet, Rosalind, Iago, Lear, Macbeth, Cleopatra among them – are extraordinary instances not only of how meaning gets started, rather than repeated, but also of how new modes of consciousness come into being.[55]

If one were to look for a single catchword that summarizes the spirit of the Renaissance, one could safely conclude that it represents an _anthropocentric_ worldview. In this respect it sharply contrasts with the medieval spirit that lingered on in Eastern Orthodoxy, which represents a _theocentric_ view of the world. Once again, the centrality of Man in the universe posits _him_ (or her), _his_ practical needs, _her_ (even idiosyncratic) preferences, _her_ individual well-being as a supreme goal to be attained by society. The Renaissance spirit rejoiced in its achievement as much as it displayed condescension and aloofness to the spirit of the Middle Ages. It is exactly in this sense that Renaissance culture bid farewell to the Orthodox spirit, which maintained its loyalty to the old values, and interpreted the uncharted waters of change not only as too perilous, but as demonic and heretical as well. But let us look at the sources.

Giorgio Vasari was certainly not a great thinker. But he reflected, accurately and obediently, the fashionable artistic _mores_ of his time. For him, the whole artistic period spanning from antiquity to the budding Renaissance was nothing but a pit of mediocrity, stagnation, and neglect. He said many a foul thing about that millennium of "decline." Largely, they can be summarized in three principal contentions: that the Middle Ages depicted the human figure in its iconographic essentials, rather than in its red-blooded fullness and luscious reality; that it miserably failed to take notice of nature; and that it was oblivious to the golden rule of moderation in pictorial (and architectural) proportions.

---

54 Few examples of Renaissance portraiture are more psychologically penetrating, and anthropocentrically oriented, than Holbein's rendering of his famous English sitters, Henry VIII and Thomas More.

55 Harold Bloom, _Shakespeare, the Invention of the Human_, New York: Riverbooks, p. xviii (1998). More will be said about Shakespeare and his perception of human nature in subsequent chapters.

Nothing at all really happened in Italian art, he held, until the ascent of the great Cimabue. His first chapter of the *Lives* actually opens in *ipsissima verba*:

The flood of misfortunes which continuously swept over and submerged the unhappy country of Italy not only destroyed everything worthy to be called a building but also, and this was of far greater consequence, completely wiped out the artists who lived there. Eventually, however, by God's providence, Giovanni Cimabue, who was destined to take the first steps in restoring the art of painting to its earlier stature, was born in the city of Florence, in the year 1240.[56]

Of all pre-Renaissance architecture he thought that,

The work produced could not have been more awkward or more lacking in the qualities of design.... Men still had to build, but all sense of form and good style had been lost.... [57]

Of the wonderful Byzantine mosaics in St. Mark's in Venice or the Cathedral in Pisa he could not find one kind word to say (Ravenna, too, did not receive much better evaluations):

Over and over again they produced figures in the same style, staring as if possessed, with outstretched hands, on the tips of their toes...the way they are drawn, they all resemble grotesques rather than what they were meant to represent.[58]

Cimabue and his immediate followers were useful, according to Vasari, to absolve society of its former despicable abyss, but not until the ascent of the great Michelangelo did Providence really smile on humankind:

Meanwhile, the benign ruler of heaven graciously looked down to earth, saw the worthlessness of what was being done, the intense but fruitless studies, and the presumption of men who were farther from true art than night is from day, and resolved to save us from our errors. So he decided to send into the world an artist, who would be skilled in each and every craft, whose work alone would teach us how to attain perfection in design (by correct drawing and by the use of contour and light and shadows, so as to obtain relief in painting), and how to use right judgment in sculpture and in architecture, create buildings which would be comfortable and secure, healthy, pleasant to look at, well-proportioned and richly ornamented.[59]

Russian Culture and Iconography

What was viewed by Vasari as an extremely uplifting artistic and conceptual achievement was dismissed with horror and resentment by generations of Orthodox theologians. Archpriest Avvakkum, reacting to the importation into

---

[56] Giorgio Vasari, *Lives of the Artists*, translated by George Bull, New York: Penguin Books, p. 49 (1965).
[57] Ibid., pp. 38–39.
[58] Ibid., p. 46.
[59] Ibid., p. 325.

Russian iconography of such Renaissance ideas as perspective or *chiaroscuro* modeling of objects, had this to say:

They depict the image of the Savior Emmanuel, with swollen face, vermilion lips, curly hair, powerful arms and muscles, swollen fingers, fat legs and hips, very stout and with a large stomach like a German; the only thing lacking is the sword attached to his side.[60]

Now Avvakkum was, of course, an Old Believer of the seventeenth century. This was an era that experimented with, for the first time, the mixing of occidental "innovations" with the existing cultural lore. Such carnal corruption of the former idiom of spiritual purity had not been seen before his time. It must have been quite a traumatic experience. It is easy to understand, and sympathize with, his profound sense of loss and his acerbic reaction. However, Avvakkum's rancorous indignation hardly abated with the passage of time, and it still echoes, with varying degrees of vehemence, from generation to generation. A pious contemporary explains the source of his consternation in these painful terms:

The gradual neglect of the Canons which govern iconography within the Orthodox Church brought about serious consequences. As a result of this neglect, one can notice an ineluctable decline and slow asphyxia in icon painting. . . . The sacred art of both East and West expressed the same realities up to the eleventh and twelfth centuries, with an identical impetus that sought to reveal those "things invisible." It was that marvelous period of Romanesque art, which unveiled a world beyond the laws of gravity, and even showed us how stone could be spiritualized. . . . In Italy, however, we see Cimabue, Giotto and Duccio for a vanguard leading to a progressive departure from the art of the Eastern Church and prompting the artistic "divorce" of the Renaissance. Turning their backs on Byzantine tradition, they initiate the "desacralization" of Western sacred art, opening the road towards an uncompromising secularization. The art of the transcendent fades with their introduction of such visuals as three-dimensional perspective, natural light and shadows, the return to a realistic portrayal of people, and the use of the emotional. . . . Until then, the icon was oriented toward the faithful, open to them, but it now became a picture living its own life; its scenes took place independently of those who contemplated it. A subjective vision of art, projected by the artist, impaired its integration into the liturgical mystery. Emotions then replaced spiritual communion; and finally, the sacred language of symbols was lost.[61,62]

The central theme, then, of all Orthodox icons is not, and cannot be, the object of observation in itself (the image of God, for instance, is distinct from

---

[60] Cited in Viktor Lazarev, *The Russian Icon*, Collegeville, MN: Liturgical Press, pp. 24–25 (1997).

[61] Michel Quenot, *The Icon*, Crestwood, NY: St. Vladimir Seminary Press, pp. 72ff (1996).

[62] One notes in passing that the marked difference in attitude between West and East toward the humanization (or secularization) of the spiritual transcends the substantive issues themselves, i.e., whether people or things should be portrayed realistically. It touches upon a subtler subject as well, and that is the attitude to the concept of change. While the West embraces change as an omen of progress, the East views it rather as a contamination of the pure. On the steadfastness of the Orthodox spirit in opposition to the concept of change see Timothy Ware, *The Orthodox Church*, London: Penguin Books, pp. 195ff (1963).

His essence). Rather, it is the radiation of the transcendent upon the material.[63] In the iconography of human beings, it is the radiation of the divine upon the flesh. A leading Orthodox theologian and art historian writes:

Destined to reflect the deification of the human being, the icon founds its aesthetic upon an eschatological realism. The psychological is banished.... Made in the image of God, humans are called to resemble him through holiness.... Darkened by the fall, the image finds its fullness only in the divine resemblance that constitutes its one and only archetype. Concentrated on the face, the icon remains radically foreign to the earthly model. A naturalistic portrait is rejected. An icon of a living person is impossible.[64]

The iconographic representation of these thoughts is quite revealing. All human representations must have faces, and all these faces must have large and protruding eyes. For in the words of Scripture,

The light of the body is the eye: if therefore thine eye be single, thy whole body shall be full of light. But if thine eye be evil, thy whole body shall be full of darkness. If therefore the light that is in thee be darkness, how great is that darkness![65]

The eyes of humans lend their subjects their spiritual meaning, because as windows to the soul they usher the subjects into communion with the divine. An eyeless, let alone faceless icon does not "exist" in the spiritual sense, even if its physical presence must be recorded as part of the narrative. Figure 10 shows the Last Supper with only Judas among the Savior and all the apostles portrayed in profile. The diminished ability of a profiled figure to maintain an eye contact with the viewer casts him out of communion, and thereby impairs his spiritual "presence." He is demoted from being a subject of the iconographic representation to being a mere object.

In the same vein, Figure 11 is a Syrian icon depicting the martyrs of Sebaste, all facing the viewers with wide eyes; only one soldier, their torturer, is entering a building and has his face hidden from the viewers' gaze, thus banishing himself from their sacramental presence. His physical imprint on the icon is devoid of any spiritual significance.[66]

In the remaining pages of this chapter I wish to call attention to two famous and influential *Russian* icons. My purpose is to establish the rejection of Man's dominion over the universe as a central tenet of the Orthodox faith and to underline the local characteristics of this proposition in the Russian heritage.

---

[63] In the mystical thought of early Christianity, this was a recurring theme. The Son of God, being the reincarnation of the Word, constituted a tangible expression of the intangible, whereby the One enters the universe of multiplicity. A sophisticated treatment of this subject can be traced back to the work of the fifth-century Syrian-Greek theologian known as the Pseudo-Dionysius. For a modern collection of his work, see *Pseudo Dionysius: The Complete Works*, translated by Colm Luibheid, Mahwah, NJ: Paulist Press (1988).

[64] Mahmud Zibawi, *The Icon, Its Meaning and History*, Collegeville, MN: Liturgical Press, p. 33 (1993).

[65] Matthew, 6, 22–23 (King James' Version).

[66] The two last examples are derived from Zibawi, ibid., pp. 38ff.

FIGURE 10. *Last Supper* (with Judas depicted in profile). Monastery of Sts. Sergius and Bacchus, Malula, Syria.

FIGURE 11. *Martyrs of Sebaste*, Church of the Forty Martyrs of Sebaste, Homs, Syria, seventeenth century.

FIGURE 12. *Our Lady of Vladimir*, early twelfth century.

Every discussion of Russian iconography must start its voyage with the venerated icon of the *Vladimirskaya*, Our Lady of Vladimir, already mentioned in the introductory chapter (see Figure 12).

The reader may recall that this famous icon, which led the Russians to battle, listened to their sacred vows, and answered their prayers, was, in actual fact, a Byzantine masterpiece that was imported to early Rus' sometime around 1130. Her name derives from her early travel from her initial Russian home in Kiev to the Cathedral of the Dormition in Vladimir in 1167, where she graced the city until 1395. By then, her urgent intervention was needed in Moscow. Her assignment was to defend the city from the onslaught of the Turk (Khan Tamerlane), which she accomplished successfully. Less than a century later she assisted the fledgling Russian army to repel the Mongol invasion of Khan Akhmet, thus terminating once and for all the Mongol domination of Holy Russia. It is only with immense seriousness, almost a sense of piety, that one can view the *Vladimirskaya* and see her for what she really is.

It is immediately apparent that she is of a mixed prototype, being at the same time a delicate example of the "Virgin *Eleousa*," or mother of tenderness, and carrying about her the sterner authority of the "*Hodigitria*," She who Shows the Way to the faithful.[67] Her mixed heritage caters simultaneously to two distinct Russian cultural traits. Her *Eleousa* nature resonates well with the indigenous cult of the mother (Mother Earth, Mother Russia, the Mother of God as well as the more down-to-earth, warm, and popular instinctive sense of motherhood).[68] Her appearance as the *Hodigitria* responds to the constant Russian yearning for a strong central authority.[69] Indeed, upon importation, she was immediately Russified and became a time-venerated symbol of patriotic pride. The *Vladimirskaya* is not a woman, although she contains distinct maternal and other womanly characteristics. Rather, she embodies in her person a whole inventory of normative *desiderata* – a deep abstract spirituality, chastity, and a secure sense of giving. The traditional stars on her headgear (the so-called "*maphorion*") and shoulders signify her eternal virginity, before, during, and after the conception of her Son. Jesus himself resembles a baby only in the proportions of his body but is otherwise an inspired adult in his facial expression and a distinguished dignitary in his elaborate attire. The icon is centered in the vicinity of Mary's heart, which rests against her Son's robust neck. The neck's supranatural width allows for the passage of plentiful air and thus stands for the Holy Spirit. Mary's elongated facial features and large, yet remote eyes invite the faithful to enter into Communion with the *spiritual* subject matter of the icon, rather than with its living persons. Indeed, the whole icon may be interpreted as the ultimate Communion between the Word, the

---

[67] On the *Vladimirskaya*'s mixed prototypical origin see Paul Evdokimov, *The Art of the Icon: A Theology of Beauty*, translated by Steven Bigham, Princeton, NJ: Princeton University Press, p. 263 (1990).

[68] The centrality of the maternal *leitmotif* in Russian religious thought is well documented in the literature. The acclaimed scholar of Russian theology, Fedotov, writes: "Differing from Greece where Theotokos was once the object of discussion, Russia laid the stress not upon the first but upon the last part of the compound name: not 'theo' but 'tokos', the Parent, the Birthgiver, the Mother. The Russian Mary is not only the Mother of God or Christ, but the universal Mother, the Mother of all mankind." See George Fedotov, *The Russian Religious Mind*, Belmont, MA: Nordland, Volume 1, p. 361 (1975). The cult of the Mother also falls in line with the characterization of Russian culture as an "icon society," a society that stresses the feminine, material aspects of the world rather than the abstract, masculine aspects. For further details see Chapter 7, *infra*.

[69] See Chapter 4, *infra*.

incarnation of the divine in the person of the Son, and the human destiny as embodied in the person of the Mother. The entire Holy Trinity marks its presence upon the scene through the clearly triangular composition of the icon. There is nothing humanly carnal, or even fleshy, tangible, or corporeal in the entire image:

> The Vladimir icon is the direct opposite of the type of Madonna painted by Raphael. Its beauty is beyond every earthly canon. Mary's face is full of heavenly majesty, woven in the transcendent features of the new and totally deified creature, but at the same time it carries all that is human.... As for Christ in the icon, he is far from the touching naiveté of the *bambino Gesú*. He is also the Word and is always dressed in adult clothing, a tunic and coat, that is *hymation*; only his size indicates that he is a child.[70]

Nor has the appeal of the Byzantine *Vladimirskaya* waned through the ages. Figure 13 is a modern-day rendition of the same subject recently executed by a modern icon painter of excellence working in the United States, Vladimir Grigorenko. Whereas the artist took the freedom to depart from the original in some minor thematic subjects, the main doctrinal features are left intact. The *Vladimirskaya* is born again with every generation of worshippers.

While the *Vladimirskaya* icon renounces the dominion of the humanist *persona* in the universe by depriving her of her distinct bodily functions[71] and remanding her into the kingdom of the ethereal, man's position near the bottom of the metaphysical power structure is revealed by other famous examples. A number of such icons are analyzed in other chapters. In this chapter I wish to examine one striking example, the icon of the Transfiguration of Christ. According to the Gospels,[72] Christ chose to reveal His divine nature to His disciples Peter, James, and John on Mount Tabor. His clothes became dazzling white, whiter than anyone in the world could bleach them. Moses and Elijah appeared on His sides and He talked to them on His impending passion. Peter told Christ that it was "good" for the apostles to bask in that glory and offered to set up three shelters – one for the Lord, one for Moses, and one for Elijah – but got no response. A shelter could be provided only through the cross, that is, through suffering and self-denial. Instead, the mortified apostles found themselves enveloped in a cloud and a voice said: "This is my Son, whom I love. Listen to Him!" Moses and Elijah evaporated into thin air, and the apostles could see only Jesus. This mystic scene (Figure 14) is traditionally portrayed with the upper part of the icon in peaceful harmony, as Jesus is encircled with a circumference of light called a *mandorla*. Although the divine light itself is considered to consist of uncreated matter, the *mandorla* represents the created

---

[70] Ibid, p. 264.

[71] This does not necessarily imply that the human body in humanist iconography was necessarily "realistic." In fact, compared to some Western medieval traditions, the humanist body was refined and idealized rather than profane and realistic. See, at much greater length, Chapter 7, infra.

[72] Mark, 9, 2–13; Matthew, 17, 1–13; Luke, 9, 28–36.

FIGURE 13. Vladimir Grigorenko, *Our Lady of Vladimir*, a recent icon in the old tradition.

universe with all its spheres. This peaceful upper part is finished with a balanced composition featuring the Savior, Moses, and Elijah. The lower part of the icon stands in sharp contrast to the dignified harmony above it. The apostles, far from being allowed to put up a shelter, are thrust upon the ground by an unfathomable violent energy. The transcendent dignity of Christ is clearly more than they can bear.[73]

To accentuate the violent interpretation of the disciples' plight, the reader might wish to contrast it with the iconographic treatment of the same subject in Renaissance Italy. Figure 15 is a typical Giovanni Bellini Transfiguration

[73] For more details on the theological significance of this icon, see Evdokimov, ibid., pp. 299ff.

FIGURE 14. Theophanes the Greek, *The Transfiguration of Christ*, early fifteenth century.

executed in 1460 in which the disciples are lovingly painted in a peaceful slumber when their Lord is transfigured on the mountain.

The powerful Russian interpretation, like all other important icons, was executed by countless generations of masters; according to Billington, its traces are clearly visible even in the pictorial representations of the contemporary Russian avant garde.[74] It was certainly used, over and over again, by the propaganda

[74] James Billington, *The Face of Russia*, New York: TV Books, p. 128 (plate number 17) (1999).

FIGURE 15. Giovanni Bellini, *The Transfiguration of Christ*, 1460.

machine in the Stalinist era. Figure 16 is a 1920 poster, entitled "Comrade Lenin Cleanses the Earth of Scum." The Godhead of the Soviet nation[75] stands atop a rounded globe (Mount Tabor is notorious for its rotundity, and so is, often, the iconic *mandorla*) flanked by a giant broom and a flying nobleman,

[75] Starting in the late teens, Lenin was often referred to in Soviet propaganda in religious terms, and even as a modern-day Christ. See Victoria Bonnell, *Iconography of Power*, Berkeley: University of California Press, pp. 141ff (1999).

FIGURE 16. Mikhail Cheremnykh and Victor Deni, poster, "Comrade Lenin Cleanses the Earth of Scum," 1920.

with the three perennial sinners aghast with pain and mortification. The gigantic stature of the leader defies all rules of perspective, also a typical theme of Russian Orthodox iconography,[76] in this case as a means to monumentalize the leader in contrast to the human "scum" he is supposed to sweep away. The choice of either subject or composition could not have been coincidental.[77]

---

[76] This topic is taken up systematically in Chapter 6, infra.

[77] The Soviet regime understood quite early on that it could not hope to maintain its power without having a strong claim on legitimacy. To achieve this goal, they had to "invent tradition," to use the brilliant phrase of Eric Hobsbawm (which was used, however, in a much broader context). In other words, they had to "inculcate certain values and norms of behavior by repetition,

This icon held the Russian people in its spell for many generations, which is a phenomenon that calls for an explanation.

In my view, its suggestive nature in the Russian mind derives from its portrayal of the individual in a state of total dependence upon a higher, unconquerable, and supreme authority. The whiteness of Christ's clothes and *mandorla* transcends the domain of the natural. It engulfs the Ruler of the Universe with His might. The apostles must heed the mysterious voice commanding: "Listen to Him!" Jesus is flanked by two extremely meaningful personalities in the Russian collective psyche. Moses, the lawgiver, is the embodiment of all authority, spelling out, with legalistic exactitude, what must be done. The character of Elijah is far more complex. Long before the baptism of Rus' in the tenth century, the pagan pantheon of the Slavs featured an admired and feared deity, the terrible thunder god Perun. Perun himself was christened with his land and assumed the figure of the prophet Elijah. Elijah was not an endearing figure in Russian folklore. Like Perun before him, he was known to ride the heavens in his fiery chariot and was capable of sending bolts of lightning and destroying entire fields. The baptized Perun did this, to be sure, in pursuit of holy motives, such as the eradication of evil spirits. But a wary eye had to be constantly cast on him nevertheless. He could also confer benefits on his worshippers; like Perun before him, he was known to carry in his chariot water to quench the thirst of the other saints, so he was also beseeched in humble prayer to spare some water for moistening the arid land.[78] Both the lawgiver and the terrible thunder god Elijah disappeared, however, as soon as the apostles found themselves engulfed in the cloud and were supposedly incorporated into the sole surviving figure of the transfigured Christ. This instantaneous fusion of the lawgiver, the Supreme Judge and the feared executioner in one glaring person; this trinity of power, complete with the command "listen to him"; the blinding light and inglorious collapse of the disciples, broadcasts, most powerfully and unequivocally, the lamentable human condition of a mere Peter, or a James, or a John in this harsh and vindictive vale of sorrows.

---

which automatically implies continuity with the past." See Eric Hobsbawm, the introductory chapter, page 1, in Eric Hobsbawm and Terence Ranger, *The Invention of Tradition*, Cambridge: Cambridge University Press (1984).

[78] Linda Ivanits, *Russian Folk Belief*, Armonk, NY: M. E. Sharpe, pp. 24ff (paperback ed., 1992). Ivanits' book also contains a number of fascinating peasant stories about Elijah's wrathful behavior toward those who failed to pay him the expected tribute of honor. Often, the peasants are delivered from his vengeful spirit only through the intervention of the kindly St. Nicholas the Wonderworker, who maintains a close and warm-hearted supervision on his human flock.

3

Individualism

The role of individualism in the formation of modern contract theory seems to depend on the historical period, which one posits at the focus of one's inquiry. In his extensive narrative of the history of the Common Law of contract, A. W. B. Simpson does not even hint at the concept of individualism, as if this concept and the evolution of contractual ideas had no point of tangency.[1] By counterdistinction, P. S. Atiyah fills hundreds of pages of his monumental treatise on the freedom of contracts with detailed discussions concerning the role of individualism in the fashioning of contractual ideas.[2] The subject of Simpson's inquiry is the rise of assumpsit, a narrative that peaked with *Slade's Case* in the early years of the seventeenth century. All post-*Slade* events, which are included in his monograph, are assigned secondary importance and do not play a major role in the formation of his theory. Atiyah, on the other hand, does not focus on the historical materials preceding the 1770s at all, as if all prior efforts to establish the reign of contracts came, in the end, to naught. The authors' differential treatments of the roles of individualism to the subjects of their respective inquiries stems, no doubt, from the fact that the concept of individualism as a word of art, a *terminus technicus*, did not gain much currency in the seventeenth century. It only started to loom large in the collective psyche after its official re-introduction by eighteenth- and nineteenth-century philosophers.[3] It would have been impossible, for the protagonists of Simpson's tale,

---

[1] A. W. B. Simpson, *A History of the Common Law of Contract: The Rise of the Action of Assumpsit*, New York: Oxford University Press (1975).

[2] P. S. Atiyah, *The Rise and Fall of Freedom of Contract*, New York: Oxford University Press (1979). Although Atiyah has only one chapter (the tenth), which is explicitly dedicated to the connection between individualism and freedom of contract, many other segments of his book are also obsessed with the same subject.

[3] Renaissance individualism manifested itself in many of its protagonists, from Petrarch to Montaigne; but many writers ascribe the official heralding of individualism into canonical thought to later centuries. See, for example, Philip Lee Ralph, *The Renaissance in Perspective*, New York: St. Martin's Press, p. 254 (1972).

to rationalize their moves by invoking the individualistic lore. It would have been equally weird for jurists of the later centuries not to. Understanding these differences, however, is not a sufficient justification for accepting their validity. Renaissance humanists were not interested, or were not *primarily* interested, in the generic traits of humankind in general. Minute attention was paid to the nongeneric, individual differences that set people apart from each other. It was necessary, in order to adhere to that brand of humanism, to acknowledge the unique, the different, the idiosyncratic of each person's sphere of existence. To be sure, in the eighteenth and nineteenth centuries the germ of Renaissance individualism generated a multitude of ever more daring, novel manifestations; the music of a Monteverdi and of a Beethoven are not exactly of the same genre. But in spite of the marked differences in the various meanings assigned to the concept of "individualism" in Western thought, there is a strong link or common denominator among them all. None of these various meanings left a lasting impression on the Russian collective psyche, which remained much more "collectivist" or "communitarian" to our day and age. I maintain that this distinction significantly contributed to the observed differences in contract jurisprudence and practice across the two cultures.

In this chapter I record the central role of individualism in the evolution of contract law, the main philosophical ideas that gave rise to it in the West, its representation in the occidental imagery of the period, and its meaningful negation in Russian culture and iconography.[4]

The Legal Scene

The *Slade's Case* itself, and its Continental counterparts, could not have seen the light of day without individualism. The writ system that preceded *Slade* did allow, of course, for various procedural avenues to address a contractual wrong. But all these distinct routes were by definition finite and not particularly numerous. *Slade* had above all a carte blanche license to forge innominate stipulations[5] that fit all idiosyncratic preferences of an infinite variety. The

---

[4] Some modern commentators observed the fact that the word "individualizm" gained much currency in the post–Soviet Russian tongue; young entrepreneurs like to read such authors as Milton Friedman and Friedrich von Hayek and to employ in their discourse such slogans as the minimal state or their own unassailable right to be free from its regulatory power. But the more thoughtful among these commentators also observed that "individualizm," in spite of its etymological pedigree, dramatically differs from its usual Western connotation, because it lacks most of its key components (as explicated in this chapter), such as the dignity of the person, her autonomy, her right of privacy, and the philosophical foundations of the will theory. In his excellent and heavily documented recent book, Oleg Kharkhordin, for example, shows that the current fascination with "indivdualizm" is mainly traceable to the Soviet tradition of focusing on the individual as a means of "self-improvement," i.e., a greater conformity with the Soviet ideology of the ideal citizen. See Oleg Kharkhordin, *The Collective and the Individual in Russia: A Study of Practices*, Berkeley: University of California Press (1999).

[5] An "innominate stipulation" (*contractus innominatus*), or a contract without a name, simply means a contract freely fashioned by the will of the parties without a need to shape it in conformity with a pre-existing mold.

difference between the medieval law of contract and *Slade* is one of principle. In the Middle Ages, individual agents had to modify their preferences in order to align them with the existing forms of action. After *Slade*, society adapted its own mode of behavior (for example, in providing its policing, judicial, and execution services) in conformity with the parties' individual preferences, as formulated by their freely negotiated contracts. This reflects above all a difference in attitude regarding the role of individual players on the social stage. But the full story is not all that laconic. I turn now to examine some of its nuances and details.

Of prime expositional importance is the distinction between lawful and unlawful contracts. From time immemorial, organized society refused to enforce promises, as well as other private entitlements, if they rested, at their source, on some form of illegality. The generic term "illegality," however, is notoriously contingent on a variety of different interpretations, ranging from sinful to immoral, contrary to statute, to precedent, to custom or to some amorphous sense of public policy. The Latin maxim captures this inherent ambiguity: *Ex turpi causa non oritur actio.*[6] In the Middle Ages there appears to be no consistent theory of what might constitute "illegality," but the mental process of identifying contractual "turpitude," being typically deductive, exhibited very little sensitivity to the individual circumstances of each case. Take, for example, the notion of usurious loans. Ecclesiastical doctrine has always held that to charge interest for lending money is sinful. Even during the Reformation, a prominent bishop declared that

[i]t is filthy gains, and work of darkness. It is a monster in nature . . . it is theft, it is the murdering of our brethren, it is the curse of God and the curse of the people.[7]

The source of this indignation can easily be traced back (at least) to Thomistic philosophy.[8] Aquinas himself thought that in the special case of money there is no ontological difference between the thing itself (the principal amount of the loan) and its use. Since the creditor gets a full repayment of the thing itself, she cannot lawfully charge the debtor a separate fee for having used the money for the duration of the loan.[9] Under his ontological presupposition, such a separate

---

[6] The maxim simply means that no enforceable cause of action may rest on grounds of "turpitude." To illustrate the ambiguity of this phrase consider, for instance, the recent English case of *Clunis v. Camden and Islington Health Authority* (1988) 2 WLR (Weekly Law Reports) 902. In that case, a convicted felon suffering from a mental condition sued the health authorities for failing to exercise reasonable care in treating him properly, and thus preventing him from committing the offense. The Court of Appeals found that this action could not be sustained for being contrary to public policy.

[7] *Works of Bishop Jewel* as cited by Simpson, ibid., p. 510.

[8] Aquinas was not the first, of course, to express a negative attitude toward the institution of interest-bearing loans. The Old Testament repeatedly proscribes the practice, although it is hard to tell whether its antagonistic attitude encompassed all kinds of interest or only the more offensive types of usurious practices. Post-biblical rabbinical authorities have always been, and still are, bent on finding extenuating circumstances that make it permissible to charge an interest for a loan (*"heiter iska"*).

[9] Simpson, ibid.

fee amounts to getting something for nothing, or, in the terminology of the later scholastic synthesizers, a contract made for such a vacuous purpose suffers from an absence of a justified cause (*causa*). Needless to say, the numerous mercantile nuclei spawned by the new urban centers of the Renaissance could not live with this Thomistic axiom, because it failed to take into account their commercial needs and the growing role of debt financing in the budding market economy. Renaissance law had to depart from the uniform Thomistic rule in its quest for more nuanced solutions.[10]

These solutions were not tardy in arrival. During the reign of Henry VIII, the first statute, paradoxically termed "An Acte against Usurye," was enacted, which made it lawful to charge an interest not exceeding 10 percent per annum.[11] Fine distinctions were then drawn between straightforward usury (which could not be tolerated) and rightful compensation for the contingency of default, which was taken to be analogous to the charging of a premium for an insured risk. This newly discovered insight – that people must be differentially compensated for assuming risks in different uncertain business environments – yielded all kinds of rules and exceptions, all of which were geared to the individual characteristics of each case.[12] The Common Law judges also jumped into the fray by speaking for and against vocational debt financing.[13] At the end of the day, they came to legitimize the right of investors to lend money for a fee, even if, in very risky situations, the fee was quite high.[14]

Another interesting illustration of the greater attention paid by Renaissance jurists to the individual exigencies of contracting concerns the law of "frustrated

[10] This story is told in detail in R. H. Tawney's famous work, *Religion and the Rise of Capitalism*, Somerset, NJ: Transaction Publishers (paperback edition, 1998; first published in 1926).

[11] 37 Henry VIII c. 9. This statute of 1545 was short-lived, having been repealed in 1552 by a "Byll against Usurye," 5&6 Edw. VI, c. 20, but was finally reinstituted in 1571, by a statute also termed an "Acte against Usurye," 13 Eliz. I c. 18. Twenty-five years later, in 1596–97, Shakespeare wrote *The Merchant of Venice*.

[12] Simpson, ibid., pp. 512ff, speaks of several kinds of legal fictions that were used to legitimize lending for gain when it was appropriate to do so. For example, the parties could enter into a complicated transaction called a *contractus trinus*, under which the lender would advance credit to the borrower under the pretext that the latter was her partner and the partnership venture involved risk. The parties would then "insure" against the contingency of default in a manner that yielded the lender a fixed interest on the funds she advanced to the partnership.

[13] Thus, in *Sanderson v. Warner* (1622) 2 Rolle Rep. 239, some judges held that "usury which is allowed by statute has obtained such strength by usage, that it would be a greater impediment to traffic and commerce if it should be impeached." Other judges, however, held that usury was always, and under all circumstances, unlawful.

[14] In an early report, *Dr. Good's Case* (1576) Cro. Eliz. 643, the court dealt with a person investing 100 pounds for a permanent income of 20 pounds per annum. The court legitimized the transaction on the grounds that the contract did not provide for the repayment of the principal of the invested funds: "if a man giveth £100 for an annuity of £20 p.a. this is not usury, for he shall never have his stock again." Modern finance theory would suggest, of course, that having a fixed maturity date for the principal of a loan (say a bond) does not affect the value of the bondholders' rights. *Dr. Good's Case* stands, therefore, more for the legitimization of annuity contracts than for the legal fiction that gave rise to this turn of events.

purpose," or impossibility. Clearly, if a promisor chooses, of her own accord, to repudiate an undertaking (or assumpsit), she may expect to confront an unequivocal legal response. But what if her best intentions were frustrated by some circumstance that was not anticipated at the time of contracting and which lay completely beyond her sway? Medieval law seems to have given promisors considerable leeway to escape liability in cases involving the doctrine of an "Act of God." An intervening Act of God was one in which natural forces rendered all performance impossible. It was considered absurd that the law should nevertheless impute to anyone an enforceable promise to perform.[15] But is it really such an indefensible outcome? Even if performance *in kind* is not feasible, the promisor could always be expected to compensate the disappointed promisee by some kind of a *monetary* remedy. If we consider the doctrine of Act of God from this perspective, it becomes clear that it rests on normative rather than on logical grounds. Essentially, it looks into the conscience of those who make promises and draws a distinction between two kinds of defaults: an excusable one, in which the defendant was not at fault, and an inexcusable one, in which default resulted from the defendant's own volition. But in hinging everything on the morality of the promisor's demeanor, this doctrine deprives the parties of the opportunity to apportion the risk of nonperformance between them as they wish. For example, an insurance company might prefer to write a risk (say, damage to a house) occasioned by natural perils (an earthquake, a flood), which are definitely instances of an Act of God. In the private ordering of legal norms, which is the domain of contracts, divine intervention should perhaps play a less dominant role.

This kind of deference to the parties' own stipulations exactly as they chose to craft them assumed body and spirit by the courts of the Renaissance. This evolution can be illustrated by the contrast between the two following cases. In the first case,[16] the plaintiff gave his castrated horse, a gelding, to the defendant, who unequivocally promised to return it on demand. The poor animal died, however, not through the defendant's fault. The latter attempted to escape liability for returning the beast to its rightful owner on the theory that its death was occasioned by an Act of God. The case was hotly contested, but in the end the defendant prevailed. This case clearly represents the medieval point of view that the adjudication of liability is essentially a matter of conscience and therefore ought to follow from moral imperatives that are completely external to the actual bargain struck by the parties.

In the second case,[17] which reflects the budding Renaissance spirit, a tenant attempted to escape liability for paying his rent, on the ground that the land was occupied by one Prince Rupert, who was described as an alien and an enemy of the king. The court recognized the act of hostile occupation by Rupert as constituting an unforeseen contingency, which lies beyond the control of

---

[15] Simpson, ibid., pp. 525ff.
[16] *Williams v. Hide* (1624) Palm. 548, W. Jones 179.
[17] *Paradine v. Jane* (1648) Aleyn 26, Style 47.

the parties. Nevertheless, it ordered the tenant to live up to his contractual promise:

[W]hen the party by his own contract creates a duty of charge upon himself he is bound to make it good, if he may, notwithstanding any accident by inevitable necessity, because he might have provided against it by his contract.

I would like to end this inquiry into the changing molds of Renaissance contract jurisprudence by taking a cursory look at the evolving doctrine of "implied contract terms." Many otherwise legally binding promises are cast into uncertainty because the parties fail to address some contingencies. A plumber might promise to fix a broken pipe but forget to stipulate the exact time of service. May the plumber fulfill his undertaking five years down the line? A cobbler might take an order for a pair of boots but not specify the kind of leather. Would it be all right for the cobbler to choose the cheapest material? Society must take a stand on these common issues, simply because these issues cannot resolve themselves.

In the Middle Ages, the law took a clear-cut position. Even slight shades of uncertainty could vitiate the whole agreement and render it void. The law's response to alleged ambiguity was totally dichotomous: If the commitment was absolutely certain and clear, it had a binding effect; if the commitment was ambiguous, it was void.

But life is far more nuanced than these two polar possibilities seem to imply. In the hypothetical cases of the plumber and the cobbler, the parties did in fact enter into a contract, because they did in fact intend the pipe to be fixed or the boots to be made. They certainly wished the pipe to be fixed within a *reasonable* period of time, not five years down the line. Similarly, they probably meant to agree that the cobbler's materials comply with some acceptable standards. If a court finds that the parties did not explicitly address these questions, but nevertheless intended to bind themselves in an ascertainable fashion, the court can read into the contract some *implied* terms. The reading of implied terms into somebody else's contract is not a trivial matter. The finder of fact must place herself in the parties' positions and read their minds. She must attune herself to the individual concerns that the parties wished to address by forging an agreement and shape the law (the arbiter's interpretation of the facts) in conformity with these concerns. The first examples of the court's willingness to do so occurred during the Renaissance.

In one such case, a defendant asked the plaintiff to deliver certain goods to his daughter and took it upon himself to pay the price. However, he failed to specify *to whom* he was to pay the price. The plaintiff brought a suit in assumpsit against the defendant, who relied on the defense of uncertainty. The court held:

An assumpsit without shewing to whom is naught . . . [but] if the jury found that the defendant assumed *modo et forma*, without saying to whom, yet it is good, and so it was held.[18]

---

[18] *Sharp v. Rolt* (1625) Noy 83, 74 E.R. 1050.

In this particular case, the specter of the medieval standard was allowed to prevail, as apparently the defendant was not found to have employed the requisite degree of specificity. Nevertheless, the court did lay down, as a matter of principle, the rule that extraneous evidence could be admitted for the purpose of filling contractual *lacunae* in conformity with the parties' real desires.

This principle was vindicated not only in principle, but also in actual practice, in another contemporary tale, *Whitlock's Case*,[19] the like of which started to proliferate as time went by. *Whitlock* concerned the validity of a lease on real estate, in which the exact duration of the lease was not specified. Rather, it was awkwardly stipulated that the lease was granted for the longevity of the latest survivor in a group of three persons, provided that none of them should outlive a specified number of years. This last proviso amounted, of course, to an upper bound on the duration of the lease, but the lease could turn out to be shorter, and in theory even momentary, if the three lives were to be cut off within a briefer interval. Admittedly, the interpretation of this unusual agreement did not require a great mental effort, let alone any form of clairvoyance, by the fact-finding tribunal, because it was understood that *in retrospect* the duration of the lease will have been clear enough. Nonetheless, at the time of contracting, the lease's duration could not be ascertained, which pitted the parties into a state of risk and uncertainty. The court in *Whitlock* did rise to the challenge and, by second-guessing the parties' intention, filled in the contractual blind spots. *Whitlock* in itself could not have been the harbinger of a new legal era, but with the passage of time it was much expanded, gained momentum, and then became universally accepted. Today the practice of second-guessing the intention of the parties is the routine practice of every civil tribunal.[20]

The Philosophical Scene

These early advances in contract jurisprudence were naturally eclipsed during the golden age of the freedom of contracts, the eighteenth and nineteenth centuries. At that later historical stage, courts in the Western world enforced nearly all contracts with few attempts to "reform" them for the sake of a higher

---

[19] (1609) Hil. 6, 77 E.R. 580.

[20] The mainstream rule of interpretation is that a good judge fills *lacunae* in the parties' agreements by attempting to mimic the kind of contract the parties would have forged of their own accord under "ideal" circumstances. These circumstances include two main features: a full awareness of all contractual contingencies, and the facility to negotiate differences without having to bear transaction costs. The resulting rule of interpretation is called a "default rule." All default rules that do not exactly match the parties' hypothetical contract under ideal circumstances are considered suboptimal, because they either put the parties into a contractual regime that is incompatible with their preferences, or they force them to wastefully spend resources in contracting around the default. Although this kind of analysis is standard in the current literature, very few commentators, if any, paid any attention to its *cultural substratum*. The received rule of interpretation conceals a tacit assumption, to wit, that a "good" default starts by a careful observation of the parties' presumed preferences and ends by an accurate reflection of these preferences in the social response, which is the rule of interpretation.

objective.[21] This policy was powered by a tacit assumption that the institution of contract reflected a set of commendable individual values, and society, as an abstract collective entity, lacked the tools, let alone the sagacity, to offer a better, more prudent, or altogether more wholesome alternative. I would like to turn now to a brief description of the ideological backdrop that sustained contracts and informed their routine enforcement in this period. In the next section of this chapter, I show how the germ of individualism was firmly sewn in Renaissance (and, *a fortiori*, in post-Renaissance) iconography but was entirely absent, and expressly rejected, in its Russian counterpart. When it made its tardy appearance with its Franco-Italianate flavor, which infected the nobility of St. Petersburg's high society, it came, like so many cultural imports to Russian soil before it, without a deep internalization of its cultural tenets. It was thus a phony presence, a mask without a *persona*, an icon without a soul. It is hardly surprising that it failed to properly be inculcated among the vast majority of the Russian people.

As Atiyah correctly points out, the two major schools of thought that contributed to the golden age of contracts in the eighteenth and nineteenth centuries in England, were the teachings of the classical economists and the philosophy of the utilitarians.[22] Classical economics triumphed for almost a full century, from the publication of Adam Smith's *The Wealth of Nations* in 1776 until John Stuart Mill's great book, *Principles of Political Economy*, first published in 1848. By a more liberal count, the period preceded Smith by a long stretch;[23] its more recent offshoots flourish to this day.[24]

---

[21] This tale is told in considerable detail by Atiyah, ibid., especially in Chapters 13–16. In the United States, the freedom of contract reigned supreme until the Great Depression, which brought to an end, once and for all, the naïve version of nineteenth-century laissez faire. The story of the rise and fall of freedom of contract *à la Americaine* is told by Morton Horwitz, *The Transformation of American Law 1870–1960: The Crisis of Legal Orthodoxy*, New York: Oxford University Press (1994).

[22] See, in general, Arthur John Taylor, *Laissez Faire and State Intervention in Nineteenth Century Britain*, New York: Palgrave Macmillan (1972).

[23] Atiyah, ibid., p. 294. As I showed before, the budding of individualistic contract jurisprudence started in the Renaissance. The godfather of all political scientists, Thomas Hobbes, was also a man of his epoch, as he propagated in his *Leviathan* (1651) the idea that all social order must have, at its origin, the traits, hopes, and aspirations of individual human beings. This idea is made apparent by the architecture of this great book. The first part, "Of Man," deals in meticulous detail with the anatomy of the mind, with what makes different people tick, with their preferences, loves and desires, hates, and fears. It is only with these diverse building blocks in mind that he proceeded to construct his grand theory of organized society.

[24] Mainstream economics in many Western nations still interpret their mission as promoting "neo-classical" ideas, that is, Smithian libertarianism tempered with the accumulated wisdom of the more recent past. A solid majority of the most influential American contract theorists, including Richard Posner, Ronald Coase, Alan Schwartz, and many others, have fervently advocated libertarian policies for reasons not entirely different in principle, although much more developed in technical sophistication, than those first proposed in the *Wealth of Nations*. For a celebrated defense of neo-classical economics, see Friedrich Hayek, *Law, Legislation and Liberty: The Political Order of a Free People*, Chicago: University of Chicago Press (paperback, 1981).

The single most important insight of the classical economists is that, under normal circumstances, *self-interest generates social welfare*. This feat is allegedly accomplished through the intermediation of what Smith called the "invisible hand."[25] By this term Smith meant that if each individual agent is left alone to look after her own best interests, without government intervention, the Public Good is inadvertently served as well. Without getting into much technical detail, the process can be illustrated by a simple example. Assume a simple economy, with a number of industries owned by capitalists and a number of workers in search of the good life. The industries differ from each other in their respective productivities, which may be declining, at the margin, with incremental labor inputs. The more efficient industries will have an incentive to offer higher wages, not exceeding the marginal productivity of their hired hands, and will, indeed, offer them to the extent necessary to outbid the competition. Under these ideal conditions,[26] the workers will be employed by the more efficient firms, thereby increasing the industrial output (and national wealth) of the entire economy, gaining high wages, and fending off unemployment. Suppose now that the capitalists pressure the government to enact *maximum* wage laws. The resulting standardized wage[27] will remove the incentive of workers to seek employment at the more efficient firms. The less efficient allocation of labor inputs will thus deplete the national output. If, on the other hand, the workers force the government to legislate *minimum* wage laws, which exceed the free-market *equilibrium*, some employers will find it detrimental to keep on the payroll the same (large) number of employees,[28] and national wealth will suffer a decline as a result of unemployment.

This is an enormously important insight, although, as we more fully realize with hindsight, it does suffer from a host of different flaws, of both the

---

[25] Smith himself used this famous term quite sparingly, as did his immediate successors. David Ricardo, for example, the great synthesizer of market economy learning and the first person to use the word "law" in reference to economic behavior, explains the invisible processes that trigger economic efficiency in these terms: "With the rise or fall of price, profits are elevated above, or depressed below, their general level; and capital is either encouraged to enter into, or is warned to depart from the particular employment in which the variation has taken place." See David Ricardo, *Principles of Political Economy and Taxation*, Amherst, NY: Prometheus Books, p. 61 (1996; the book was first published in 1817).

[26] To make these conditions really "ideal," one ought to assume that all market agents are well informed of all employment opportunities (a sustainable assumption in a small economy) and that the costs of labor mobility are negligible (if moving from one employer to the next generates high costs, in learning, adaptation, and defraying the expenses of the actual move, the conditions of freely competitive markets are impaired).

[27] The standardization of wages will result from the fact that the more efficient industries will, on the one hand, outbid the competition by offering higher wages, but they will only do it to the minimum extent necessary to fend off the less competitive industries.

[28] The competition among firms implies that, absent minimum wage laws, some firms will already have paid their employees a wage equal to, or approaching, their marginal productivity. If minimum wages exceed this rate, these firms will be able to keep all their former employees on their payroll only at a loss.

positive[29] and normative[30] varieties. However, to the extent that one is inclined to believe in its veracity, as most eighteenth- and nineteenth-century economists did, the astuteness of enforcing every agreement, just as the parties chose to forge it, looms as a very attractive proposition. Contracts radiate individual choice, and the best strategy that an enlightened government can pursue is not to stand in the way of the invisible hand, that is, like a good waiter in a restaurant, to cater to the patrons' individual choices but not to stay around the table and pontificate over the meal.[31]

The other school of thought that powered the freedom of contracts to its peak in the relevant period was utilitarianism. There are many silly foibles in the "felicific calculus" proclaimed by Jeremy Bentham[32] and his coterie during this golden age of utilitarianism. For to determine which policy promotes the greatest happiness to the greatest number of people, one has to possess a clear unit (like a pound for weight or a yard for distance) for measuring bliss or anguish, of which there is obviously none. One must also be able to get into the bloodstream of all living people in order to engage in fruitful interpersonal comparisons (if we take a widget from A and give it to B, does B's bliss exceed, is equal to, or is less than A's anguish?). As a moral philosophy, it suffers from one additional affliction – its total lack of judgmental observation. (If C derives a pleasure from killing D, the act of murder must be considered "socially good," unless C's pleasure is more than eclipsed by D's misery, which may or may not be the case.[33]) But for all its imperfections, Benthamite utilitarianism has

---

[29] For example, this model does not take into account that contracts that may be perfectly efficient from the point of view of the contracting parties themselves might inflict losses on third parties. This may happen, e.g., if most workers choose to be employed by a firm that is the worst air polluter among its rivals and causes health hazards to the surrounding community.

[30] The example used in the text merely shows that the size of the pie might be larger under laissez faire, but it does not establish that it is carved equitably between firms and employees.

[31] This includes, of course, the enforcement of promises. Atiyah, ibid., pp. 329ff, seems to think that laissez faire economics does not square well with an active role of government at the stage of enforcement. This alleged paradox is illusory, of course. The Smithian invisible hand is a mechanism that translates self-interest into the Social Good. If individual actors are aware at the *ex ante* stage that organized society will not enforce their bargains, their interest to strike superior deals withers away, and the whole model collapses. The certainty of coerced compliance is thus an inseparable part of the theory of free markets and the invisible hand.

[32] The "principle of utility" was proclaimed by Bentham in his *Introduction to the Principles of Morals and Legislation*, first published in 1789. In his first chapter he writes: "By the principle of utility is meant that principle which approves or disapproves of every action whatsoever, according to the tendency it appears to have to augment or diminish the happiness of the party whose interest is in question.... The interest of the community then ... what is it? The sum of the interests of the several members who compose it." This initial formulation is a theme upon which many variations can be, and actually have been, attempted. For example, a society may strive to maximize the sum total of all its individual utilities or the average utility of all its members.

[33] The shortcomings of utilitarianism from a normative perspective are admirably discussed by Richard Posner, "Utilitarianism, Economics and Legal Theory," *Journal Legal Studies* 8:103 (1979), a paper that triggered a deluge of writing on both utilitarian theory and about Posner's own modification of it, which he terms "wealth maximization."

one major attractive feature – it defines the Public Good as being dependent on individual well-being and on absolutely nothing else.[34] Society as such does not have preferences of its own. It is not, as with some German thinkers,[35] a living organism that has to be reckoned with, either as a primary guide to moral choice or even alongside the well-being of real people, those who have "a body to be kicked or a soul to be saved." Utilitarianism is a brand of humanism (not humanitarianism) at its extreme form. It is the antithesis of Fascism, Statism, and a whole lot of other forms of corrupt communitarian principles.

It also has one additional advantage: All, or nearly all, of its deficiencies evaporate into thin air when it comes to contracts. Consider, for example, the case of a person who strikes a bargain to exchange a stallion for a stack of cash. Since both the buyer and the seller enter into the transaction voluntarily, their revealed preference indicates that the buyer values the stallion more than her money, and the seller would rather have the money than the horse.[36] Since both parties are made better off by the deal, one can safely conclude that society experienced an increase in its aggregate sense of happiness. This conclusion is reached without having to assign cardinal units of measurement to bliss or anguish and without having to plunge oneself into the impossible terrain of interpersonal comparisons. Moreover, if *everyone* is made better off, how can society, as the embodiment of the Public Good, suffer a detriment? Contract, then, is not only convenient, or efficient, or even desirable: Contract is moral, too.

This surviving domain of the old utilitarian lore – the domain of contractual relations – came to the fore about a century ago in the work of the Italian economist Vilfredo Pareto, who wrote his *Manuale di Economia Politica* in

[34] Modern economists were able to condense the utilitarian ideal into the concise formula, $W = \Sigma U_i$, where W, the Social Welfare, is obtained by the sigma, or sum total, of the individual utilities (the U_i's) of every individual on the index of existing persons in the community. John Harsanyi, in his "Cardinal Utility in Welfare Economics and in the Theory of Risk Taking," *Journal Political Economy* 61:434 (1953), was even able to identify a set of axioms under which the social superiority of utilitarian governance to other moral principles could be rigorously proven.

[35] German collectivism need not be associated with its more corrupt ramifications, which led to the despicable horrors of the twentieth century. For a much more urbane version of collectivism, see, for example, Otto von Gierke's great work, *Das deutsche Genossenschaftsrecht*, which is partially available in English in its translation by the legal historian Frederick Maitland, under the title *Political Theories of the Middle Age*, Cambridge: Cambridge University Press (reprint edition, 1996). In his treatment of the business corporation, for example, Gierke held that it had a "real" person, not a fictitious one, which can be conceptualized as being distinct from its shareholders and other claimants.

[36] Faith in the perfect fit between revealed and actual preferences was equally shared by the classical economists and the utilitarians. David Ricardo, for example, explains: "Why ... does an individual wish to sell his land? It is because he has another employment in view in which his funds will be more productive. Why does another wish to purchase this same land? It is to employ a capital which brings him too little. ... This exchange will increase the general income, since it increases the income of these parties." See his *Principles of Political Economy and Taxation*, p. 108.

1906.[37] All economists in the modern era routinely use his normative criterion, known as "Pareto efficiency," although, one suspects, the vast majority of
economists never held his book in their hands, nor understood its intellectual
pedigree. An allocation of goods or services is considered "Pareto efficient"
if it cannot be altered without causing at least one individual some degree of
disutility. If, on the other hand, an allocation can be altered, thereby conferring
a benefit on at least one individual and inflicting losses on none, there is room
for a "Pareto improvement." Many neo-classical projects are informed by the
desire to achieve some social improvement according to this Paretian criterion
of efficiency. Now, in the real world, very few undertakings can be rationalized
by this kind of logic. Almost any act of social engineering will be displeasing to
at least a small portion of the general population, and thus pursuing it cannot
achieve a social improvement in the Pareto sense. But, once again, contracts
constitute one glaring exception. Society as a whole consists of countless members, and they cannot all agree on mutually advantageous strategies. However,
when just two (or some other small number of) players strike a bargain, the
bargain not only *can*, but actually *does*, improve the lot of every single player,
or else it would not have been struck in the first place.[38] Thus, it does affect
a social improvement in the Pareto sense. Indeed, a Pareto efficient allocation,
one that does not suggest an opportunity for further voluntary exchange, is
said to be part of the "core," or "contract line." The contract line is nothing
but the set of all Pareto efficient allocations, namely all allocations that cannot be departed from without adversely affecting the well-being of at least one
potential trader.

Is this story really convincing? I find this question beside the point. It is sufficient that it *be considered* convincing within a given society to generate an ethos
under which private contracts must not be tampered with and the government,
with its endless corps of regulators, must be kept at bay. To enshrine contracts,
according to this ethos, is not merely to facilitate "efficient" outcomes. It also
ushers in a totally humanist interpretation of the notion of justice. The interference with the parties' attempt to effectuate Pareto improvements denies society
an opportunity to maximize aggregate pleasure or minimize pain. To a classical
utilitarian, this would be *morally* reprehensible.

The cult of the individual was further spirited by a strong school of
Social Darwinism that flourished in England (and elsewhere) during the nineteenth century. This school of thought sought to extend the evolutionist's

---

[37] Pareto's book has been translated into English, *Manual of Political Economy*, edited by Alfred
Page and translated by Ann Schweir, Augustus M. Kelley, Publishers (1969).

[38] One assumes, of course, that the parties know what is good for them and are willing to take
rational steps for the attainment of their goals. Many modern critics take issue with this assumption, primarily on the grounds that individual actors are prone to commit cognitive errors and
fail to identify optimal strategies for promoting their own interests. It is not necessary to critically
evaluate these modern objections, simply because my aim is to record the intellectual mood that
was prevalent in Pareto's time, and not 100 years later. This subject is explored a little further
in Chapter 6, infra.

insight[39] about the physical world into the social sphere. The proponents of this line of reasoning fathomed that the circumstance of living organisms, whose random mutations furnish only the fittest with the means to survive in a tough competitive environment, is mirrored in the social arena. They believed that superior strategies, if unhindered by a central authority, are destined to prevail over blunders and all kinds of folly. As in the case of genetic mutations, which blindly give an advantage to the fittest of the species by *natural* selection, rather than by external fiat, so must be the case with human society. There is no legitimate role to be played by a central planner in casting individual players into position on the stage. It is for them alone to rise or fall by their own devices. Successful strategists will prevail; shortsighted ones will vanish. This natural selection is too important to be delegated to the bureaucracy, lest it favor, and ultimately perpetuate, the weak over the strong, the socially corrupt over the collectively advantageous.

Even without penetrating deep beneath the surface, the relevance of Social Darwinism to contract is self-evident. If game-theoretic equilibria[40] are to be treated like genetic transformations, surely all players must be left alone, free from government interference. The normative justification of the freedom of contract lies in the trust that one reposes in the forces of natural selection.

Thus phrased, Social Darwinism fell out of grace among many a modern commentator, for it was sensed that there is no sufficient evidence to support the analogy between the natural world and the social fry. The leading force of Social Darwinism in the nineteenth century, Herbert Spencer, was ridiculed for his blind faith in this analogy and remanded to the dustbin of history.[41] But this summary dispensation of Spencer seems to me not only too harsh, but also shortsighted. The inviolable common *leitmotif* of Darwin's reflections on the natural world and of his followers' conclusions about human society lies in the great notion of *change*. The painstaking, gradual triumph of the fittest (in the natural world) cannot occur in a static state. The species must mutate, transform, and adapt. It is this constancy of change that tests the seaworthiness of all vessels in the foamy seas of existence and escorts only the most wholesome to safe harbor. It is this insight, of not only the legitimacy, but also the utter imperative of change, that is most analogous to the process of contracting. All prototypical *formulas* must yield to the different. All canonical truth goes stale in the presence of individual idiosyncrasies and personal whims. It is this

---

[39] Charles Darwin published his *On the Origin of the Species* in 1859.

[40] All concluded contracts among rational agents could be safely assumed to be the resulting stable equilibria of games. Contractual parties offer and counteroffer their tentative proposals until they both realize that no Pareto superior allocation lurks behind the corner. The selected allocation is a "stable equilibrium" because it is Pareto efficient, i.e., it cannot be departed from with the mutual consent of all the contracting parties.

[41] Atiyah, ibid., p. 323, not a great devotee of libertarian ideas, to be sure, fumes: "But it is not worth devoting any more attention to Herbert Spencer. Probably few modern English lawyers have even heard of him, and he may be allowed to remain in the obscurity into which he has deservedly fallen."

feature, not the gross parallel with genetic mutations, that animated the vision of Herbert Spencer:

It is a trite enough remark that change is the law of all things: true equally of a single object and of the universe. Nature in its infinite complexity is ever growing to a new development. Each successive result becomes the parent of an additional influence, destined in some degree to modify all future results.... As we turn over the leaves of the earth's primeval history, as we interpret the hieroglyphics in which are recorded the events of the unknown past, we find this same ever-beginning, never ceasing change.... Where once rolled a fathomless ocean now tower the snow-covered peaks of a widespread, richly clothed country teeming with existence; and where a vast continent once stretched, there remain but a few lonely coral islets to mark the graves of its submerged mountains.... Strange indeed would it be if, in the midst of this universal mutation, man alone were constant, unchangeable. But it is not so. He also obeys the laws of indefinite variation. His circumstances are ever altering, and he is ever adapting himself to them. Between the naked houseless savage and the Shakespeares and Newtons of a civilized state lie unnumbered degrees of difference.[42]

Government must be attuned to and respectful of these nuances between people. It is inherently wrong for government to ignore them, and to the extent that it does so, it is the legitimate privilege of the affected individuals to profess insubordination:

For if legislative authority is deputed, it follows that those from whom it proceeds are the masters of those on whom it is conferred.... As a government can rightly act for the people only when empowered by them, so also can it rightly act for the individual only when empowered by him. If A, B, and C debate whether they shall employ an agent to perform for them a certain service, and if while A and B are to do so C dissents, C cannot equitably be made a party to the agreement in spite of himself.[43]

The application to contract seems straightforward. It is the natural liberty of each person to offer, refuse, or accept all contractual stipulations. This seems to guarantee that only the "fittest will contract" or, alternatively, that all contracts will inure to the best interests of society as a whole.[44]

---

[42] Herbert Spencer, *Social Statics*, Robert Schalkenbach Foundation, pp. 31–32 (1970); the book was first published in 1850, almost a full decade before *On the Origin of the Species*. One notes, however, that Mr. Darwin was (secretly) hibernating over his main discovery since the 1830s, and other evolutionary theories were floating in the air among the natural scientists for quite some time before the publication of *Social Statics*.

[43] Ibid., p. 187.

[44] A modern example may shed some light on this insight. Suppose that party A owns an agricultural machine (say a tractor) and wishes to sell it. She may sell it to party B, a New York attorney, or to party C, an Iowa farmer. The freedom of the potential offerees to either accept or refuse the offer ensures that by the end of the day the tractor will be owned by party C, the farmer. The marginal product of the machine is likely to be greater if employed by her than by the New York attorney, and thus she will have an incentive to overbid the attorney and purchase the tractor. Obviously, the tractor may not be sold at all, which will occur if the marginal product of the tractor at the hands of A is, in fact, the greatest. In either case, the freedom of contract guarantees that all assets are optimally allocated.

The passive role of government in this game follows quite trivially:

Evidently, each is free to offer; each is free to accept; each is free to refuse; for each may do these to any extent without preventing his neighbors from doing the like to the same extent and at the same time. But no one may do more; no one may force another to part with his goods; no one may force another to take a specified price; for no one can do so without assuming more liberty of action than the man whom he thus treats. If everyone is free to offer, to accept, and to refuse, but to do nothing more, it is clear that, under the circumstances above put, the closing of an agreement between two of the parties implies no infringement on the claims of the disappointed ones.... As a corollary from this, all interference between those who would traffic with each other amounts to a breach of equity.... Harmonizing as it does with the settled convictions of thinking people, the foregoing conclusion may safely be left to stand unsupported.[45]

The underlying link between all British-spawned forms of individualism, to wit market economics, utilitarianism, and Social Darwinism, as well as their lasting effect on Western culture, were duly noted, somewhat *sotto voce* I suspect, by the modern philosopher John Dewey. Dewey was quick to observe that the modern corporate state presented a serious threat to the older forms of individualism. Its large organizations, the inundation of the individual in impersonal corporate cultures, and the cult of the uniform and standardized seem inimical on their face to the blossoming of individual concerns. He thought, however, that this threat must be of a superficial nature, because individualism consists not only of the *substance* of putting forward one's unique *desiderata*, but, inexorably, also of the *procedure* of responding to new environmental *stimuli* by a constant stream of adaptations. To ignore this, he writes, "treats individualism as if it were something static, having a uniform content. It ignores the fact that the mental and moral structure of individuals, the pattern of their desires and purposes, change with every great change in social constitution."[46] The standardization wrought on the human race by the machine age, he adds, is only skin deep: "At a given time ... conformity is the rule. In a time span, taken longitudinally, instability and flux dominate."[47]

So let it be with contracts. It came to the fore because Western culture learned to respect individual aspirations, market-driven ambitions, and, above all, diversity and change. Contract, being a private ordering of legal norms, is inherently decentralized. Each person, with her wants and desires, is an autonomous hothouse for the generation of contractual relations. But this notion of contractual *autonomy* calls for a separate account.

The market economy, the felicific calculus, and the survival of the fittest all flow out from the British Isles. Personal autonomy as a driving force in the ethos of contract emanates from elsewhere. It is mainly attributable to the

---

[45] *Social Statics*, pp. 131–32.
[46] John Dewey, *Individualism Old and New*, New York: Prometheus Books, p. 40 (1999). The contents of this book were first published as a series of articles in the late 1920s and early 1930s.
[47] Ibid., p. 42.

great influence of Kantian and Hegelian philosophy on the theory of Western thought.

There are great differences, perhaps, between the view of man in Hobbes, in Adam Smith, in Herbert Spencer, or in the political philosophy of Jeremy Bentham. But there is one major thread in the holdings of all those great Britons – the underlying belief that social redemption can be achieved only through individual self-seeking. To use, once again, the central Smithian insight, an invisible hand was trusted with the miracle of transforming narrowly interested patterns of behavior into the morally enlightened Social Good. In this respect, Kantian philosophy is radically different. Kant staunchly believed that any quest of happiness is, as such,[48] devoid of any moral merit. Morality implies principled choice. What are the options that conform to those axioms of the Good? These are the options that, in the opinion of the chooser, would have been universally selected by all other rational agents, if it befell to them to make the relevant choices, and if they were completely oblivious to their own personal agendas. Kant was aware, of course, that in actual fact not all choices conform to this high standard of morality. He thought, however, that nonconforming choices were not truly "free" or "autonomous" and did not confer on their practitioners a true sense of human "dignity." The analytic link between freedom, autonomy, and morality is not self-evident, and Kantian scholars spilled oceans of ink to make it more transparent.[49] Perhaps the most convincing formulation of this vision is that agents who subordinate their choices to self-interest, or even to the considerations pertaining to the phenomenal world (the world perceived through our senses, rather than through a priori spheres of reason) are not free and autonomous agents. Their preferences, in lacking the universality required of all moral choices, are not "legislating" to the world (that is, to themselves as well as to others). The individual becomes an autonomous *nucleus* of dignity only if she assumes the role of such a universal legislator.[50] The language of Kant himself, though not an exemplar of stylistic clarity, is well worth quoting:

---

[48] But Kant did not advocate suffering, either. In fact, it is quite plausible that in choosing options that make people better off, the principles of morality may be better served. See Patrick Riley, *Will and Political Legitimacy*, Lincoln, NE: Universe, pp. 125ff (1982).

[49] See, for example, Henry Allison, *Kant's Theory of Freedom*, Cambridge: Cambridge University Press, p. 134 (1990). Allison explains that the link seems to lie in Kant's definition of "freedom." If the definition of this term excludes agents acting contrary to principle, then it would be true to hold that "if one regards oneself as a rational agent, then one must also regard oneself as free and therefore as standing under the moral law."

[50] Carl Friedrich, *The Philosophy of Kant*, New York: Modern Library, p. XXXVI (1949). Friedrich writes: "The idea of autonomy is central to Kant's problem of freedom and obligation. Autonomous, or self-legislative, is a will, which is not subject to any restraining set of external 'laws'. Hence all ends which depend upon the workings of the phenomenal world for their realization, such as happiness or power or even peace, must not be involved in true autonomy. The only free will is that which acts according to 'moral laws' derived from the basic moral law embodied in the categorical imperative."

It can easily be explained how it happens that, although in the concept of duty we think of subjection to law,[51] we do nevertheless ascribe a certain sublimity and dignity to the person who fulfills all his duties. For though there is no sublimity in him in so far as he is subject to the moral law, yet he is sublime in so far as he is legislative with reference to the law and subject to it only for this reason. . . . Autonomy of the will is that property of it by which it is a law to itself independently of any property of objects of volition. Hence the principle of autonomy is: Never choose except in such a way that the maxims of the choice are comprehended in the same volition as a universal law.[52]

The relevance of these notions to contract law is rather straightforward. To begin with, Kant himself thought them relevant and went into meticulous detail in abstracting from his principles practical guidelines for the determination of contract disputes.[53] Second, and most importantly, the whole Kantian approach to the metaphysics of morals is imbued with the centrality of human will as a standard for good and evil.[54] Contract law, more than any other legal discipline (think, by contrast, of criminal law), renounces central authority to accommodate (decentralized) individual preferences, or the human will. It is, in fact, just as Kant visualized it – an individually centered fountainhead of legislation. In the highly individualistic mood of the eighteenth and nineteenth centuries, it could not but take firm root.

It seems odd to me that some[55] leading commentators do not accept this simple conclusion. Gordley, for example, attempts to trivialize the Kantian influence on the development of German contract jurisprudence of his period. He shows that some of the leading jurists of the day chose to base their teachings

---

[51] The word "law" is not used here to refer to an actual statute, or even to an idea akin to the Rule of Law. Rather, the word "law" stands here for the moral principle that ought to govern, in the ideal world, the choices actually made by individual "free" agents.

[52] Immanuel Kant, *Foundations of the Metaphysics of Morals*, translated by Lewis White Beck, Indianapolis, IN: Bobbs-Merrill, pp. 58–59 (1959; first published in 1785). In this seminal work, and especially in his treatment of what he calls "the elements of justice" (Sections 19–21), Kant speaks of a contract as an embodiment of "trans-empirical" morality. These kinds of contractual *desiderata* are normatively attractive, because the parties manifest their respect for the autonomous dignity of their contractual counterparts.

[53] Kant believed, for instance, that his moral principles could be used to solve such questions as whether an offer and an acceptance need be simultaneous, or to what extent, if any, may a promisor withdraw her promise before it was "met" by the promisee's acceptance. For this rather well-known proposition, see, for example, Leslie Mulholland, *Kant's System of Rights*, New York: Columbia University Press, pp. 261ff (1990).

[54] The first section of his *Foundations of the Metaphysics of Morals*, ibid., p. 9, starts with these words: "Nothing in the world – indeed nothing even beyond the world – [In the phrase "beyond the world" Kant is referring to the divine – U.P.] can possibly be conceived which could be called good without qualification except a *good will*. Intelligence, wit, judgment, and the other talents of the mind, however they may be named, or courage, resoluteness, and perseverance as qualities of temperament, are doubtless in many respects good and desirable. But they can become extremely bad and harmful if the will, which is to make use of these gifts of nature and which in its special constitution is called character, is not good."

[55] But most of them do. For an early example, see Samuel Williston, "Freedom of Contract," *Cornell Law Quarterly* 6:365 (1921).

on alternative, non-Kantian premises. His most convincing example concerns the work of the great German jurist of the nineteenth century, Friedrich Karl von Savigny.[56] Although Gordley acknowledges that Savigny was *personally* saturated with Kantian notions of autonomy and freedom, he believes that he managed to completely banish the essence of these notions from his philosophy of law.[57] This was due to the fact that Savigny thought that all laws, and entire legal systems, should not be crafted to reflect universal values at all. Rather, they should be fashioned after the particular values (and in their entirety, the "spirit" – *Geist*) of the given nation in which they developed and took form – in his own case, the Germanic spirit. His ability to accept Kantian notions on the personal level but to renounce them in his legal philosophy stemmed from his (slightly comic) belief that the categories of law and philosophy are quite distinct, and considerations pertinent to the one ought not to contaminate the purity of the other. The role of the lawyer, he held, is to read and critically interpret texts, not to philosophize about them. But this formulation speaks more about Savigny than it does about the German legal system. All interpreters of texts, including Savigny (and, to be sure, Gordley, or me, or the reader), cannot disengage themselves, in the act of interpretation, from what they believe to be a worthy mental picture of the Good. Given the universally high esteem of the Kantian notions of morality, freedom, and will in nineteenth-century Germany, the rapid development of contract jurisprudence at that time on that particular soil can hardly be viewed as an odd coincidence.

It would be impossible to conclude this (necessarily cursory) survey of nineteenth-century will theory on the development of Western contract law without making a reference to Hegelian philosophy. In Hegel's mind, the concepts of property and contract are intimately intertwined. Hegel did not subscribe to the teachings of some contractarian philosophers, that each person is endowed with some property (at least, say, over her own person) in the state of nature, and that the process of contracting is a mere method of exchanging *preexisting* entitlements.[58] Rather, he believed that objects initially exist just as "things," not as anybody's exclusively owned property. Things can be transformed into "property," into objects that "belong" to individual subjects, only if they are willed to be so transformed by the mutual assent of free individuals.[59] Since Hegel also held that ownership of objects, including ownership of a person over herself, is essential to the definition of "personhood"

---

[56] Savigny's masterpiece, *System des Heutigen Römischen Rechts*, was first published between 1840 and 1848.

[57] Gordley, ibid., pp. 225ff.

[58] See, for instance, John Locke, *Second Treatise of Government*, c. 5, §27 (originally published in 1690). In that section Locke writes: "Every Man has a Property in his own Person . . . the Labour of his Body, and the Work of his Hands. . . ."

[59] Peter Stillman, "Property, Contract and Ethical Life in Hegel's Philosophy of Right," in Drucilla Cornell, Michel Rosenfeld, and David Gray Carlson (eds.), *Hegel and Legal Theory*, New York: Routledge, p. 205 (1991).

(*Persönlichkeit*),[60] he reasoned that contracts were necessary for the mental construction of the self.[61]

Hegel's language, though stylistically inelegant, is clear enough on this subject:[62]

In contract property is no longer viewed on the side of its external reality, as a mere thing, but rather as containing the elements of will, another's as well as my own. . . . The necessary nature of the conception is thus realized in a unity of different wills, which, nevertheless, give up their differences and peculiarities. But this identity implies not that one will is identical with the other, but rather that each at this stage remains an independent and private will.[63]

Since the driving force behind the legitimacy of contract is the human will, it matters little to Hegel whether a willed stipulation was already fulfilled, or it still remains, to use the Common Law vocabulary, a mere "executory contract." The object of the exchange immediately vests in the promisee and becomes his "property":

Stipulation is already the embodiment of my volition. I have disposed of my property; it has ceased to be mine, and I recognize it as already belonging to another. The Roman distinction between *pactum* and *contractus* is not sound. Fichte once laid it down that the obligation to hold to the contract began for me only when the other party began to do his share. . . . The trouble is that stipulation is not merely external, but involves a common will, which has already done away with mere intention and change of mind. The other party may of course change his mind after the engagement, but has he any right to do so?[64]

To be sure, Hegel's thinking about the idea of contract was much more opulent than can be assembled from these scanty lines. Contract is necessary, for instance, not only as a means for the acquisition of property (and thus of personhood), but also as a means of dumping it, or willing it away, as one's preferences change, and a repudiation of the status quo for greener pastures is called for. Likewise, the meeting of two minds in the formation of an *individual* contract is not only a means for obtaining self-respect through the acquiescence

---

[60] The most distinguished legal scholar utilizing Hegelian notions in theorizing about the modern law of property appears to be Margaret Jane Radin. See, for instance, her book, *Reinterpreting Property*, Chicago: University of Chicago Press (1994).

[61] Hegel's philosophy has a strong "communitarian" streak; one of its manifestations is that a person's own dignity, indeed her sense of personhood, is derived, inter alia, by its recognition by other people. In this respect, contracts play a major role, because they make room for the mutual recognition of individual persons' rights to property. See David Carlson, "How to Do Things with Hegel," *Texas Law Review* 78:1377 (2000).

[62] Readers who wish to avail themselves of a linguistically lucid account of this passage, and of its pride of place among the other ideas about contractual relations in Hegel's philosophy, are referred to Alan Wood, *Hegel's Ethical Thought*, New York: Cambridge University Press, pp. 94ff (1990).

[63] Georg Wilhelm Friedrich Hegel, *Philosophy of Right*, translated by S. W. Dyde, Amherst, NY: Prometheus Books, §§72–73 (1996; originally published in 1821).

[64] Ibid., §79.

of the other; it is also a didactic first move, which attains its ultimate triumph in the *universal* meeting of all rational minds in the concept of the state.[65] But be it as it may, it is clear that will theory took center stage in justifying the binding effect of contracts. Hegel was convinced that contract was a vital link between the willing person and all external objects. It thus made it possible for all individual agents to assert their claim to personhood, and to assume a sense of dignity and self-worth.[66]

All these philosophical ideas (and ideals) – the market economy, the invisible hand, utilitarian maximization, Social Darwinism, Kantian autonomy, Hegelian will, as well as a host of other, related notions of the self,[67] its centrality in the universe, or its prized individualism – never presented themselves to the Russian mind. It falls outside the scope of this chapter to show what did present itself, and was accepted as ruling ideology, during these fateful centuries from the onset of the Renaissance to the present day. This task will be undertaken in later chapters.[68] At this stage I would like to proceed, without further ado, to the manifestation of these polar opposites, in the West and in Eternal Russia, through their respective pictorial iconography.

Iconography

The incorporation of individualistic values into Western iconography is universally recognized. It was also an age in which portraiture in general, and self-portraiture in particular, assumed in the eyes of the artists and their sitters alike a particularly important role.[69] I will touch on this rich subject with the utmost brevity. The most articulate champions of individualistic iconography

---

[65] Mark Tunick, *Hegel's Political Philosophy*, Princeton, NJ: Princeton University Press, pp. 48ff (1992).

[66] "Property is the realization of a self-conscious will in an external thing. Since mind is essentially a self-revealing system, it must give itself an outward existence and maintain its freedom in a world of things": Hugh Reyborn, *The Ethical Theory of Hegel: A Study of the Philosophy of Right*, Gloucestershire: Clarendon Press, p. 125 (1921). "Property, taken by itself, is the most abstract phase; it states explicitly only the relation of the individual will to a particular thing. But we have seen that this relationship is conditioned by a rational community, and involves the recognition of one will by others. In contract this context begins to appear: Each individual recognized the right of the other contracting individual, and a common will is established." Ibid., p. 139.

[67] My text omits, for instance, all discussions of social contract theories. The greatest contributors to this philosophical school who come to mind include the greatest of them all, Thomas Hobbes, or the most influential on ideological formation of trans-Atlantic democracies, John Locke, or on the French revolution, Jean-Jacques Rousseau.

[68] See especially Chapters 4 and 5, infra.

[69] See, for example, Joanna Woods-Marsden, *Renaissance Self-Portraiture: The Visual Construction of Identity and the Social Status of the Artist*, New Haven, CT: Yale University Press (1999). The discovery of the great value of self-portraiture far exceeded the visual arts. Michel de Montaigne, for example, interpreted the whole *corpus* of his celebrated *Essays* as a literary form of a self-portrait. For a concise yet accurate treatment of this fascinating subject, see the translator's introduction to Michel de Montaigne, *Essays*, translated by J. M. Cohen, New York: Penguin Books (1958); the *Essays* first saw the light of day in 1580.

were, once again, the great masters of the Renaissance. As Leonardo famously put it:

To know and to will are two operations of the human mind. To discern, to judge, to reflect, are actions of the human mind. . . . Represent your figures in such actions as may be fitted to express what purpose is in their minds; otherwise your art will not be good.[70]

The practical implications of heeding this advice are to craft each human figure in a different mold, typical only of itself. In his notes about painting the disciples in the *Last Supper*, Leonardo reflects on what might properly be their relative positions and mental moods:

One who was drinking and has left the glass in its position and turned his head towards the speaker. Another twisting the fingers of his hands, turns with stern brows to his companion. Another with his hands spread shows the palms, and shrugs his shoulders up to his ears, making a mouth of astonishment. Another speaks into his neighbor's ear and as he listens, turns towards him to lend an ear while holding a knife in one hand, and in the other the loaf half cut through. Another as he turns with a knife in his hand upsets a glass on the table. Another lays his hands on the table and is looking. Another blows his eyes with his hands. Another draws back behind the one who leans forward, and sees the speaker between the wall and the man who is leaning.[71]

The same point of view is admirably expressed by a precursor of Leonardo as a humanist and as a typical Renaissance person, Leon Battista Alberti,[72] in his famous treatise on painting.[73] In this treatise Alberti set out a list of painterly traits that he deemed necessary for the achievement of pictorial greatness. One of the most important traits is *varietà*, variety, which assists the painter in fleshing out the uniqueness in each individual object contained in his enterprise. *Varietà* is not a synonym for copiousness. Copiousness exists where a painting exhibits a large number of objects, like men, women, children, animals and things. *Varietà*, on the other hand, consists of "ornate" (*ornata*) copiousness by diversity, as when the figures display a difference of attitude and exhibit various parts of their bodies and of their mental attitudes. It then befalls the artist, in Alberti's book, to link the various objects, each marked by its own *varietà* in a unifying pictorial theme, a fruit of his own imagination, which

[70] *The Notebooks of Leonardo Da Vinci*, selected and edited by Irma Richter, New York: Oxford World's Classics Paperback, p. 177 (1998; first published in 1952).

[71] Ibid., p. 180. Does this description fit Leonardo's famous fresco in the Convent of Santa Maria delle Grazie? Not necessarily. Always reflective in his personal life as well, Leonardo must have had second thoughts concerning some of the relevant figures.

[72] For a short account of Alberti the humanist and Renaissance Man, see Sir Anthony Blunt, *Artistic Theory in Italy, 1450–1600*, Gloucestershire: Clarendon Press, Chapter I (1940).

[73] Alberti's treatise, *Della Pittura*, was written in Latin in 1436 and translated by the author into Italian to make it accessible to his great contemporary, Filippo Brunelleschi (Vasari attributes the translation to Lodovico Domenichi). In general, there were few persons in the whole of human history who had a better well-rounded erudition in all the available spheres of human knowledge than this Renaissance Man, Leon Battista Alberti. Alberti's treatise is available in English translation: Leon Battista Alberti, *On Painting*, translated by John Spencer, New Haven, CT: Yale University Press (1956).

Alberti calls "*composizione.*" The role of this composition is to discipline the otherwise too loosely crafted objects blazed by *varietà*, while their role, in turn, is to nourish the wholesomeness of the composition.[74] *Varietà* also implies originality. Mimicking the example of other artists is pedestrian; Alberti writes:

Some copy figures of other painters. Here they seek the praise given to Calamis, the sculptor who sculpted two cups, as is recorded, in which he copied things similarly done by Zenodorus so that no difference could be seen between them. Our painters will certainly be in great error if they do not know that ... things taken from nature [are painted] sweetly and correctly. ... Nothing more can be acquired from paintings but the knowledge of how to imitate them.[75]

Michael Baxandall illustrates the propensity of Renaissance imagery to convey different states of mind through visible bodily gestures by analyzing, quite convincingly, I think, the iconography of the Annunciation. Mary was differentially portrayed in this famous scene as having experienced at least five distinct states of mind, each having its own standard iconography. The first of these psychological phases is disquiet, depicting the Virgin's alarm at being visited by divinity and being conscious of her "mere" human nature. A second rendition of the scene catches her in a reflective mood, a totally introspective humor showing the Virgin assessing the new surprising situation. A third pictorial approach involves inquiry, focusing on Mary considering the plausibility of her Immaculate Conception. The next state of mind is submission, depicting the virgin accepting her destiny; and, finally, merit, a mixture of gratification and awe at being instantly conceived with God Incarnate.[76] Although the number of these renditions is finite, and not excessively large, Renaissance *mores* encouraged individual artists to assign to every humor a personal interpretation, completely novel and different from everybody else's. Baxandall contrasts, for instance, Filippo Lippi's gentle and sweet interpretation of Mary's disquiet with Botticelli's almost violent one, where the announcing angel seems to frighten the "disquieted" Virgin nearly out of her senses (see Figures 17 and 18).

The importance of *varietà* was such that, for many Renaissance theorists, it justified subjecting artists to the most rigorous educational accountability. Only learned artists, it was believed, could faithfully draw on their erudition to generate distinct representations of reality in such important matters as diversity of nationality, historical moment, taste, and costume.[77] Portraiture was considered an elevated form of pictorial representation (second only to the representation of historical scenes), because it licensed the artist to plunge into

---

[74] Michael Baxandall, *Painting and Experience in Fifteen Century Italy*, Oxford: Oxford University Press, pp. 133ff (1972).

[75] Alberti, ibid., p.94.

[76] Baxandall, ibid., pp. 48ff. Baxandall ascribes the identification of Mary's distinct states of mind to the fifteenth-century Florentine preacher, Fra Roberto Caracciolo. It was common among the preachers of that age to sensitize their flock to the interpretive nuances of painted moods.

[77] See, for instance, Rensselaer Lee, *Ut Pictura Poesis*, New York: Norton, pp. 41ff (1967).

FIGURE 17. Filippo Lippi, *Annunciation*, circa 1442.

the domain of different individual traits.[78] Differentiation and individualism dominated not only the theory of pictorial representation, but also Renaissance interpretation of human emotions in general. John Martin, for example,

---

[78] Rembrandt's pupil, Samuel van Hoogstraten (1627–1678), shared this view, although he thought that portraiture had to be reviled, too, for its commitment to unimaginative naturalism and for the greed of its practitioners. See Mariët Westermann, *A Worldly Art, the Dutch Republic 1585–1718*, New York: Palgrave, p. 64 (1996).

FIGURE 18. Sandro Botticelli, *Annunciation*, 1489–90.

does a superb job of demonstrating the many facets of prudence and sincerity in Renaissance thought.[79] Literary development, too, often took the route of liberating the narrative of individual lives from the chains of overarching structural patterns.[80] The Western story, in short, is clear enough.

Things could not have been more different in Eastern Orthodoxy, and especially in Eternal Russia. Russian icons have a great deal of *individuality* but no *individualism*. Their individuality results from the simple fact that they are the handicraft of disparate painters, each artist reporting to work at his easel with his own unique baggage of genetic matter, life history, and artistic genius.[81] However, the moral and religious doctrines relating to icons interpret the

[79] John Martin, "Inventing Sincerity, Refashioning Prudence: The Discovery of the Individual in Renaissance Europe," *American Historical Review* 102:102 (1997), reprinted in Keith Whitlock (ed.), *The Renaissance in Europe*, New Haven, CT: Yale University Press, pp. 11ff (2000).

[80] See Michael McKeon, *The Origins of the English Novel 1600–1740*, Baltimore, MD: Johns Hopkins University Press, pp. 90ff (1987).

[81] In addition, individual differences are attributable to the different "schools" of icon painting. In Russia, the main schools, after the loss of Kiev to hordes of nomadic tribes, were located in Moscow, Novgorod, Pskov, and, to a lesser extent, in a variety of larger and provincial towns. The distinct tastes of each school reflected those of the relevant principality, bishopric, metropolitan seat, or even individual monasteries. See, in general, Engelina Smirnova, "Moscow

principle of individualism as evil and corrupt. Orthodox hostility to individualism is animated by two main themes – the theological value of mimicking old types and the transcendental meaning of time.

The most striking feature of the Orthodox, especially the Russian, attitude to the painting of icons is that older icons, as well as other older doctrinal manifestations, represent a more authentic version of the True Faith than any conceivable modern permutation.[82] The practical implication of this insight is that contemporary painters of all generations are expected to look up to the example set for them by their predecessors and to faithfully copy their iconography. On its broadest philosophical footing this attitude supposes that truth, and especially divine truth, is eternal in its nature and cannot be modified by transitory interpretations, by fashion or by whim. If old icons are viewed as "windows to heaven," as a reflection of some divine truth, and if this truth is assumed to be immutable, it logically follows that iconographic innovations must be condemned as a form of heresy.

Robin Cormack demonstrated a wonderful early illustration of this principle.[83] Figure 19 reproduces a page from a ninth-century Byzantine manuscript, known as the *Sacra Parallela*. The subject of this image is an icon painter, a monk, engaged in the holy work of producing a new icon by copying an old one. We are thus entrusted into a close universe ruled by three icons. This notional "triptych," consisting of the work itself and its two subjects, posits the old icon as a model, and the new one is shown in the process of production. The cloning of fresh icons by older inspiration thus assumes, in itself, iconic value, which is fortified, for good measure, by an explicit conspicuous script. This text reads:

As painters when they paint icons from icons, looking closely at the model, are eager to transfer the character of the model to their own work, so he who strives to perfect himself in all branches of virtue must look to the lives of saints as if to moving and living images, and make their virtue his own by imitation.

Faithful to its philosophy that higher spiritual value is to be found in more ancient role modes, the text itself is not original. Although the icon was made in the ninth century, the text is borrowed, according to Cormack, from much earlier patristic sources, in this case from the writings of St. Basil, who was active in the fourth century.[84]

The practice of producing icons by copying other icons has another valuable theological explanation, which will be dwelt on at some length in Chapter 6, infra. It is repeated here in shorthand to buttress the argument that mimicking

Icon Painting from the 14th to the 16th Century," in *The Art of Holy Russia, Icons from Moscow 1400–1600*, Exhibition Catalog, Royal Academy of Arts, London, pp. 45ff (1998).

[82] Timothy Ware, a bishop in the Orthodox faith and an Oxford don, gives many examples of the apparent changelessness of Orthodoxy. One quaint example concerns the deacon crying out during the Liturgy the words "The Doors! The Doors!," in an unbroken tradition from the early days of Christianity when the doors had to be guarded against the pagan oppressors. Ware cogently argues, however, that the repetition of old rituals need not be interpreted as

FIGURE 19. Byzantine manuscript (*Sacra Parallela*) (ninth century) showing a monk in the act of copying icons.

a role model is more virtuous than creating one from scratch. Creating a new icon may engage the artist in looking for his inspiration at the world. But since the object of icons is held to transcend reality, as it involves such mysteries as the Holy Trinity, the Incarnation, or the Transfiguration of Christ, the artist's

---

"parrotlike" and must be given a new meaning in every generation. See Timothy Ware, *The Orthodox Church*, pp. 195ff (1997).

[83] Robin Cormack, *Painting the Soul*, Chicago: Reaktion Books, pp. 74ff (1997).

[84] Ibid.

FIGURE 20. El Greco, *St. Luke Painting the Virgin and Child from Life*, between 1560 and 1567.

sensory *stimuli* cannot be used as appropriate vehicles for its pictorial transmutation. The artist must be inspired by stimuli other than empirical reality and be assisted by the introspective methods used by former iconographers. In fact, I am aware of only one kind of iconographic representation in which the artist was "licensed" to explore outside phenomena as his inspirational material. Figure 20, an early painting by El Greco, executed in his youthful years, when he was still really a Greek icon painter, shows St. Luke, the evangelist, who was, by tradition, an icon painter, too, making an icon of Mary and the infant Jesus *from life*, although one notes in passing that the Virgin and Child in this famous format assume an absolutely iconic appearance. The reason for the exception is rooted in the iconoclastic wars of the eighth and ninth centuries. The belief in the historical validity of this story, that is, that the Virgin and the Child themselves agreed to sit for St. Luke, was used by the iconodules as a powerful argument for the legitimacy of icons. In this image, El Greco depicts St. Luke in the process of portraying the Virgin and the Child with a gesture suggesting that his arduous labor needs only one final touch to attain perfection. Both "sitters" are clearly delineated on the panel, again, in a strikingly iconic format, *but none appears within the frame itself*. St. Luke is clearly sighting a scene in which the viewers are not invited to partake. The absence of the "sitters" from a scene, in which their presence was supposed to trump the argument in the iconoclastic debate, suggests that even in this special case one ought to look within oneself in quest of the deeper truth. The uniform nature of this devotional truth[85] is self-evident in the icon (within an icon) of the Virgin and the Child.

The myth of St. Luke as the portraitist of the *Hodigitria* is so robust that legends of his efforts still abound in modern Christian Orthodoxy and allow for some modest naturalism in the depiction of the sitter. Figure 21, for example, is claimed to have been executed by St. Luke himself, although the connoisseur will not find it difficult to discern its late execution. This minor difficulty notwithstanding, the faithful (in this case the tiny Syriac community in the old city of Jerusalem) dispense its healing powers to afflicted pilgrims, who travel long distances to avail themselves of the cure.

Assigning special merit to reproduction and the rejection of innovation is a fairly pan-Orthodox theological trait. But it appears to have assumed special emphasis on Russian soil. A sixteenth-century Russian ecclesiastical source, which contains, *inter alia*, a variety of dogmas concerning the painting of icons, reads:

Iconographers must frequently have recourse to spiritual fathers and seek their advice in everything and live in accordance with their rules and their teachings in fasting, praying, and abstinence in all humility and without scandal or violence. And with great diligence they are to draw the image of our Lord Jesus Christ and of the Immaculate Mother of God [and other saints] . . . in the image and likeness and in conformity with the substance and best examples of ancient iconographers . . . and those iconographers are respected . . . and more honored than other men. Noble and ordinary people should show utter respect to iconographers because of the noble images they paint. And in their respective territories, bishops must make sure that the fine iconographers and their disciples paint according to the principles of ancient models and that they do not represent the divinity according to their own creativity and their own ideas.[86]

In keeping with this caveat, individual injunctions were issued from time to time concerning the sanctity of particularly well-executed icons. The

---

[85] The paradigm is, of course, the Panagia Hodigitria, where the Virgin points to Jesus with her right hand, thereby showing the way to the faithful.

[86] From the forty-third chapter of the Council of the Hundred Chapters (1551), cited by Viktor Lazarev, *The Russian Icon*, translated by Colette Joy Dees, Collegeville, MN: Liturgical Press, p. 24 (1997).

FIGURE 21. Anonymous artist (claimed to be St. Luke), *The Virgin and Child Painted by St. Luke* (ostensibly an early twentieth-century canvass).

best-known example concerns Rublev's famous rendition of *The Holy Trinity* and the concomitant obligation of living artists to copy it just as it is, without any modifications.[87] The discussion of this icon and its many theological aspects is deferred, however, to Chapter 6.

[87] This particular injunction was also contained in the Church Council of 1551, known as the Council of the Hundred Chapters.

Russian icons lack individualism not only because mimicking an existing type was considered a virtue, but also because of the Orthodox conception of *time* (and, to a lesser extent, space). Time is an elusive concept. To imagine that time matters, one has to presuppose that evolution and progress are feasible, that it is possible to surpass an ancient paradigm by some kind of an evolutionary process, by trying harder, or by possessing a greater talent. If, on the other hand, an ancient paradigm is assumed to be divinely inspired or to reflect eternal grace, wisdom, or bliss, the passage of time can herald no evolution, no progress, and no growth.

Now the dry facts are that Russian, as well as other Orthodox, icons are never (or almost never) dated, nor are they signed by their iconographers. They are designed to convey a sense of timelessness. The personal traits of their makers are deliberately effaced, thereby producing a fusion of the individual artist within the transcendental mystery of his mission.

Timothy Ware, in a recent book in which he is featured in his official capacity as an Orthodox bishop, mystically explains the notion of Orthodox time as being captured by the geometrical shape of a circle or a spiral. He then contrasts it with the Hebraic (as he calls it) notion of time, which is more like an arrow or a straight line. The linear model of the Hebrews implies that time moves forward, never treading again on the same spot, while Orthodox continuity implies repetition and the consecration of the old.[88] The closest that Ware gets to a rational explanation of this mystery is his assertion, a "basic truth" as he calls it, that "time and eternity are not opposed but interdependent, not mutually exclusive but complementary."[89] Clearly, it is the eternal element of time that renounces its transience. To the Western (Hebraic?) mind, which links individual expression to transient personalities, the Orthodox temporal transcendence may seem suffocating. By the same token, to the Eastern mind, the "Hebraic" subordination of the eternal to the transient may seem pedestrian, and its practitioners may be pitied for missing out on something pertaining to the higher spheres of human existence.

The Orthodox interpretation of the essence of time cannot be fully understood without its parallel interpretation of space, or its *theology of presence*. An icon cannot be used for its liturgical function until it is approved and blessed by an authorized priest. Once it is thus inaugurated to its theophanic ministry, its subject matter (the image of God or of the saints) is believed to conquer the material, to dominate the panel. It is they, God and the saints, who assume a "real" existence, whereas the panel and its image, that is, the wood and the pigment, the gilding and the varnish, lose their epistemic "reality." A modern doctrinal authority explains:

It is certainly true that the icon has no reality of its own. In itself, it is only a wooden board. The icon gets all its theophanic value from its participation in the Wholly Other;

---

[88] Bishop Kallistos Ware, *The Inner Kingdom*, Crestwood, NY: St. Vladimir's Seminary Press, pp. 181ff (2000).

[89] Ibid., p. 184.

the icon is the mirror of the Wholly Other. It can therefore contain nothing in itself but becomes rather a grid, a structure through which the Other shines forth. The absence of three-dimensional volume in two-dimensional icons excludes all materialization. The icon thus expresses an energetic presence which is not localized nor enclosed but which shines out from a point of condensation.[90]

The iconographer, then, is a mere vehicle for assisting the Eternal to glow in His own image. The wooden panel itself, which the iconographer holds in his hands and painstakingly transforms into an icon, becomes, by this very process, devoid of "reality." How can the artist, then, hope to portray not only Him, who is the subject of His image, but also the particularized, transient, and totally human foibles of his own hand? Even the artist's inspiration is not believed to be his own. The artist is instrumental. His labor is noble and dignified, but he himself is banished from its glory.[91]

I would like to wrap up the discussion of this chapter by tracing the stylistic developments of one icon, the Nativity of Christ. This famous image, like, in fact, almost any other major icon, illustrates both the propensity of the Orthodox mind to consecrate the prototype and the invincible human spirit, which, in spite of all doctrinal injunctions, slithers its way through to individual expression. It thus demonstrates more eloquently than words the ubiquitous distinction between *individualism* and *individuality*.

The immutable prototype of this icon is held to date back to an image painted by an artist commissioned by Emperor Constantine on the site of the Nativity in the fourth century.[92] This ancient prototype was, and still is, faithfully copied by generations of icon painters. Thus, in a famous fifteenth-century Muscovite icon, the Virgin elegantly rests at the center of the panel and is certainly its main protagonist. She is enclosed by an ovally diagonal red shape, which sets her apart from all the others. Everyone else (including her own Son) is either derived from her or is seen in the light of her miraculous conception. The infant Jesus is represented twice. He lies above his mother, at the mouth of a cave, thus hinting not only to the manger of His birth but also to the depth of Hades into which He is destined to descend in His future role as Savior. He also rests in the arms of a midwife, who pours water over Him, thus presaging His baptismal ministration. At the lower left side Joseph is seen brooding over the mystery of the conception, tempted by a devil to entertain impure suspicions. The prophet Isaiah is seen at the right with a tree and a shepherd at his side, signifying the connection between heaven and earth, the spirit and the flesh, and pointing to the Infant of his prophesy. The Magi ride up to the occasion on the upper left side of the panel, and the angels are exalting the Nativity from both directions. A trifurcated source of light, signifying the Trinity, basks the whole scene with a serene light of redemption.

---

[90] Paul Evdokimov, *The Art of the Icon: A Theology of Beauty*, translated by Fr. Steven Bigham, Princeton, NJ: Princeton University Press, p. 179 (1990; first published in French in 1972).

[91] Ibid., p. 177.

[92] Evdokimov, ibid., p. 271.

FIGURE 22. Monk Gregory Kroug, *The Nativity of Christ*, twentieth century.

   Nothing of significance has ever been changed in this form of imagery. One might consider, for example, a famous icon executed a full century later in the city of Novgorod. The Novgorod style is considered less refined, and more folkloristic, than its Muscovite counterpart, reflecting, as it were, the "Northern Manners" of the colonized north. The iconography of this latter panel is, however, by and large identical, although one notices some slight variations in the staging of some protagonists (Isaiah is positioned at the lower right side, Jesus is washed by a midwife closer to the center, and the shepherds come along accompanied by their livestock). Mary retains her privileged pose

FIGURE 23. Georgii Kibardin, poster – "Lenin and the Airships," 1931.

at the center of the panel and almost[93] all the theological messages remain intact.

The same imagery is still copied faithfully today. Figure 22 was executed by Monk Gregory Kroug (1909–1969), a prominent contemporary iconographer. Obviously not an exact copy of either the Muscovite or the Novgorod type, the thematic resemblance of all these icons, including in the centrality of the Theotokos and the theological bundle of messages, is self-evident.

Unsurprisingly, the same theological message of the iconography of the Nativity was carried forward to the propagandist imagery of the Soviet dictatorship. In a political poster from the darkest days of the Bolshevist era, entitled *Lenin and the Airships* (Figure 23), executed in 1931, we essentially

---

[93] There are slight variations. The location of the washed Jesus in the Muscovite icon, for instance, dissects the panel in a geometrical proportion that mimics the ratio of the horizontal and vertical bars of the cross. This implicit reference to the cross is missing in the Novgorod panel.

see the same iconographic elements. The place of Mary is now usurped by the grim icon of tovarish Ulyanov (Lenin). The diagonal shape enclosing the Virgin is substituted by the diagonal shapes of futuristic airships, bearing the inscription "Lenin." An invisible rising sun basks the scene with serene light, celebrating the nativity of a new faith. The Magi, the shepherds, and the angels are transformed into hordes of admirers, clumped together at the bottom of the image, who flock to the site of the Nativity with a clear sense of redemption. The communist Savior has already lowered himself into the capitalistic Hades, to bring new life to the suffering souls of yore.

4

Authority

Vast legal domains are imbued with authority. The law of crimes, for example, is nothing but a list of injunctions, mandating people to do, or not to do, specified sorts of things. In autocratic regimes these injunctions emanate from a sovereign, who may or may not be responsive to the individual concerns of her subjects. In democratic regimes these injunctions, as well as the rest of the legal structure, are supposed to emanate from the people. But given the heterogeneity of individual preferences, the ultimate determination of their "collective will" is bound to be arbitrary, coercive, and authoritarian.[1] This insight is not confined to the law of crimes. Even constitutional law, which is designed to guarantee the values of individual freedom more than any other branch of the law, imposes itself on every subject, whether she likes its ultimate outcomes or not. Constitutional decisions of the highest order of magnitude are determined by fiat, rather than by choice. This includes questions relating to the right to live (of the unborn, of convicted felons), to die (of the critically ill or suffering), to partake in the political process, and, in general, to strike a balance between diametrically opposed social goals.

Western contract law is one small haven of individual choice in an ocean of regulated order. The authority of the state is used for the enforcement of consensual agreements, but not otherwise. In this vein, contact law is best understood not in stating what it does, but in what it does not do. It strips the state of its authority to call the shots. Except bearing its enforcement responsibilities, it is supposed to do nothing. Even in its enforcement functions, it is not supposed

---

[1] This is so for a variety of reasons. One leading reason is that society, as such, does not have preferences of its own. The aggregation of individual preferences into a single social outcome, even if one assumes away official corruption or bad judgment, does not necessarily correspond with what the individuals themselves desire. The greatest contemporary debunker of any possible links between individual utilities and social outcomes is Kenneth Arrow, in his famous "impossibility theorem": Kenneth Arrow, *Social Choice and Individual Values* (2d. ed., 1970). In addition, official corruption can hardly be assumed away. A leading modern exponent of this theme is Mancur Olson, *The Logic of Collective Action* (1971).

to serve its own goals, but the goals pronounced by ordinary people in their private stipulations. This voluntary divestiture of state power in the service of individual *desiderata* reflects, when it transpires, recognition of the limited role of government and its lack of legitimacy to pry into the private domain. It is harder to come by in authoritarian societies, where the role of government is more encompassing and less contingent on context or circumstance.

Russian society is, by long tradition, extremely authoritarian and hierarchical. The main theme of this chapter is to record this fact, with special emphasis on its legal implications; to contrast it with the more limited role of authority in the West; and to illustrate it by iconographic means. Without a doubt, the failure of contract in contemporary Russian society can be traced back to this central tenet of its culture. An all-pervasive government and consensual self-regulation, like oil and water, make poor ingredients for a wholesome mix.

An appendix to this chapter examines the architecture of the fair City of St. Petersburg. Intended, as it was, to reflect the Western values of the Renaissance and the Baroque, it was nonetheless transformed by its builders, Peter the Great and his despotic successors, into an icon of power and central authority. This stark realism clearly radiates, I contend, through the thin veneer of its Franco-Italianate architectural style.

What Is Authority?

The concept of authority is best captured by its post-Renaissance conventional image, a *lingua franca* shared by all Europeans of the period. Cesare Ripa, in his *magnum opus* on the conventional imagery of his time,[2] describes Spiritual Authority as a splendidly attired, mature handsome lady sitting on a throne, holding a scepter in one hand and keys in the other. An inscription taken from Cicero announces that weapons must give way to the toga, a symbol of her dignity. The keys are held up in recognition of their supremacy over the other objects reflected in the image: the scepter (temporal power), the weapons of war, books (mere learning), a bundle of lictors' rods (means of punishment), banners (allegiance to competing causes), and trophies (success in life). The Hertel edition[3] (see Figure 24) adds a *fatto* (a pictorial illustration of the main icon) showing Christ presenting Peter with the keys to the heavenly kingdom. *Ecclesia* is thus presented with the (delegated) supreme power to reward the just. The authority to castigate the guilty is not delegated; subjecting others to pain – and anticipating their submission and ultimate surrender – can be expected only from the Highest Authority. In Ripa's work, Authority is seated, to command the respect of her admirers. She is mature in years, for authority does not fit with the young. The dignity of Spiritual Authority is not derived of

---

[2] Cesare Ripa, *Baroque and Rococo Pictorial Imagery* (the 1758–60 Hertel Edition, translated for Dover Publications by Edward Maser, 1971), image number 177

[3] Ripa's text was illustrated numerous times, but the Hertel edition is considered the "best" and it is in terms of its pictorial language that it is customary to think of Ripa's descriptions.

FIGURE 24. Cesare Ripa, *Spiritual Authority*, Hertel Edition, 1758–60.

her wisdom (books), might (weapons), coercive power (rods), or lure of reward (trophies). It asserts its supremacy by voiding the cogency of rival claims (banners). It seals it by denying the legitimacy of all other forms of clout (the rejected scepter).

As the Ripa icon demonstrates, authority cannot rest on brutish force alone. A mugger's claim to a commuter's purse in the subway may well be obeyed by the commuter, but the commuter need not acknowledge the mugger's authority to pursue his claim. Naked violence is transformed into authority when coupled with some *justificatory* argument whose legitimacy is affirmed by the conforming individuals.[4] By the same token, not all justified claims can be based on

---

[4] J. Ladenson, "In Defense of a Hobbesian Conception of Law," in Joseph Raz (ed.), *Authority*, pp. 32ff (1990).

the authority of the person asserting them. It might be justified, for example, to commit violence in the interest of self-defense, but the actor's violence need not rest on her claim to authority nor on the victim's recognition of such a claim.[5] Authority, then, is a state of maintaining a jurisdiction over the destinies of other people. It implies both sheer power to force one's will on others and a common understanding that this power must be exercised, and is in fact exercised, for the attainment of a justified cause.

Now cultures vary greatly in their understanding of what may constitute the use of coercion for the attainment of a justified cause. Autocratic cultures define the domain of justified causes broadly, thereby allocating political power to the source of authority (e.g., a sovereign) and away from those subject to its claims (the people). Anarchistic cultures may deny the very existence of a core of justified causes, thereby freeing the individuals living in such societies from the heavy yoke of being ruled by others.[6] Pure anarchy hardly exists, but contract societies are obviously closer to the pole of anarchy than they are to the pole of autocracy. In contract societies, individual members are recognized as the owners of valuable entitlements and are free to trade them at will. Noncontractual societies deny individuals their independent claim to numerous entitlements. Even when individual actors are tolerated by the source of authority to possess some entitlements, they are less free to exchange them for the entitlements possessed by others. All rights descend from the top down, rather than ascend from the bottom up. No recipient can better her position and accumulate fresh entitlements by using her vested rights and trading them at her pleasure. Western legal systems have opted for contract, thereby diminishing the domain of justified causes for the exercise of political clout. The Russian culture opted out of contract by maintaining its autocratic structure. This choice is reflected in Russian history, art, and law.

Political Authority in Russia

It is not easy to determine with certainty at what historical period the confused hodgepodge of Slavs, Lithuanians, Huns, Finns, and Scythians, to name just a few ethnic groups, first fused and crystallized into a single Russian nation. For the purpose of this narrative it would not be bad to start the count with the baptism of Kievian Rus' in the year 989.[7] The heathen Prince Vladimir sought out a new faith for his vast principality. Legend has it that he sent emissaries

---

[5] J. Raz, "Authority and Justification," ibid., pp. 115ff.

[6] R. P. Wolff, "The Conflict Between Authority and Autonomy," ibid., pp. 20ff.

[7] Once baptized, it became impossible for a Russian to interpret the meaning of her own personhood except in terms of her being an Orthodox practitioner. Followers of other religions, e.g., "Russian" Jews, were never accepted as part and parcel of the Russian nation. For a suggestive literary example of the interconnection of personhood and Orthodoxy in medieval Cossack society, see Nicholas Gogol's famous short novel, *Taras Bulba* (1834), in which the Orthodox Cossack protagonists fight the hordes of Asiatic nomads (the Tatars) and the congregations of

to the four corners of the earth to inquire about the relative merits of the main religions. His delegates to the kingdoms of Islam, Judaism, and Roman Catholicism came back crestfallen and dejected. Not so the messengers he sent to the imperial court at Byzantium. This is what they reported:

The Greeks led us to the edifices where they worship their God, and we knew not whether we were in heaven or on earth. For on earth there is no such splendor or such beauty, and we are at a loss how to describe it. We know only that God dwells there among men, and their service is fairer than the ceremonies of other nations. For we cannot forget that beauty. Every man, after tasting something sweet, is afterward unwilling to accept that which is bitter, and therefore we cannot dwell longer here.[8]

Vladimir must have been very impressed by this report, but apparently not impressed enough to stop him from launching a military campaign against Byzantium. He even threatened to sack the capital, but in the ensuing negotiations between him and the besieged emperor, a deal was struck that changed the course of history. Vladimir agreed to back off, carrying the emperor's sister as his bride and trophy of war. To seal the agreement (and strengthen the bond with Byzantium), he consented to be baptized and accept the rites of Orthodoxy. For good measure, he baptized his entire population, mainly in the Dnieper and in the other rivers flowing in Rus'. The entire feat was accomplished swiftly and expeditiously. The ancient legend, once again:

When the prince arrived at his capital, he directed that the idols should be overthrown and that some should be cut to pieces and others burned with fire. He thus ordered that Perun should be bound to a horse's tail and dragged along Borichev to the river. He appointed twelve men to beat the idol with sticks.... Thereafter Vladimir sent heralds throughout the whole city to proclaim that if any inhabitant, rich or poor, did not betake himself to the river, he would risk the prince's displeasure. When the people heard these words, they wept for joy, and exclaimed in their enthusiasm: "If this were not good, the prince and his boyars would not have accepted it"...they all went into the water...there was joy in heaven and upon earth to behold so many souls saved.[9]

To be sure, many a heathen practitioner actually resented this sudden surge of Christian piety,[10] and not a small number of them kept on nurturing their pre-Christian heritage to our own day and age.[11] Nevertheless, it appears that

---

"Papist" Poles with equal fervor. Neither enemy (the same holds true for the Jewish merchants of this tale) is perceived as fully human.

[8] This legend was reported in real time in the so-called *Primary Chronicle* or *Tale of Bygone Years* in the year 987. The English translation is reprinted in Serge Zenkovsky, *Medieval Russia's Epics, Chronicles and Tales*, New York: Plume, pp. 67–68 (2d ed., 1974).

[9] Ibid., pp. 70–71

[10] There appears to be some evidence, for example, that the city of Novgorod accepted Christianity "with fire and sword." See Bernard Pares, *A History of Russia*, New York: Knopf, p. 32 (1953).

[11] Ample evidence for lingering pagan practices among the Russian peasantry is offered in Linda Ivanits, *Russian Folk Belief*, Armonk, NY: M. E. Sharpe (1992).

by and large the population accepted the prince's authority to determine their spiritual destiny. They could have rebelled against this unilateral imposition of the prince's will but instead opted for submission. They simply chose to obey.[12] This *leitmotif* of accepting the sovereign's will, sometimes to the complete obliteration of the independent will of his or her subjects, keeps repeating itself throughout Russian history.[13]

Some Russian sovereigns have resorted to systematic coercion for the purpose of satisfying their own personal cravings. The most frightening illustration of this genre of coercion is offered by the Stalinist regime, which found ingenious methods[14] to slave-drive large segments of the population to the brink of extinction. The great sovereigns of pre-Revolutionary Russia normally had a mixed bag of private and public-spirited agendas.[15] But their taste for coercive measures, and the corresponding willingness of the population to accept the yoke of authority, runs like a red thread amongst them all. This is true of the greatest reformer of modern Russia, Peter I "the Great," a cruel and bloodthirsty monarch who was not loved by his subjects but universally obeyed by them all.[16] Peter also cemented the stratification of Russian society by introducing a table of ranks in which high-ranking officials dominated, at times to a

---

[12] Pares, ibid., p. 31.

[13] James Billington, in his famous book, *The Icon and the Axe*, London: Vintage (1970), writes (at page 35): "The 'political theory' that developed in early Russia has been well described as a belief that 'the Tsar is, as it were, the living icon of God, just as the whole Orthodox Empire is the icon of the heavenly world'. The icon screen provided...a model for the hierarchical order of Russian society. Each figure occupied a prescribed position in a prescribed way, but all were unified by the common distance from the God of the sanctuary, and by their dependent relationship to the central panel of Christ enthroned."

[14] Less ingenious autocrats, including in Russia itself, had difficulties convincing the population to slave away for the attainment of their goals, because people do not have an incentive to generate wealth that will be entirely taken away from them. Stalin's method was to lower normal salaries almost to zero, thereby imposing an almost 100% (implicit) tax rate on normal labor quotas. The effective tax rate on production exceeding these (heavy) quotas was negligible. Since workers could not subsist on their disposable income from their regular quotas, they had to generate additional units of production, which they could essentially keep for themselves. Thus, the Soviet Union had the most regressive tax structure in the whole world. It bled the population dry, yet kept it toiling, for hard work (and theft) remained its only means of survival. See Mancur Olson, *Power and Prosperity*, New York: Basic Books (2000).

[15] Consider the case of Catherine the Great's attitude to the ideas of the Enlightenment. There was no one who did more than she to introduce these "advanced" ideas to Russian society. But as soon as the French Revolution broke out, and especially after her beloved friend Marie Antoinette was roughed up and then guillotined, all liberal discourse in Russia instantly stopped. Catherine turned around and became, as if by a touch of a magic wand, an archconservative. Her pet French intellectuals were dubbed the foes of Russia, their writings were banned, and all association with many of them was treated as subversive activities.

[16] A good introductory study of the Petrine revolution, through progress and toil, benevolence and coercion, is Evgenii Anisimov, *The Reforms of Peter the Great, Progess Through Coercion in Russia*, translated by John Alexander, Armonk, NY: M. E. Sharpe (1993). Anisimov's study is considered "revisionist" in light of the unmitigated admiration that Peter received during the Stalinist regime (Stalin was a great admirer of Ivan the Terrible as well).

ludicrous extent,[17] the lives and destinies of all those holding lesser dignities.[18] More about Peter and his political heritage is offered in the appendix to this chapter.

The Petrine tradition of defining society in authoritative terms was embraced even by the most enlightened of his successors. Thus Catherine II "the Great," the most ostensibly liberal sovereign of her day, was nevertheless the most exacting, iron-fisted, and despotic autocrat imaginable.[19] One of Catherine's finest achievements was to pontificate over an assembly of statesmen who prepared her famous "Nakaz," or Instructions, for a comprehensive codex of laws for Russia. The Nakaz never assumed binding legal force, nor was it later translated into concrete fragments of legislation. Nevertheless, it symbolized Catherine's avowed dedication to some form of lawfulness, as distinct from sheer clout and brutal force. Indeed, Section 15 of the Nakaz festively declares that:

The intention and the end of Monarchy, is the Glory of the Citizens, of the State, and of the Sovereign.

For, as Section 3 provides,

Every Individual Citizen in particular must wish to see himself protected by Laws, which should not distress him in his Circumstances, but, on the Contrary, should defend him from all Attempts of others, that are repugnant to this fundamental Rule.

Does this mean that "individual citizens" could, in fact, look forward to the protection of the laws against authority itself, against the privileged status of their sovereign? Did the Nakaz make a bona fide attempt to institutionalize the rule of law, rather than the rule of men (or women; three of the most prominent of Peter's immediate successors were, in fact, powerful czarinas)? Here is the Nakaz again:

Society cannot exist without government; and the government most in conformity with nature is that whose character corresponds most closely with the character of the nation for which it is established. The combination of all the particular powers of a state comprises what is called the Constitution of a State. In Russia, this overall power is

---

[17] The greatest satirist of the Petrine rank system was, without a doubt, the inimitable Nicholas Gogol, who nevertheless maintained, in his private life, reactionary czarist convictions. For hilarious illustrations of the submission of junior rank holders by individuals holding only a slightly higher rank, see, for example, his *Inspector General* (1836) and his fantastic short story, "The Nose" (1835).

[18] Thus, the Civil Service included the following ranks: Chancellor, Active Privy Counselor, Privy Counselor, Active State Counselor, State Counselor, Collegiate Counselor, Court Counselor, Collegiate Assessor (these first eight ranks conferred hereditary nobility on those who achieved it), Titular Counselor, Collegiate Secretary, Naval Secretary, District Secretary, Provincial Secretary, and Collegiate Registrar. A parallel ladder of ranks existed in the Army, and yet another in the Navy. It is hard to think about this kind of society except in "vertical" terms, a stark contrast to even the most rudimentary "horizontal" structure of an egalitarian civic democracy.

[19] Catherine's colorful personality, as well as her legendary sexual appetite, generated numerous, often conflicting, narratives of her life and character. A level-headed account is provided by John Alexander, *Catherine the Great, Life and Legend*, New York: Oxford University Press (1989).

entrusted to one person; and this is Russia's natural constitution in accordance with the rules of Public Law appropriate to this Empire, which would cease to be powerful if it were ruled in any other manner.

Catherine was devoted to the act of legislation. Indeed, she described her own spasms of legalistic craftsmanship as "legislomania."[20] Nevertheless, it mattered very little to her what the law, even of her own doing, actually provided, if she found herself in opposition to its tenor. She was above the law. For all her sweet, elegant, and "enlightened" small talk with such luminaries as Voltaire and Diderot, for all her fascination with the quest for knowledge of the Encyclopedic movement, or of the reigning free spirit of the *Philosophes*, hers was *not* a constitutional monarchy. An eyewitness testifies (with the typical sexist idiom of the day):

Generally speaking, women are more prone to despotism than men; and as far as she is concerned, it can justly be averred that she is in this particular a woman among women. Nothing can irritate her more than when making some report to her, men quote the laws in opposition to her will. Immediately the retort flies from her lips: "Can I not do this irrespective of the laws?" But she has found no one with the courage to answer that she can indeed, but only as a despot, and to the detriment of her glory.[21]

To illustrate how well Catherine could handle political dissent, it is best to let her speak for herself. The following is an excerpt of an official decree to the senate, signed by the Empress, from 1790, a year after the famous indiscretions that took place on French soil. It concerns a book authored by one Radischev that contains critical innuendos about the regime:

Collegiate Assessor...Radishchev has violated his oath of allegiance and his duty as a subject by the publication of a book entitled *A Journey from St. Petersburg to Moscow*, full of the most harmful ideas, undermining law and order, belittling due respect for the authorities, aiming at occasioning discontent among the people against their governors and the government, and finally, full of offensive and intemperate expressions against the rank and authority of the monarch.... For this offense...he was sentenced to death...and although by reason of the nature and gravity of the offence, he deserves this penalty, in accordance with our principle of combining justice with mercy, and for the sake of the general rejoicing which our faithful subjects share with us at the present time...we reprieve him from sentence of death, and order instead that he be stripped of his official ranks...and be banished to Siberia...for ten years without remission...and that his property...be held in trust for his children...[22]

The most striking evidence of the stratified, authoritarian nature of Russian society can be collated from the die-hard system of serfdom, which was not abolished until Alexander II's Act of Emancipation of 1861. Steven Hoch, a

---

[20] Ibid., Chapter 8.

[21] A secret memoir, published posthumously, of Prince M. M. Shcherbatov, reprinted in A. Lentin, *Enlightened Absolutism*, Newcastle upon Tyne: Avero Publications, p. 39 (1985).

[22] Imperial decree to the Senate (which acted as the highest judicial tribunal), dated September 4, 1790, ibid., pp. 116–17.

modern historian, painstakingly records what life was like in a typical Russian estate in the nineteenth century. His account dispels a number of myths about serf society. The evidence suggests a great deal of egalitarian distribution of wealth among the serfs, as arable land was constantly redistributed by the landowning boyars according to the labor capacity of each individual household (*dvor*). The purpose of the frequent transfers was not any kind of concern about equality or fairness, but the desire to maximize labor-related products (mainly cereals), which ultimately inured to the benefit of the landlord. Obviously, allocating too many or too few factors of production to any production unit was not compatible with this goal. The boyars had to deal with a perennial problem, how to maintain this serf society functioning in their service, given the natural inclination of the serfs to escape their hard destiny.

Hoch shows that this objective was realized through the combined effect of elder-patriarch collaboration and punitive measures. The particular estate that was the subject of his inquiry was supervised by a bailiff, acting for the absentee landlord. Headquarters were stationed in Moscow. Although interfamily wealth was evenly distributed in the peasant society, there was a great deal of economic disparity *within* the family. Patriarchs enjoyed a position of authority, which they could only maintain in the rigid, seemingly immutable, serf society. This position entitled them to the warmest bed in winter. It also gave them a secure claim to be seated during the family meals underneath the icons in the beautiful corner at home, to an exclusive right to communicate with the house *domovoi* (the house spirit, which was also keen, so they were told, to punish all manners of deviation). For good measure, they also were entitled to a fair number of straightforward economic emoluments. These perquisites consisted mainly of benefits associated with the marriage market, whereby daughters were sold for rich dowries and sons "acquiring" brides were allocated land for cultivation. Since the extended family lived off the land, patriarchs benefited from marriages and wished to perpetuate this system as long as it yielded exclusive benefits in their favor. Serf servility was thus obtained through a combination of patriarch authority and material benefits associated with that authority. In addition, punitive measures were commonplace, including flogging, public ridicule, loss of status, recruitment to the army (twenty-five years was a normal term), and exile to Siberia. Since serf life was ridden with tension, want, superstition, and exploitation, serf society was violent, shirking was common, theft practiced everywhere (both from the estate and from fellow serfs), and social cohesiveness was weak.[23] The cultural ethos that facilitated the perpetuation of this exploitative society is easily traceable to Catherine the Great and to her supposedly liberal Nakaz.[24] It is also typical of all her Romanov successors, including the emancipators of the serfs, all the way down to the great

---

[23] Steven Hoch, *Serfdom and Social Control in Russia*, Chicago: University of Chicago Press (1986).

[24] Section 250 of the Nakaz declares: "Civil society, like everything else, requires a certain order. There must be persons who govern and command, and others who obey. ... One should not suddenly and through general law create a large number of free men."

October Revolution (and beyond).[25] The stratified, authoritarian nature of Russian society manifests itself clearly both in law[26] and in iconography.

Continental Europe (as distinguished from the British Isles) has a long tradition of legal codification, that is, the formal gathering of legal norms in comprehensive statutory form. This tradition can be traced back at least to the great codification effort of the Emperor Justinian (527–565 A.D.).[27] Now many of the cultural assets of the Byzantine Empire were incorporated, if not in substance at least in form, in early Rus'. First and foremost, Rus' was christened after the fashion of Byzantine Orthodoxy. But this tidal wave of imported culture failed to include the legal system. The first legal code ever promulgated in Christian Russia is the so-called *Russkaya Pravda* (literally, "Russian truth"), an essentially penal statute compiled under Yaroslav the Wise, who ruled Rus' from 1015 to 1054. The *Russkaya Pravda* is a statutory compilation of local customs; it bears no resemblance to contemporary Byzantine sources, and it fails to make any mention of civil law in general or of contract law in particular.[28] The next compilation of all existing statutes occurred at the end of the fifteenth century.[29] "In the year 1497, in the month of September, the Grand Prince of all Rus' Ivan Vasilievich [i.e., Ivan III – U.P.], with his children and boyars, compiled a code of law on how boyars and *okol'nichie* [the highest ranking boyars – U.P.] are to administer justice."[30] This code did not deal with substantive private entitlements (rights and obligations) either. A sole exception provides that if a person commits his labor for a particular cause and quits before the completion of the job, his wages may be confiscated. The next legal

---

[25] Some commentators discern a strong common denominator among *all* rulers of Russia since Ivan IV "the Terrible" (1530–1584), from whom this "tradition" of coercion and totalitarianism descends. See, for example, Alexander Yanov, *The Origins of Autocracy: Ivan the Terrible in Russian History*, Berkeley: University of California Press (1981). It is a little early on to make predictions about the current Putin administration in Russia, but it is not hard to identify streaks of authoritarian despotism among his predecessors, including, of course, Boris Yeltsin.

[26] Thanks are due to my friend and student, Karl Bikhman, for his invaluable assistance in reading and understanding the statutory materials discussed in the following few pages. It is interesting to note that although Ivan the Terrible will forever be remembered by his fully deserved nickname, the Soviet authorities were keen on rehabilitating him as a legitimate political figure. Sergei Eisenstein, the renowned filmmaker of the Stalinist era, crafted two very beautiful movies, *Ivan the Terrible, Part One* (1944) and *Ivan the Terrible, Part Two* (1946), as a tribute to his personality. This trend was doubtlessly motivated by the great admiration of a person of indisputable and forceful authority; this unusual duo followed another great movie in the same vein, *Alexander Nevsky*, which Eisenstein had already presented to the public in 1938.

[27] There were some earlier precedents, e.g., the Theodossian Code of 438. Justinian himself completed his Codex Justinianus in 529 (but only a later edition, of 534, survived) and his path-breaking *Digesta* in 533.

[28] Although it does contain one section providing for the obligation to pay bridge builders their fees. For a fuller description of this statute, see George Vernadsky, *Medieval Russian Laws*, London: Octagon Books, p. 4 (1947; reprinted 1965).

[29] The code was dubbed the *Sudebnik*, a word that is etymologically related both to "sud" (a court) and to "sudit" (a judge).

[30] George Vernadsky, *A Source Book for Russian History from Early Times to 1917*, New Haven, CT: Yale University Press, Volume 1, p. 118 (1972).

code, the *Svobodnoe Ulozhenie* ("free code") was enacted under Czar Alexis Mikhailovitch in 1649 and survived for more than two centuries. This statute contains twenty-five lengthy parts, covering such diverse topics as penal law, military governance, and court procedure. Substantive rights and obligations are left out entirely. Many emperors, especially since Peter the Great, intended to reform this essentially antiquated compilation. This same motive informed Catherine the Great's attempt to "instruct" her subjects in her abortive Nakaz. None succeeded until the reign of Alexander II (1855–1881). Alexander was, indeed, a great reformer,[31] but his *Basic Principles Concerning the Reform of the Judicial Administration in Russia* of 1862, which resulted in a comprehensive code two years later and which survived all the way to the Russian Revolution, generated only an anemic echo of the great contemporary European codes.[32] The most striking feature of this comprehensive "reform" is that it is almost entirely about procedure, as, in fact, is implied by its very name.[33] The predominance of procedure over substance appears, then, to be a staple feature of *all* Russian codes from the eleventh to the early twentieth centuries. This is a striking phenomenon. The canonization of procedure without substance essentially implies that litigants could bring their dispute for adjudication, but the final arbiter was not bound by any predetermined rules, since the parties did not possess any *ex ante* entitlements. This is tantamount to conferring on the final arbiter unfettered discretion to determine every dispute as she sees fit. Her discretion comes in lieu of the law, as she herself becomes the embodiment of law, the fountainhead of authority, and the source of substantive rights. Litigants can thus pray for legal remedies but insist on none. What a different course did legal history take on European soil! I shall turn to this comparative subject shortly. Before doing that, however, I would like to restate, or recapitulate, the Russian theme in the time-honored poetry of the Russian icon.

Figure 8 (shown in Chapter 1, supra) is an extremely popular and well-beloved icon in Russia, St. George doing battle with the dragon. This image is quite common in Western iconography as well.[34] The two kinds of image, the Western and the Russian, do bear a deceptive resemblance; however, they are vastly different. The Russian composition is pierced by a diagonal lance, which implies a ladder. The ladder symbolizes a cosmic hierarchy, neatly divided by an

---

[31] See John Van Der Kiste, *The Romanovs 1818–1959: Alexander II of Russia and His Family*, Phoenix Mill, UK: Alan Sutton Publishing (2000). For instance, it was he who finally liberated the serfs.

[32] For example, the Great Code Napoleon was written between 1804 and 1807; it is without a doubt a great achievement of the human spirit in ways far transcending the technically legal domain.

[33] The code is named simply *Sudebnie Ustavy*, meaning Court Rules. See Vernadsky, *A Source Book for Russian History from Early Times to 1917*, New Haven, CT: Yale University Press, p. 614.

[34] The cult of St. George (*megalomartyros*) originated in Cappadocia around the fifth century, a little more than a century after his martyrdom at Lydda. St. George was lovingly Russified during the reign of Yaroslav the Wise in the eleventh century.

octave of universal rank. At the upper right angle of the icon the highest rank makes itself visible in the image of God's hands. The next rank is the heavenly spheres, the area separating the Divine Providence and the flowing cloak of the saint. The cloak itself constitutes the third sphere. Underneath this protecting veil, the saint himself, the image of Man, is in the fourth sphere. The saint gallops astride a white charger, whose exaggerated anatomical features as well as the burning solar shield that hangs about the saint evoke the memory of Dazhbog, the ancient sun-god of the pre-Christian Russian North. At the charger's feet we encounter the sixth rank, the dragon, which seems to smile benevolently at his assailant, as both attacker and victim are contentedly fulfilling their assigned roles in the universe. The base earth supports the giant reptile from underneath, dominating, in this cosmic order, only the subterranean depth that bares its hollows at the bottom right angle of the icon. In some versions of this otherwise fearsome image, the young virgin saved by the saint appears on the scene, calmly holding the dragon on a leash, completely oblivious to the gory fate that she so narrowly escaped. With or without the virgin, the whole composition implies that, far from being an embittered battle, the scene reflects a balanced state of equilibrium, a perfect harmony resulting from the secure staging of each person, animal, or thing within their intended station in life.[35]

Russian iconography is replete with explicit images of authority. In one well-known icon, *In Thee Rejoices All Creation,* the mother of God is seen sitting in majesty, holding the Christ Child in her hands and surrounded by a *mandorla.* In a neat venerating posture encircling this forbidden space, the Theotokos is flanked by the archangels. They, too, are arranged by the dignity of their rank. The foreground is filled, to the exclusion of everyone else, by the admiring prophets, priests, bishops, holy monks, apostles, martyrs, kings, nuns, and patriarchs. The overarching architecture of a stylized church does extend an invitation to individual persons to be admitted into Holy Communion, but their lowly station does not allow for their actual representation in the icon. The icon of the Theotokos does not make room for ordinary folks, because her majestic authority does not derive its legitimacy from the presence of the faithful. This kind of authority is immutable, precisely because ordinary people did not author it, did not will it, and were not consulted in forging her jurisdiction, nor will they be tolerated to suggest modifications. Authority is uncreated matter; it predates all creations and will survive their eventual demise.

The ultimate submission to authority is sublimely imparted to the viewer in the *Presentation of Our Lord* icon, which is also very common in occidental cultures (see Figure 25). Its theme was quickly assimilated in Russian iconography and is prevalent throughout Orthodoxy.

The Law of Moses (Leviticus, 12) ordains that new mothers purify themselves for forty days following the delivery of a male son and then proceed to the Temple to sacrifice a lamb "for a burnt offering." In the case of first-born sons, the

---

[35] See Dick Temple, "Icons," in *Russian and Greek Icons, Van Daren Gallery,* Salem, OR: Book Bin, p. 12 (1982).

FIGURE 25. Duccio, *Presentation of Our Lord in the Temple*, 1311.

latter have to be sanctified by a priest (in lieu of actually sacrificing them to the Lord).[36] The last verse concluding the chapter (Leviticus, 12,8) provides that "if she [the mother – U.P.] cannot afford a lamb, then she shall take two turtledoves or two young pigeons, one for a burnt offering and the other for a sin offering, and the priest shall make atonement of her, and she shall be clean." The icon shows Mary presenting herself at the Temple, as prescribed by Leviticus, 12, 8. She hands over the infant Jesus to the priest Simeon, who recognizes in Him, alongside with the elder prophetess Anne, immediately behind him, the true Lord and Savior. In this act of Presentation, *the Word of God, who is the author of the Law, Himself fulfills the Law*.[37] Now obviously the Immaculate One hardly needed any "cleansing" as "atonement" for her "sin." Such acts of absolution were meant for the sinful, not for the Son of Man or for His most holy mother. Nevertheless, the author of the Law chooses to uphold it. The authority of law must be respected without regard to circumstance. A superficial reading of this mesmerizing story might imply that the *Presentation* glorifies the Rule of Law in its Western sense, the subordination of the mighty (even God Himself) to a constitutional order, to a republican form of government. For how else can we justify the Presentation of Him who Himself authored the Law? It is submitted that there is nothing further from the truth than this interpretation. In constitutional democracies, the subordination of human dignitaries to the Rule of Law stems from the common understanding that authority emanates from the supremacy of norms, rather than from the supremacy of men. The law rules the mighty *because* they did not author it. All binding norms are commonly believed to have been forged at the grass-root level by ordinary people who, by authority of law, rank equally with the mighty and form, alongside

---

[36] The latter ritual is still practiced among Jews. First-born sons are redeemed by the parents by paying a symbolic tribute to a Rabbi (*"pidyon ha'ben"*), instead of sacrificing the child to God.

[37] The story of the Presentation is narrated in Luke, 2, 22–40. The dogma of the Lord fulfilling the law of His own creation is contained in the Vespers and Matins of the feast.

with them, the source of all legitimacy. The *Presentation* offers a diametrically opposed theology of legitimacy whereby the Lord *is* the Word, and therefore obeying the Word parallels an act of submission to the Lord. In upholding the letter of the law, the Lord does not obey anyone but Himself, who is the Divine author of the Word and the ultimate source of legitimacy. His otherwise futile act of obeying Himself ought to be understood as a didactic gesture instructing the faithful as to *their* proper way of comporting themselves. If He Himself senselessly follows in His own footsteps, how humbling a lesson it must be for the rest of us! Like Him, we must not inquire as to the reason or justification of following authority, but must abide by its letter and joyfully harness ourselves to its yoke.

Political Authority in the West

The Russian model of a complete subjugation of individual persons to the over-riding will of a person or institution of authority did not originate in Russia. It was prevalent throughout Western Europe for most of its medieval history. Medieval sovereigns reigned supreme. Seigniorial rights could not be fruitfully disputed. The individual was born into her station in life, from which all departures were not tolerated.[38] The world was well structured. As the individual has not yet discovered herself, she had no right to assert her desires,[39] to claim recognition, or to modify the world in recognition of her own personal aspirations. But this robust hierarchical structure started to give way in the late Middle Ages; it was seriously breached during the Renaissance; and it was completely demolished in the age of modern constitutionalism.

The very first warnings that the concept of authority was put in jeopardy could be detected in some fourteenth-century juridical sources, both on the Continent and on the British Isles. In this vein, it is interesting to peruse the work of one Durandus of St. Pourçain, who wrote a well-known treatise entitled *Tractatus de Legibus*. Durandus posed the question of whether licit government, as well as licit rights of dominion over things (*res*) "descended" from God, as was the traditional medieval approach, or "ascended" from human needs and were grounded in some notion of natural law. The former possibility, the medieval

---

[38] This substantive differentiation among people based on their original station in life is well reflected in medieval and even Renaissance artistic style. Each class could be artistically portrayed only by using unique stylistic features, which could not be used for the portrayal of other classes. For example, tragic literary roles were traditionally reserved for members of the aristocracy, while plebeians had to make do with comical roles. See Erich Auerbach, *Mimesis: The Representation of Reality in Western Literature*, translated by Willard Trask, Princeton, NJ: Princeton University Press, p. 328 (1953; first published in 1946).

[39] Gregorian chant was strictly monophonic, because the Church ordained that to indulge in the aesthetic pleasure of polyphonic music was too sinful. Obviously, the latent motive for the rejection of polyphony was the fear of contrapuntal diversity, a threat to the unison of voices expected from the faithful. Indeed, diversity fosters pleasure, and pleasure is sinful because it is autonomous and does not derive from a central ecclesiastical dispenser of grace.

one, recognized the legitimacy of all individual rights only if they could be traced back to a central source of authority. The latter possibility, being humanist in its drive and purpose, could be achieved only through the impairment of divine authority as the primary source of all licit claims. Durandus was not bold enough to deny that the ultimate source of authority "descended" from God. But he did have the courage to pose the question, and even was ready to concede, as a practical matter, that human judges were licensed to interpret some licit claims *as if* they "ascended" from the bottom up, that is, as if they originated "naturally" at the grass roots.[40] English contemporaries were even bolder. The notion that the King of England lacked authority to unilaterally tax the people but needed Parliamentary, that is, popular, support, was legislated in 1340.[41] The consent of the governed was thus formulated as the rationale for the legitimacy of government, more than three centuries *before* Hobbes irretrievably changed the world by penning his great masterpiece, *Leviathan* (1660). Thus, the medieval jurist Pecock wrote in his *Folower to the Donet* (1453), that

Whanne a lawe is iustli maad bi consent of al peple or of the more parti of the peple...each persoon of thilk peple is bounden bi resoun and in lawe of kynde to kepe it.[42]

Pecock's views were shared by some of his compatriots (the most notorious being Fortescue) as well as by some Continental jurists of the period (e.g., Nicholas de Cusa and Pierre D'Ailly).[43] In England, some of these ideas were vested with quasi-constitutional entrenchment, as, for instance when it was legislated by the last decade of Edward III's reign (1369) that all statutes purporting to derogate from the *Magna Carta* were void.[44]

But all these were just feeble beginnings. The sense of authority started to disintegrate for real only a couple of centuries later, during the Renaissance, with the introspective invention of the self. Some came upon this discovery with relish and an exquisite sense of *joie de vivre*. No one expresses this better than the inimitable Michel de Montaigne. Can we trust the authority of any giver of laws? Can we trust the Bible itself as a source of authority? He responds:

The conclusions that we seek to draw from the likeness of events are unreliable, because events are always unlike. There is no quality so universal in the appearance of things as their diversity and variety.... I hardly agree, therefore, with the opinion of that man [Justinian – U.P.] who tried to curb the authority of his judges by a multitude of laws, thus cutting up their meat for them. He did not understand that there is as much liberty

---

[40] Brian Tierney, "Public Expediency and Natural Law: A Fourteenth-Century Discussion on the Origins of Government and Property," in Brian Tierney and Peter Linehan (eds.), *Authority and Power*, New York: Cambridge University Press, p. 167 (1980).

[41] 14 Ed. III c. 1.

[42] Cited by Norman Doe, *Fundamental Authority in Late Medieval English Law*, New York: Cambridge University Press, p. 18 (1990).

[43] Ibid.

[44] 42 Edward III. c. 3.

and latitude in the interpretation as in the making of them. And those men who think they can lessen and check our disputes by referring us to the actual words of the Bible are deluding themselves, since our mind finds just as wide a field for controverting other men's meanings as for delivering its own. Could there be less spite and bitterness in comment than in invention? We can see how mistaken he was. For we have in France more laws than the rest of the world put together, and more than would be necessary for all the worlds of Epicurus . . . and yet we have left so much for judges to consider and decide, that there has never been such complete and uncontrolled freedom. . . . There is little relation between our actions, which are perpetually changing, and fixed immutable laws.[45]

And about books he adds:

When did we ever agree in saying: "This book has had enough. There is nothing more to be said about it?" This is best seen in the practice of law. We attribute binding authority to innumerable doctors, to innumerable decrees, and to as many interpretations. And yet do we find any end to the need for interpreting? Is there any progress to be seen, any advance towards peace? Do we need any fewer pleaders and judges than when this great mass of law was still in its infancy? On the contrary, we obscure and bury the meaning; we can no longer discover it without negotiating many fences and barriers.[46]

So what is it, he asks, that makes us succumb to authority, makes us accept an authoritarian point of view in spite of its clear inadequacy to address our real concerns? Here is Montaigne again:

It is nothing but our personal weakness that makes us content with what others, or we ourselves, have discovered in this hunt for knowledge . . . there is always a different road to follow. There is no end to our investigations. . . . No generous spirit stays within itself; it constantly aspires and rises above its own strength. It leaps beyond its attainments. If it does not advance, and push forward, if it does not strengthen itself, and struggle with itself, it is only half alive. Its pursuits have no bounds or rules; its food is wonder, search and ambiguity.[47]

So much for Montaigne. Some other Renaissance pioneers approached the same issue with less frivolity, even with a somber air of tragic loss, but they too inched their way to the same final destination. James Boyd White has forcefully shown how the Renaissance sense of ruptured authority is reflected in the *oeuvre* of William Shakespeare, especially in his *Richard II*. Richard Plantagenet, the legitimate sovereign of England, is deposed by a usurper, Henry Bolingbroke, eventually Henry IV. Henry has a multitude of good reasons to ascend to Richard's throne. Richard is a shoddy and unjust ruler, devoid of either wisdom or magnanimity. His reign is harmful to his subjects and ruinous to England. These are all *constitutional* grounds for a change of stewardship. Richard,

[45] Michel de Montaigne, "On Experience," in his *Essays*, translated by J. M. Cohen, New York: Penguin Books, pp. 344–45 (1958; first published in 1580).
[46] Ibid., p. 347.
[47] Ibid., p. 348.

however, does not consider himself to be a mere custodian, holding his power for the sake of the governed. He is the Crown, authority incarnate. His claim to the throne is based on his birthright, on the very immutable foundation of medieval society. The supremacy of either desert or birthright as a preemptive claim to the throne cannot be decided by logic alone. "The crown by its nature cannot have an apologist or advocate," says White, "But it can have a poet; and this is the role of Richard in this play, to create a poetry of kingship."[48] In Shakespeare's play, Henry's seemingly victorious depredation of that poetic claim could not be but self-defeating in the end, because, once destroyed, it could no longer support Henry's own interest to perpetuate his privilege; authority fell victim to the vulgar forces of meritocracy. White concludes his analysis by claiming that the collapse of authority gave rise to the modern constitutional order. The authority of Richard is gone. No one can restore it. Therefore, no one wields authority in Shakespeare's play. But the play itself has authority. It shows, with authority, that no single voice has an absolute claim to be heard. We must attune ourselves to the voices, and to the music, of alternative contenders. The play sounds a tune of indeterminacy, and hence of tolerance, which is the touchstone of constitutional discourse. Without knowing it, Shakespeare presaged the authority of the constitution.[49]

It is perhaps possible to augment White's brilliant reading of *Richard II* by adding two additional comments. As Harold Bloom has noted, there is more to *Richard II* than just including the voice of the "other" in a richly polyphonic constitutional discourse (White's point). Richard's poetry, which exists side by side with his human wickedness and incompetence, creates a fissure between human dignity (which is lacking, in his case) and aesthetic dignity (which he elevates to the point of perfection).[50] Human dignity is about substantive values and is reserved for Richard's adversaries, the "modern" (i.e., Renaissance) protagonists of the play.[51] Aesthetic dignity, which concerns form, is reserved for Richard alone, this magnificently poetic spokesman of the Middle Ages. As we have seen, and will stress again in the following pages, medieval law underscored authority by focusing on pure form (procedure) and neglecting *substantive* entitlements. Richard is echoing this medieval focus by stressing

---

[48] James Boyd White, "Shakespeare's Richard II: Imagining the Modern World," in *Acts of Hope, Creating Authority in Literature, Law and Politics*, Chicago: University of Chicago Press, p. 64 (1994).

[49] Ibid.

[50] Harold Bloom, *Shakespeare, The Invention of the Human*, Riverhead, NY: Riverhead Books, Chapter 16 (1998).

[51] Gaunt, for instance, denounces Richard's reign on the grounds of its moral turpitude. In doing so, Gaunt (especially in his dying scene) lays the foundations for merit as the sole legitimate ground for human dignity, even in the case of royalty. In a similar fashion, the gardener's scene, in comparing a kingdom to a well-tended garden in which the vegetation withers away if not diligently cared for, makes licit authority contingent on the fulfillment of the sovereign's obligations to his subjects. The poetry of absolute privilege is thus subordinated to the inclusionary claims of ordinary people.

the poetry of kingship *sans* its merit,[52] by showing ornament without its supporting pith.[53] The second point is that both the fissure of human and aesthetic authority and the reinterpretation of Henry's ascension to the throne as presaging constitutional consciousness are entirely of Shakespearean origin. Henry II as a *historical* figure died in 1400, well before the formation of these Renaissance notions of complexity and inclusion. With all the dramatic overtones of Richard's demise and Henry's usurpation of the throne, their living contemporaries, still immersed in the English Middle Ages, have not been alerted to these interpretations.[54] It was the Renaissance self-fashioning of Elizabethan England, not the historical narrative of 1400, which triggered the demise of authority and the rise of individual rights.

The Renaissance insight that authority – any authority – can literally be willed away, that it depends for its survival on some sort of human acquiescence, was fraught with an alarming sense of peril. *Richard II* itself shows it clearly enough. It is even more dramatically reflected in Christopher Marlowe's *Doctor Faustus*, which was first published in 1604.[55] This famous narrative concerns a pact between a historical figure, Johann Faust of Würtemberg, a magician and an astrologer, and Lucifer, the prince of the devils. The devil takes possession of Faust's soul and destines it for eternal damnation. Faust, on his part, is willingly giving away his claim to salvation in exchange for temporary glory, wealth and fame, and, above all, infinite erudition. He is taken by his surroundings to be a mighty sorcerer, for they cannot otherwise account for his never-erring trickery. He is *truly* a powerful magician, but not for that reason. Faustus employs contract, and his will and his thirst for masterminding the universe, to

---

[52] When Richard finds out that Henry has landed on English soil and that all his men have deserted to Henry's camp, he still finds it incomprehensible that his "absolute" claim to the throne should be compromised, regardless of the causes that provoked his impending downfall. In his words, "Not all the water in the rough rude sea/ Can wash the balm off from an anointed king./ The breath of worldly men cannot depose/ The deputy elected by the Lord./ For every man that Boolingbrooke hath press'd/ To lift shrewd steel against our golden crown/ God for his Richard hath in heavenly pay/ A glorious angel. Then, if angels fight,/ Weak men must fall, for heaven still guards the right" (*Richard II*, Act III, Scene 2). In his speech, Richard reveals another important medieval trait. It is a total confusion between the descriptive and the normative. Descriptively, it takes less than an ocean of salty water to wash the balm off his anointed head. Since he believes, however, that this treacherous act *ought* not to be undertaken, he cannot believe that it *will*.

[53] All iconography of power both displays and hides. It exhibits the visible symbols of power and obscures from view the vacant nature of that which is symbolized. See Costas Douzinas, "Prosopon and Antiprosopon, Prolegomena for a Legal Iconology," in Costas Douzinas and Lynda Nead (eds.), *Law and the Image, The Authority of Art and the Aesthetics of Law*, Chicago: University of Chicago Press, p. 36 (1999). Ornament per se may also serve as an independent instrument of authority. See Piyel Haldar, "The Function of the Ornament in Quintilian, Alberti, and Court Architecture," ibid., p. 117.

[54] A good historical account of Richard's life and tribulations is offered by Nigel Saul, *Richard II*, especially in Chapter 17 (1997).

[55] The first (posthumous) version published in 1604, called "the A text," came out just two years after the court announced its landmark decision in *Slade's Case*. A later version, "the B text," saw the light of day in 1616.

render damnation itself, a hitherto exclusive domain of divine intervention, fair game for human manipulation and free choice. Divine authority (and, *a fortiori*, temporal authority) thus succumbs to the will of the chooser: Faustus is not a Renaissance villain but a Renaissance hero.[56] To be sure, Faustus had to pay a high price for corrupting the integrity of power; he "was a Renaissance man who had to pay the medieval price for being one."[57] But his ability – anyone's ability – to contract away clout, fear, and social stratification could not be tolerated to run rampant, to go on a free reign. During the same year of the play's initial publication, 1604, Parliament passed, for the first time in English history, an explicit statute making it a criminal offence to conclude a pact with the devil.[58]

The Renaissance renunciation of the notion of authority did not manifest itself only in literary works. It actually amounted to a total repudiation of the medieval scholastic claim that the very act of *reasoning* must be fundamentally grounded on some ultimate authority. This scholastic claim extended to all forms of authority, not only to religious dogma or political clout. It covered, for instance, the authority of the ancients, of the sages (say, Aristotle), of the scriptures, of the Church, of its vicars, or of precedent. It even spawned the optimistic view that the entire human condition could be satisfactorily explained away on the basis of the existing stock of knowledge.[59] Renaissance Man made a giant leap forward in treating all these authoritative sources with the utmost disdain. Hence, for example, the fantastic ground breaking achieved in this period in the natural sciences.[60] Hence also the tremendous surge in the musical world,[61] with the concomitant demolition of the monophonic tradition and the introduction of polyphony and counterpoint; but to these musical themes I shall return in Chapter 6, infra.

[56] See, in general, Luke Wilson, *Theatres of Intention*, Stanford: Stanford University Press, pp. 184ff (2000).
[57] This famous epigram was authored by Professor R. M. Dawkins. For a short, but authoritative anthology concerning Faustus' humanist pedigree, see the introduction and articles contained in Christopher Marlowe, *Doctor Faustus*, Sylvan Barnet, ed., New York: Signet Classics (2001).
[58] 1 Jac. I c. 12 (1604). There have been previous prohibitions on using witchcraft for illicit purposes (*maleficium*), but it was in the first year of the Jacobean reign that the very act of contracting with the devil was made a criminal offence in England. See Keith Thomas, *Religion and the Decline of Magic*, New York: Penguin Books, p. 525 (1991; first published in 1971).
[59] On the basic assumption of scholastic thought and on the centrality of the notion of authority in scholastic culture, see John Baldwin, *The Scholastic Culture of the Middle Ages, 1000–1300*, Long Grove, IL: Waveland Press (1997).
[60] The most celebrated natural scientist to have repudiated Church authority is probably Galileo Galilei. For a good introduction to Galilean reasoning and to the ways in which it bids farewell to the prevailing scholastic culture, see Maurice Finacchiaro, *Galileo and the Art of Reasoning, Rhetorical Foundations of Logic and Scientific Method*, Dordrecht, Holland, and Boston: Reidel (1980).
[61] Perhaps the best account of this musical revolution in cultural terms is Gary Tomlinson, *Monteverdi and the End of the Renaissance*, Berkeley: University of California Press (1987). This book merits a much fuller discussion, but this is deferred to Chapter 6, infra.

The germs of liberty-from-authority spirit that were sewn in the Renaissance came to full bloom during the Protestant Reformation [62] and colored the entire development of the great republican governments of the modern era. The details of this double narrative are too well known to be herein discussed in full, but some aspects of it are treated in Chapter 5, infra, and are succinctly footnoted here.[63] In the remaining pages of this chapter I explore some manifestations of these ideas on procedure, contract, and artistic imagery.

[62] The single most important theological teaching of the Reformation was that individual persons are accountable for their own deeds. Even their dealings with Divine Providence do not depend on ecclesiastical intermediation, as they essentially lie within the sphere of their own individual choice. The assignment of responsibility to the deeds of an individual actor to the actor himself, a responsibility that he cannot escape by being instructed by others, vacates the authority of external agents to initiate such instruction and reposes the brunt of authority within the self. For a brief introduction see Timothy George, *Theology of the Reformers*, Nashville, TN: B & H Publishing (1999) (surveying the lives and teachings of the main Reformers from the vantage point of a modern follower). See also Jaroslav Pelikan, *Spirit Versus Structure: Luther and the Institutions of the Church*, New York: Harper & Row (1968).

[63] For a general introduction concerning American republicanism, see Lawrence Freedman, *The Republic of Choice, Law, Authority and Culture*, Cambridge, MA: Harvard University Press (1990) (asserting that all Western law, and American law in particular, is focused on the repudiation of authority and the centrality of individual values). A fascinating study showing the great impact of individualistic notions and the repudiation of authority on the American Republic at its formative stage is offered by Lawrence Leder, *Liberty and Authority, Early American Political Ideology, 1689–1763*, Chicago: Quadrangle Books (1968). Leder shows that early Americans rejected the Hobbesian and embraced the Lockean conception of the state of nature as a justification for the authority of the state. Hobbes presupposed the evil nature of man. Leviathan was necessary to redeem him from the absolute vicissitude of that state, a redemption that could be bought only at the price of total subjection to the authority of the sovereign. Locke, on the other hand, who viewed the state of nature as a historical period rather than as a philosophical construct, held that it had some rudimentary rules of civic behavior, where subjects were already endowed with some natural rights. This state was replete with danger, to be sure, and thus had to be supplemented, or better protected, by organized society. Society could not demand total submission in return, because the players' fallback position was a relatively benign state of nature. A sovereign that requires his subjects to make a greater sacrifice should expect a justified revolution: ibid, pp. 37ff. The colonists were also obsessed with the idea of constitutionalism, as a form of limiting government authority. The single most important historical event that triggered this interest was the English Glorious Revolution of 1688: ibid., pp. 79ff. The Roman Catholic James II, who ascended to the throne in 1660, sought to restore Catholicism as the dominant faith in England, by mass conversion, packing important institutions with his nominees and resorting to other coercive measures. Both the Tories and the Whigs, who shared a Protestant allegiance, invited his Dutch son-in-law, William of Orange, and his consort, the Protestant Princess Mary, to assume the throne. William landed in England in 1688, and James fled to France after his forces deserted him. The newcomers were enthroned as co-sovereigns, William III and Mary II, upon the explicit condition that they ceded much of their power to Parliament, never to be reclaimed by the crown. This started a slow process of turning Britain into a constitutional monarchy. The revolution was attained without bloodshed. As Leder convincingly shows, this piece of English history had a formative impact on the development of American liberties and the shaping of the nascent Constitution. Finally, the colonists were also influenced by the haughty English stance that the colonies were not equal in status to the mother country, in spite of the national origin of most of its inhabitants; this sense was further intensified with the growing immigration from countries other than England. Having come to revere the

The Empty Shell of Procedure and the Emergence of Substantive Law

In the Middle Ages, authority was either directly divine (the authority of God) or divinely inspired (the authority of the crown, by the Grace of God). In the secularized Renaissance and post-Renaissance worlds, the seat of authority passed on to the state, and to its coercive agent, the Law.[64] The authority of the state, however, cannot remain intact if successfully assaulted by the rise of contract. Contract erodes authority because it delegitimizes the monopolistic claim of the state to craft binding rules of conduct and delegates this function to the subjects of the realm. Modern states differ from each other in terms of their response to contract. Some states are more willing to acquiesce in the erosion of their own power wrought upon the social scene by willing individuals. *These are contract states.* Some do not, or do so only to a diminished extent. *The latter are authoritarian states*, because they wish to fend off individually crafted rules of behavior, wishing to maintain their own monopoly in this game of power.

Mirjan Damaška, the leading legal comparative scholar, developed this theme in a recent *magnum opus*.[65] "The reactive state," he writes, is one that "is limited to providing supporting framework within which its citizens pursue their chosen goals." Such a state rests on the idea of contract. Even laws passed by the legislature are normally *jus dispositivum*, that is, mere default rules that can be contracted away by willing individuals. "Where individual preferences are sovereign, the most suitable norm-creating devices are various types of agreement, contracts and pacts."[66] Not all nations have reactive states. Some states are "activist." The activist state "espouses or strives toward a comprehensive theory of the good life and tries to use it as a basis for a conceptually all-encompassing program of material and moral betterment of its citizens." Since the activist state does not trust the judgment of its own citizens, "the controlling image of the law is that of the state decree, wholly divorced from contractarian notions."[67] Numerous acts of the legislature are *jus cogens*, that is, cannot be opted out of by any contractual means. To illustrate the practical ramifications of this distinction, one can think of contractarian law as a system of resolving disputes between the parties. Both the substantive rights of the parties and the mode of fleshing them out in a court of law are left to the discretion of the affected individuals. The judge (or any other symbol of authority) is not supposed to superimpose her own values, or the values of society at large, on the warring disputants. The procedure is "adversary." Each party is a champion of her own cause and the judge simply referees who has the upper hand. In

---

English constitution and to assume equal treatment thereunder, the denial of these equal rights cast a shadow on the very concept of authority: ibid., pp. 131ff.

[64] For a psychoanalytic interpretation of the coercive power of law as authority, see, e.g., Peter Goodrich, *Oedipus Lex*, Berkeley: University of California Press, especially Chapter 7 (1995).

[65] Mirjan Damaška, *The Faces of Justice and State Authority*, New Haven, CT: Yale University Press (1986).

[66] Ibid., pp. 73–75.

[67] Ibid., pp. 80–82.

activist states, on the other hand, the parties have to conform to a set of higher values, which is represented by the source of authority (embodied in the person of the judge). The judge is not only the conductor of the orchestra; she is the concert soloist as well. The procedure is "inquisitorial." It is conducted from the bench, not from the bar.

The distinction between reactive and activist states fleshes itself out in the differences between Western democracies and authoritarian regimes. Western legal systems, especially Common Law jurisdictions, are reactive states. Russia (as well as some Western jurisdictions, at certain stages of their history)[68] has never been a reactive state. There is obviously no need to waste ink on classifying the Soviet regime as an activist state (but Damaška does it anyway).[69] More interestingly, he shows that Czarist Russia has never been different in this respect, in spite of the pronounced inclination of post-Petrine Russian autocrats to hold themselves out as being a part of the Enlightenment movement or as having a liberal worldview. In general, Russian judges have always been authorized to disregard the parties' actual pleadings and to seek, on their own accord, what constituted "the truth."[70]

The sense that judges are the custodians of the truth also implies that not only contractual rights, but the entire *corpus* of substantive law, the parties' own set of entitlements, is a poor repository, an empty chest, unworthy of the task of its own enforcement. The traditional Russian practice of law has always been focused, as has been shown above, on *procedure*, on the exercise of legal clout by its sacerdotal caretakers. Procedural law is essentially about questions such as, "Who may bring suit and under what circumstances? Which tribunal is authorized to adjudicate disputes? How should the parties structure their arguments and what may be admissible in evidence to support their cause?" A

---

[68] The obvious example is Germany, especially (but not only) under the Third Reich. The most articulate German legal philosopher to have embraced the concept of the activist state is the famous Third Reich legal ideologue, Carl Schmitt. See his *Political Theology, Four Chapters on the Concept of Sovereignty*, translated by George Schwab, Cambridge, MA: MIT Press (1985; first published in 1922). The single most important concept in Schmitt's philosophy is the notion of the "exception." Succinctly put, an exception is an extraordinary, unforeseeable situation. Due to its unforeseen nature, exceptions cannot be addressed by existing legal norms and must be delegated to the discretion of a higher authority. Since exceptions occur frequently, an important bulk of all legal altercations must be concluded by administrative fiat. See Oren Gross, "The Normless and Exceptional Exception: Carl Schmitt's Theory of Emergency Powers and the 'Norm-Exception' Dichotomy," *Cardozo Law Review* 21:1825 (2000).

[69] Ibid., pp. 194ff. Soviet criminal procedure, for instance, banned all kinds of evidentiary privilege (e.g., a privilege given to consultations between an attorney and her client). Defendants were denied the right to counsel at the early stages of the criminal process. Refusal to give evidence was considered a serious crime. Investigators were charged with the obligation to conclude the guilt or innocence of the defendant much before the case went to trial. This, in turn, diminished the weight given to the proceeding in open court, because once the defendant was required to face the charges he was already assumed to have committed the crime. Procedural defenses (what is called in America "procedural due process") were regarded as a formalistic quibble and ostracized as leading to obstruction of justice.

[70] Damaška, ibid., pp. 201ff.

legal system without substantive provisions does not generate predetermined answers to such questions as, "Who is entitled to exercise dominion over some form of wealth? How do rights come into existence? How can they licitly be employed by their owners?" An empty chest of substantive rights empowers the custodians of the law to mete out personalized justice. In purely procedural systems, individual subjects are treated as if their rights depend on the goodwill and discretion of their secular or religious pastors. Rights are thought of as manifestations of government largesse rather than something that belongs to them spontaneously or "naturally."[71] Rights *result* from adjudication rather than *precede* it. In short, people are trained to think that rights (their own) depend on privilege (the source of authority), rather than, as is customary to think in Rule of Law societies, that privilege depends on right, on desert, or on merit.

The Russian ineptitude in discerning the value of substantive rights, and the willingness of Russians to accept authority as a substitute, is best illustrated by Dostoyevsky's reflections about civil liberties, contained in his *Diary of a Writer*:

Civil liberties may be established in Russia on an integral scale, more complete than anywhere in the world, whether in Europe or even in North America, and precisely on the same adamant foundation. It will be based not upon a written sheet of paper, but upon the children's affection of the people of the Czar, as their father, since children may be permitted many a thing which is inconceivable in the case of a contractual nation; they may be entrusted with much that has nowhere been encountered, since children will not betray their father, and, being children, they will lovingly accept from him any correction of their errors.[72]

The predominance of procedure over substance characterized medieval Western law as well. As is ably demonstrated by Desmond Manderson,[73] all pre–sixteenth-century English statutes dealt primarily with the division of power between the potentates of the era (the crown and the nobility) and the structure of the feudal system. Law was completely devoid of substantive provisions. Prominent examples include King John's Magna Carta of 1215 and King Edward I's Statutes of Westminster, which followed each other in rapid succession in 1275, 1285, and 1290.[74] These early statutes were all written in Law-Latin, an enigmatic tongue that only a small and privileged minority

---

[71] By contrast, supporters of the "natural law" school of jurisprudence believe that rights are endemic to the human race, do not depend on a grant by government, and are immune from being trampled upon by central (even divine) authority.

[72] Cited by Ernest Simmons, "Some Thoughts on the Soviet Concept of Authority and Freedom," in Lyman Bryson, Louis Finkelstein, R. M. MacIver, and Richard McKeon (eds.), *Freedom and Authority in Our Time*, New York: Harper, pp. 147, 148 (1953).

[73] Desmond Manderson, *Songs Without Music*, Berkeley: University of California Press, pp. 58ff (2000).

[74] Manderson's claim may be somewhat exaggerated on this score. The Statutes of Westminster, although directly affecting the feudal system and the privileges of the nobility, also affect the nature of freeholding in real estate and are thus related to substantive rights in land.

could access and decipher. This linguistic smokescreen implied that the vast majority of the people were denied view to the inner temple of the law, except through the mediation of its appointed vicars, lay or ecclesiastical. If this fact is compounded with the emptiness of the core itself, the absence of substantive entitlements, it becomes clear that early English medieval law braced and intensified the central authority of the lawgiver. It took very little interest in fostering the substantive rights of the people as the ultimate beneficiaries of the legal system.[75] Manderson's insight is naturally not confined to statutory law. Case law, too, being cultivated through the forms of action, a wholly procedural device, was fully compatible with the other attributes of the legal structure until the forms of action finally caved in with the sudden rise of assumpsit.

Western Iconography

The Western legal Renaissance, of permitting substance to permeate the law and thus to erode the procedural concept of unmitigated authority, is easily demonstrable in Western iconography.

I proceed in three stages, showing the iconographic interpretation of authority in humanist Italy before, during, and after the Renaissance.

The medieval Sienese artist Ambrogio Lorenzetti (1285 ca.–1348) executed his famous frescoes of the Good and Bad Government around 1338–40. These murals pioneer the disdainful approach to unmitigated clout (i.e., tyranny) in all Western iconography.[76] The paintings adorn the walls of the Council Room (*Sale della Pace*, or *Sale dei Nove*), in Siena's City Hall (*Palazzo Pubblico*) (approximately 14×7 meters). The smaller, northern wall of the room represents *The Allegory of Good Government* (Figure 26). The long, eastern wall on its right demonstrates *The Effects of Good Government on Life in the City and in the Country*. Figure 27 shows a detail of this fresco (the effects of good government in the city). The prolonged western wall to the left shows both *The*

---

[75] In Kafka's *The Trial*, this seems to be one of the central themes. The law is guarded by a person of authority (or his henchmen; perhaps, there isn't any person of authority – only his henchmen are there to exercise the absentee person's clout). Individual persons cannot access the law. They do not possess an entitlement to be treated fairly. There is no evidence for the existence of legal substance on the other side of the guardians' outpost, but the law's vacuous nature is kept as a dark secret, it is not admitted in loud voice. The citizen's remedy is totally contingent on the good will (or lack thereof) of the guardians. See Dominique Gros, *Le "Gardien de la Loi" Selon Kafka*, an unpublished paper presented at the International Conference of Law and Literature, Nice, 2001. Whereas Kafka is hardly a narrator of the Middle Ages, his tale mourns the debacle of modernity and predicts the total eradication of substantive rights.

[76] The nuance of Lorenzetti's political message is subject to many interpretations. Some discover in these murals a subtextual endorsement of Aristotelian and Thomistic ideas. See Nicolai Rubinstein, "Political Ideas in Sienese Art: The Frescoes by Ambrogio Lorenzetti and Taddeo di Bartolo in the Palazzo Pubblico," *Journal of the Warburg and Courtauld Institutes* 21:179 (1959). For a more modern interpretation, see Quentin Skinner, "Ambrogio Lorenzetti: The Artist as a Political Philosopher," *Proceedings of the British Academy* 72:1 (1986).

FIGURE 26. Ambrogio Lorenzetti, *The Allegory of Good Government*, 1338–40.

Allegory of Bad Government and *The Effects of Bad Government on Life in the City and in the Country.*[77]

The cycle was commissioned and executed when Siena experienced a unique kind of a proto-republican form of government. The city economy was already based on commercial and free-market foundations, assisted by a brisk banking industry. In spite of its smallness, the city accommodated a broad range of different constituencies (merchants, knights, "liberal" and "mechanical" artisans) and was torn between the rising power of its own citizenry, the "people" (*popolo*), and the claims made upon it by outsiders (the pro-papal Guelph party and its head, the French king of Naples, and its own chief city executive, also nominated by nonpopular constituencies – the *podestà*). The popular power was concentrated in the hands of nine governors, representing the checks and balances of the city's diverse constituencies. These governors met and exercised their power in the *Sale dei Nove* (literally, the Hall of the Nine), presumably just underneath *The Allegory of Good Government.*[78]

The entire mural cycle radiates a strikingly republican message to its audience about the meaning of political power. Authority is interpreted in every

[77] All these names are modern. Lorenzetti himself called good and bad government "peace" and "war," respectively.

[78] For a popular, yet learned explanation of the cycle and its political and ideological backdrop, see Randolph Starn, *Ambrogio Lorenzetti, the Palazzo Pubblico, Siena*, New York: George Braziller (1994).

FIGURE 27. Ambrogio Lorenzetti, *The Effects of Good Government in the City and in the Country*. Detail: *The Effects of Good Government in the City* (1338–40).

one of these murals, not so much for *what it is*, but for what are *its expected effects* on the lives of ordinary citizens. The focus of attention is thus immediately diverted from the *grandeur* of the mighty, as an end unto itself, to the gratification of the meek, those who are the ultimate beneficiaries of prudent dominion.[79] Unlike in the Shakespearean poetry of King Richard II, dominion cannot be "good" unless it has good effects. To be sure, the guaranteed beneficial effects of the Sienese inclusionary politics on the actual lives of the citizens are hardly borne out by historical fact. As Lorenzetti was ready to deliver his masterpiece in 1340, the city was struck by a devastating famine. Eight years later it was visited by the Black Death, which claimed the lives of one-third of the population, including Lorenzetti himself. The struggling republic found it increasingly harder to resist foreign expansionism and eventually capitulated to its main archenemy, Florence (1555).

Ambrogio Lorenzetti will never be forgotten, however. He is, I submit, the mirror image of Richard II as interpreted by White. Exactly as Richard's

[79] According to one interpreter, one has to pay special attention to a common cord held by the happy citizens standing next to the image of *Concordia*, symbolizing a contractual bond amongst them that is based on moral justice. The Rule of Law reigns supreme in this imagery, as the image of *Justitia* and *Sapientia* dominates even the image of the allegorical King. See Gunther Teubner, "Contracting Worlds: The Many Autonomies of Private Law," *Social and Legal Studies* 9:339 (2000). Compare Quentin Skinner, "Ambrogio Lorenzetti: The Artist as Political Philosopher," *Proceedings of the British Academy* 72:1 (1986).

FIGURE 28. Ambrogio Lorenzetti, *The Effects of Good Government in the City* (detail: dancing citizens, 1338–40).

kingship could not be rescued, save for his *poetry* of kingship, Lorenzetti was able to coin a poetry, a veiled dream, of the republican spirit in a world that was not quite ripe for such a daring adventure. Under the reign of his good government, happy citizens are seen dancing in the streets, although actual festivities of this nature were probably not allowed in his time (see Figure 28); other citizens are shown engaging in lively commerce, a great matter of civic pride in the fourteenth century (Figure 29). The countryside is celebrated for its lush and plentiful harvest, in defiance of the approaching famine (see Figure 30). Lorenzetti's lyric aspirations were a mere vow for the future, but they were eventually acted upon, and turned into political reality, in the ensuing centuries, as is sketched out in the concluding sections of this chapter.

FIGURE 29. Ambrogio Lorenzetti, *The Effects of Good Government in the City* (detail: shops and commerce, 1338–40).

I chose Botticelli's allegorical painting, *The Calumny of Apelles* (Figure 31), as a possible illustration of the imagery of authority in the Quattrocento. Apelles, the great fourth-century B.C. Greek artist, painted an allegory about calumny, but the painting itself, as well as the rest of his lifetime *oeuvre*, did not survive. The praise of Apelles comes down to us secondhand. His *Calumny* was meticulously described by Lucian (second century A.D.) and, through him, by Alberti in his *On Painting*. This was the version known to Botticelli, on which he based his own interpretation of the scene. The elevated figure in the painting is a royal judge, perhaps King Midas. On either side of the king stand two women, representing Ignorance and Suspicion, whispering their venomous missive in his ass-like ears. Calumny herself is seen in her approach. She is a beautiful but crafty woman, dragging along an innocent person, with his hands held up for justice, to face his bitter destiny. She is led in her effort by an ugly and filthy man, Hatred, and is assisted by two other female helpers, Envy and Fraud. An old darkly clad woman, Penitence, is casting a backward glance at a young, beautiful, and naked girl, Truth.

Now Botticelli has gone through dramatic transformations in his personal and artistic biography. His first allegories (*Primavera, The Birth of Venus*) bring to the fore a classical, humanist, pagan, sunny, yet dreamy worldview of untold refinement. These allegories reflect the liberated Renaissance spirit in which he reveled in his formative period. In his later years, Botticelli fell under the darker spell of the unrelenting Savonarola, and his imagery became more austere and, indeed, joyless. *The Calumny of Apelles* belongs to this second period. The only

FIGURE 30. Ambrogio Lorenzetti, *The Effects of Good Government in the Country* (detail), 1338–40.

figure reminiscent of the famous allegories of his former style is Truth, whose posture, body language, and general appearance closely mimic the *Venus* of his youth. One is strained to wonder, then, what is the role of this pagan beauty in the imagery of corrupted justice?

According to the Greek mythology, which was well known to Botticelli, Venus was conceived when the Titan Cronus (time) castrated his father, Uranus, and then cast his severed testicles unto the foamy brine. Her mother's womb was the vast ocean, which was inseminated by the very act of patricide. She was given life by the mutilation of her male ancestor. With his authority gone, her beauty came into being; and in Botticelli's *Calumny*, with the king's authority corrupted by the Vices, she is the one who holds out hope, for she is not only striking in her appearance; she also personifies Truth itself. Venus was not the

FIGURE 31. Sandro Botticelli, *The Calumny of Apelles*, 1495.

only one among her kin to have been given life (or suffered death) by Oedipal longings. Uranus himself was created without male assistance by his mother, Gaea, the great primordial womb (earth). He became the lord of the sky and, by embracing the horizon from all sides, mounted his own mother and became her husband. Gaea was displeased with her lover, because he was cruel to their children and imprisoned them in deep cavities within her womb. It was with her complicity that their son, Cronus, rose against his father, her husband, and hurled his genitals to the waves. Cronus himself did not excel in his parental responsibilities. He was mortified of his own offspring and, to fend off the danger, devoured them at birth. This time it took his own wife's complicity to cheat him out of eating one of their sons, Zeus, who eventually disposed of him to establish the dynasty of the Olympians.

Venus, then, is the luscious fruit of patricide. Zeus himself had not achieved his magnificence by a lesser deed. Is Botticelli, then, telling us that to seek out the truth (to create Venus) one needs to destroy the fountainhead of authority? That the king is not capable of delivering a sound judgment? That being swayed away from his charges by the debasing effect of the Vices, he, the King, the Father, the Ruler of Men, must be swept aside to enable Truth, a wisp of a girl, a delight to the senses, to give a measure of comfort to her suitors?

Admittedly, this is a speculative interpretation. But it is not devoid of some remarkable corroboration. E. H. Gombrich was successful in bringing to light a rich narrative concerning the genesis of *The Birth of Venus*, to which I will turn shortly.[80] Although Gombrich carefully limits his analysis to the iconography of

---

[80] E. H. Gombrich, *Symbolic Images, Studies in the Art of the Renaissance*, New York: Phaidon/Praeger, pp. 31ff (1972).

the goddess as of the time (and circumstances) of her painting (ca. 1485–86),[81] the close resemblance between her original rendition[82] and her later appearance in the *Calumny* (1495) makes it unlikely that she came to symbolize an altogether different set of ideas.

The original Venus was painted under the patronage of an adolescent, Lorenzo di Pierfrancesco de' Medici (1463–1503), a second cousin of his magnificent namesake. The painting was commissioned to adorn the young patron's new villa at Castello. Gombrich gathers his main clues about this commission from a letter sent by Marcilio Ficino, the renowned humanist, to the youthful recipient of the painting, instructing him as to its proper meaning and what it ought to imply for his own social conduct. Ficino even took special measures to insure that Lorenzo's tutors should force him to memorize his injunctions by rote. The letter spells out, in astrological terms, the significance of Venus among her celestial companions. It reads:

First Luna – what else can she signify in us but that continuous motion of the soul and of the body? Mars stands for speed, Saturn for tardiness, Sol for God, Jupiter for the Law, Mercury for Reason, and Venus for Humanity (*Humanitas*).

It then goes on to state the proper relationship between Luna, the movement of the soul, and the diverse celestial planets, reserving the fair Venus, like a child might hold on to a rare delicacy, for the very end:

Finally she [Luna – U.P.] should fix her eyes on Venus herself, that is to say on Humanity. This serves us as exhortation and reminder that we cannot possess anything great on this earth without possessing the men themselves from whose favor all earthly things spring. Men, moreover, cannot be caught by any other bait but that of Humanity. Be careful, therefore, not to despise it, thinking perhaps that "humanitas" is of earthly origin. For Humanity herself is a nymph of excellent comeliness born of heaven and more than others beloved by God all highest. Her soul and mind are Love and Charity, her eyes Dignity and Magnanimity, the hands Liberality and Magnificence, the feet Comeliness and Modesty. The whole, then, is Temperance and Honesty, Charm and Splendor.[83]

History does not recount whether the minor Lorenzo heeded Ficino's admonition to elevate *humanitas* above all virtues. But Botticelli himself, her creator, seemed to have trailed it, and then surpassed it, not only to the letter, but also to the very poetical spirit of its intention. He could not have forgotten his mission when the time came to revive her once more, dejected yet magnificent, in the left-hand corner of the allegory of his *Calumny*.

In the presence of Truth, who carries about her person, naturally and effortlessly, magnanimity and splendor, dignity and magnificence, not much is left to

---

[81] Ibid., p. 40.
[82] According to Gombrich (ibid.) her "original" rendition is not only in the *Birth of Venus* but also in the central figure of the *Primavera*. It thus seems that the association between her person and the notion of *humanitas*, as explained in the text immediately following, is not case-specific and permeates all of Botticelli's renditions of her lovely image.
[83] Ibid., pp. 41–42.

support the authority of the poor king, lending his ass-like ears to badmouthing and slander. The innocent man in the painting may not win his day in court, but the violence that is visited upon him is clearly devoid of authority. The beautiful goddess, once again, mutilated in her human dignity the legitimate birthright of her progenitor.

Finally, I would like to turn our attention toward one illustration of the imagery of power in the era of the Baroque. Cardinal Maffeo Barberini (1568–1644), a member of the Florentine branch of his wealthy family, was elected to the papal throne in 1623. Prior to his time, the conclave of cardinals used to fill vacancies to the Holy See by oral discussion, without a secret ballot. Powerful cardinals used to proclaim their top choices without fair warning, thus stampeding the opposition out of sight, for fear that the victorious incumbent might not look kindly on their demurrer. Gregory XV, the pope immediately preceding Maffeo Barberini, reformed the system by introducing, by a papal bull, the secret ballot, an election method that was regarded with considerable suspicion by the members of the conservative conclave. When Gregory died in 1623, two main contenders aspired to the Holy See, Cardinal Ludovisi and Cardinal Borghese. The secret ballot proved just as hazardous as predicted: The conclave was deadlocked and a compromise candidate had to be spirited to the throne. Barberini's name was mentioned, but due to his lack of social rank (his family did not belong to the old nobility) he was not considered "*papabile*." To complicate matters, an outbreak of malaria struck at the secluded conference of cardinals and several of them actually perished. *Papabile* or not, Barberini's name was put on the roster of candidates once again; the realization that no other aspirant could break the deadlock, the suffocating heat at the sequestered gathering, and the mounting death toll convinced the cardinals to lend their support to this uninspiring bidder. When the votes were counted, one of the ballots was missing, and the opposition was claiming that it smelled a rat. With Barberini's acquiescence, a second counting was administered, which produced, this time, the ascension of Barberini to the throne as Pope Urban VIII. Urban held in his hands the very keys of St. Peter, but not his authority. Authority had to be refashioned by artificial means.[84]

This he attempted to do by a clever combination of architectural and artistic imagery, and a verbal indoctrination of his flock. Under his supervision, the Palazzo Barberini was constructed; it easily overshadowed all secular palaces in Rome in its sheer size, lavish opulence, and detailed ornament. The best artists were hired to embellish this architectural symbol of prosperity and clout. In sheer grandeur, this palace was second to none. But something more was missing. It was felt necessary to wed the poetry of legitimacy to the prosaic assertion of might. Figure 32 is a detail of one of the numerous ceiling paintings inside the palazzo. It was executed by one of the leading Baroque artists, Pietro da

[84] Many of the materials concerning Urban VIII and his quest of legitimacy are borrowed from John Beldon Scott, *Images of Nepotism*, Princeton, NJ: Princeton University Press (1991).

FIGURE 32. Pietro da Cortona, *Ceiling Fresco with Divine Providence* (detail), 1633–39.

Cortona. It portrays Divine Providence, nimbly floating in the heavenly spheres, hanging on to the coat of arms of the Barberini family (the crossed keys). It clearly implies that Urban's ascension to the throne was not a mere coincidence, occasioned by an unusual combination of circumstances, but the fruit of a meditated divine intervention, the guiding hand of Providence herself. Large bees are clearly visible underneath the flying figure. Contemporary sources, embraced by the Barberini family, explain the connection:

A few days before his election, a great group of bees entered the Vatican Palace from that part facing the meadows that look out toward Tuscany, and the swarm rested on the wall of the room in which was the cell of Barberini. If this happens by chance, it can be said a remarkable encounter that a little before the assumption to the papal throne of a Tuscan, whose coat of arms is made up of bees, a swarm came from Tuscany and settled over his cell in the conclave.... It can be said that this sign had been sent by God to demonstrate his will with regard to the person who ought to be elected and to enlighten the electors in the midst of such darkness of private interests and dissension.[85]

Barberini was seemingly not a bad pontiff.[86] But he had one major fault, nepotism. To favor one's kin and promote them to positions of power and affluence was hardly his own invention, but Urban seemed to have refined the practice to a point of perfection.[87] In other words, he was abusing his authority.[88] This he did by converting the material assets of his stewardship into his (or his relatives') private dominion. For all his efforts to secure his sway, his contemporaries were not quick to embrace the legitimacy of his reign.[89] Perhaps he himself sensed that it could not withstand the critical tide of time, for before he died he summoned a council of theologians to pass judgment on his deeds. The council found no fault in his behavior. Nevertheless, when his spirit left its temporary habitation, the streets of Rome were filled with jubilation.

It is submitted that the intrinsically broken staff of Urban's authority can be discerned in its own imagery. The doctrine that pontiffs rule by the grace of God was fairly current in his time and hardly needed iconographic support.[90] The actual depiction of Divine Providence surrounded by a swarm of bees looks contrived, because it evokes fear for her safe landing amidst this insect-infested environment, more than it inspires awe for the *persona* symbolized by these creatures. Unlike the Russian *St. George*, whose Authority is derived from the hierarchy of the very spheres, from an intrinsically wholesome world where everyone and everything has its proper place, Urban's authority is all confusion. Unlike the Virgin Mary making her appearance at the Temple because Authority had to be obeyed no matter what, Urban's authority relies for its validity on

---

[85] This source, which was kept by the Barberini family and cherished for its contents, is cited ibid., p. 184.

[86] For a balanced evaluation of his reign, see Laurie Nussdorfer, *Civic Politics in the Rome of Urban VIII*, Princeton, NJ: Princeton University Press (1992).

[87] Scott, ibid.

[88] He particularly loved two of his nephews, Francesco and Antonio, who were summarily appointed cardinals and held positions of power in his court. A third nephew, Matteo, was made Prince of Palestrina and Prefect of Rome. His brother Antonio was not neglected and was appointed a cardinal as well.

[89] See Gregorio Leti, *Il Nipotismo di Roma*, Amsterdam (1667).

[90] All popes were denoted "*Divina Providentia Pontifex Maximus*," but this theological assumption was rarely, if ever, made explicit in the visual arts.

an obviously insipid[91] tale of multiple flying figures, an open window and its portentous location, and an uninvited swarm of bees.

[91] The conclave of cardinals in the early seventeenth century consisted of savvy politicians who were consumed by ambition and completely conscious of the tricks of their trade. It is hard to believe that even if some bees were spotted in the arena of their deliberations, any of them would have assigned to this fact the slightest significance.

Appendix to Chapter 4

St. Petersburg

> There are, my dear Nastenka, in case you don't know, some rather strange corners in Petersburg. It's as if the sun that warms the rest of the city never shines on them, and instead another sun, especially designed for them, supplies them with a different light. Fyodor Dostoyevsky, *White Nights* (translation: Andrew MacAndrew).

The Imperial City of St. Petersburg and its manifold cultural manifestations stand out as the single most common refutation of the exclusively Slavophile spirit of eternal Russia. Whereas Moscow is often portrayed as traditionally Russian, Orthodox, Eastern, and, at root, plebeian, St. Petersburg gained the reputation of a European, cosmopolitan, occidental, and aristocratic center. Whereas Moscow looks inwardly, into the Russian soul, St. Petersburg is commonly portrayed as a window to the West, an extended arm integrating old Rus' with the Enlightenment, the liberal spirit, and indeed the Renaissance of Western Europe.

This remarkable city distinguished itself in almost every artistic form known to the human race. Its literary giants (Pushkin, Dostoyevsky, Gogol) are second to none. Its great composers (Moussorgsky, Balakirev, Borodin, Rimsky-Korsakov, Cui)[1] attained the most highly acclaimed musical praise. Its greatest claim to fame, however, derives from its sheer beauty: a palace-lined marvel of architectural magnificence, regally laid out upon a network of rivers and canals, with spacious avenues, broad plazas, and opulent Italianate *palazzi*.

The simple question is this: If St. Petersburg can truly be conceived as a window to the West, why did it not give rise to capitalist institutions in general and to contract in particular? Why were these institutions singled out from all the manifestations of the human spirit and banished from its intellectual forging ground, while art and music, stage and dance, the *belles-lettres* and architecture, all flourished, Western style, and attained such an unrivaled magnificence?

In this short appendix I wish to argue that St. Petersburg may, indeed, be a *window*, a sighting post, from which the West can be viewed from a distance,

---

[1] This group went down in history as the "Mighty Five."

admired, dreamt about, idealized, or put in rhyme and verse. But all of this falls short, very short, I contend, of transforming this metropolis into a veritable Western capital. I explore some aspects of the avowedly Westernized architectural style of the city as my (only) proxy for the larger claim.

Before turning to look at the actual architectural design of this urban *extravaganza* and trying to decode the cultural message it was plotted to convey to the eye of the beholder, a few threshold remarks are called for.

St. Petersburg, much more than any other Russian town, is the city of despots. The general tyrannical traits of its designer, Peter the Great, in matters of state are universally known. But he was the most obnoxious intruder of seemingly trivial and mundane matters as well, and this psychological inclination, to encompass *everything* in his sway, was carried over to all his deeds, including, as we shall shortly see, the building of his new imperial capital. Bernard Pares reports:

Under his direction was brought out the first textbook on social behavior, in which his subjects were ordered to be amiable, modest, and respectful, to learn languages, to look people in the face, take off their hats, not to dance in boots, or to spit on the floor, or sing too loud, put the finger in the nose, rub the lips with the hand, lean on the table, swing the legs, lick the fingers, gnaw a bone when at dinner, scratch one's head, talk with one's mouth full; and his assemblies or social gatherings, at which he made attendance compulsory, were the first crude school of European conventions. Russia was to be Europeanized by the knout.[2]

A formative decision in the building of a city – any city – is the choice of its geographical location. Some city builders choose their site for its proximity to important trade routes (say, a navigable river). Others may be inspired by the natural sweetness of the climate, the fertility of the land, or the richness of the natural resources. Many modern capitals are conveniently positioned in the geographical hub of a large realm, to make communications with the periphery more accessible. None of these blessings can be associated with the wretched site of Peter's capital. Petersburg is located at the far northwestern corner of the vastest landmass of all earthly dominions. Its marshy terrain is muddy, soggy, unstable, and overwhelmed by periodic floods of biblical proportions. Its water is not potable. In winter, it falls into an endless night of polar gloom. In summer, its swamps come to life with clouds of fever-carrying insects. It was selected for its proximity to the sea, for Peter (vainly) dreamt of transforming his land-locked empire into a seafaring nation, just like the paradigm of his fantasies, Holland (Petersburg was meant to mimic the canal-pierced cityscape of his admired Amsterdam). To manifest this Dutch infatuation, Peter named his new capital Sankt Pieter Burkh,[3] as a linguistic homage to his source of inspiration. Its immediate proximity to Sweden, with which Peter waged an endless succession of wars, added, I think, additional attraction to the choice of the

---

[2] Bernard Pares, *History of Russia*, New York: Knopf, p. 225 (1953).

[3] The current name, St. Petersburg, was given to the city by Peter's successors. It was later named Petrograd, Leningrad, and again St. Petersburg, as a changing mirror of the tide of time.

locale. It symbolized his defiance of the powerful foreign foe and the very act of turning a backwater feudal society into a powerful "Europeanized" nation ("If I can beat a European superpower, I must be a European superpower myself"). The treacherous delta of the Neva River was selected, then, as the future center stage for acting out all future Russian events of historical proportions simply because Peter willed it so.[4] There was absolutely no other reason.

Two little obstacles had to be overcome: the unavailability of a willing labor force, to actually build the city, and the resentment of its prospective residents to call this loathsome place home. None of these annoying factors caused Peter to budge. All his laborers were simply forced to fulfill his ambition, often at the sacrifice of their own lives. They were recruited primarily from three sources: serfs, prisoners of war (especially Swedes), and common bona fide convicted felons. In other words, Petersburg was built by forced slave labor. Bruce Lincoln describes the inevitably cheerful atmosphere at the building site:

Every year, Peter ordered between ten and thirty thousand serfs, prisoners of war, and common criminals to be marched to the Neva delta to drain marshes, drive piles, and build St. Petersburg's first buildings. These men worked with the crudest tools under conditions that killed them by the thousands. Some dug dirt with their hands and carried it away in containers made from their shirts and coats, while others hacked at the swampy ground with roughly made picks and wooden shovels. Cholera and giardiasis threatened everyone who entered the region, and the bad water that caused these ailments has condemned St. Petersburg's residents to endure those sicknesses ever since. "It would be difficult to find in the annals of military history any battle that claimed more lives than the number of workers who died in [the building of] St. Petersburg," the historian Kliuchevsky wrote at the end of the nineteenth century. For the men who built Russia's new capital, he concluded, the new city "turned out to be nothing but a huge graveyard."[5]

The problem of populating the new city was solved with similar dispatch. Peter ordered a thousand leading aristocrats to move immediately, with their entire households, to St. Petersburg. Similar orders ensued to hordes of artisans, merchants, and barracks upon barracks of soldiers.[6] He himself moved to the new city in 1710, some six or seven years after the construction of the first wooden houses there, and made it the capital of Russia soon thereafter (1712).[7] I find the conversion of Christianity's Third Rome (Moscow) into the

---

4 Could such a choice of location occur in the Renaissance? In his life of Leon Battista Alberti, the great Renaissance architectural theorist, Vasari comments, right at the beginning of his narrative: "Everyone knows . . . that when choosing a site for a new building one must take account of what natural science has to say about avoiding places where there are destructive winds, an unhealthy atmosphere, or stench and exhalations from impure and stagnant waters." See Giorgio Vasari, *Lives of the Great Artists*, translated by George Bull, New York: Penguin Books, p. 208 (1965; Vasari's original revised edition was published in 1568).

5 Bruce Lincoln, *Sunlight at Midnight: St. Petersburg and the Rise of Modern Russia*, New York: Basic Books, pp. 20–21 (2000).

6 See Lindsey Hughes, *Russia in the Age of Peter the Great*, New Haven, CT: Yale University Press, p. 215 (1998).

7 Perhaps it would not be entirely false to add to the official reasons for Peter's selection of Petersburg as his new capital his intense dislike of the old capital, Moscow. His father, Czar

secular imperial capital of the realm highly reminiscent of its polar opposite, the conversion of old Rus' from paganism to Christianity, some eight centuries earlier: swift, unyielding, total and tyrannical. De-Russifiying Rus' could not have been attempted, and then crowned with such an astounding success, by anyone but a thoroughly Russian prince.

It would have been a miracle if a city willed by one individual, built by slave labor, and peopled by forced mass transfers of civilians and military personnel could transform itself into a Florence or an Amsterdam. This is one miracle that actually did not transpire. In fact, the city's own rank and file (as distinguished from its top aristocracy) could hardly relate to the new urban idiom. Like other artistic art forms, which were artificially borrowed from the West, it created an ugly rift between Man and his environment, and eventually pitted ruler and subject into a collision course of tragic consequences. George Heard Hamilton comments:

In ancient Russia the arts had been the arts of the people.... With rare exceptions the builders of Russian churches, the painters of icons, and the manufacturers who were also the designers of the works of spiritual art – all these had come from the people. After the establishment of St. Petersburg as the capital in 1712, the Russians were usually students of foreign artists. Such a state of affairs inevitably alienated the people from the art of the Court, which they could neither create nor comprehend. The loss of cultural unity eventually reached the proportions of national tragedy, until an embittered populace took terrible revenge upon the upper classes for having deprived them of their right and proper place in the nation's economic, political and cultural life.[8]

St. Petersburg was built as a political statement. The sympathetic Billington comments on Petrine architecture:

The new architecture was called *regulyarnaya*, meaning both "regular" and "regulated." It sought to impose rigid rectilinear order on nature as well as on the irregularities of previous construction.... In place of Moscow's chaotic, curvilinear streets and circular

Alexis Mikhailovitch, had two successive wives. Among his children from his first czarina were Princess Sophia and Princes Fyodor and Ivan; both princes were weaklings, not fit to rule the empire. Peter was born to the czar from his second wife, and thus was younger than all his half-siblings. When Alexis died, Fyodor succeeded him, but soon fulfilled his obligations to the fatherland and perished. The boyars recognized Ivan's fastidious nature and elected the younger Peter to the throne (Sophia was not considered because of her gender). The relatives of Alexis' first wife, however, refused to let their kin be passed over in the traditional line of succession. Sophia organized the Palace Guard (*Streltsy*) to mount a gory revolt, which took place in the presence of Peter. Ivan was proclaimed Czar alongside with Peter, and the regency was entrusted in the (able) hands of Sophia. As her dominion over the realm solidified, so did her suspicions of Peter's imposing character, and she plotted to assassinate his mother, forcing Peter to escape. By that time he was savvy enough, and the boyars were disgusted enough of her rule, to prepare the ground for a coalition among them; stripped of all her military support, she capitulated without bloodshed and was dispatched to a monastery. Peter assumed the throne as the sole ruler of the empire, but he could never forget, nor forgive, the gory scenes of his boyhood, which remained forever associated with the scene of the crime. See generally Bernard Pares, *A History of Russia*, New York: Knopf, p. 193 (1953).

[8] George Heard Hamilton, *The Art and Achitecture of Russia*, New Haven, CT: Yale University Press, p. 260 (1954, reprinted 1983).

FIGURE 33. The Fortress of Peter and Paul, St. Petersburg.

religious processions, Petersburg built broad, straight boulevards or "prospects" suitable for military parades.... Petersburg soon became a city of monumental ensembles. Aristocrats from the provinces built palaces there in order to secure or improve their position in the new Table of Ranks....[9]

Significantly, the very first structure to have been built in stone[10] in Peter's new capital is the Peter and Paul Fortress. Besides being a fortified outpost on the erstwhile deserted Hare Island, on the northern shore of the Neva, it has two additional functions, a cathedral church and a jail. The fortress is extremely prominent in Petersburg's cityscape (the more imposing tower stands at 404 feet, the tallest in the city). It has been like this from the beginning. It is still like this today. It sends to its viewers an unmistakable political message, to which I now turn (see Figure 33).

The architectural design of the cathedral is vastly different from the prevailing Muscovite style at the beginning of the eighteenth century. Whereas Moscow featured tent-like roofs and the traditional gilded, or lovingly painted, onion-shaped domes of the Orthodox Church, St. Peter and Paul boasts two straight towers. They are crafted in the Western style,[11] like so many other church spires in Europe. They perfectly mesh into the grand design of the regularized, rectilinear layout of the whole city and of the swiftly flowing, wide river in its midst. The interior of the church is bright and roomy, letting in plenty of

[9] James Billington, *The Face of Russia*, New York: TV Books, pp. 84ff (1999).

[10] The cathedral was originally built of earth and wood, like almost all other public buildings during the lifetime of Peter, but was later covered with stone.

[11] The architect was Domenico Trezzini, a Swiss-Italian, who seems to have been Peter's favorite. It is hard to tell whether Trezzini was designing his structures out of innocent ignorance of the indigenous style or out of deliberate desire to appease Peter's choice of westernizing his city "by the knout."

sunlight through its wide windows. It mimics the atmosphere of a Protestant temple, thus defying the Orthodox taste for the mystery of candle-lit interiors. The baroque iconostasis, separating, as always, the nave form the altar, looks out of place, a gauche lip service to Orthodox devotion. Superficially, Peter's opting out of the Orthodox building conventions attests to his intentions to bask and flourish in Western culture. Indeed, this interpretation reflects the conventional wisdom on this point and is not entirely false.[12] But one must also try to imagine what impression it must have made on his contemporaries, that he took the liberty to ignore the Orthodox building conventions and to replace them by the style of his choice. It was nothing short, I submit, of taking into his own hands the privilege of speaking for the Church.[13] The straight towers proclaim their message in a different voice than the Church's own. The Church would have gravitated to its own traditions, if anyone were obliging enough to let it speak for itself.[14] The straight towers have a European appearance, but

[12] The more sophisticated commentators usually treat Petersburg as a hybrid city, floating in limbo between East and West. The original myth of the dual nature of St. Petersburg is commonly attributed to its greatest poet, Alexander Pushkin, in his famous prose poem, "The Bronze Horseman" (1833). This poem narrates the fate of an ordinary person, Evgenii, caught in a devastating flood. Although Evgenii finds refuge near the elevated equestrian statue of Peter (executed by the French artists Maurice Falconet and Marie Collet between 1766 and 1778, and mounted on a block of granite weighing 1600 tons), he later discovers that his paramour was swept away by the waves. The horrific statue seems to scorn the protagonist's misery, and from the secure post of its solid reign it continues to haunt him to his death. The peculiar thing about "The Bronze Horseman" is that Peter's role was commonly read by generations of its interpreters as both good and evil, despotic and fatherly, Asiatic and occidental, repressive and inspiring all at the same time. The manner in which Pushkin achieved this feat defies description and reveals the genius of his art.

[13] Obviously, this architectural statement was nothing but a dim reflection of Peter's attitude to matters of church and state in general. On the one hand, Peter exhibited religious tolerance unequalled by his predecessors, i.e., in allowing the small Catholic community, as well as Lutheran and Calvinist parishioners, to practice their faith on Russian soil. But these negligible minority groups obviously did not present a serious threat to the homogeneity of his reign. On the contrary, the greater toleration exhibited to these weaker factions assisted him in solidifying his grip on the single powerful religious group that jeopardized the exclusivity of his power, the Orthodox Church. To better control this powerful religious establishment he launched a series of dramatic and far-reaching reforms. When the Patriarch Adrian died in 1700, Peter simply did not appoint anyone to succeed him. For a full generation, the Church was denied a leader to hinder the secure course of the Petrine revolution. Finally, in 1721, he appointed a Holy Synod in lieu of the patriarchate. The members of the Synod were appointed by the emperor and led by a lay procurator. In addition, Peter curtailed the jurisdiction of the ecclesiastical courts and supervised the appointment of bishops. He was not satisfied to cripple only the authority of the Church; he coveted its wealth, too. He conducted a census of the vast monastic properties and income and appropriated parts of it to the secular use of the state. See David Ogg, *Europe in the Seventeen Century*, p. 511 (6th revised ed., 1956). Many clergymen accepted the yoke of his reforms willingly. The Old Believers, for whom he personified the Antichrist, and who actually opposed his policies, were subjected to persecution, torture, and death. For a fuller account of the Petrine religious reforms, see Evgenii Anisimov, *The Reforms of Peter the Great*, New York: M. E. Sharpe, pp. 203ff (1993).

[14] Tents and domes come in handy, of course, in snowy weather. But Russian architecture was not partial to them just to suit the elements. They also assumed a traditional liturgical significance. Tent-like roofs suggested Moses' Tabernacle in the desert, and an onion is the vegetable used

only superficially so. They look "Western" because church towers in the West are straight as well. But whereas the West, much before Peter's time, moved away from authoritarianism and became more humanist, decentralized, and individualistic, Peter's upward thrusting spires monopolize state clout in his royal hands, to the exclusion of all other voices in government.

Lest the message of the straight towers remain in the eye of *some* beholders too ambiguous, the architecture of the whole compound removes this ambiguity. It does so loud and clear by packaging together, in the same fortress grounds, church and jail, spiritual and coercive power. Dark and forbidding, thick-walled, damp and freezing in the winter, the Hare Island jail (see Figure 34) was in active service for centuries. One of its wretched inmates was Fyodor Dostoyevsky, counting his days before execution, only to find out, while actually facing a firing squad, that the czar, in his infinite generosity, commuted his sentence to imprisonment with hard labor in Siberia.[15] The most important political prisoner to have perished there in Peter's time was his own independent-minded son, Aleksey, who suffered death as a result of interrogation under torture, thus mimicking the gory death of Ivan the Terrible's only son, who also died at the behest of his father. Other famous political prisoners included, in later generations, Maxim Gorky, Leon Trotsky, and Lenin's brother, Alexander. This was an imposing structure indeed.[16]

The authority of the Orthodox Church to control the spiritual life of its flock was already handed a blow by the cathedral structure. The proximity of the jail to the symbol of compromised Church authority focuses on the coercive nature of this combination and reflects on the bitter destiny of potential free thinkers or dissenters of all kinds.

Petrine architecture was not confined, of course, to the fortress alone. But a detailed description of the other surviving or vanished structures dating back to his reign falls outside the ambit of this short appendix.[17] Suffice it to say that there was nothing joyous or frivolous about Peter's capital in its early days. Peter was a great admirer of Amsterdam, both for its architecture and for its seafaring thrust. Consequently, Sankt Pieter Burkh was originally built

---

by the Virgin to haul sinners out of hell. It is not in vain that the Russian Orthodox Church, when given a free reign, used these traditional motives in structures outside Russia, even in hot climates (e.g., Jerusalem), and even in its much more recent history.

[15] Dostoyevsky's biographical notes from his prison years are contained in his work, *The House of the Dead* (1859–61).

[16] Bruce Lincoln, *Sunlight at Midnight: St. Petersburg and the Rise of Modern Russia*, New York: Basic Books, pp. 171–73 (2000). In these pages Lincoln narrates how the fortress came to symbolize repression and torture for generations to come.

[17] Significantly, these structures include the Admiralty, a huge structure facing the fortress on the side of the mainland; the "Twelve Colleges" (later corrupted, but not destroyed by the Bolsheviks) on Vasily Ostrov, which Trezzini built to house the Senate, the Synod, and the government ministries; and a variety of private palaces built by the members of the aristocracy. The single most conspicuous element in all these structures is their rectilinear conformity with the master plan of the whole city at this stage of its development. They exude an air of practicality, order, and lack of grace.

FIGURE 34. The Hair Island Jail: Main corridor leading to inmates' cells.

as a naval base with a distinctly northern appearance. It was as lovely as the interior of a Dutch Reform Kirk.

Arguably, it is not surprising that Peter failed in his attempt to instantly transform Russia into a Western nation by simply willing it. He was anything but Western himself, and one cannot pull oneself up by tugging at one's own shoestrings. But many of his successors were born into luxury and comfort and were better suited than he to successfully import Western culture to the eastern Slavs. His daughter Elizabeth was such a person, and it was she who gave free reign to the ostensibly greatest architect of the new capital, the Italian-born Bartolomeo Rastrelli.[18] Rastrelli designed and executed, at Elizabeth's behest, the three most imposing palaces ever built in the whole of Russia.[19] These are the Winter Palace along the Neva, at the very heart of town, and two palaces at the outskirts, the palace at Czarskoe Selo (now renamed Pushkin) and the

[18] Rastrelli came to Russia as a young lad, accompanying his father, a sculptor and architect of garden variety, who nevertheless was employed on a number of important commissions in the rapidly spreading city. The younger Rastrelli started his career building significant structures for the Czarina Anna (1731–41), but most of his work was executed during the reign of the Italianate Czarina Elizabeth (1741–61). When Catherine the Great, a consummate Francophile, ascended to the throne, Elizabeth's artistic inclinations fell out of grace, and Rastrelli, by that time a permanent resident of the capital, found himself unemployed. He lived off a meager pension and died in misery and despair.

[19] Elizabeth herself did not live to see the completion of these pioneering stone structures. She died in a temporary wooden palace while the permanent stone structure on the Neva was still under construction.

FIGURE 35. Ivan Vladimirov, *Execution of Workers in Front of the Winter Palace in St. Petersburg, 9 January 1905.*

palace at Peterhof. All three palaces share a common rococo architectural style. It was Rastrelli's style, to which I shall turn shortly, that transformed the city from its formerly grim, Dutch-looking seafaring outpost of Peter's beginnings to its supposedly lighthearted Italianate marvel of the Elizabethan reign. The best known of these three structures is the Winter Palace, also known as the *Hermitage*, which was later transformed into one of the finest art collections on the face of the earth. In the next few lines I dwell on the architectural characterization of this grandiose edifice. Figure 35 is an artistic impression of this huge structure, complete with one of the bloodier deeds that was committed in its vicinity.

The first and strongest impression of Rastrelli's *Hermitage* is wrought upon the mind by its sheer size. To allow Rastrelli to lay the foundations for this huge structure, Elizabeth gave him a full year's worth of her salt and liquor tax collections, both looming very large among her overall fiscal revenues. The grand total was obviously much larger. The lavish expense poured on this edifice hardly resulted from the high cost of labor. The cost of constructing a single window, out of the two thousand–odd windows in the entire structure, was roughly equivalent to the wages earned by a common laborer in ten years. The cost of a single interior door could be earned in thirty (there are 1,786 such doors in the palace). The palace stretches out for almost 200 meters along the Neva,[20] which is its main façade, but it has long and imposing façades along its other three sides, each complete with matching squares and vast open urban spaces to resonate in tandem with its dignity. The palace is girdled by a main cornice, which totals almost two kilometers in circumference. The palace has

[20] The main façade at Czarskoe Selo is approximately twice as long!

1,054 rooms. They are connected by 117 internal sets of stairs. Being a royal residence, it was first and foremost among all the city's *dvors*, or living spaces and reception facilities for the local aristocracy and foreign guests. Religious practices took place within the *dvor*, and thus the structure contained devotional areas, entirely dwarfed, needless to say, relative to their surrounding majesty; the church was just one of three different rooms adjacent to the central grand staircase at the heart of the interior structure. Some 250 stately columns adorn its exterior walls. Its rooftop boasts about 180 statues, all of them totally foreign to the Russian tradition. They seem to be winking, in their nudity, at the remote and sunny shores of Rastrelli's ancestral land.[21] Now from an aesthetic point of view Rastrelli's greatest challenge seems to have been how to harmonize the endless length of the structure and its monotonous appearance with its moderate height – only three storys in all.[22] For better or for worse, he attempted to meet this challenge by dividing the stretch into five parts, further partitioned by "bays." There are thirty seven such bays just on the Neva side (and even more on the west side), allowing for some projections and recessions, as well as alternations in the positioning of the windows and the columns. The obvious intention was to give each bay an appearance of a quasi-independent unit, which would restore some sense of proportion between it and the unimposing height of the structure. The ultimate success of this heroic effort is in the eye of the beholder. I am inclined to agree with those whose sense of proportion was not appeased, simply because, in spite of the projections and the recessions, the partitions and the alternations, the entire structure is conceived as one unit, endlessly repeating itself in its own ritual of change.[23] The more obvious response would have been to build a more restrained structure overall. Rastrelli was a much better architect of smaller buildings,[24] but none of the post-Petrine czarinas would stand for such an unpretentious solution, as they were all bent on showing off their power via architectural extravaganza. It is, perhaps, more than just historical irony that the power of the czars was ultimately broken, in the month of October 1917, by the storming and occupation of the *Hermitage* by the revolutionary masses.[25]

The Winter Palace, then, is the embodiment of the architecture of power.[26] In humanist societies any declaration of might, in life and in art, is mitigated

[21] George Heard Hamilton, *The Art and Architecture of Russia*, New Haven, CT: Yale University Press, pp. 283ff (3rd ed., 1983). See also, James Billington, *The Face of Russia*, pp. 94ff (1999); Bruce Lincoln, *Sunlight at Midnight*, pp. 41ff (2000).

[22] It was not fashionable to build vertically in St. Petersburg. By decree of Czar Nicloai I, which was not repealed until 1905, all other buildings in town had to be at least two meters shorter than the *Hermitage*, which thus dominated the city skyscape for many years.

[23] Hamilton, ibid.

[24] A good example is Rastrelli's Smolny Convent, also in St. Petersburg, which is an infinitely more satisfying structure, in my opinion, than the larger Palace on the Neva.

[25] In his famous movie *October*, the communist filmmaker Sergei Eisenstein portrays these historical events from his party's perspective, thereby reaffirming the popular conception of the Winter Palace as the symbol of tyrannical authority in czarist Russia.

[26] On the uneasy relationship of power and structure size, see John Ruskin, *The Seven Lamps of Architecture*, New York: Dover Publications, pp. 70ff (1989, republication of the second edition

by recognition of the other, and the privilege of other people to contribute a balancing voice of their own. In public law and in politics, the blending of voices generates a constitutional order. In private law, it makes room for contract. In art, it ushers in a sense of proportion. In the art of architecture, it balances space against space, line against line, wall against window. The clamorous message of Rastrelli's architecture is more clearly fathomed when one contrasts it with the paradigm of Renaissance architecture.[27] Thus the Pazzi family, the fierce opponents of the Medici in the Florentine *Quattrocento*, who eventually led an abortive conspiracy against the *Magnifico*, recruited a team of architects, led by Filippo Brunelleschi (he of the Duomo Dome) to construct the Pazzi Chapel, the most exquisitely humanist structure ever built:

[Brunelleschi] used a cube measuring twenty *braccia* on each side, as well as pendentives and a melon dome. Classical membering in *pietra serena* again creates an ordering armature that divides stuccoed wall surfaces into carefully proportioned fields.... One can easily perceive the architect's geometric conception. The central cube has, essentially, four modules to a side.... The self-containment of and centrality of the space are emphasized by the correspondences in the fields and the membering – rectangle answers rectangle, arch answers arch, blind arch answers window – as well as by the horizontal continuity of the entablature and the monk's bench, which bind together the main room and the sanctuary.[28]

The Pazzi's yearning for political predominance and their desire to project their claim into the public domain was moderated and refined by their architect's sense of proportion. Elizabeth's declaration turned, at Rastrelli's hands, into an unrestrained (all its embellishments notwithstanding) assertion of brutish force. Nor was Rastrelli resigned to this ignominy, as is clearly evidenced by his seemingly abortive attempt to compensate for size by subdivision. His capitulation to the Empress' mandate to sacrifice refinement for size and subtlety for sheer power reveals the true nature of the finished product, an empty shell of Western manners without the core of Western values.

There is one final architectural attribute of the Winter Palace that carries over to the entire urban mood and betrays its peremptory message: Its main ornament is lavished upon its exterior walls. Rastrelli's external façades are copiously adorned by columns and bas-reliefs, cornices, pilasters, and statues. This promiscuity of external ornament prompts the viewer to admire the magnificence of the sovereign without having to look inside for what the palace has to offer to its residents and their guests. Whereas humanist structures are

of the original work from 1880). Ruskin warns against excessive size, especially in the case of ornamented buildings.

[27] It is not entirely fair, of course, to contrast Rastrelli's mid-eighteenth-century rococo style to the architecture of Renaissance Florence. But the great Renaissance architectural builders and theorists laid the foundations for generations of post-Renaissance architects in Western Europe, who departed from the simplicity of their proportioned measurements but often retained their underlying values.

[28] Glen Andres, John Hunisak, and Richard Turner, *The Art of Florence*, New York: Artabras, Volume 1, p. 357 (1988).

normally geared to provide comfort and warmth for its own users,[29] Rastrelli's architecture communicates with strangers.[30] It is a self-aggrandizing style of ornament that departs not only from the architectural paradigm of the Renaissance, but also from its former medieval roots.[31] It is like codifying procedure without substance, like wearing one's intimate clothes on top of one's tailored suit, like enshrining the façade of power to the neglect of its justifying cause. St. Petersburg as a whole echoes this choice by a general proliferation of façades

[29] Alberti, the first Renaissance architectural theorist, explains in the preface to his main work: "Him I call an Architect, who, by sure and wonderful Art and Method, is able, both with Thought and Invention, to devise, and, with Execution, to compleat all those Works, which, by means of the Movement of great Weights, and the Conjunction and Amassment of Bodies, can, with the greatest Beauty, be adapted to the Uses of Mankind. . . . But the only Obligation we have to the Architect is not for his providing us with safe and pleasant Places, where we may shelter ourselves from the Heat of the Sun, from Cold and Tempest . . . but for having besides contrived many other Things . . . of the highest Use and Convenience to the Life of Man." See Leon Battista Alberti, *The Ten Books of Architecture*, preface (the 1755 Leoni edition, reprinted for Dover Publications, New York, 1986. The book was originally published, posthumously, in 1485). The Albertian credo was reiterated a century later by Andrea Palladio. Although Palladio himself was a man of the (late) Renaissance, his architectural ideas were much admired throughout the seventeenth and eighteenth centuries, and some mimic his elegant style to this day and age, which makes his ideas a fairer point of departure for a comparison with Elizabethan Petersburg. Palladio pays tribute in his preface to both Alberti and to the perennial source of humanist architecture, Vitruvius. In his treatment of private houses (for which he was most famous) Palladio writes: "For that house only ought to be called convenient, which is suitable to the quality of him that is to dwell in it, and whose parts correspond to the whole and to each other." See Andrea Palladio, *The Four Books of Architecture*, p. 37 (the 1738 Isaac Ware edition, reprinted for Dover Publications, New York, 1965; the original work was published in Venice in 1570).

[30] Even the ancients sensed clearly that excessive, extroverted ornaments had to be avoided, because they corrupted the rhetorical power of art and it only fit the barbarians ("Asians," in their Eurocentric lingo). See, for example, Marcus Fabius Quintilianus, *Institutio Oratoria: Books I–III*, translated by H. E. Butler (1980; first published circa 95 A.D.). The denunciation of excessive ornaments appears also in the work of Pliny, who thought that *luxuria*, being excessive and "Asiatic," cannot be made compatible with *dignitas*. See Piyel Haldar, "The Function of the Ornament in Quintilian, Alberti, and Court Architecture," in Costas Douzinas and Lynda Nead (eds.), *Law and the Image: The Authority of Art and the Aesthetics of Law*, Chicago: University of Chicago Press, p. 117 (1999).

[31] Thus John Ruskin, the great defender of medieval architecture who thought of the style of the Renaissance as a decadent corruption of medieval elegance, has this to say about the role of ornaments: "For observe, the function of ornament is to make you happy. Now in what are you rightly happy? Not in thinking of what you have done yourself; not in your own pride; not your own birth; not in your own being, or your own will, but in looking at God; watching what He does; what He is; and obeying His law, and yielding yourself to His will." See John Ruskin, *The Stones of Venice*, Cambridge, MA: De Capo Press, p. 101 (1960; first published in 1853). And about overabundance of ornaments he adds: "I have already said, again and again, you cannot have too much of it to be good. . . . But you may easily have too much, if you have more than you have sense to manage. For every added order of ornament increases the difficulty of discipline. It is exactly the same as in war; you cannot, as an abstract law, have too many soldiers . . . and every regiment which you cannot manage will, on the day of battle, be in your way, and encumber the movements it is not in disposition to sustain." See ibid., p. 116.

of all kinds. It marshals in a series of sharp contrasts between outside opulence and domestic gloom. Its splendid palatial glimmer lives side by side with its dismal urban blight. The evidence of its former aristocratic grandeur is matched by the misery of its plebeian residences, its unsafe streets, and its dilapidated neighborhoods – all things that do not constitute a part of its centrally located, highly visible urban showcase.[32] It is a Potemkin Village magnified a million times. It is the seat of power, authority incarnate. It is not less Russian than the immense medieval village looking inwardly and pondering its own soul, the third and last Rome, Moscow.

One could well raise the objection that it is not fair to compare a huge architectural mammoth like the Winter Palace to an understated, well-proportioned, and delicate icon of the Renaissance such as the Pazzi Chapel in Florence. To gain cogency, a comparison ought to be drawn between the Winter Palace and ambitious buildings on a similarly large scale in Western Europe. In scanning all possible analogies, the best I could come up with is the seat of power to end all seat powers, Louis XIV's palace at Versailles. It would be silly, of course, to aver that Versailles was not intended to reflect the glory of the Sun King, or that the expression of authority was not intended as one of the principal architectural *leitmotifs* of the Palace. How else could one interpret, for instance, the painted central panel in the ceiling of the Hall of Mirrors, showing, with pomp and magnificence, *The Assumption of Personal Rule by Louis XIV*? With this said, there is a host of telling differences between the two structures. I leave it to the reader's judgment to evaluate their significance in the overall architectural message conveyed by the two palaces.

The dreaded circumstances of building the Winter Palace (and the entire city of St. Petersburg) and of securing its finances have already been narrated. The construction of Versailles during the reign of Louis XIV was entrusted, by counterdistinction, to a shrewd financier, M. Colbert, who simultaneously served as the royal finance minister. The money was raised by relentless efforts to stimulate the national economy. The effort was launched at a time when it was widely believed that France was the richest nation on earth and not only could *afford*, but *owed* it to posterity, to mark its grandeur by physical means and on a large scale.[33] Although the personal reign of Louis XIV is reflected from every corner, there is, perhaps, a parallel message of an even stronger persuasion, that the structure is dominated by *the reign of reason*. The Sun

---

[32] In his short masterpiece, *The Overcoat* (1835), Nicholas Gogol pits the meekness of his protagonist, Akakii Akakeivitch, against the haughtiness of the "important personages" with whom he comes in contact. This contrast is echoed by the clear distinction between the urban glamour of the rich residences and the squalid gloom of Akakii's neighborhood, where the heartbreaking crime of stealing his new overcoat is committed. Akakii's world of socio-economic stratification has not changed much with the passing years. Although the income level in Petersburg, as in the rest of Russia, is rather low, the inequality in the distribution of income is substantial. Almost a full quarter of the Petersburg population lives in total destitution and more than 40 percent are below the poverty level.

[33] Guy Walton, *Louis XIV's Versailles*, Chicago: University of Chicago Press, Chapter 4 (1986).

King forbade the teaching of Descartes in the Sorbonne, but he was a devout Cartesian practitioner in his personal taste. Every little detail had to be planned in advance to ensure that rational order would prevail everywhere. Everything in Versailles is symmetrical. There is no tilting of emphasis to either direction. This was secured by entrusting all architectural decisions to committees of experts that were supervised by the King's Building Office. The committees consisted of qualified architects, but also of administrators with a good working understanding of architecture as well as of budgetary constraints, of the practical needs of the future residents of the palace, and of the current artistic idioms.[34] The king himself was part of this order *and did not stand above it.* In repudiation of any public-private divide that might have been preferred by some less devoted royalty, Louis situated his bedroom right next to the Hall of Mirrors – the most public *situs* in the whole palace, and the interior of his dining room was observable by all passersby.[35] Louis had primarily a royal Person, which was everyone's to share, rather than a private person belonging to him alone. His totally transparent reign transformed his famous uttering, *L'etat c'est moi*, into the opposite proposition, as if he said "there is only a State, not a personal statesman." By the same token, the personal needs of his own private person and his huge private family, consisting of his wife, numerous mistresses, legitimate and illegitimate children, grandchildren and great-grandchildren, the spouses of all these kinsmen, not to mention courtiers and ladies of attendance, were very well planned for and rationalized to a certain extent the large proportions of the structure. The palace also contained fragments of humanist messages, such as, for instance, the supremacy of humankind over nature, which was symbolized by the cultivated and carefully controlled gardens.[36] Its vast sculptural iconography, unlike its *Hermitage* counterpart, was entirely derived of its own endemic sources, and particularly of Ripa's *Iconographia*, which, as has been stressed before, served as an iconographic *lingua franca* across Europe of the late Baroque and the early Rococo. Although these external sculptures adorned the façade of the structure, an identical or similar décor was carried forward to the interior and formed the main architectural ornament from within.[37] With these considerations in mind, I maintain that the common denominator between Versailles and the Winter Palace is much eroded. Rastrelli's masterpiece is thus reduced, for all of its magnificence, to a parody of the real thing, and Versailles, for all of its megalomaniac pomp, is part and parcel of that real thing.

[34] Ibid., Chapter 2.
[35] Ibid., Chapter 3.
[36] Ibid.
[37] Ibid., Chapter 7.

5

Wealth

When money speaks, the truth is silent
Russian Proverb

Contract is a vehicle for the satisfaction of personal preferences. This is tautologically true of any form of exchange. The owner of an apple would not trade it for a pear, unless she values, at the margin, pears more than apples. The owner of the pear will refuse to satisfy the other person's craving for the pear, which she is invited to sacrifice, unless she values, at the margin, apples more than pears. The freedom to contract implies the liberty to eschew contract. If both parties choose to cooperate, and exchange (some parts of) their original endowments, they clearly manifest, by their overt choice, the Pareto superiority of exchange.[1] They are both better off with than without contracting. In sophisticated economies individual agents do not often exchange pears for apples (or lectures on Wittgenstein for a haircut; some barbers might be resistant to the offer). Exchange takes place through the intermediation of money. Agent A may be paid for her Wittgenstein scholarship and use (some of) her compensation to solicit agent B's consent to give her a haircut. The intensity of one's preferences can often be judged by the amount of money one is willing to spend for their procurement (or to forego for not parting with something that one already owns). To maximize one's utility, then, often entails maximizing one's wealth: The accumulation of money paves the way for the gratification of individual wants.

Now *executory* contracts vastly expand the opportunities for contracting. They import into the domain of exchange all things that do not even exist at the time of contracting (say, next year's crops), as well as all things that are not readily available for an instantaneous barter (an item that is not currently in stock). They provide incentives for the formation of novel species of wealth that would not have materialized without contracting (say, a research and development project). They promote saving (I will forego some part of my income today

[1] On the meaning of Pareto comparisons, see Chapter 3, supra.

to allow for greater spending and consumption tomorrow; for instance, I will invest my money in a pension plan). Saving promotes utility (as measured by money) because savers rank future consumption, at the margin, more than they value current consumption. Executory contracts encourage investment (I will buy some stocks and bonds and look forward to future returns; firms will use the money thus raised to purchase capital assets and to expand production and gain). A society without executory contracts is doomed to poverty. Given the connection between wealth and utility, a society without executory contracts is doomed to suffering and anguish. The main contention in this chapter is that Russian culture sharply differs from its Western counterpart in its attitude to both wealth and happiness. Whereas Western culture, especially since the Reformation, interpreted wealth as a value, Russian society underscored the virtues of poverty. Whereas Western culture set itself upon the course of utility maximization, Russian culture responded by the cult of suffering.

The first part of this chapter is about wealth and happiness in the West. It shows that whereas in the Middle Ages both the dominion of worldly possessions and the quest for personal bliss were viewed with a great deal of ambiguity, a slow process began during the Renaissance and the Reformation that changed all that. Unsurprisingly, this was the formative period for the consecration of contract in Western society. The second part of this chapter explores the parallel developments on Russian soil. It shows that although many individual Russians have always been bent on the accumulation of personal assets as well as on hedonistic consumption, success in these ventures has never been considered normatively "good," let alone morally desirable. Rather, a strong Russian ethos has always viewed the state of want, both material and psychological, as having a purifying effect on the spirit, and normatively praiseworthy as such. In the third and last part of this chapter I visit again the attempts that were made during the centuries to introduce contract (and the corporate form of conducting business) into the Russian scene and offer a partial[2] explanation for their dismal failure based on the negative Russian approach to both wealth and personal satisfaction.

The Western Scene

Many early Christian sources are very ambiguous when they refer to the accumulation of riches. For those who wish to interpret the New Testament as the Poor Man's password to paradise there is no shortage of authority. The best-known example is embedded in Christ's admonition that it's easier to squeeze a camel through the eye of a needle than to admit a wealthy person to paradise.[3]

---

[2] The full explanation does not rest on any given culture's attitude to wealth and happiness alone. It is grounded, rather, on the combined effect of *all* the cultural variables examined in this book. The more or less detailed analysis of the corporate scene is integrated into this chapter, because corporations are especially associated with the accumulation of personal wealth (for their founders and investors) and with capital formation (for the economy as a whole).

[3] See Matthew, 19, 24; Mark, 10, 25; Luke 18, 25.

"If any man would come after me," He preached, "let him deny himself and take up his cross and follow me."[4] In a way, Christ's preaching is unmistakably straightforward. The Eastern Orthodox Church has, in fact, interpreted these words in light of their literal meaning and has never changed course in its long and eventful history. It often teaches that taking up one's cross in the footsteps of Christ implies voluntary assumption of suffering and self-denial. Man is contaminated by the Original Sin; but poverty and anguish purify and provide the faithful with their only hope for salvation.[5]

Similar voices have often been raised in Western Catholicism. The Holy See has by and large refused to subscribe to these ideas,[6] but they were often followed by a variety of ascetic sects, as well as by the example set for the faithful by a long list of canonized sufferers. This tradition goes back to the early martyrs, who were prosecuted for their Christian faith by the heathen authorities; these early martyrs took up their passion, and suffered death, with a gay spirit, being assured that their temporal grief paves the way for their eternal salvation.[7] When Christianity gained the upper hand and became the official state religion, it faced the risk of losing the charismatic appeal bestowed upon it by the early saints; martyrdom was simply no longer needed to uphold the Truth against its heathen foes. This turn of events gave rise to *self-inflicted* asceticism. Voluntary forms of torment became accepted as independent spiritual *desiderata*, to be sought after for their own sake.[8] Some self-induced martyrs opted for extreme masochistic practices in the name of Christ.[9] Some sectarian orders, notably (but by no means only) the Franciscans, took up a voluntary regimen of poverty and suffering, although the authenticity of the *stigmata* suffered by

---

4 See Matthew, 16, 24; Mark, 8, 34; Luke, 9, 23.

5 For a modern-day guidance in this direction within the Russian Orthodox Church, see Bishop Innocent of Kamchatka and the Kurilian and Aleutian Islands, *Indication of the Way into the Kingdom of Heaven*, published by the Eastern Orthodox Foundation, Indiana, PA (the book is not dated; since Truth is dogmatically assumed to transcend time, the Western habit of dating objects with liturgical significance, such as icons, is not favored by the Eastern Church).

6 The greatest proponents of the doctrine of the poverty of Christ and of the apostles were the Franciscans, especially toward the end of the first quarter of the fourteenth century, during the great Papal Schism. They based their argument on scriptural and patristic texts; their political ambition was to oppose the accumulation of wealth by the Catholic Church. See Hervaeus Natalis, *The Poverty of Christ and the Apostles*, translated by John Jones, Toronto: Pontifical Institute of Mediaeval Studies (1998). Mainstream theologians, including St. Thomas Aquinas himself, repudiated the Franciscan point of view. See his *An Apology for the Religious Orders*, translated by J. Procter, London: Sands and Co. (1950). Not surprisingly, the affluent Catholic Church did not subscribe to the Franciscan point of view, and the Holy See, especially Pope John XXII from Avignon, ruled that the Franciscan doctrine was heretical (see his bull *cum inter nonnulos* from 1323).

7 See, for example, Joyce Salisbury, *Perpetua's Passion: The Death and Memory of a Young Roman Woman*, New York: Routledge (1997).

8 See Aviad Kleinberg, *Fra Ginepro's Leg of Pork, Christian Saints' Stories and Their Cultural Role*, New York: Routledge (2000, in Hebrew).

9 A famous example is the holy man Symeon Stylites, who chose to spend a lifetime on top of a pole, never washing his decaying flesh and forever suffering the most horrible forms of pain and deprivation. See Susan Ashbrook Harvey, *Asceticism and Society in Crisis: John of Ephesus and the Lives of the Eastern Saints*, Berkeley: University of California Press, pp. 15ff (1990).

St. Francis himself has always been taken by many Catholic believers with a healthy grain of salt.[10] St. Francis's followers who chose to take his teachings literally and led the life of suffering paupers may have not lost their claim to sainthood but were often regarded as holy fools.[11]

The New Testament, however, is a fairly long document, and what one chooses to find in it is largely in the eye of the beholder. If we move forward in the tunnel of time and station ourselves, say, in the Dutch Republic of the seventeenth century, that is, in the formative period of contract law and of commercial expansion and economic growth, we can easily discern that the gospels were searched, at that period, for the justification of totally different dogmatic principles. Figure 36, *Old Woman Reading*,[12] is a typical Dutch portrait of the 1630s perfectly executed by Gerard Dou.

The sitter is seen reading the nineteenth chapter of Luke, which tells the story of Jesus' entry to Jericho. The sitter's pious act of being engrossed in reading the Bible was considered as a passable pretext for painting human figures (graven images!) even during this stark iconoclastic spell in Dutch history.[13] Luke 19 tells the story of a tax collector called Zacchae'us who was short of stature and needed to climb a tree to gain a better view of Jesus' entry into the city. Jesus observed him and asked him to descend and host Him in his house. Zacchae'us joyfully rose to the challenge, revealing in the process that he was really a righteous man. Jesus' association with this man puzzled the Jericho townsfolk, because tax collectors were considered as collaborators with the enemy and corrupt. But Jesus said: "Today salvation has come to his house. . . . For the Son of Man came to seek and to save the lost."[14] How can a person whose profession immerses him in money be pure? How can he be righteous? Jesus addresses this issue by telling His audience (verses 12–26) the following parable:

12 He said therefore, "A nobleman went into a far country to receive a kingdom and then return. 13 Calling ten of his servants, he gave them ten pounds, and said to them, 'Trade with these till I come.' 14 But his citizens hated him and sent an embassy after him, saying, 'We do not want this man to reign over us.' 15 When he returned, having received the kingdom, he commanded these servants, to whom he had given the money, to be called to him, that he might know what they had gained by trading. 16 The first came before him, saying, 'Lord, your pound has made ten pounds more.' 17 And he

[10] See Chiara Frugoni, *Francesco e l'Invenzione Delle Stimmate: Una Storia Per Parole e Immagini Fino a Bonaventura e Giotto*, Torino: G. Einaudi (1993).

[11] A looming example is St. Francis's disciple, brother Ginepro, who was probably a real idiot and whose following of the Franciscan rhetoric bestowed on him an amazing glory of saintliness. See Giorgio Petrocchi (ed.), *La Vita di Frate Ginepro*, Bologna: Commissione Per i Testi di Lingua (1960).

[12] Dou's portrait is often referred to also as "Rembrandt's mother."

[13] See Mariët Westermann, *A Worldly Art: The Dutch Republic 1585-1718*, London: Weidenfeld and Nicolson, p. 47 (1996). Obviously, the history of Dutch painting in the seventeenth century went through several more lenient phases as well, in which the graphical representation of human figures did not meet with hostility and suspicion. See, for example, the numerous wonderful portraits of Pieter de Hooch, who did not need any Biblical pretexts for executing his portraits.

[14] Luke 19, 9–10.

FIGURE 36. Gerard Dou, *Old Woman Reading*, 1630–40.

said to him, 'Well done, good servant! Because you have been faithful in a very little, you shall have authority over ten cities.' 18 And the second came, saying, 'Lord, your pound has made five pounds.' 19 And he said to him, 'And you are to be over five cities.' 20 Then another came, saying, 'Lord, here is your pound, which I kept laid away in a napkin; 21 for I was afraid of you, because you are a severe man; you take up what you did not lay down, and reap what you did not sow.' 22 He said to him, 'I will condemn you out of your own mouth, you wicked servant! You knew that I was a severe man, taking up what I did not lay down and reaping what I did not sow? 23 Why then did you not put my money into the bank, and at my coming I should have collected it with interest?' 24 And he said to those who stood by, 'Take the pound from him, and give it to him who has the ten pounds.' 25 (And they said to him, 'Lord, he has ten pounds!')

26 'I tell you, that to every one who has will more be given; but from him who has not, even what he has will be taken away."

Gerard Dou's sitter seems to have internalized Christ's lesson quite successfully. She is sumptuously attired in expensive, yet comfortable garments. Her collar is adorned with a precious stone and her head is snugly encased in a fluffy fur hat. Yet there is nothing vain about her. In spite of her obvious material success, she seems to be seriously interested in the otherworldly morals of Christ's teachings. Her wrinkled hand suggests that she does not shun manual labor and her deeply lined forehead implies spiritual alertness. For this pleasantly pensive lady, wealth is a wholesome thing and she has every intention of using it for worthy purposes.

In the mainstream, nonascetic Catholic world, the quest for material possessions both preceded the Renaissance and the Reformation and survived them. The Catholic attitude to the dominion of worldly goods differed from the Protestant approach because people were delighted with their riches and did not feel either anxiety or guilt if they allowed themselves to show them off or to consume them with pleasure and abandon. Figure 37 is the celebrated *Arnolfini Marriage (Giovanni Arnolfini and his Wife Giovanna Cenami)* executed in 1434 by the Flemish master Jan Van Eyck.

This double portrait is endlessly enigmatic, as has been often recognized in the literature.[15] Some chose to interpret this portrait as a symbol of a harmonious union between husband and wife, basing their assertion on such symbols as the little dog (fidelity), the single burning candle (the union of the two spouses; or God's all-seeing eye; or an icon of St. Margaret, the patron saint of women giving birth), the bed (intimacy), or the slippers (domestic tranquility). This sweet interpretation strikes me as totally romanticized. Following Lisa Jardine, I see in this portrait not a true couple, but only one person, Giovanni Arnolfini. Giovanni, a rich Italian merchant and apparently a personal friend of the artist who came to the Netherlands on a business mission, is the only realistically portrayed person on this canvass. His bride, Giovanna Cenami, looks like a porcelain figurine, featuring prototypical traits of a young and beautiful lady, but not any distinguishing characteristics of her own. It is easy to see that her presence is totally "commodified" and is proudly marshaled alongside the other expensive commodities – the brass chandelier; the precious fabrics, clothes, linen, and curtains; the exquisite little dog; the comfortable dwelling – all belonging, as it were, to him who is the master of this small universe, the merchant Giovanni Arnolfini. Giovanni is not looking at his bride, any more than he is looking at any of his other possessions. He is staring right at the beholder, showing off the consequences of his lucrative trade, and thus claiming for himself his rightful place as the sole speaker in this pictorial

[15] See Edwin Hall, *The Arnolfini Betrothal: Medieval Marriage and the Enigma of Van Eyck's Double Portrait*, Berkeley: University of California Press (1997). For more general modern scholarship on Van Eyck, which puts the *Arnolfini Marriage* in a broader context, see Craig Harbison, *Jan Van Eyck: The Play of Realism*, London: Reaktion Books (1997).

FIGURE 37. Jan Van Eyck, *Giovanni Arnolfini and His Wife Giovanna Cenami*, 1434.

narrative. The left hand outstretched by Giovanni to his bride is not offered in recognition of their union, but is rather pointing to one of his most precious possessions, his porcelain bride,[16] as is also evidenced by the invitation to pay

---

[16] This commodification of women is often present in other famous Renaissance double portraits. For example, Piero della Francesca executed around 1465 an astounding double portrait of the rulers of Urbino, Duke Federico da Montefeltro, who was robust, brownish and realistic, featuring a broken warrior's nose, moles, and blemishes on his skin and a majestic air, and his spouse, Duchess Battista Sforza, featuring her expensive jewels, her elaborate hairdo, and total

attention performed by his raised right hand. Giovanni's delight in his worldly possessions is loud, vulgar, and clear.[17]

Most Catholic and Protestant European nations had, in the course of modern history, their economic ups and downs, but in the long run they both made enormous progress on the road to prosperity; most Western Christian societies developed capitalistic cultures fully compatible with their high regard for the accumulation of material goods. But it is commonly believed that *Protestant* communities were much ahead of everyone else in this race for riches and were more instrumental in the fashioning of a commercial ethos and the development of a contractual civilization. What might be the explanation for this historical observation?

In my opinion, the single most powerful rationalization was suggested a full century ago by Max Weber in two seminal papers[18] published around 1905, and later in countless editions in book form.[19] It holds in one sentence (a fuller exposition follows) that the spirit of capitalism sprouted out of Calvinist theology. It came to be known as the "Max Weber Hypothesis." The hypothesis was explored from all possible vantage points,[20] often

lack of character. In this case, too, it is easy to come to the conclusion that the duchess's expensive gear and jewelry, along with her own person, are marshaled by Piero as a demonstration to the viewer of Federico's good material luck.

[17] Lisa Jardine, *Worldly Goods: A New History of the Renaissance*, Glasgow: HarperCollins, p. 14 (1996). The romanticized interpretation of the Arnolfini narrative is attributable to a large extent to the influential work of Erwin Panofsky, who read the whole picture as describing the sacrament of marriage. Panofsky underscored Van Eyck's innovation in fusing sacred art and profane art by setting this sacrament, as it were, within the domestic milieu of a bedroom. In his reading of the *Arnolfini Marriage*, the outstretched left hand stands for the *fides manualis* of the parties to this sacrament, and the raised right hand stands for the *fides levata*, both derived from Catholic nuptial dogma. Panofsky explains away the unusual locale – a private bedroom – for holding this ceremony by invoking the early Catholic doctrine that the sacrament of marriage (unlike all other sacraments) did not depend for its validity on priestly intermediation and could be contracted in the intimate presence of the bride and bridegroom alone. See Erwin Panofsky, *Early Netherlandish Painting*, Volume 1, New York: Icons Editions, Harper and Row Publishers, pp. 202ff (1971; the book first saw the light of day in 1953). I find it difficult to accept this interpretation not only because I read Giovanni's whole attitude as addressing some invisible audience (presumably, the viewers of the picture) and introducing to it the evidence of his material success. In addition, it is very clear that the couple was not alone in this picture; the artist was also present in the room, as is evidenced both by the express inscription *Johannes de Eyck fuit hic* – Jan Van Eyck was here – and by his reflection, along with that of another unnamed person, in the convex mirror facing the entrance to the room.

[18] Weber expanded his thesis in a number of other seminal publications. For an overview of his entire opus, see Anthony Giddens, *Capitalism and Modern Social Theory, an Analysis of Marx, Durkheim and Max Weber*, New York: Cambridge University Press (1971).

[19] A good translation is Max Weber, *The Protestant Ethic and the Spirit of Capitalism*, translated by Talcott Parsons, London: Unwin Hyman (1930).

[20] Some of the most recent reevaluations of Weber's thesis include: Malcolm MacKinnon, "Part I: Calvinism and the Infallible Assurance of Grace: The Weber Thesis Reconsidered" and "Part II: Weber's Exploration of Calvinism: The Undiscovered Provenance of Capitalism," *British Journal of Sociology* 29:1 (1989); Hartmut Lehman and Guenther Roth (eds.), *Weber's Protestant Ethic: Origins, Evidence, Contexts*, New York: Cambridge University Press (1985); Stanley

exalted,[21] and sometimes dissented from and even ridiculed.[22] With hindsight, most of us recognize some of its possible lapses of judgment, its pronounced Eurocentricity, and its commitment to the idiom of his days. Its very fame made it somewhat hackneyed to deal with, much like hanging a reproduction of Van Gogh's *Sunflowers* in someone's living room or listening to Beethoven's *Symphony Number 9*. With this said, it is impossible to proceed with this chapter's business without scrutinizing the Max Weber Hypothesis.

Max Weber's *Protestant Ethic* is crafted to solve a puzzle: how to explain the fact that in lands with a mixed Protestant and non-Protestant population, most of the wealth is concentrated in Protestant hands, and, more generally, Protestant countries tend to be wealthier than countries dominated by other religious groups. A related question is how to explain the fact that Protestant congregations were historically quicker to adopt a capitalistic way of life, or to adapt to it if imported from the outside.[23]

The *Protestant Ethic* draws attention to a few theological doctrines that informed the spiritual teachings of Martin Luther and, much more significantly, of John Calvin and his followers. The Protestant world, unlike its Catholic counterpart, is not a hierarchical formation leading from God to the Holy See to a variety of cardinals, bishops, and priests and then all the way down to the common folks. It is rather a horizontal structure, where each person is responsible before God for her own actions, unmediated by lord or vicar.[24]

Engerman, "Max Weber as Economist and Economic Historian," in Stephen Turner (ed.), *Cambridge Companion to Weber*, Cambridge: Cambridge University Press (2000).

[21] An erudite enthusiastic supporter is, e.g., David Little in his excellent volume, *Religion Order and Law*, New York: Harper & Row (1969).

[22] See, for example, H. R. Trevor-Roper, "Religion, the Reformation and Social Change," in G. A. Hayes-McCoy (ed.), *Historical Studies, IV: Papers Read Before the Fifth Irish Conference of Historians*, London: Bowes and Bowes, p. 18 (1963) (alleging that Calvinism could not have generated the spirit of capitalism, because the industrial revolution preceded Calvin); André Biéler, *La Pensée Économique et Sociale de Calvin*, Genève: Librairie de l'université, p. 493 (1959) (denying the connection between the original Calvinist theology and the theology of the affluent capitalistic centers of Northern Europe and North America); Michael Walzer, *Revolution of the Saints*, New York: Aetheneum Press (1971; originally published in 1965) (stressing the oppressive nature of the Puritan way of life and doubting its ability to generate the spirit of free markets).

[23] It ought to be apparent on the threshold that the empirical foundations of the Protestant Ethic can be justified only *grosso modo*, as some important Catholic centers, e.g., in Florence or in Flanders, evolved very early on as important capitalistic hubs in Renaissance Europe. Nevertheless, the empirical foundations of Weber's views are largely supported by the relative wealth of Calvinist centers in England, Scotland, France, Germany, Holland, Switzerland, and even Poland and Hungary, as well as of course among the different Puritan sects in America. More on Catholic capitalism is said in this chapter, infra. The question of Jewish capitalism is deliberately glossed over, because Jewish tradesmen were historically *forced* to join the entrepreneurial professions, given the ban imposed on their participation in many other trades. More materials on the constrained choice of Jewish tradesmen within the Russian context are offered in the following pages as well.

[24] This "horizontal structure" of human society was a central tenet of Luther's teachings right from the start. Thus, in an early document, "An Appeal to the Ruling Class of German Nationality as

All humans are equally important in God's eyes. Providence "calls" upon each and every one of us to live in Christ in accordance with our respective, and diverse, powers and abilities. This "doctrine of the calling" finds its scriptural foundations in the teachings of St. Paul himself, who held that:

Every one should remain in the state in which he was called. Were you a slave when called? Never mind.... For he who was called in the Lord as a slave is a freedman of the Lord. Likewise he who was free when called is a slave of Christ.[25]

Indeed, unlike Catholicism, which placed St. Peter on center stage among all the apostles, Protestantism favored St. Paul. It deduced from his teachings that each person is subject to a direct, unmediated, religious obligation to be attentive to the role assigned to her by Divine Providence, and to fulfill her calling conscientiously.[26] The doctrine of the calling was instrumental in christening everyday life. The performance of a person's calling (milking one's cows, trading in one's goods) thus became a *religious* obligation, acting in the service of Christ and for His eternal glory.

According to Catholic dogma, if a person lives the life of the righteous (in Protestant terms, is conscientiously obedient in her calling), she may look forward to being rewarded in the afterlife and inherit eternal bliss. Even sinners,

to the Amelioration of the State of Christendom," translated by Bertram Lee Woolf, reprinted in *Luther, Selections from His Writings*, edited by John Dillenberger, Garden City, NY: Anchor Press (1961), where Luther calls for the reform of the church, he writes (at pp. 403ff): "When under the threat of a secular force, [the Romanists] have stood firm and declared that secular force had no jurisdiction over them, rather the opposite was the case, and the spiritual was superior to the secular.... May God help us, and give us one of these trumpets with which the walls of Jericho were overthrown ... and set free the Christian, corrective measures to punish sin, and to bring the devil's deceits and wiles to the light of day.... [A]ll Christians whatsoever really and truly belong to the same religious class and there is no difference among them except in so far as they do different work. That is St. Paul's meaning, in 1 Corinthians 12 when he says: 'We are all one body, yet each member hath his own work for serving others.' ... Those who exercise secular authority have been baptized like the rest of us, and have the same faith and the same gospel; therefore we must admit that they are all priests and bishops." Luther's horizontal universe also makes itself evident in his famed "two kingdoms" theology. According to this theological principle, all Christians are full citizens of two kingdoms, the temporal earthly kingdom and the eternal or heavenly one. The temporal kingdom is ruled by reason and law, and is subject to human magistrates who administer their own system of temporal justice. The heavenly kingdom is ruled by love and grace, where the faithful are free to be guided only by their conscience. The division of the universe into two parallel kingdoms ended for its practitioners the hierarchical, secure, and mystical worldview of the Catholic faith and thrust the world unto an entirely new course. See John Witte, *Law and Protestantism*, New York: Cambridge University Press, pp. 5ff (2002).

[25] 1 Corinthians 7, 20–22.

[26] The political implications of this "horizontal" worldview were clearly reflected in the civic governance of Calvin's model city of God, Geneva. It was not ruled by either prince or vicar. Although it was clearly dominated by the clergy, the clergy exercised its authority through the ministry of a Presbytery consisting of both religious pastors and lay leaders. From the start, it created an easy coalition between celestial and worldly concerns and was strongly supported by the local merchants and entrepreneurs.

who might otherwise burn in hell, have the chance to atone for their transgressions and by true repentance, and then confession and absolution (and, alas, an elaborate set of indulgences), change their own destiny and go to paradise instead. The Protestant movement rejected this hypothesis. Rather, it created its unique "doctrine of predestination." This doctrine holds that a person's faith is sealed before she was born, and was fixed from the first day of Creation. This doctrinal divorce, between a person's "good works" and her eventual salvation, was also based on the teachings of St. Paul. Both Luther and Calvin relied on the apostle's teachings in Romans, 9, 10–20, where it says:

> When Rebecca had conceived children by one man, our forefather Isaac, though they were not yet born and had done nothing either good or bad, in order that God's purpose of election might continue, not because of works but because of his call, she was told, "The elder will serve the younger." As it is written, "Jacob I loved, but Esau I hated." What shall we say then? Is there injustice on God's part? By no means! For he says to Moses, "I will have mercy on whom I have mercy, and I will have compassion on whom I have compassion." So it depends not upon man's will or exertion, but upon God's mercy.... You will say to me then, "Why does he still find fault? For who can resist his will?" But who are you, a man, to answer back to God? Will what is molded say to its molder, "Why have you made me thus?"

In Lutheran theology, the doctrine of predestination coupled with the obligation of every Christian to accept her calling abruptly ended the notion that deliberate poverty could have an improving effect on the spirit. Voluntary idleness was nothing more than an act of simple shirking. It was a sin, not a virtue. Nor could the act of assisting the poor (or supporting mendicancy) advance the interests of the giver, or her chances of salvation: Her fate was sealed and could not be altered by works.[27]

Calvin gave the doctrine of predestination an even greater emphasis. In his main theological *opus*, the *Institutes*,[28] he writes:

> God has once for all determined whom He would admit to salvation and whom He would condemn to destruction. We affirm that this counsel, as far as concerns the elect, is founded on His gratuitous mercy, totally irrespective of human merit.[29]

Consequently, there is no purgatory in Calvin's theology. Punishment is eternal. There is no useful purpose to be served by praying for the dead. One of the strengths of this doctrine lies in its fierce logic. It emanates in a straightforward fashion from the more basic dogma of God's eternal perfection (which one is invited to accept axiomatically); if we assumed that God's judgment could be modified by human will or by good works, it would not have been compatible with His immutable flawlessness. What is perfect cannot be changed and

---

[27] See John Witte, *Law and Protestantism*, New York: Cambridge University Press, pp. 20ff (2002).

[28] Calvin's *Christianae Religionis Institutio* saw the light of day in 1536, was often revised and then was published in the vernacular by Calvin himself in 1541. References to this magnum opus are usually made to this edition.

[29] *Institutes*, II, pp. xxi, 7.

retain its former splendor. It is that simple. In spite of its logic, the doctrine of predestination is chillingly frightening. It holds that only the elect few can look forward to salvation, whereas the vast multitudes of the human race are predestined to perdition. Moreover, each person must face his horrible destiny alone, and *there is nothing, absolutely nothing, that he can do about it.* He cannot change it by good works. He cannot be assisted by priest or vicar. Even Christ died not for him but for the elected few.[30] It casts the individual in a lonely role, where no one can come to her rescue. But here is the worst part: There is nothing, absolutely nothing, that a person can do to find out if she was predestined to salvation, as only a handful of individuals have been, or doomed to eternal suffering, as is the lot of the vast majority of the human race. The congregations of Calvinist saints were thus doomed to a life of anxiety, compulsion, and terror.

I am inclined to think that Calvin chose to hold his followers *in terrorem*, because he himself was a haunted person, held in terror by his numerous and severe anxieties. For him, a life of anxiety was not a sanction imposed on someone, but a simple mirror of an appalling reality. He was an honest man, who was committed to telling only those narratives in which he genuinely believed. Thus, Calvin was terrorized by the natural elements (e.g., thunder, stormy seas, which made him shudder with fear). He thought that water was lighter than other materials and had a natural inclination to submerge the earth. It was miraculously kept in check by God's will, but could, and perhaps would, at any moment, flood the earth, because there was no reason for God to hold on and not change His mind, thereby drowning all of His miserable creatures in one instant. Calvin equally distrusted human conduct, as being conducive to disorder, in his vocabulary synonymous with sin. "We throw heaven and earth into confusion by our sins," he wrote, "for if we were rightly disposed to obey God, all the elements would certainly serve us, and we would discern an almost angelic harmony in the world."[31] Calvin abhorred mixtures. His opposition to the papacy lay mainly in his understanding that it mixed earthly and heavenly matters. His love for order and loathing of mixtures prompted in him a necessity to see clearly the boundaries between opposites. Everything in life had to be bounded. God himself created these boundaries (e.g., geographical boundaries between nations) and mortals had to accept those boundaries as His divine ordination. His craving for boundaries also generated in him intolerance for one gender taking on activities, or modes of behavior, that were bounded or ordained, as it were, for the other. Clear boundaries had to be established between light and darkness, the "community" and the "other," right and wrong.[32] His desire to incorporate everything in his theology was

---

[30] Weber makes this point very clear in Chapter 4 of his *Protestant Ethic*.

[31] See William Bouwsma, *John Calvin, a Sixteenth Century Portrait*, New York: Oxford University Press, p. 34 (1988).

[32] Many commentators make the point that the clear line of demarcation implied in Calvinist theology between right and wrong laid the foundations for the modern concept of the Rule of

motivated by a desire to exercise control on that which otherwise might be out of bounds. This also gave rise to the neat division of humankind to the saved and the damned, where no trespassing was ever permitted to the residents of either domain.[33]

That was John Calvin the man. But among the latter Calvinists, he was merely a *primus inter pares*. That was true in his own days, and *a fortiori* in later generations, in Europe and America, when the memory of his strong personality faded into partial oblivion. For his common followers, ordinary people of all walks of life, Calvin's prescription of a lifetime of anxiety, with no possible hint of salvation or damnation, was too much to bear: *They wanted to know*. To attain this goal, only a small modification to Calvin's original doctrine of predestination was necessary. According to this slightly modified holding, one had to be sure of one's salvation. Not being sure was considered, according to this modified doctrine, as lack of faith, in itself a clear evidence of damnation. Thus, material success, that is, *successful* attempts to aggrandize God's creation, came to be regarded as an omen of divine grace ("doctrine of proof"). To alleviate one's theological anxieties and obtain this premonition of grace, as well as to protect the faith, one had to immerse oneself in worldly affairs. Those who succeeded in rationalizing the universe (giving it clear boundaries) and in making it more pleasantly affluent stood a chance of attaining an *unio mystica* with God, so working hard to increase the glory of God could give its practitioners

Law. See David Little, *Religion Order and Law*, New York: Harper & Row, pp. 167ff (1969). Little pays a lot of attention to Sir Edward Coke, the main champion of the Common Law. Coke was born in 1552 and educated at Trinity College, Cambridge, at a time when the Anglican-Puritan ferment was at its height. Although he never abandoned the Anglican faith, he was sympathetic to Puritan ideas and in due course defended their cause *ex officio*. The single most important ideological divide between sixteenth- and seventeenth-century Anglicans and Puritans was embedded in their different theology of order. For the Anglicans, order descended from the Crown and was hierarchical and authoritative. For the Puritans, since each person was bound by his calling, which descended directly from God, all human beings were ordered horizontally, which gave rise to the Rule of Law and to the recognition of rights. Coke was appointed as the Chief Justice of the Common Pleas in 1606 and as Chief Justice of the King's Bench in 1613 until his dismissal in 1616 by his arch rival, James I. But he continued to carry on his defense of the Common Law in Parliament and was more influential than anyone in establishing its supremacy over all human, including royal, prerogative. He was not a learned man. He was a master of the Common Law and maintained that every legal question could be resolved by a methodical application of existing precedents. Thus, paradoxically, he employed ancient precedents in his quest for innovation, the subordination of prerogative to the general law of the realm. The prerogative of the Crown developed from the times of Edward I, as the feudal system started to collapse in the thirteenth century, and the Crown managed to fill the void by strengthening its own position. Parliament, in these early days, acted as sort of a legal tribunal, where the peers and commons were the king's servants, although the king's power did not extend to confiscation of private property without Parliamentary consent. Although Coke was a loyal subject and recognized, in principle, the existence of royal prerogative, he had a unified view of the law such that it was all incorporated in the Common Law. He liked to cite Bracton, who said that "*quo Rex non debet esse sub homine sed sub deo et lege.*" It was this kind of rhetoric that caused James I to dismiss Coke in 1616.

[33] Bouwsma, ibid.

their desired *certitudo salutis*, or the assurance of one's salvation. In practice, this meant that God helps those who help themselves. The faithful do not toil *in order* to gain salvation, but simply to be sure of it, that is, to destroy their anxieties.[34] The Lutherans, never too generous in their interpretation of Calvinist doctrine, accused the Reformed Church of introducing salvation by good works as a practical doctrine through the rear door. But it must be stressed in the Calvinists' defense that theirs was an entirely different brand of good works. For the Catholics, each action could be judged separately. Man could attain salvation in spite of sin, through repentance, confession, and absolution. These mechanisms were lacking in Calvinism. One had to do his good works absolutely, at all times, and with no respite. One's works had to be methodical (the insistence on methodical commitment gave rise, in time, to the emergence of the Methodist Church). The faithful were supposed to be serving God's glory, rather than toiling in their own narrower interests. This gave rise to one more doctrine, holding that the accumulation of riches could safely be interpreted as an omen of divine grace, *but the resulting material possessions could not be used for pleasures of the flesh*, that is, for the personal consumption of their owners. The faithful had to maintain a frugal, ascetic way of life. Only thus could they attain assurance that all their good works were performed in Christ, and not for their own personal gratification.[35] In this respect, there is a marked difference between the attitude of the Calvinist world to worldly riches and that of the Catholic Renaissance. In the latter case, people were not only permitted, but also socially encouraged to amass wealth for consumption as well as for conspicuous display.[36] Calvinists, on the other hand, acquired possessions in their calling and reinvested them to generate more possessions.[37] True, some

---

[34] Some commentators differ. In his elegantly written primer, Ronald Bainton maintains that the people of the Reformation, especially in its early phases of the sixteenth century, worked hard out of religious sentiment (wishing to create a holier place to live) and not out of fear of damnation or because of a psychological need to obtain the proof. Their rate of saving (the portion of their income not used for consumption) was so high because their strong commitment to otherworldly affairs made them disinterested in the frivolities of everyday existence. See Ronald Bainton, *The Reformation of the Sixteenth Century*, Boston: Beacon Press, Chapter 13 (1952).

[35] In this respect Calvinism departed from the old humanist tradition that put human needs (including spiritual needs, to be sure) at the center of the universe (see Chapter Two, supra). It is hardly surprising that the greatest humanists of the period, e.g., Erasmus of Rotterdam and Thomas More of England, refused to abandon the good old Catholic faith. By dampening the enthusiasm for humanist ideas, Calvinism could not have done a great service to the development of a contractual culture. But this effect cannot be studied in isolation. Besides its direct impact on the attitude toward wealth, Calvinism was instrumental in the development of individualism, rationality, and a great drive for the domination of a "word" culture over an "image" culture. For the impact of these notions on the development of contractual ideas see, respectively, Chapters 2, 6, and 7. When traditional Calvinism eventually shed its resistance to hedonistic principles (see in this chapter, infra), the victory of contract was complete.

[36] See Lisa Jardine, *Worldly Goods, a New History of the Renaissance*, New York: Nan A. Talese (1996).

[37] For a modern critique of this set of beliefs, see Jeanne Schroeder, "The Midas Touch: The Lethal Effect of Wealth Maximization," *Wisconsin Law Review* 687 (1999). Schroeder makes

Catholics opted, just like them, for an ascetic way of life. But Catholic asceticism, when it transpired, was of a totally different feather. It actually meant to totally sever one's ties with all worldly affairs, perhaps to withdraw to the desert or to a remote monastery (or to live on a pole). Calvinism chose the opposite path, that of personal modesty combined with a deep involvement in the real world and its activities. In Catholicism the ascetic way of life was reserved for monks and holy recluses, who thus removed themselves from the humdrum of "normal" society. In Calvinism, asceticism became a way of life for the masses, and thus became strongly intertwined with economic activities and with the emergence of flourishing markets.[38]

With this last sentence the Weberian puzzle can be put to rest. If a community dedicates itself to hard work and is driven to accumulate riches on pain of damnation, but once accumulated these riches must not be spent in vain, a solid base is laid for capital formation and, indeed, for a thriving capitalistic society. In my mind, it also draws a sharp line of demarcation between the Protestant societies of the West and the pseudo-capitalistic ventures that are being pursued in Russia today. The Calvinist spirit, although fraught with anxiety, compulsion, and fear, is also graced by a silver lining of deep morality, and a surplus element of contractual lineage that differentiates the free market both from the state of nature[39] and from an unscrupulous race for the accumulation of riches, Russian style. Capitalistic societies endowed with this kind of ethical behavior grow into democracies. Without it, they become mere "kleptocracies."[40]

The connection between Protestant ethics and the institution of contract was made evident right from the start. Even in Lutheran theology there is great emphasis on the need of the citizenry to adopt a covenant, a social contract, to liberate humankind from the vicissitudes of the State of Nature, to uphold

the cogent point that the accumulation of wealth without a psychological license to enjoy it is self-defeating, because wealth (Midas' gold) lacks an independent value of its own. Schroeder's critique is mainly directed at secular thinkers (e.g., Richard Posner in his celebrated 1979 article, "Utilitarianism, Economics and Legal Theory," *Journal of Legal Studies* 8:103) for whom the accumulation of wealth does not have a (conscious) theological significance. I think her analysis is inapposite in the original Calvinist context, because for Calvinists the accumulation of wealth generates *certitudo salutis*, which is in itself a valuable good of consumption.

[38] Max Weber, ibid., Chapter 4.

[39] The essential role of contract (not "*social* contract"; just "contract") as a defining element in a civic society, an element that is indispensable for substituting it for the state of nature, was fully recognized by Hobbes. See Thomas Hobbes, *Leviathan*, edited by Edwin Curley, Indianapolis, IN: Hackett Publishing, Chapter XV, Section 5 (1999; the first Latin edition was published in 1668). In the following section, Section 6, Hobbes writes: "As for the instance of gaining the secure and perpetual felicity of heaven by any way, it is frivolous, there being but one way imaginable, and that is not breaking, but keeping of covenant."

[40] The terms "kleptocrats" and "kleptocracy" came into common usage in post-Communist Russia. A "kleptocrat" is a member of the new commercial elite, with wide-ranging connections with both licit business endeavors, usually on a very large scale, and with organized crime (the Russian Mafia). On the corrupting effect of kleptocratic hegemony in modern Russia, see Bernard Black, Reinier Kraakman, and Anna Tarassova, "Russian Privatization and Corporate Governance: What Went Wrong?," *Stanford Law Review* 52:1731 (2000).

the Rule of Law, and to lay the foundations for the keeping of promises.[41] This juridical proclivity was even more obvious in Calvin's grim City of God. To fortify the bond between the citizenry of Geneva and their faith, Calvin mandated all citizens in 1537 to make a public confession of the faith, thereby committing their souls, by conscious choice, to uphold it. Although Calvin hardly tolerated any dissent and had the means of forcing his will on the citizenry by sheer fiat, he chose to cement this bond by consent. He thereby laid the foundations for the idea that the source of authority was not prerogative but conscience, individually carved out of a willing spirit. The mirror image of the same proposition is that authority is precluded from exercising its prerogative unconscionably, and if it attempts to do so, it gives rise to a licit liberty of the subjects to resist it. This revolutionary idea has some (feeble, in my mind) basis in the Scriptures,[42] but at any rate was strongly advocated by the first generation of Calvin's disciples.[43] Eventually, these ideas gave rise to the notion that not only licit authority is grounded in contract, but also that contract itself must find its justification in the will, or consent, of the parties, rather than in the whim of a sovereign. A lucid example concerns a seemingly technical question – the appropriate procedure for the formation of companies. In the Middle Ages, corporations could be founded only by royal charters or other forms of "concessions" granted by the source of temporal or spiritual power (hence, the so-called "concessionist" approach to incorporation). In modern times, corporations are formed by consent of the founders, where the state's role in the process of incorporation is limited to technical *minutiae* and public officials are precluded from using their discretion to bar lawful attempts to form companies. Since every corporation is basically a *nexus* of contracts among its various constituencies (e.g., shareholders, managers, creditors, or employees), selecting the procedure of incorporation, by concession or by consent, reflects the attitude of a given society to the role of contract within the body politick.

---

[41] These ideas were explicitly taught at the Marburg jurisprudential circle, around the middle of the sixteenth century, especially thanks to its founder and greatest contributor, Johannes Eisermann (1485–1558). On Eisermann's legal philosophy as an early Lutheran social contractarian, see John Witte, *Law and Protestantism*, New York: Cambridge University Press, pp. 140ff (2002).

[42] See Romans, 13, 5, where it says: "Therefore one must be subject, not only to avoid God's wrath but also for the sake of conscience," from whence it could be deduced that the obligation of subjects to obey their magistrates is constrained by their obligation to listen to their own conscience.

[43] First and foremost among them is Theodore Beza, who thus became one of the first spokesmen in modern history to advocate civil disobedience on appropriate occasions. See Theodore Beza, *Concerning the Rights of Rulers Over Their Subjects and the Duty of Subjects Towards Their Rulers*, translated by Henri-Louis Gonin, Cape Town: H.A.U.M. (1956; original edition published in 1574). Beza's bold ideas were no doubt formulated, *inter alia*, as an emotional response to the massacre of French Huguenots on Saint Bartholomew's Day in 1572. But the same idea took root and appeared, again and again, in Calvinist centers everywhere, e.g., in a work by George Buchanan about the rights of the crown of Scotland, published in 1579, and in a much later theoretical work by Samuel Rutherford about royal prerogative, published in 1644.

FIGURE 38. Adriaen Van Ostade, *The Alchemist's Shop*, 1661.

Autocracies are inclined to favor the concessionist approach; democracies opt for contract. When Calvinist ideas started to proliferate, it sounded the death knell for the concessionist approach to incorporation. When Sir Edward Coke was appointed as Chief Justice of the King's Bench in 1613, one of his principal campaigns against the prerogative of the Crown was to divest the Crown of its exclusive power to license companies by royal charter and to allow incorporation by consent. Ironically, Coke was not even a Puritan, although he was rightly hailed as a liberal defender of the Puritan cause.[44]

An iconographic summary of the *Protestant Ethic* can be found in a common theme, an alchemist's shop, as painted by Reformed artists. Figure 38, executed by the eminent artist Adriaen Van Ostade in 1661, depicts the owner of this notably ungainful occupation, the alchemist, as a clear imbecile toiling in vain for no redeeming purpose. His untidy surroundings (in Calvinist terms, there are no "boundaries" there) suggest the unsmiling response of Providence to his lack of productivity, the consequences of which are also visited upon his dependents. A prematurely elderly woman, presumably his wife, is injuring her eyesight doing needlework in a darkened corner of their den, and a chubby child, perhaps a mongoloid, is eating off the floor a chunk of unsightly matter.[45]

---

[44] David Little, *Religion Order and Law*, New York: Harper & Row, pp. 189ff. See also note 26, supra.

[45] It is rather clear that the alchemist's stupidity does not consist of his failure to generate goods for his own consumption, but rather of his failure to generate wealth for a redeeming purpose. This distinction is made evident when we examine another common theme of seventeenth-century Netherlandish art, *vanitas*. *Vanitas* is a still life, filled with items alluding to the transient nature of human existence, such as skeletal parts, hour glasses, crystal balls, and decaying

FIGURE 39. Gabriel Metsu, *Vegetable Market in Amsterdam*, early 1660s.

Contrast Van Ostade's painting with an equally distinguished canvass, *Vegetable Market in Amsterdam* (Figure 39), executed by Gabriel Metsu in the early 1660s. In this painting, every person is engaged as a participant, or a potential participant, in some market transaction. At the forefront of the painting, Metsu displays the produce itself, the subject matter of contractual dealings, with a particular emphasis on vegetables (such as cauliflower), which were considered expensive delicacies in that period. The human figures move about the pictorial space with an air of natural dignity; everyone is well fed and adequately

fruit. Yet they are also filled with precious possessions like golden goblets and fine jewelry. The combined message of the *vanitas* theme alludes to the desire to amass worldly possessions, coupled with a disdain for treating them as goods of consumption. Thus, in Pieter Claesz's *Vanitas*, the viewer is invited to appreciate, simultaneously, the preciousness of the golden goblet at the center of the image, but also its uselessness as a vehicle for hedonistic pursuits.

(but not lavishly) dressed, exuding a sense of civic pride and contentment. This market activity is made possible by the system of canals (visible in the middle distance) connecting the Dutch communities *inter se* and the Dutch Republic with its expanding trade routes and global overseas interests. A quietly elegant structure at the background attests to the freshly discovered urbane culture of an economic, free-market empire on the rise.[46]

Sometime during the seventeenth century a major transformation started to take shape in the Protestant lands of the West. The earlier Calvinist spirit of anxiety, frugality, and asceticism matured into a mellower form of wealth seeking, in which the acquisition of worldly goods was attended by a growing awareness of the pleasure of acquisitions and by a nascent ethos of a hedonistic culture. How did this change come about? Clearly, there is no single "correct" answer to this question, although, one is inclined to believe, there can be very little dispute that the transformation actually transpired.

Calvinist Protestantism started out as the most invasive, wide-ranging regimentation of each believer's life. In Calvin's Geneva, frivolous, gay, or immodest modes of behavior were strictly censured. Discipline was everything (again, every move had to be "bounded" within the rules).[47] The demands of discipline assaulted every sphere of human existence (e.g., parents could be sent to jail for choosing a name for their children not out of the Old Testament). Elders made yearly visits to every home to ensure compliance with the rules. But this strict regimentation contained in it the seeds for its own destruction. Since human society was organized "horizontally," and each person had to fend for herself and be responsible for her own salvation, the conveniently communitarian sense of mutual support prevalent in the Middle Ages was eventually replaced by fierce individualism. To put it in the words of William Haller, writing on the Puritan revolution of mid-seventeenth-century England, "It is one thing to launch men on a quest for the New Jerusalem, quite another to stop them when they have gone far enough.... All attempts in 1644 to impose a Presbyterian frame upon revolutionary Puritanism served simply to evoke the many-headed hydra of English dissent."[48] The same effect was caused by the intolerant Calvinist approach to differences of opinion. At the beginning, Calvinism preached the compulsory annexation of all souls under the auspices of a single Reformed Church. In later years, it took the opposite direction and oozed out revulsion for those exhibiting signs of damnation and contaminating the community of the pure. This in turn evolved into the proliferation of sects and denominations, whereby each one (Methodism, Pietism, Baptism, the Mennonites, the Quakers, and other Puritan denominations) considered the

---

[46] Mariët Westermann, *A Worldly Art, The Dutch Republic 1585–1718*, London: Weidenfeld and Nicolson, pp. 108ff (1996).

[47] Michael Walzer, *The Revolution of the Saints*, Cambridge, MA: Harvard University Press, Atheneum, pp. 54ff (1971; originally published in 1965).

[48] William Haller, *Liberty and Reformation in the Puritan Revolution*, New York: Columbia University Press, p. 142 (1955).

others impure. The monopoly of Calvinist Truth shattered into a competitive environment among opposing points of view. The final arbiter was each individual person making this choice, like all other moral choices in life, in the solitude of her inner soul. In other words, the extremity of the religious demands made by the Calvinist Faith gave rise to diversity, and then to independent thinking and to secularism. In my view, the introduction of hedonistic principles into the Protestant world was made possible because people simply lost their faith, or, at least, their faith lost its exclusive grip on their decision-making processes. These people found themselves immersed in riches, and then, applying their reason, their common sense and their individual judgment became disposed to enjoy them.

This psychological mutation found doctrinal support in the ideas espoused by the philosophers of the period (or maybe the philosophers reflected in their work the changing *mores* of the time, which would have cropped up even without their assistance). The single most important among them was John Locke, especially in his famed *Second Treatise of Government*, published in 1690. In this opus Locke accepted the Calvinist doctrine that Man had to apply himself, intelligently and diligently, in his calling, seeking to accomplish some useful goal (like finding land that lies fallow and, by his hard labor, make it blossom).[49] But unlike the original Calvinist Man, whose good works were not rewarded and his fate was sealed from the first day of Creation, Locke firmly believed in reward and retribution. In His infinite goodness (he held), God knows that this Earth's fallen souls would better accomplish His cosmic design, as well as promote their own chances of salvation, if they obey His command and accept their responsibility in their calling. Being aware of their frail (and very human) self-interested inclinations, He had to make it known, to all human actors (who are taken to respond to stimuli in a rational manner) that sinners would be punished and the righteous would be saved. Locke was accused by his critics that by coloring his theology with the mercantile tints of reward and damnation, he was reducing faith to a mercenary role, because those who accepted his views were no longer motivated by faith, but rather by their hope to gain salvation or escape damnation. But Locke emphasized the superior moral stance of his own version of work in the calling. Although the faithful were promoting their own self-interest, both in this world (by accumulating riches) and in the next (by saving their souls), they were also promoting the cosmic design of their Creator (by fulfilling His command) and assisting their fellow human beings (by making the world at large a better place to live in). Thus, the very vulgarization of theology, the interpretation of normative human action as an instrumental, and, indeed, as a hedonistic exertion of the spirit, had, at the same time, many redeeming qualities. It tied the gratification of human desires to the amelioration of other people's

---

[49] John Dunn, *The Political Thought of John Locke*, London: Cambridge University Press, pp. 16ff (1969).

FIGURE 40. Jean-Honoré Fragonard, *The Swing*, 1766.

destinies; it graced all self-regarding motivations by aligning them with the Social Good.[50]

In the latter decades of the seventeenth century, and more so as time rushed on into the eighteenth, it became apparent that all the great Western industrial and commercial nations, including those with strong Calvinist traditions, not only discovered the principle of pleasure, but were deeply immersed in a constant quest for the good life. Figure 40, *The Swing*, is a frivolously carefree masterpiece by Jean-Honoré Fragonard (1732–1806), executed in 1766. It

---

[50] For a very thoughtful analysis of the Lockean revolution of English Puritanism, see Richard Taylor, *Sources of the Self*, Cambridge, MA: Harvard University Press, pp. 234ff (1989). Taylor also records (ibid., pp. 248ff) the grounds proposed by Locke's contemporaries in opposition to his views, mainly the vulgarization of theology through instrumentalism.

is typical of the French Rococo style that he, along with his contemporary Jean-Antoine Watteau (1684–1721) and his erstwhile teacher, François Boucher (1703–1770), brought to perfection.

There is nothing but lighthearted playfulness in this elegantly attired young aristocrat on the swing. Nature herself is at her feet. The flowery, mysteriously lit garden perfumes the air while her male companions are plainly stationed in their positions for the sole purpose of tendering their good services and conveying their unremitting admiration. Even antiquity itself is vulgarized into the neo-classical style of the garden statues, to join the merry pack of her admirers. The past is thus condensed into the present, and the moment reigns supreme.[51]

Side by side with the exaltation of pleasure, the seventeenth century already displayed the first signs of viewing pain with horror and antipathy.[52] Figure 41, *Dolor*, is Ripa's conventional iconography of Pain, which was considered standard during the Baroque and the Rococo. The aged man at the forefront of the etching wears a black robe and black shoes, which were commonly understood in the period to symbolize the lack of joy. The extinguished candle in his hands stands for the broken spirit of the sufferer, and the lingering smoke is the first harbinger of death. Pain is not romanticized or spiritualized in any way. It is an evil happenstance and it must be avoided like the plague.[53]

The ethos of pleasure and the abhorrence of pain were not typical only of Catholic France (or other Catholic nations), but spread to Protestant lands as well. Even in these sterner climates, wealth was no longer pursued in the calling, nor desired as a portent of grace, or at least not exclusively so. It was also desired for its potential to alleviate pain and propagate happiness. When Jeremy Bentham proclaimed his famous utilitarian principle in 1789 – the greatest happiness for the greatest number of people – the age was ripe for such ideas. It was hardly a case of jumping one's gun.[54] Adam Smith, perhaps the

---

[51] The truth of the matter is that Fragonard's art had much more to it than met the naked eye. His epoch was fraught, of course, with momentous historical events, for which he had very little taste. In his later years he fell to obscurity as a direct result of refusing to join the fashionable revolutionary style. I always considered him as a principled fighter for his (artistic) cause, which is somewhat counterintuitive given the frivolity of his subjects. For a good treatise on Fragonard see Mary Sheriff, *Fragonard: Art and Eroticism*, Chicago: University of Chicago Press (1990).

[52] Along with these early signs, the seventeenth century has not freed itself from the glorification of pain, as is evident, for example, in the pictorial examples of Caravaggio, Rembrandt, and some of the better works of Peter Paul Rubens.

[53] Cesare Ripa, *Baroque and Rococo Pictorial Imagery* (the 1758–60 Hertel Edition, translated for Dover Publications, New York, by Edward Maser, 1971), image number 25.

[54] Bentham's *Introduction to the Principles of Morals and Legislation*, New York: Hafner Publications (1789), the other English utilitarians, and the significance of their work to the development of contractual ideas are discussed and analyzed in Chapter 3, *supra*. It should be stressed at this point that even orthodox utilitarians cannot give themselves a carte blanche license to pursue their own pleasure or minimize their own displeasure as a goal unto itself, because in the real world strategies of this nature may cause unhappiness to others, and utilitarians are called upon to maximize aggregate, not just personal, happiness. With this said, it is also true that Benthamite morals regard, *ceteris paribus*, personal happiness as a welcome contribution to the Social Good, whereas theorists and practitioners of *kenôsis* would take the opposite position. The prevalence of externalities in the real world confront utilitarians with hard practical choices,

*Hippocratem Podager longo varioque dolore,
implorat fessus, quo mala dura levet.*

FIGURE 41. Cesare Ripa, *Dolor*, Hertel Edition, 1758–60.

leading figure of the Scottish Enlightenment, had already announced the advent of his proverbial "invisible hand." It established a crisply fresh proposition that if each agent pursues her own private interest, then, barring administrative meddling, the "invisible hand" can be trusted to transform the diffused set

especially due to the lack of scientific tools to measure cardinal utility, but this technical difficulty cannot diminish the vigor of the utilitarian ideal, that it is happiness, not anguish, that the moral person is called upon to maximize.

of individually earned private gains into an optimal aggregation of the Social Good.[55] The ethos of the invisible hand taught its cohorts that by following their natural inclination to seek pleasure and avoid pain, then far from harming society at large they are actually conferring on it a great benefit. Self-seeking and other-regarding motivations miraculously merge into a single moral path.[56]

On the face of it, any quest for riches stripped of its original Calvinist spirit of sacrifice and self-denial is less conducive to capital formation, because it is bound to reduce savings and hamper investment.[57] But by the end of the eighteenth century, when Smith and Bentham were drumming up the moral justifications for their self-seeking injunctions, the spirit of capitalism had already been so deeply entrenched within the Western industrial centers that the ascetic mood that gave rise to it was no longer necessary to keep it going. In addition, the vast technological advances that were gained in the meantime made it possible to increase both saving and consumption at the same time. The goals of wealth and happiness could finally be united. When this was made possible, the introduction of a hedonistic principle to the accepted list of social *desiderata* did not hinder the capitalistic spirit. On the contrary, it enhanced it, because now economic actors were seeking their luck with a licit,[58] newly discovered *joie de vivre*.

The Russian Scene

Many Russians are greedy, but very few of them bothered to internalize the ideas, so aptly described in the *Protestant Ethic*, that gave rise to the accumulation of riches in the West, and then to investment, to individualism, and to the emergence of a true capitalistic culture.

An interesting starting point to consider the Russian attitude to worldly possessions and to hedonistic principles can be found in the chilling novel of the indomitable Fyodor Dostoyevsky, *The Gambler*. A compulsive gambler himself, Dostoyevsky considers the relative merits of amassing riches as an alternative to squandering them away. The novel's (clearly autobiographical) protagonist travels to a German casino town and muses on the German habits of thrift and frugality:

There is here [in Germany] in every house a *vater* horribly virtuous and extraordinarily honest – so honest that you are afraid to go near him. I can't endure honest people whom one is afraid to go near. Every such German *vater* has a family, and in the evening they read improving books aloud. Elms and chestnut trees rustle over the house. The sun

---

[55] Adam Smith published the most important economic book ever, *The Wealth of Nations*, in 1776.

[56] Many follow these moral injunctions today, too. See, for example, Richard Posner, *Economic Analysis of Law*, 5th ed., Frederick, MD: Aspen Law & Business, pp. 284ff (1998).

[57] In the aggregate, overall household savings equal the overall investment of firms in capital goods, and thus fewer savings implies less investment.

[58] By "licit" I mean both that this new quest for personal gratification met with social approval and that it was pursued without sacrificing the tradition established in the previous centuries that personal integrity was a necessary element in commercial affairs.

is setting, there is a stork on the roof, and everything is extraordinarily practical and touching.... And in what complete bondage and submission every such family is here. They all work like oxen and all save money like Jews. Suppose the *vater* has saved up so many guldens and is reckoning on giving his son a trade or a bit of land; to do so, he gives his daughter no dowry, and she becomes an old maid. To do so, the youngest son is sold into bondage or into the army, and the money is added to the family capital.... All this is done from nothing but honesty, from such intense honesty that the younger son who is sold believes that he is sold from nothing but honesty.... The elder son is no better off: He has an Amalia and their hearts are united, but they can't be married because the pile of guldens is not large enough. They, too, wait with perfect morality and good faith, and go to the sacrifice with a smile. Amalia's cheeks grow thin and hollow. At last, in twenty years, their prosperity is increased. The guldens have been honestly and virtually accumulating. The *vater* gives his blessing to the forty-year-old son and his Amalia of thirty-five, whose chest has grown hollow and whose nose has turned red.... With that he weeps, reads them a moral sermon, and dies. The eldest son becomes himself a virtuous *vater* and begins the same story over again.[59]

Not content to leave the parable in its raw form, Dostoyevsky goes on to reformulate his proposition in abstract and general terms:

The faculty of amassing capital has, with the progress of history, taken place – an almost foremost place – among the virtues and merits of the civilized man of the West. The Russian is not only incapable of amassing capital, but dissipates it in a reckless and unseemly way.[60]

It is not entirely clear that Dostoyevsky is actually speaking for Russia on this score. I think one should interpret this excerpt more as an apologetic testimonial of the author's own penchant for gambling away his fortune than as a considered assessment of the "authentic" Russian spirit. The proverbial *vater* is depicted not only as a caricature of a frugal miser in constant quest of piling up the family *guldens*, but also as a suffering victim of his own thrift, willing to forego the juiciest parts of life for the sake of his "improving" abstractions. This composite portrait of Western man as both a pathetic miser and a sufferer erroneously implies that his polar opposite, the generous Slavophile Russian, holds wealth in deep contempt but vies for pleasure and felicity. Unlike the miserable Germanic *vater*, who saves (and is despised) like a Jew, the Russian *pater familias* comes out of this comparison as a jolly *bon vivant*, who knows to use his riches to improve his lot in this world, rather than purify his soul in anticipation of the next. This chapter shows, however, the darker side of the Russian soul, to which Dostoyevsky himself was painfully well attuned. The Germanic *vater* may indeed reflect in his choices a pronounced proclivity not

---

[59] Fyodor Dostoyevsky, *The Gambler*, edited by Philip Smith, New York: Dover Books, p. 19 (1996; first published in 1866).
[60] Ibid. The reader cannot escape the suspicion that Dostoyevsky's long tirade against the *vater's* frugality serves his private agenda of lending an air of respectability to his own spendthrift's proclivities. Nevertheless, his acute psychological observation did not fail him on this score either, as will be revealed in this chapter.

to squander away his riches. It is also true that most Russians do not share this trait. But by the same token, the evidence does not support the view that Russians act as if they were seriously interested in enjoying their good fortune. Certainly, if one is willing to adopt a result-oriented approach, it is hard to miss the point that most Russians have always been, and still are today, deeply immersed in a hopeless quagmire of suffering and self-denial.[61]

Fierce reports about suffering in Russia date back to the dawn of Russian history. According to popular legend, the first attempt to convert the indigenous Russian population to Christianity was undertaken by the Apostle St. Andrew (in actual fact, this legend anticipates the actual event by a full millennium). The legend ascribes to the apostle the following account of what he saw on his journey:

I saw the land of the Slavs, and while I was among them, I noticed their wooden bath-houses. They warm them to extreme heat, and then undress, and after anointing themselves with tallow, they take young reeds and lash their bodies. They actually lash themselves so violently that they barely escape alive. Then they drench themselves with cold water, and thus are revived. . . . They make the act not a mere washing but a veritable torment.[62]

The interesting part in this legendary account is that the bathers' mortal danger was not inflicted on them by others. They chose to submit to this punishment by their own hand. This tale is consistent with the view that much of the anguish suffered by the Russian people in the course of history was not, as some superficial commentators suggested, generated by a succession of cruel autocrats (say, Joseph Stalin). It is true, of course, that many of these rulers were authoritarian, ruthless, and evil. Authority, however, entails not only the actual dominion of one person (the autocrat) over another person (the subject), but also the subject's voluntary assumption of this yoke.[63] Most commentators agree that Russian autocrats were successful in imposing so much suffering on their subjects only because the latter exhibited such little resistance to the attempt. The historian Nicholas Vakar writes:

Historians who have written that the tyranny of the Czars conditioned the nation to accept the tyranny of the Communists have missed the fact that Russian habits of obedience have been the cause, not the result, of political authority.[64]

---

[61] Modern Russian literature often glorifies the suffering person and equates her with the pure, virtuous, and even saintly. Although on many instances this equation has a redeeming social purpose, to improve the lot of sufferers, it is hard to escape the impression that anguish is masochistically glorified for its own sake. A typical example is Maxim Gorky, the suffering person's champion (see, for instance, his best-known short novel, *Twenty-Six Men and a Girl*, Letchworth: Bradda Books (1899)), whose poetics of torture are without a doubt the strongest point in his literary output.

[62] Cited in Serge Zenkovsky (ed. and trans.), *Medieval Russia's Epics, Chronicles and Tales*, revised and enlarged edition, New York: Penguin Books, p. 47 (1974).

[63] See Chapter 4, supra.

[64] Nicholas Vakar, *The Taproot of Soviet Society*, New York: Harper, p. 40 (1961).

Another commentator adds:

Russia is customarily characterized as an "authoritarian" or "patriarchal" culture. This is no doubt true, but the very terms tend to attract blame toward those exercising "authority" and draw analytic attention away from those who do the suffering and who might possibly be complicitous in the "authoritarianism."[65]

In the following pages I record some of the ideological roots of want and suffering in the collective Russian psyche, and then move on to demonstrate some of its practical implications for the economy, the body politick, and law.

Russian theology, of both the religious and secular varieties, recognizes in the human body and in the pleasures of the flesh a source of evil that righteous persons should try to avoid. This ancient model of "self-emptying," of vacating the *persona*, the external mask, of its internal fleshy contents has some scriptural support in the doctrine of *kenôsis*, enigmatically formulated in the words of St. Paul in Phillipians, 2, 5–10:

5 Have this mind among yourselves, which is yours in Christ Jesus, 6 who, though he was in the form of God, did not count equality with God a thing to be grasped, 7 but emptied himself, taking the form of a servant, being born in the likeness of men. 8 And being found in human form he humbled himself and became obedient unto death, even death on a cross. 9 Therefore God has highly exalted him and bestowed on him the name which is above every name, 10 that at the name of Jesus every knee should bow, in heaven and on earth and under the earth.

Taken (more or less) literally, St. Paul's prescription invites the faithful to discard their pleasure-producing sensitivities and to reduce themselves to a servile state of anguish. However, this seemingly simple advice generated diverse interpretations in the history of Christian thought.[66] To the best of my knowledge, *kenôsis* was first explored as an *analytic* Christological problem by Protestant theologians of the mid-nineteenth century.[67] The object of the exploration was to determine whether the Incarnation of Christ, which allowed Him to "abase" (lower) Himself to the *human* condition of birth, growing up, and physical and spiritual pain, and eventually human death on the cross, divested Him of His *divine* nature, or at least permitted Him to voluntarily suspend its immunity upon His feelings. For the Western theologians, this issue was of particularly analytic interest, because of its potential to make logical dents in the mainstream Doctrine of the Incarnation, which held that the assumption of a *human* nature did not devalue the fully *divine* attributes of Christ; the rub, of course, was

---

[65] Daniel Rancour-Laferriere, *The Slave Soul of Russia, Moral Masochism and the Cult of Suffering*, New York: New York University Press, p. 2 (1995).

[66] For a good summary of Patristic, Lutheran, and Reformed interpretations, see Alex Bruce, *The Humiliation of Christ*, Edinburg: T & T Clark (1881).

[67] See Claude Welch (ed.), *God and Incarnation in Mid-Nineteenth Century German Theology*, New York: Oxford University Press (1965).

that if Christ did maintain His fully *divine* attributes, it is hard to see why His passion was not trivialized, because without shedding His *divine* immunity ("emptying" Himself of His *divine* attributes) He could not have agonized in His *human* condition.

This is an entirely Protestant manner to approach this question, however, because the very act of posing it tacitly assumes a logical universe in which even the mystery of the Incarnation is expected to be "bounded" by the reign of reason. Orthodox theology (as well as the original Patristic sources) does not risk falling into this pitfall because it is more content to accept the Incarnation as a veiled form of reality that cannot be penetrated by the blunt tools of human logic.

The banishment of the flesh from the domain of the worthy is clearly reflected in the Orthodox iconography of faces. Mahmud Zibawi explains:

Destined to reflect the deification of the human being, the icon founds its aesthetic upon an eschatological realism. The psychological is banished... made in the image of God, humans are called to resemble him through holiness.... Darkened by the fall, the image finds its fullness only in the divine resemblance that constitutes its one and only archetype. Concentrated on the face, the icon remains radically foreign to the earthly model. A naturalistic portrait is rejected. An icon of a living person is impossible.[68]

Consider for instance Figure 42, *The Holy Face*, an important Novgorodian icon from the late twelfth century or perhaps the beginning of the thirteenth century (now at the Tretyakov Gallery in Moscow).

Just as Zibawi describes it, this face is purified of all its carnal elements. Its most striking feature is in Christ's expressive gaze, accentuated by the asymmetric formation of the eyebrows. This expressiveness is wholly spiritual, as *kenôsis* successfully emptied the shell of all of its erotic, lustful, or, indeed, fleshy parts. The shell echoes the prototype, which in the case of Christ is the Word, *logos*, that which has no body, no desires, and no worldly aspirations. *The Holy Face* is not just an icon. According to legend, it is the first historical icon, an *acheiropoetos*, an icon of an icon "not made by human hands." King Abgar of Edessa, a contemporary of Christ, was afflicted with a serious illness. Having faith in Christ, he sent emissaries to paint His portrait. According to one tradition, Christ Himself fulfilled the order and painted His own likeness; according to another, it was imprinted upon a shroud when Jesus wiped His face with it. When shipped back to the king, it cured him of his ailments as a reward for his faith in the Lord. The face of faces, then, does not merely banish the "psychological," the carnal, from the eye of the beholder; it is not even contaminated by being made by a carnal hand, as the ritual of *kenôsis* empties the shell of both the cause (the painting hand) and the effect (the painted face)

---

[68] Mahmud Zibawi, *The Icon, Its Meaning and History*, Collegeville, MN: Liturgical Press, p. 33 (1993).

FIGURE 42. *The Holy Face* icon, late twelfth century.

of all human existence.[69] The acceptance of this dogma spells salvation, as is clearly evident in King Abgar's healing from his serious afflictions.[70]

Pavel Florensky, a leading Orthodox leader during Bolshevism who was incarcerated by the authorities in the Gulag and finally murdered in 1937,

[69] A mock mirror image of the Holy Face is the Russian Holy Fool, an explicit model of someone who was "emptied" of all of his pleasure-seeking faculties and leads the life of a hermit in the midst of "normal" society. A complete analysis of this uniquely Russian phenomenon, its distinguishing features from Western holy fools, and its relevance to the development of contract law in Russia is deferred to Chapter 6, infra.

[70] Another proclamation of one's obligation to empty oneself when one deals with the holy icons is suggested in Andrei Tarkovsky's poetic movie, *Andrei Rublev* (the film was first released in 1969 and was soon banned by the Soviet authorities). The movie is a long (185 minutes) narration of Russia's greatest icon painter's life story. It flows on in an extremely slow pace, like a big, wide and deep river, engulfing the viewer with a sense of the timelessness of both icon painting and suffering. At one point the protagonist declares that it is impossible to paint icons "with a full stomach." This short sentence captures the act of *kenôsis* in its most explicit form and also contrasts the emptiness, or void, within the artist's physical person and the spiritual fullness of his artistic achievement.

explores a similar theme. Florensky holds that all "essence" (carnal existence) that attempts to "collapse into appearance" (hold its ground independently of its spiritual prototype) is sinful essence. He maintains that *entirely carnal objects are entirely empty*, where "emptiness" and "evil," or "sin," are used as interchangeable terms. The theology behind this otherwise opaque claim is, in fact, not complicated. It simply avers that natural objects derive their significance from their "spirit," which is the Platonic idea, or the prototype, of which they are mere reflections. Since Orthodox theology preaches that the prototype of all natural persons is in Christ, any corporeal existence *not* perceived through the prototype is a "collapsed" existence, a big hollow, or void, or sin, a *persona* without a face. He explains:

[This] sin possesses a personality, and as the face ceased to be a window through which God's radiance shines... the face separates from the personality... and loses its vitality in becoming a chilling mask of possession by the passions.[71]

To liberate himself from this sin, the artist need mirror in his work the spiritual prototype, a process that requires him to internalize the repudiation of the flesh, because bearing witness affirming the Truth of Christ cannot be achieved by any other means:

High spiritual attainment transforms the face into a light bearing countenance by driving away all darkness, revealing everything that was under-revealed... and the countenance then becomes an artistic self-portrait whose living material details arise from the art of arts. This art is the practice of selfless asceticism, wherein the devoted practitioner, the ascetic, comes... to *bear witness* and prove the truth of authentic reality.[72]

Florensky is not unusual in his theology. His holdings find support everywhere in Russian folklore, religion, and culture. In Russian folklore, there exists one significant object that does not have a spiritual prototype, the concept of the *void*, or nothingness.[73] Voids exist in all kinds of apertures. An aperture might be an open well, or a cave, or even someone yawning. Popular belief has it that the devil, who is ubiquitous, likes to crawl into apertures of all kinds and

---

71 Pavel Florensky, *Iconostasis*, translated by Donald Sheehan and Olga Andrejev, Crestwood, NY: St. Vladimir Seminary Press, p. 55 (1996; first published in 1922).

72 Ibid., p. 56. Florensky goes on to denounce Protestant iconography, especially in prints and etchings, as being based on reason rather than on "canonic truth." The Protestant flimsy theology is echoed, he thinks, by the perishable material (paper) of their prints and etchings, which Florensky compares to the solidity of wooden plates of the Russian icon (pages 98ff). The paper–wood dichotomy is, perhaps, not very convincing, but Florensky may have had a good intuition is sensing that the logic and order of Protestant reasoning, as reflected in their iconography, are not good vehicles for defending the faith against the rising tide of modern secularism.

73 Recall the icon of St. George and the Dragon (Chapter 4, supra, Figure 8). The icon reflects a hierarchy of the spheres, leading from the hand of the Creator in the upper corner of the icon all the way to the subterranean hollows at the bottom of the hierarchy (and the lower corner of the icon). Exactly as the highest sphere symbolizes holiness, the lowest sphere stands for sin. The devil crawls into the hollows through a clearly visible aperture, and by his very threatening presence gives significance to the battle of St. George against the forces of evil.

lurk in wait for the unwary, unleashing on them a host of his unclean charges, withered souls, suicides, stillborn babies, and people who suffered a premature and violent death. Any Christian encountering an aperture must therefore make the sign of the cross to fend off the assault of nothingness.[74] One cannot avoid the suspicion that bodily apertures, including those that are instrumental in lovemaking and intimacy, are no exception to the general rule. If this be so, the repudiation of the human body could not be more complete. Bishop Kallistos Ware, perhaps the leading contemporary figure combining traditional Orthodox theology and academic scholarship, sheds some light on this speculation by holding that the general injunction applying to all Orthodox believers, that *kenôsis* implies asceticism and constant martyrdom, is of particular importance within the family. Although the Orthodox marrying couple is blessed with happiness, it is, in his words, "the happiness of the cross." The couple is made to understand that:

[W]ithout inward martyrdom, without willingly accepted suffering, there can be no true marriage. As the newly crowned couple goes processionally three times round in a circle, the priest carries the cross in front of them, and the choir sings a hymn in honor of the holy martyrs, "you who have fought the good fight and have received your crowns."[75]

I do not believe that Bishop Kallistos was thinking psychoanalytically, but his words are eerily suggestive of the folkloristic injunction to make the sign of the cross in the presence of open cavities.

The cult of bodily deprivation, as well as of the repudiation of riches, is deeply rooted in the most ancient (as well as modern)[76] literary texts of Russian Christianity. When Prince Vladimir, who was chiefly responsible for the conversion of Kievan Rus' to Christianity, died, his son Boris was engaged in a skirmish against the tribe of the Pechenegs. Hurrying back to Kiev, he heard news that his brother Sviatopolk plotted to kill him, alongside with his other brother Gleb, still a boy, in order to ensure his succession to the throne. Rather than mount a belligerent effort for survival, which he had an option to try, Boris chose to peacefully submit, thereby accepting the fate of a martyr. He passed the night in prayer, awaiting his assassins. After chopping Boris to pieces, Sviatopolk's henchmen proceeded to apprehend Gleb, who refused to escape, giving too little credence to the reports concerning Sviatopolk's wickedness. The murderers caught up with him and, after finishing him off in the most brutal manner, threw his remains into the forest. Gleb may have been, in this

---

[74] Linda Ivanits, *Russian Folk Belief*, Armonk, NY: M. E. Sharpe, pp. 38ff (1992).

[75] Bishop Kallistos Ware, *The Inner Kingdom*, Crestwood, NY: St. Vladimir's Seminary Press p. 121 (2000).

[76] Alexander Blok (1880–1921) captured this spirit in a poem: "A buzzard flies the drowsy field,/Smooth circle after circle weaving./He scans bare lands. A shack revealed;/A mother for her son is grieving./'Here, take this bread and suck this tit./Mind! Grow! Here's your cross; carry it!'/Centuries pass, the war's at hand,/Rebellion came; each village sears,/And you are still the same, my land,/In your old beauty, stained with tears./O how long must the mother grieve?/How long-the circling buzzard weave?" cited in Daniel Rancour-Laferriere, *The Slave Soul of Russia, Moral Masochism and the Cult of Suffering*, New York: New York University Press, p. 231 (1995).

gory tale, a simple symbol of innocence,[77] but Boris was a thinking agent who, according to an anonymous legend, was able to articulate his tragic choice:

If I go to the house of my father, many people will pervert my heart that I may expel my brother, as my father had done before the holy baptism, for the sake of glory and the kingdom of this world which passes away and is thinner than a cobweb. . . . What had gained both my father's brothers and my father himself? Where are their lives and the glory of this world and the purple mantels and ornaments, silver and gold, wine and mead, tasty food and swift steeds, high and stately houses, many possessions and tributes and honor without measure, and the pride of their boyars? All this, as if never existed for them, all has disappeared with them. . . . Therefore, Solomon, having passed through all and acquired everything, said: vanity of vanities, all is vanity; the only hope is from good works, from true faith and from sincere love.[78]

Immediately after their deaths, in 1015, the veneration of these two "arch-martyrs" (see Figure 7) spread throughout Rus' (Sviatopolk was not around to obstruct the practice, as he was soon disposed of and replaced by one of the more righteous surviving siblings). A strong grassroot pressure was then exerted on the Greek-Byzantine supreme prelate of Rus' to canonize the brothers. He was understandably reluctant to do so, not only because this was the first move to canonize *anyone* in Rus', but chiefly because in the tradition of the Church it was customary to canonize only those who suffered their death in defending their Faith against a heathen foe, while Boris and Gleb did not experience any kind of religious passion. They were not even heroic in their deeds, but rather defenseless, meek, passive, and accepting. Nevertheless, the prelate soon found out that he could not resist the pressure, and the two siblings became the first canonized indigenous Russians, and the most important ones ever since.[79] They have also been extensively studied due to the centrality of their myths, legends, and folk stories in the early stages of Russian literature.[80] In their icon they are elegantly attired as a symbol of their royal blood, but their unassuming, complacent posture miraculously transforms their princely garments, in the eye of the beholder, almost to monastic habits, their downward-pointing swords to the walking staff of the hermit. They embody in their respective persons (always together, in spite of the arguably different roles they both played in the story of their martyrdom) a unified dismissing stance to both worldly possessions and to the joy of living.

Their spirits still live today. Some of Dostoyevsky's greatest characters, Prince Mishkin in *The Idiot*, Alexey (Alyosha) Karamazov in *The Brothers Karamazov*, and many others took their inspiration from the ascetic tradition of the Russian sufferer. St. Tikhon of Zadonsk (1722–1793, canonized in 1861), a

---

[77] Although, according to legend, after pleading in vain with his assassins to spare his young and innocent life, and pledging in vain his allegiance and servility to his horrific brother, Gleb committed an act of piety by accepting his bitter fate and entrusting his soul to the Lord.

[78] Cited by George Sedotov, *The Russian Religious Mind*, Belmont, MA: Nordland Publishing, Volume 1, p. 98 (1975).

[79] Ibid., pp. 94ff.

[80] See Gail Lenhoff, *The Martyred Princes Boris and Gleb: A Social-Cultural Study of the Cult and the Texts*, Columbus, OH: Slavica Publishers (1989).

leading practitioner[81] and teacher[82] of *kenôsis*, became the inspirational figure for conjuring up the character of the Elder Zossima in *Karamzov*.[83] Zossima's saintly figure was the kindly Alyosha's role model in life. A magical scene unfolds when, at the death of Zossima, his flesh starts to decay, exuding unpleasant odors in every direction. Simple souls around the monastery interpret this turn of events as a testimony of Zossima's false claim to saintliness. They figure that if his reputation were well deserved, his decaying body would have exuded much more delicate scents. Alyosha, on the other hand, continues to hold his dead master's memory in high esteem, but nevertheless leaves the monastery and goes to the "world." Everybody's reaction to the dead body's foul odors reflects, although with marked differences in nuance, a deeply ingrained disbelief that the human body, frail, decaying, and sometimes smelly as it is, may give shelter and contain the sanctity of human existence.

The glorified attitude to human suffering is poetically elucidated by Iulia de Beausobre, a Russian aristocrat of deeply religious convictions who was detained and interrogated and indeed severely tortured by the Bolsheviks in Lubyanka Prison in 1932. Eventually she was released and expatriated to England, where she lived for the rest of her life. In 1940 she broke her silence and told her tale, connecting it to ancient legends and to the everlasting fascination of the Russian people with suffering and want. According to popular legend, she writes, the victorious St. George raised his lance with an intention to kill the devil. He was prevented from doing so by some higher power that stayed his hand. Some choose to believe that it was Antichrist intervening on behalf of the devil. The better tradition ascribes this to Christ Himself, because He knew that without the devil there can be no suffering and, in the end, no redemption or salvation. De Beausobre goes on to speculate about the distinction between Russian and English benevolence. When the English wish to assist the needy, to redeem them from the depth of their lower existence, they stoop down to them and lend a helping hand; but uppercrust Englishmen never dream of actually descending to the abyss of the lower classes' existence, as the stratified formation of society cannot be broken. For a Russian, on the other hand, there is no practical way of assisting the needy, doing the good works, unless she descends to the needy, mingles with them, and partakes in their suffering. This was the way of Christ. This is the way of Russia.[84]

---

[81] A famous popular story narrates an occasion in which St. Tikhon was struck in the face by an angry boyar for having pleaded too urgently on behalf of his maltreated serfs. The saint prostrated himself at the feet of his assailant, pleading forgiveness for having put him to an arduous test, in which he failed. The boyar was so impressed by his meekness that he agreed immediately to ameliorate the condition of his serfs.

[82] See, for instance, his book *Journey to Heaven: Counsels on the Particular Duties of Every Christian*, Jordanville, NY: Holy Trinity Monastery (1994).

[83] Nadejda Gorodetzky, *St. Tikhon of Zadonsk: Inspirer of Dostoyevsky*, Crestwood, NY: St. Vladimir's Seminary Press (1976).

[84] Iulia de Beausobre, *Creative Suffering*, Oxford: SLG Press (1984; the original work was published in 1940).

A few words might be in order about exceptions. Many notable Russians will always be remembered for their hedonistic tastes. The late Romanovs, for example, were the most important clients of the House of Fabergé, the ultimate fin de siècle designers of frivolous little things. Their gilded Russian Easter eggs, pretty little clocks, figurines, jewelry, and domestic articles had nothing in them except pure form. There was no complex prototype–icon relationship there, as each exquisite item did not represent anything except itself. If they deserve a footnote in the annals of art history, one could perhaps say that they took the spirit of Fragonard a few steps forward, vacating it of its hidden complexities and turning it into a trivial experience of the palate, like sugared *confetti* or a glass of Rhine wine. And yet they were favored by the late czars who lived and died with them.[85] If one is allowed to take the Fabergé example as a proxy for the general case, one can easily dismiss the significance of the exceptions. Obviously, there was nothing uniquely *Russian* in M. Fabergé's constant flow of Russified fantasies. Indeed, it was the scent of its foreign taste that appealed to Nicholas II, the last of the Romanovs, and to his German czaritsa; she who could never master the language of her subjects, sympathize with their plight, appreciate their soaring spirit, or, indeed, comprehend why they hated her so much. Nor was too much popular affection wasted on her royal spouse – not by the disgruntled peasants, who longed for, but never lived to see, some *real* agrarian reform of the kind that would liberate them from their endless state of serfdom not only *de jure* but also in actual fact; nor by the intellectuals and liberals, for whom he was a conservative reactionary; nor for the conservative reactionaries, for whom he was a weakling, a Westernizer, and a henpecked husband. When he finally was forced to abdicate on March 15, 1917, he did it in the name of national unity.[86] He was commonly believed to have experienced a great sense of relief, as did the vast majority of his resentful subjects.

Implications for Corporate Law, Commercialization, and Privatization

With this background in mind, we are ready to examine some of the recent, and not so recent, developments on the Russian legal scene. Much has been said in previous chapters on the development of the law of contract, or the

---

[85] The house of Fabergé, headquartered in St. Petersburg, soon vanished in 1917, as the grueling Bolshevik commissars had just about the same kind of admiration for its *art nouveau* whimsical style as they had for those who patronized it. Although the chief craftsman, Karl Gustavovitch Fabergé, a second-generation Russian of French Huguenot descent, fled to the West, his epoch was ended with the Russian Revolution, and his style died with it.

[86] In his (typically pompous) words: "The cruel enemy is making his last efforts and the moment is near when our valiant Army, in concert with our glorious Allies, will finally overthrow the enemy. In these decisive days in the life of Russia we have thought that we owed to our people the close union and organization of all its forces for the realization of a rapid victory; for which reason, in agreement with the Imperial Duma, we have recognized that it is for the good of the country that we should abdicate the Crown of the Russian State and lay down the Supreme Power."

absence thereof, on Russian soil. In this chapter I wish to pay special attention to the development (or lack thereof) of a special brand of contract, the corporate form.[87] Whereas the previous parts of this chapter can be read as having a particularly theoretic interest, this part is intended to draw some practical conclusions. It shows that, contrary to what current reformers believe, the road to profound changes in the economic and corporate structure of modern Russia is much rockier than they anticipated.

The English word "company" is derived from a Latin composite expression, *com-panis* (literally "bread together"), which really alludes to an institution, or venue, where different people can break together their bread. *Panis* stands for the paradigmatic economic good, a staple necessity of the marketplace, and *com* is the term that implies a trade. The modern corporation is, just as is suggested by its etymological root, a *nexus* of contracts.[88] It is, primarily, a partnership of inputs between stockholders who lack the qualifications to manage their own money and managers who do possess these qualifications but lack the sufficient resources to manage their own funds. This is a potentially strained contractual relationship, because as soon as the investors' money is entrusted to the managers, the latter have an incentive to use it for their own purposes, rather than for the purposes of their principals.[89] If the company is partially financed by some nonstockholder constituencies (i.e., creditors), another potential conflict of interest ensues, between the stockholders (who prefer riskier business strategies) and the creditors (who prefer more conservative strategies).[90] Other conflicts exist in the relationship between large block holders and minority holders of stock, between stockholders and employees, between secured and unsecured creditors, or between the owners of derivative financial products (such as options) and everyone else. A sophisticated *corpus* of corporate norms

---

[87] For the reasons for including this discussion in this chapter, see note 2, supra.

[88] See, for example, Frank Easterbrook, and Daniel Fischel, "The Corporate Contract," *Columbia Law Review* 89:1416 (1989).

[89] This problem, commonly referred to as the "divorce of ownership and control," was first recognized by Adolf Berle and Gardiner Means, *The Modern Corporation and Private Property*, New York: Macmillan (1932). Berle and Means thought that the separation of ownership and control left the investors at the mercy of the corporate managers, who have an incentive to use the funds entrusted to them for their own benefit. Later scholarship revealed that the managers are constrained by a combination of structural, legal, and market forces that are crafted to align their objective function with that of their principals.

[90] Creditors have only a fixed claim in the enterprise (the capital lent to the firm, with interest) and therefore have no desire to increase profit volatility, even if doing so increases the overall expected return on the firm's capital (for example, rather than make a sure profit on $1 million a year, have a 50 percent chance of losing $1 million dollars a year and a 50 percent chance of making a profit of $5 million a year). This is so because, if a downside scenario materializes (the firm loses money), they may not be able to recoup their claims (the firm may become insolvent), while if an upside scenario materializes (the firm makes much more money than before), they do not share in the residual profit, because they still get only their fixed claims and all the residual profits go to the shareholders. Shareholders are less risk averse, because in an upside turn they have a claim for all the residual profits, and in a downside turn they use the shield of limited liability to "externalize" some of their costs to the creditors.

regulates these "agency problems."[91] It is imperative that the regulatory structure be fair and efficient, because otherwise cautious investors will be loath to repose their trust in strangers. This complex web of knotty relationships among the different corporate constituencies is mostly taken care of by contract, although statutory[92] and judge-made[93] law also assist in formulating the overall regulatory product. The roles of statutes and precedents are to supply the parties with "default" contract arrangements, that is, rules that control their relationship in the absence of explicit contractual language. Viewed in this light, statutes and precedents too may be regarded as contractual devices of sorts. In some (fewer) cases, corporate rules are mandatory (cannot be contracted out of). Wise legislators confine mandatory rules to cases of "market failure," in which rational parties, transacting at arm's length, cannot reach optimal decisions without external assistance. In a sense, even mandatory rules are hypothetical contracts, that is, contracts that the parties would have drafted for themselves, if the contracting process were costless and free of all kinds of market failures. The modern corporation, then, is a highly developed contractual concept as well as a principal instrument of capitalism. If the economy, of some country or of the world, were run by households or mini-firms alone, the small scale of the economic units would not have allowed for the exploitation of economies of scale, and no significant wealth formation would have materialized. The drive to maximize the pie, the social *panis*, and to divide the resulting wealth among the market participants is what powers the formation, growth, and proliferation of the modern corporate state.

European corporations existed in the Middle Ages but were of an entirely different feather. The Catholic Church and the City of London provide two germane examples. These entities assumed their corporate nature by being recognized as independent "legal persons," that is, having legal capacity to hold rights and owe obligations that are distinct from the rights and obligations of the natural persons surrounding them. For instance, the vast possessions of the Catholic Church did not "belong" to the pope or cardinals. Rather, they belonged to the Church. The Church could contract, commit a civil tort or suffer a tort being committed against "it," inherit property, or stand in its own right in legal process. Unlike natural persons, whose days in this world are numbered, corporations may live forever, as the entries and exists of their human stewards do not affect the perpetuity of their own existence. This kind of legal person, however, could not have assumed an important role in the rise of capitalism. To accomplish that goal, three additional properties of the corporate form are necessary. The first and most obvious one is that corporations

[91] The classical article on this subject has been and remains Michael Jensen and William Meckling, "Theory of the Firm: Managerial Behavior, Agency Costs and Ownership Structure," *Journal of Financial Economics* 3:305 (1976).

[92] Philipe Aghion and Benjamin Hermalin, "Legal Restrictions on Private Contracts May Enhance Efficiency," *Journal of Law, Economics and Organization* 6:381 (1990).

[93] John Coffee, "The Mandatory-Enabling Balance in Corporate Law: An Essay on the Judicial Role," *Columbia Law Review* 89:1618 (1989).

be used for the accumulation of private gain. This is the main distinctive feature, differentiating the medieval not-for-profit associations from the modern business enterprise. The second element requires that corporations reflect the consensual preferences of their founders, rather than the will of a sovereign. Since the corporate contract regulates a complex set of potentially conflicting interests among numerous constituencies, as noted above, it ought to be based on their own agreement, rather than on administrative fiat. This can be achieved by letting the parties form their own companies, with their own rules of conduct (subject to the mandatory provisions of the legal system). Truly consensual corporate forms are not consistent with the "concessionist" approach to incorporation, which conditions corporate life on the acquiescence of some higher authority, or which lets a higher authority determine the details of each company's internal governance. Finally, modern corporations feature one of the greatest inventions of the enterprising spirit, limited liability. This doctrine limits the risk of investors to the value of their investment without exposing their personal assets to the peril of being dissipated in satisfaction of a corporate debt. Without that shield, public stockholders would have shunned the securities markets, because they would have lacked the capacity to either monitor an approaching calamity (for which they would have been personally liable) or fend it off when it transpired. By giving public investors the assurance of limited liability, vast sums can be raised from the public, thus laying the foundations for large enterprises enjoying huge economies of scale and transforming a successful capitalistic economy from dream to reality. The combination of these three modern features – for-profit enterprises, consensual incorporation, and limited liability – are of relatively recent pedigree even in the West. When they materialized, they transformed an erstwhile embryonic capitalistic system into the modern corporate state. But they never materialized on Russian soil.

The history of Russian corporate law is thoughtfully narrated by Thomas Owen, writing on the period from 1800 to the 1917 Revolution.[94] This is really the most interesting period to explore, because prior to 1800 corporate ideas were not very well developed in the West either, and in the seventy years or so of Communism there was obviously very little to explore. Owen's study, published in 1991, left untouched the years following *Perestroika* and *Glasnost*. I attempt to bridge this gap in the closing paragraphs of this chapter.

In his introductory overview of his study, Owen reports that in the whole history of Russian corporate law until the Revolution, a mere 6,000 companies were established. This is an amazingly small number. How can it be accounted for? The czarist regime did understand the importance of capitalistic institutions for the furtherance of its own causes, but it really had no idea what made successful companies tick. The intentions of the czars were basically military. They wished to modernize their economy as a means for financing their war efforts and for making the country better suited to face military challenges.

---

[94] Thomas Owen, *The Corporation Under Russian Law, 1800-1917*, New York: Cambridge University Press (1991).

They did not pay much attention to the question of what might prompt rational investors to risk their money and underwrite the intentions of their rulers. In other words, they overlooked the fact that modern corporations are *for-profit* organizations, rather than cash cows in the service of a military regime. As a result, the czars and their financial lieutenants created so many barriers to entry, and imposed such heavy restrictions on existing companies, that only very few were able to access the market and hold their ground. Given the high rate of "taxation by regulation,"[95] companies could survive in this heavily regulated environment only by illicit activities involving graft and corruption. Nor did large enterprises fare well in popular culture. For the great masses of the Russian people, to be an industrialist was tantamount to being corrupt, which is fully consistent with the traditional cultural attitude to the concept of wealth. Most households continued to rely on traditional forms of doing business (as family enterprises) and had little taste for formal contracting, let alone any sophisticated forms of commercial activities.[96] Similar blunders were committed vis-à-vis the labor force. The industrialization effort in czarist Russia was largely made possible by the coerced labor of the Russian peasant. Peasants were literally forced to produce their quota, and their fees were taxed to the point of starvation. Only during the very last years of the reign of the Romanovs, during the Stolypin reforms (see infra), did the peasants get, for the first time, some economic incentives not to shirk or steal from their employers, but even this late reform was largely motivated by a desire to diffuse peasant hostility and protect the government from political uprising.[97]

Until 1825 only very few companies were in existence.[98] Each one had to be chartered by a complex bureaucratic procedure, and only those that curried favor with the authorities were chartered. The great "westernizing" emperors did not understand the benefits of corporations. Only four companies were chartered during the long reign of Catharine the Great. In 1805, Alexander I made a significant step forward by issuing a decree conferring limited liability on investors in joint stock companies. But his enterprising spirit did not go far enough to allow free incorporation without a charter, except for partnerships and similar family businesses.[99]

In 1836, Czar Nicholas I enacted a corporate code that was inspired by the West and by the labor of his finance minister, Igor Kankrin (1774–1845).

---

[95] Every form of regulation may impose some costs on the regulated industries. These costs may be interpreted as a form of taxation. The heavier the regulatory structure (czarist Russia is a prime example), the more onerous is this implicit tax. On the characterization of the costs of regulation as "taxes," see Richard Posner, "Taxation by Regulation," *Bell Journal of Economics*, 2:22 (1971).

[96] Owen, ibid., Preface.

[97] William Blackwell, *The Industrialization of Russia*, New York: Thomas Y. Crowell, 2d ed., Chapter 2 (1982).

[98] Part of the explanation lies no doubt in the fact that, until the middle of the nineteenth century, only about 8 percent of the Russian population were city dwellers. See Blackwell, ibid., p. 16.

[99] Owen, ibid., pp. 6ff.

Kankrin was a frugal soldier with a scant understanding of economics. His attitude to modernization can be gathered from his famous utterance on the mobilization of goods and raw materials in Russia, which, one recalls, is the vastest land mass on the face of the earth: "Railroads do not always result from natural necessity, but are more often an object of artificial need or luxury. They encourage unnecessary travel from place to place, which is entirely typical of our time, and also fleece the public of excess funds." The law of 1836 reflected Kankrin's abhorrence of previously unregulated corporate bubbles, which caused financial ruin to their investors. The law prescribed limited liability for all companies, but also bestowed on them monopoly privileges and other concessions, which made them highly inefficient. It was frighteningly restrictive. All companies had to be chartered. A chartered company had to renew its license if it wished to change its objects or introduce other modifications in the original charter. No trading in corporate shares was allowed until all shares had been issued, and insiders could not own more than a 20 percent stake in the business. All policy issues had to be decided by the general meeting of stockholders (as a means of avoiding self-interested deals). All promises to sell shares not accompanied by instantaneous delivery were both void and criminally punishable. *This highly restrictive statute was the only comprehensive corporate law ever enacted in Czarist Russia.*[100]

Many key players sensed that the 1836 law had a deadly effect on the companies it purported to regulate. In almost every decade a major effort was mounted to significantly amend it. None succeeded. Here are a few examples. Around the middle of the 1850s, following the Russian military defeat in the Crimean War, it finally occurred to the czar and his advisors that Russia could not win wars without modernizing its economy. This caused Czar Alexander II (1855–81) and his finance ministers (Peter Brok, 1852–58; Alexander Kniazhevich, 1858–62; and Mikhail Reutern, 1862–78) to seek new ways to encourage private enterprise. But Alexander and his advisors were adamant on the issue of chartering, and the decision of whom to charter, being made by a notoriously inefficient and corrupt administration, favored inefficient and corrupt candidates.[101] Like Peter the Great before him, who was often hailed for opening a window to the West but remained traditionally Russian in his bones,[102] Alexander too, who was often praised for being an enlightened reformer (mainly for liberating the serfs), could not deliver when he had a chance. This was certainly true in the corporate domain, and many commentators believe that his overall record as a reformer was not much better.[103]

Enter the 1860s. In this decade it was perceived that the 1836 law had to be reformed in conformity with the European model of free incorporation and less restrictive legislation. In 1863 it was permitted by statute, for the first

[100] Ibid., pp. 14ff.
[101] Ibid., pp. 30ff.
[102] See Appendix to Chapter 4, supra.
[103] See Daniel Field, *The End of Serfdom*, Cambridge, MA: Harvard University Press (1976).

time, to engage in commerce even if someone was not a "merchant." Access to commerce was opened "to persons of both sexes, Russian subjects of all ranks, and foreigners."[104] This was a step in the abolition of the medieval guild system whereby only recognized artisans were admitted as practitioners of a given trade. A decree of 1873 gave even Old Believers a footstep in commerce, although a full emancipation of all schismatic sects had to wait until 1905. But the attempts to reform the law of 1836 itself came to naught. Free incorporation was still a dream.[105]

Enter the 1870s. In 1874, the minister of finance, Reutern, resolved to stop paying lip service to reformist ideas. He ruled that the time was not ripe for such a bold move, announcing that "no further action was taken in view of the state's difficult financial situation and the apprehension that the less difficult procedure for establishing joint-stock companies would result in the undesirable development of small companies."[106] True to his word, Reutern fostered a policy of "tutelage" whereby all corporate activities were closely regulated by the state, including its strict adherence to the concessionist theory. Since each charter was enacted separately into a *lex specialis*, it actually superseded the law of 1836, and, in practical effect, there was no corporate code, just a series of individually enacted statutes as arbitrarily decided by the regulatory agencies.[107] An eyewitness observed: "Bribery, personal funds, violations of legal procedure, etc, went to extremes in Petersburg. Everything was possible, but at the same time one could be refused the most just and lawful [request].... The immorality, unscrupulousness, and foolishness of the upper administration surpassed all the swindling and stupidity of the provincial and district bureaucrats."[108]

Reutern was succeeded by Vyshnegradskii and then by Witte. They both maintained the same philosophy of tutelage. This unwise policy was seriously exacerbated due to the xenophobic attitude of nearly everyone in Russian government and their bigotry towards foreigners, Jews, and religious dissidents within their own faith (especially the Old Believers). Whereas in the West it was recognized from times immemorial that trade and industry could not be contained within the geographical limits, or social *milieu*, of a single ethnic group,[109] Russians have always been suspicious of the unfamiliar perils of

---

[104] Section 21 of the 1863 Law.

[105] Owen, pp. 57ff.

[106] Ibid., pp. 75ff.

[107] This evidence falls in line with one of the major assertions in Chapter 4, supra, that Russian law did not develop substantive entitlements, just procedural avenues for seeking redress. In that chapter I made the point that this heavy emphasis on procedure, rather than on vested rights, is inimical to the development of the Rule of Law and is consistent with the fundamental autocratic nature of Russian culture. The policy adopted by Finance Minister Reutern implies that one could not find one's law in the law books and had to make do with whatever "concessions" were offered to one by the authorities.

[108] This testimony was offered by an eyewitness, Aleksandr Koshelev, cited in Owen, pp. 79ff.

[109] The original *Lex Mercatoria* (Law Merchant) has it roots in antiquity. For a British version of this universal concept dating back to the end of the eighteenth century, see Wyndham Beawes, *Lex Mercatoria Rediviva* (two volumes, 1795). In this extensive treatise the author surveys the

forging a business partnership or a joint venture with non-Russians or with Russians of some other religious persuasion.[110] In keeping with this xenophobic tradition, severe restrictions were imposed on corporate land ownership of all corporations having foreign, Jewish, or Polish stewards. Some of these restrictions were not regulated by statute but simply by an arbitrary, but consistent application of the concessionist system. An exclusionary statute was passed in 1869 barring foreigners from participating in corporate shipping ventures. This restriction spread like cancer to railroad, insurance, mining, and other companies. A series of exclusionary land laws was passed in the 1880s. Gold mines and petroleum followed suit. International trade became, for many foreign entrepreneurs, virtually impossible.[111] The exclusion of Jews may have been the most extreme. It was Catherine the Great who first initiated the decree mandating all Jews within her empire to reside within a more or less well-defined "pale of settlement," thus making even physical contact among Jewish and gentile traders immensely cumbersome. The geographical boundaries of the pale largely depended on the whims of each particular sovereign. As late as 1881, Czar Alexander III expanded the pale barring the Jewish population from living in the Province or City of Moscow. The 1897 censure revealed that among Russia's more than 5 million Jews, only 200,000 were permitted to live outside the pale. The restrictions were not formally lifted until the Romanovs left power.

The other xenophobic tendencies of the Russian authorities lingered all the way to the Revolution as well. When Count Józef Potocki, a Polish Jew of impeccable reputation, proposed to build a railroad, both Prime Minister Stolypin and Transportation Minister Sergei Rukhlov refused to charter the company on the basis of his foreign ancestry.[112] Eventually, the czar overruled them but the charter did not allow the company to elect more than one non-Russian director and one non-Russian alternate member of the board. Witte tried to resist this tendency but to no avail. Only in 1906 did the czar give his consent for corporations to buy land even if they had Jewish directors, provided that these Jewish incumbents should not own the land itself or be responsible for its management. In 1910, Jews were allowed to manage land in some, but not all, parts of the Empire. Other efforts to reform the law, and especially those intended to get rid of the concessionist system, failed. Explaining his reasons

laws of the main commercial nations, their common features (these common features constitute the core of the *lex mercatoria*), and the way to conduct international trade between citizens and aliens.

[110] See Walther Kirchner, *Commercial Relations between Russia and Europe 1400 to 1800*, Bloomington: Indiana University Press (1966).

[111] Owen, ibid., pp. 116ff. For a vivid description of an Englishman's business tribulations under Witte, see James Whishaw, *Memoirs of James Whishaw*, London: Methuen (1935).

[112] Stolypin, too, is often hailed as a liberal reformer, but it is rather hard to accept this view when one considers the evidence contained in the text. A more balanced recent account of Stolypin's character and accomplishments can be found in Abraham Ascher, *P. A. Stolypin: The Search for Stability in Late Imperial Russia*, Stanford: Stanford University Press (2000).

for refusing to adopt this kind of reform, the Minister of Trade and Industry, Timashev, announced that it would lead to "the evasion of a whole series of statutes limiting the acquisition of nonurban real estate by certain categories of individuals."[113]

In 1913, reactionary factions had the upper hand and foreigners, especially Jews, were excluded more than before. In the same year a series of anti-Semitic laws were made; the famous Mendel Beilis trial took place, in which the defendant was accused, and finally acquitted, of ritual murder of a gentile child. Some leaders proposed the total expulsion of Jews from the empire, and many Jews were divested of their property, professions, and market participation.[114] In 1915, the war prompted the government to extend its exclusion of foreigners to German, Austrian, Hungarian, and Turkish subjects.[115] For good measure, existing corporations belonging to or managed by people of these ethnic origins were wound up, to the detriment of the Russian economy. After the 1917 Revolution, all ethnic restrictions were lifted and many corporations could be formed without charters; but obviously, as the central planning economy tightened its grip, these reforms lost all their practical significance.

Today the Russian Federation seeks to join the ranks of the Western industrial nations and do what it takes to privatize its economy. Obviously, no such moves are even remotely possible without large and reliable public corporations and a smoothly functioning corporate code, and none was enacted in Russia since the ill-fated 1836 Law. The Russian nation has always been blessed with highly intelligent people with a penetrating mind and a creative spirit. Nonetheless, the Russian government saw fit to delegate the professional responsibility for crafting a brand new corporate code to two foreign jurists, Bernard Black from Stanford and Reinier Kraakman from Harvard. Both are well-known and highly regarded scholars in American legal academia. In due course, Black and Kraakman proposed a model, and the government swiftly acted on it and passed a corporate code for the Russian Federation.[116] It was a dismal failure.[117]

[113] Owen, ibid., p. 164.

[114] For a fuller account of the czarist attitude to Jewish capitalists of all sorts, see Arcadius Kahan, *Notes on Jewish Entrepreneurship in Tsarist Russia*, Washington, DC: Wilson Center, Kennan Institute for Advanced Russian Studies (1978).

[115] In spite of all their efforts, the Russian finance ministers did not succeed in eradicating the dominance of minority groups among the country's top industrialists. During the period from 1890 to 1914, most moneyed industrialists in the Moscow area were Old Believers, St. Petersburg was dominated by German industrialists, and Western Russia was dominated by Industrialists of Jewish extraction. See William Blackwell, *The Industrialization of Russia*, New York: Thomas Y. Crowell, 2nd ed., pp. 35ff (1982).

[116] The Federal Law on Joint Stock Companies, enacted by the Duma in 1995, entered into effect on January 1, 1996.

[117] This was readily conceded, with admirable candor, by its own authors. See Bernard Black, Reinier Kraakman, and Anna Tarassova, "Russian Privatization and Corporate Governance: What Went Wrong?," *Stanford Law Review* 52:1731 (2000). I shall return to the reasons for this failure, both those imagined by the authors and my own, in short order.

When the proposed statutory product was in its final formative stages, the authors wished to share their insights with the world, so that its guiding principles would be known to all and sundry. They called their model a "self-enforcing" one, to signal their awareness that any legal norm that depends on *external* support from the institutions of organized society in contemporary Russia is doomed to failure; in their paper, Black and Kraakman describe in detail what might be the self-enforcing mechanisms of their proposed code.[118] The common denominator among all these proposals is that they are nothing but a set of executory promises, packaged together with remedies for breach. They thus fail to come to grips with the most fundamental problem of Russian *corporate* law – its failure to accept the basic cultural underpinnings of *contract* law. For example, the authors suggest to confer on the company's shareholders "call options," the right to buy additional shares in specified contingencies (such as when the company wishes to issue additional shares; the call option is meant to shield the existing shareholders from a dilution of their holdings); obviously, a call option is a contract, and its value depends on the likelihood of its enforcement. In a similar vein, they suggest to confer on the shareholders some "put options," the right to sell their shares on specified events (such as when the company is acquired by a new entrant). Put options are contracts as well, and their value, too, depends on their enforceability. They suggest instituting what is called "cumulative voting for directors," which is a fancy legal term allowing minority block holders to gain proportional representation on the board (rather than allow the majority of shareholders to elect *all* members of the board). But they fail to take into account that the exercise of the shareholders' voting rights is wholly contractual as well. Or they suggest mandating that corporate incumbents disclose all material information about their firms, forgetting that this mandatory injunction creates an obligation that is yet to be enforced. They further suggest that the directors and managers of large firms be subordinated to the will of large shareholders (to minimize agency costs), overlooking the simple fact that the directors and managers might not be willing to sacrifice their control only because the law mandates them to do so. Interestingly, they prescribe "bright line rules," legal standards that are easy to administer without getting entangled in "gray areas" of linguistic ambiguity, but are not alarmed by the prospect that whoever is called upon to follow those rules might simply refuse to abide by them. Finally, in recognition of the lesser likelihood of detection and enforcement of norms, they propose onerous sanctions for breach, suggesting that the high penalties in cases of enforcement will induce optimal behavior overall; but they commit the error of discounting the possibility that none, or only a negligible ratio of, the entire number of cases involving breach of contract or other forms of wrongdoing will be resolved by legal redress.

---

[118] Bernard Black and Reinier Kraakman, "A Self-Enforcing Model of Corporate Law," *Harvard Law Review* 109:1912 (1996).

In their attempt to rationalize what went wrong, the authors put the blame on the deep corruption of the ex-Soviet "kleptocrats." They contend that the government made an error in privatizing its industries first and dealing with conflicts of duty and interest later, rather than the other way around. Even when initial acquirers of the privatized ventures happened to be honest people, they ended up selling their enterprises to corrupt kleptocrats. This is because, the authors explain, corrupt owners can always outbid honest ones, because they pay less taxes, are better connected to organized crime (the Russian Mafia), and can look forward to financing their shady deals by stealing from the corporate coffers.[119]

I find this explanation plausible, but incomplete. Given the insecurity of property rights in Russia, that is, the ability of kleptocrats to appropriate other people's money, not to contribute to the public *fiscus*, or to use the Mafia for extortion and intimidation, it is, indeed, hardly surprising that things "went wrong" and that an otherwise well-thought-out corporate code failed to achieve its intended purpose. But the fundamental question to ask is, Why aren't property rights secure in Russia in the first place? The authors' speculation that things could have gone "right" if the government were to simply take care of "corruption" first and privatization later implies that they believe that "corruption" could be eliminated by some swift action, for example, more aggressive policing of deviant activities. But harsh measures against offenders have been the usual practice in Russia from the inception of its history,[120] and it is yet to generate the desired results. It is submitted that turning Russia into a market economy will take more than just crafting and imposing severe penalties for kleptocrats.

Nor am I sure that the use of the term "corruption" is necessarily appropriate in this context. It implies something that used to be wholesome and then sunk into the abyss of depravity. But is this really the case? Not holding wealth in high esteem is just as much of a "value" as holding wealth in high esteem. This chapter records the philosophical and theological roots of this alternative

[119] There seems to be plenty of evidence suggesting that the acquisition of Russian firms is often motivated by "softer" forms of corruption. For example, it seems that media corporations are often coveted not for their potential to generate profits as much as for their capacity to mold political destinies and, indirectly, to generate social and economic clout. See, for example, Elena Vartanova, "Corporate Transformation of the Russian Media," in Monroe Price, Andrei Richter, and Peter Yu (eds.), *Russian Media Law and Policy in the Yeltsin Decade*, The Hague and London: Kluwer Law International, p. 249 (2002).

[120] According to the accounts of the famous literary citric-at-large Georg Brandes, who wrote his impressions of his Russian travels in 1887, each little provincial town in Imperial Russia was sure to boast a prison of its own, usually teeming with inmates. See Georg Brandes, *Impressions of Russia*, translated by Samuel Eastman, p. 6 (1966; reprint of the 1889 Thomas Y. Crowell edition). The severity of punishment inflicted on the inmates in late Imperial Russia is chronicled by Dostoyevsky, in his *House of the Dead* (1862). No one in her right mind would suggest to restore law and order to contemporary Russian society by surpassing the severity of the punitive measures that were commonly practiced, apparently with little or no consequences, by every single one of Russia's former regimes.

path, which were consecrated by the intense suffering of millions of Russians for many generations. A culture of poverty and the poetics of suffering simply do not provide a fertile environment for capitalistic, or, indeed, hedonistic, transplants. If change were to be made, it ought to take place in schools, not penitentiaries. And if a lengthy process of "re-education" were to succeed some day, the resulting blending of Russian culture into the mainstream flux of Western consumerism would certainly be a victory achieved with a large grain of salt.

6

Truth

This chapter is not designed to offer a new philosophical insight of what truth might consist of. Rather, its aim is to record the prevailing views about this subject *in the formative periods* in the history of contract. This set of beliefs about the validity of propositions, and the way in which they were gradually transformed in the minds of scientists and persons of letters, vary dramatically in Russia and in the West. It is submitted that considerable attention has to be paid to this crucial difference in attempting to comprehend the observed differences in contract law and practice across the two cultures.

Let me start with a parable. Suppose that a judge has to make a factual finding, for example, whether the victim was actually killed by the person charged with the crime or whether it was the plaintiff or the defendant who first found a $10 bill tucked in a dark street corner. Clearly, the reality, which the fact finder is expected to reconstruct, is no longer in existence; it vanished into the past and is masked from the eye of the beholder. To overcome this hurdle, the judge must rely on some other data, external to the disputed fact itself, which she believes are strongly suggestive of its actual occurrence. Thus, she may infer that the accused visited the scene of the crime, and *ergo* that he might have been implicated in its commission, by examining the microscopic *flora* that stuck to the soles of his shoes, or she may infer that the plaintiff was the first one to have found the $10 bill by being unfavorably impressed by the blushing or stuttering of the defendant. This mental process of inferring from the existence of state of the world A that the state of the world B actually transpired is perennially present in the work of all judicial tribunals. This "problem of proof" is commonly addressed by the combined effect of probing the external *phenomenal evidence* and drawing on some internal process of *reasoning*.

Suppose, however, that the fact-finder firmly believes in the active role played by Divine Providence in the fact-finding process and in God's commitment to unequivocally bare the truth to its seekers. Such, for example, was the disposition of medieval (and some modern) judges sitting in ordeals by fire, in which certain physical consequences of exposing the human flesh of the "witness" to extreme heat (e.g., speedy recovery) were taken as sure signs of certain factual propositions (e.g., the reliability of the "witness"). Other forms of ordeals were quite common as well, for example, ordeal by water, or ordeal by battle, in person or through the engagement of vocational champions.[1] For a fact-finder adhering to these views, it would be silly to rely on the ambiguous, and sometimes false, probative value of either empirical evidence or human reasoning, due to his greater faith in the reliability of *judicium Dei*.

The problem of judicial proof is a mere parable for a broader proposition. The larger claim is that one can construct one's view of the world by drawing on one's experience, whether it emanates from external or innate sources. But this is not the only possible way. In the alternative, one could draw on one's faith in God or, indeed, on one's faith in a secular source of authority. One could, for instance, believe that proposition P is true because Aristotle said so, or because it was endorsed by some famous columnist in the *New York Times*. Furthermore, one could hold on to this view even in the face of conflicting scientific or other empirical evidence, as well as in violation of some axioms of rationality, for one could repose more trust in the pronouncement of her chosen source of knowledge than in the conclusions of scientific proof or rational inference.[2] Finally, one need not confine her trust in her chosen source of authority to past events (e.g., whether it rained in Fiji on some specified date in the past), but also to all kinds of testable hypotheses (e.g., whether oil and water are easy to mix). This is so because the refuting force of the conflicting evidence may not be sufficient for such a believer to make her change her mind in disregard

---

[1] The leading historian of English Law, W. S. Holdsworth, calls ordeals by battle *judicium Dei par excellence*, and then adds, with regard to all forms of ordeals: "Without taking account of less important forms of the ordeal, we find that the person who can carry red-hot iron, who can plunge his hand or his arm into boiling water, who will sink when thrown into the water, is deemed to have right on his side. The belief is so natural that very modern illustrations of it are not wanting." See W. S. Holdsworth, *A History of English Law*, Andover, UK: Sweet & Maxwell, Volume 1, pp. 310ff (1922). The "very modern" illustration cited by Mr. Holdsworth occurred in Italy in 1811. A breathtaking eyewitness account of ordeal by fire among twentieth-century Bedouins in the Sinai is provided By Austin Kennett in his book, *Bedouin Justice*, London: Kegan Paul, pp. 107ff (1925). The Bedouin practice is to make a person lick with his tongue a red-hot spoon. He is pronounced "clean," and his story is authenticated, if the tongue is not severely damaged by the heat. I was able to verify that this practice goes on in the Sinai (and elsewhere) even today, and is believed by its practitioners to generate equitable results.

[2] Why does a given believer, B, accept the validity of a certain proposition, P, when her source of authority, A, holds that P is true? Conceivably, B may believe that A is endowed with supreme reasoning faculties. Hence, P is deemed to be true not because A said so, but because if A said so, it is reasonable to conclude that P is indeed true. But this need not be the case. B may not hold any beliefs regarding A's reasoning faculties, or even ascribe to A mystical characteristics that have nothing to do with the concept of reason, and yet accept P as being true precisely because A said so. Reposing her trust in A liberates B from the task of either deciding for herself what is reasonable or trying to find some hidden logic in A's holding. It embodies the sweet submission to someone else's will, it frees the spirit of its own inquisitive burdens, and it gives B an opportunity to fend off some anxieties that commonly result from the state of uncertainty.

of her counselor's instructions. As Henri Bergson famously said, "the eye sees only that which the mind is prepared to comprehend."

The main contention in this chapter is that contractual culture is intimately linked with an empirical and rational interpretation of the world. This interpretation is based on a premise – that observation and scientific logic (or rationality) play a key role in the conduct of human affairs in general, and in the validation of propositions in particular. This worldview emerged in Western Europe during the Renaissance and the Reformation, gained much prominence in the seventeenth and eighteenth centuries, and lingered on, in one form or another, throughout the nineteenth century, and conceivably much longer. On the other hand, it made only weak inroads into the collective Russian psyche. Thus, the shaky foundations of contract law and contractual behavior in the Russian Federation can be attributed, *inter alia*, to this fundamental cultural difference.

I start my analysis by offering an explanation as to why Western contract is, or rather has been, basically conceived of as an empirically driven concept and in which ways it drew its vitality from the axioms of rational choice. I proceed to illustrate how empiricism and rationality came of age in Western culture as mutually complementary concepts, and in what ways their combined effect was instrumental in the history of ideas in general and in contract jurisprudence in particular. I then turn to the Russian scene and highlight its fascinating *alternative* approaches to both empiricism and rationality. Like in so many other fields, Russia has a lot to offer in terms of its own spiritual inspiration, but there is, alas, a price to be paid for this inspiration. Diminishing prospects for a sanguine contractual culture constitute a part of that price tag. The differential treatment of both observation and rationality as accepted methods for the validation of propositions manifests itself with the utmost clarity in the art of Russia and of the West. In recognition of this difference I conclude this chapter with a section on visual (and musical!) perspective and demonstrate how this artistic technique reflects the sharp divide between the two cultures.

Contract, Rationality, and Empirical Evidence

It is not immediately apparent why a given society should prefer to use contract as a vehicle for the formation of its legal norms. On the face of it, contract does not loom large as an attractive option, given the choice to forge legal norms by legislation or by administrative fiat. Organized society has much vaster resources to invest in the process of lawmaking than the average citizen, as well as easier access to information and expert assistance. Since many legal norms can easily be recycled in similar, recurring situations, centralized lawmaking may yield significant economies of scale, because the fixed cost of learning, comparing alternatives, choosing, and drafting are incurred in one go (rather than in a series of duplicative efforts undertaken, without coordination, by private individuals). The fixed cost of centralized lawmaking implies efficiency in production, because it is spread thin over an enormously large number of transactions.

Nevertheless, Western societies opt to be governed by a vast number of private contracts (side by side with additional sources of law).[3] The obvious question is, Why? Superficially, one could dismiss this question out of hand by suggesting that only individually crafted contracts, and certainly not centralized decrees, can be tailor-made to address the legal concerns of individual players. After all, how could the legislature, or the prince of the realm, be sensitized to the special concerns of each individual subject? However, this answer presupposes that the individuals in question *can* succeed where prince or parliament fail. More specifically, the assumption is that individual players can correctly identify their own concerns and rationally devise means to address them. But is this a realistic hope? Can private individuals live up to these expectations? In this chapter, I do not attempt to offer a "correct" answer to this difficult question. However, if one is willing to subscribe to a certain set of behavioral and cultural assumptions, then the private ordering of law comes into view as a much more appealing scheme. Conceivably, this set of beliefs, which I term the *combined empiricist and rationalist assumption*, is just a story that some of us are fond of telling each other or a set of leaps of faith with little substance behind them. But if this story is considered credible in a given culture, the belief in its veracity may generate far-reaching consequences for its legal institutions.

The essential elements of this combined empiricist and rationalist assumption presuppose that people are endowed with bundles of commodities, including tangible and intangible objects and skills of various kinds. They can evaluate, albeit not with mathematical precision, what level of utility they can derive from their bundles and then seek opportunities to improve their lot by trading some of their possessions in exchange for something more desirable that is initially owned by other agents.[4] According to this assumption, they have a good chance of doing well in their endeavor for the following reasons. First and foremost, what they are looking for, a "best outcome," or a "correct" strategy, "exists," or, at least, in the economic setting, it exists for any given budget constraint. This holds for all propositions in general, and for ideal legal outcomes in particular. It is further assumed that what one is looking for is not only "out there," but is

---

[3] Accepted wisdom has it that even large segments of statutory law are nothing but contractual arrangements in disguise. This is true particularly of so-called "default rules" (*jus dispositivum*), i.e., rules that apply whenever the parties do not explicitly overrule them by explicit stipulations. Why does the legislature produce default rules, given the carte blanche permission to contract around them? Because had they not been produced by the legislature, the parties would have to do it on their own and to incur, in the process, the high costs of production. For this mainstream interpretation of default rules as a mirror of the parties' presumed intention see, for instance, Ronald Gilson, "Evaluating Dual Class Common Stock – The Relevance of Substitutes," *Virginia Law Review* 73:897 (1987).

[4] More precisely, agents need not even know "how much" utility (in cardinal terms) they and other agents derive from their bundles. It is sufficient that they be able to evaluate whether they can derive more or less utility (in ordinal terms) by engaging in a process of exchange.

also observable by sensory means. Since we are all endowed with adequate sensory organs, we are all well positioned, at least in principle, to be rewarded for diligent observation by a realistic chance to obtain a good grasp of the phenomenal world. But whereas experience (or experimental observation) is a necessary condition for finding out what one is looking for, it is not a sufficient condition. To reach one's destination, one has to harness one's experimental knowledge to the reign of reason. The faculties of reason are supposed to be hard-wired in our minds, and many of us can actually use them in quest of the truth. In short, a *well-reasoned* dispensation of one's sensory *stimuli* is the "right" way of acquiring knowledge and a reasonable means of approaching the truth. When it comes to evaluating one's bundles of goods and commodities, comparing them to the bundles owned by other individuals, and making informed exchange decisions, governments and sovereigns, however enlightened, cannot replace the judgment of the concerned individuals. Only the latter know how they feel, what they covet, or what is reasonable to give up in exchange for their objects of desire. Consequently, only private agents can use both their sensory powers and their innate reasoning capacity to engage in contract.

The contract narrative may or may not be convincing. As Isaiah Berlin pointed out, the canonic belief in the existence of a single correct outcome, or of Truth in general, was shattered with the Romantic movement of the nineteenth century.[5] I find it unsurprising that the nineteenth century also marked the beginning of the decline of the reign of contract.[6] In this sense the Romantic movement of the nineteenth century paved the way to the various post-modern philosophies of the twentieth century, which cast doubts on the very concept of objective reality, let alone on the permanency of any scientific allegation in general[7] and within the legal domain in particular.[8] Again, it is not surprising

---

[5] See Isaiah Berlin, *The Roots of Romanticism*, Princeton, NJ: Princeton University Press (1999). See also his book, *The Crooked Timber of Humanity*, London: John Murray, pp. 207ff (1990; first edition published in 1959). Berlin seems to think that the first philosopher to have sewn the seeds that destroyed the canonic belief in a single Truth was Giambattista Vico in his book *Scienza nuova* (*The New Science*), whose definitive third edition was published posthumously in 1744. *The New Science* was translated to English by Thomas Bergin and Max Fisch for Cornell University Press in 1948 and reissued in 1984. Vico could not stand the conformist methods of instruction and substantive, totally unimaginative canonic beliefs of the scholarly community surrounding him (eighteenth-century Naples) and was an important first harbinger of cultural diversity. For Berlin's reading of Vico's role in this matter, see Berlin, ibid., pp. 49ff.

[6] The story of the gradual decline of contract in modern times is narrated, perhaps with too much emphasis, by Patrick Atiyah in the last part of his monumental volume on the history of contract. See P. S. Atiyah, *The Rise and Fall of Freedom of Contract*, New York: Oxford University Press (1979).

[7] Jacques Derrida has famously laid the foundation, in his *De la Grammatologie* (1967), to the proposition that modes of speech in general and written symbols in particular are "closed structures" that signify themselves rather than "real" external objects.

[8] The post-modern trend gained momentum especially among "critical legal theorists" who deny the scientific foundation of jurisprudence and maintain that all legal norms reflect the end result of a political struggle between factions and interest groups. See, for instance, Roberto Unger, *The Critical Legal Studies Movement*, Cambridge, MA: Harvard University Press (1986).

that modern "critical legal scholars" address such ideas as the freedom or the sanctity of contract with open hostility, mainly because they view traditional contract law as the end product of an unfair power struggle rather than as a fair and balanced pact forged by equally informed rational agents.[9] When these post-modern skeptics burst upon the scene, however, all Western countries had already been committed for a number of centuries to their respective privatized economies. Furthermore, I do not claim that the essentials of the empiricist and rationalist assumption generate a fair description of what people actually *do*. On the contrary, given all the evidence we now have both from psychoana- lytic theory and practice and from the plethora of recent experiments in the field of cognitive psychology, its explicit and hidden assumptions look rather contrived. Nevertheless, it existed, if nowhere else, at least in the eyes of most beholders during the formative periods of Western contract law. The rationality of the human race, and the ability of people to gather empirical evidence and to draw from the collected data informed and beneficial decisions, emerged as canonic truth during the heady days of the late Renaissance. They completely dominated Western philosophy in the seventeenth and eighteenth centuries, and were still very much in circulation during the entire nineteenth century as well. It still echoes quite vigorously in our day and age.[10] When psychoanalytic

---

[9] See, for instance, Morton Horwitz, *The Transformation of American Law, 1870–1960*, New York: Oxford University Press, Chapter 2 (1992).

[10] This rather orthodox faith in the rationality of contractual players and in their skills of gathering and processing of information gave rise to the modern view, which still persists in the twenty-first century, that contract is "efficient." An outcome is deemed efficient if, compared to its feasible alternatives, it achieves some desirable goals with the minimum of sacrifice or eliminates some costs without impairing any achievements. Translated to terms of individual utility or state of personal bliss, outcome A is more efficient than outcome B if some people (at least one) are happier under A than under B, and none is happier under B than under A. The prevailing view among economic analysts of contract law is that contract is "efficient," and so are the remedies afforded for its breach. Concerning substantive contractual doctrines and their efficiency, see, for example, Anthony Kronman, "Mistake, Disclosure, Information and the Law of Contract," *Journal of Legal Studies* 7:1 (1978). Concerning contract remedies see, for example, John Barton, "The Economic Basis of Damages for Breach of Contract," *Journal of Legal Studies* 1:277 (1972). Both Kronman's and Barton's articles have been expanded and, perhaps, corrected by more recent contributions to the literature, but the great bulk of the current theoretical wisdom still favors the view that the leading rationale of contract lies in its efficiency. The idea of efficiency is also captured by the so-called Coase Theorem, molded by Ronald Coase in his seminal article, "The Problem of Social Cost," *Journal of Law and Economics* 3:1 (1960). The theorem shows that in an ideal environment, with rational players, full information, and zero transaction costs, private parties will trade with their bundles and voluntarily reach an efficient endowment structure, i.e., an allocation of resources such that each player will end up with the bundle she prefers and is willing to pay for. For an easy exposition of the theorem, see, for instance, Mitchell Polinsky, *An Introduction to Law and Economics,* 2nd ed., Frederick, MD: Aspen Law & Business, p. 11 (1989). Closely associated with the idea that given full information and rational players contracts are deemed to be efficient are the so-called two basic theorems of welfare economics. They state that if the parties are left to their own devices, all contracts are bound to gravitate to Pareto efficient allocations of goods and services, and that any such Pareto efficient allocation is attainable, given an appropriate initial endowment structure. For the meaning of

theory[11] and much later cognitive psychology[12] made their first serious inroads into the citadel of rationality, the victory of Western contract was already a fait accompli. Russia, on the other hand, was ushered into the age of the *id* and of cognitive errors before it had a realistic chance to inculcate contract and integrate it into her culture.[13] For Russians, contract came too late.

The Retina and the Mind

The twin process of training one's eyes to take in the phenomenal universe and one's mind to figure it out has its roots in the pan-European Renaissance; it lingered on until the end of the nineteenth century. The development of this state of mind thus spanned the entire formative period of Western contract.

Pareto efficiency, see a fuller discussion in Chapter 3, supra. The first modern formulation of the notion that contract is intimately linked with Pareto efficiency was made by Francis Edgeworth in his famous book, *Mathematical Psychics: An Essay on the Application of Mathematics to the Moral Sciences* (1881). By the end of the nineteenth century, when the book was published, the vast majority of people still believed in the reign of reason and in the advancement of learning by experimental means, a belief that was not to be shattered until the onslaught of the First World War. This optimistic naiveté explains the great popularity of Edgeworth's work among his contemporaries. Old habits account for the continued inclusion of its main insights in almost any rigorous intermediate-level microeconomic course in all Western nations. The formal proof that every competitive equilibrium is Pareto optimal, and that every Pareto optimal result can be obtained in a competitive environment (given an appropriate reshuffling of the initial endowments), was first offered by Kenneth Arrow in his seminal article, "An Extension of the Basic Theorems of Classical Economics," in J. Neyman (ed.), *Second Berkeley Symposium on Mathematical Statistics and Probability*, Berkeley: University of California Press, and New York: Cambridge University Press, p. 507 (1951).

[11] Sigmund Freud published his *Interpretation of Dreams* in 1900 and his *The Ego and the Id* some twenty-three years later.

[12] The main experimental evidence about the prevalence and seriousness of cognitive errors is mostly attributable to Amos Tversky and Daniel Kahneman. See, for example, their article, "Rational Choice and the Framing of Decisions," *Journal of Business* 59:251 (1986). In my opinion, it is still too early to evaluate the lasting significance of these experimental results on our understanding of the human mind. Although very impressive in their own right, these results do not rest on clear theoretical foundations. A final evaluation of their true meaning will necessarily have to await the emergence of a convincing theory.

[13] I already recorded, especially in Chapter 4, supra, that Czarist Russia never had substantive contract legislation. Paradoxically, the first serious attempt to consider the role of contract in the governance of commerce and industry came during the 1920s as Lenin came to realize that his so-called "New Economic Policy" needed to take into account the problem of incentives on people's behavior. But unlike the Edgeworth-like discourse that views contract as a vehicle for social (Pareto) improvement, Lenin's plan interpreted it as a necessary evil that had to be endured for the achievement of the ultimate cause. See Michael Head, "The Passionate Legal Debates of the Early Years of the Russian Revolution," *Canadian Journal of Law and Jurisprudence* 14:3 (2001). Even that halfhearted tribute to capitalistic propensities irritated the left wing of the Party. See, for example, Leon Trotsky, *The Revolution Betrayed: What Is the Soviet Union and Where Is It Going?* 5th ed., translated by Max Eastman, New York: Pathfinder Press (1996). Although Trotsky did not fare so well in the Soviet Union, it seems that his call to abort all semblances of contract and property was better reflected in actual practice than the "moderate" Leninist view.

In this section I focus only on the "West." Russia's (very different) intellectual history comes up in the following section.

One of the greatest achievements of the Renaissance is, without a doubt, the so-called "empirical revolution," the propensity of its key figures to interpret the universe on the basis of experimental observations. This has not always been the case. Throughout the medieval millennium, the validity of most propositions could only be tested by comparing them to canonic "Truth," either sacred or profane.

Leonardo's sketchy, but revealing *Notebooks* say it all in the typical argumentative style of the period:

Many will think that they can with reason blame me, alleging that my proofs are contrary to the authority of certain men held in great reverence by their inexperienced judgments, not considering that my works are the issue of simple and plain experience which is the true mistress... though I have no power to quote from authors as they have, I shall rely on a far bigger and more worthy thing – on experience, the instructress of their masters.... All our knowledge has its origin in our perceptions. The eye, which is called the window of the soul, is the chief means whereby the understanding may most fully and abundantly appreciate the infinite work of nature.... To me it seems that all sciences are vain and full of errors that are not born of Experience; that is to say, that do not at their origin, middle, or end, pass through any of the five senses.[14]

And then again:

All true sciences are the result of Experience which has passed through our senses, thus silencing the tongues of litigants. Experience does not feed investigators on dreams, but always proceeds from accurately determined first principles, step by step in true sequences to the end; as can be seen in the elements of mathematics.... Here no one argues as to whether twice three is more or less than six or whether the angles of a triangle are less than two right angles. Here all arguments are ended by eternal silence and these sciences can be enjoyed by their devotees in peace. This the deceptive purely speculative sciences cannot achieve.[15]

In scribbling down these reflections Leonardo was clearly rebelling against "the sages" and their canonic "truth." The bastard son of a country notary, Leonardo did not enjoy a thorough liberal education; his mastery of the Latin tongue – the *only* language of respected scholarship – was definitely inadequate, and he must have been painfully aware of his inferior status vis-à-vis the "learned" humanists of his time. But he had the audacity, and the genius, to allow experience to trump authority and prevail.

For all his genius, he was not alone in professing this new revelation. A mesmerizing example of how scientific exploration was harnessed to expose the falseness of canonic wisdom is Lorenzo Valla's *Treatise on the Donation*

---

[14] *The Notebooks of Leonardo da Vinci*, selected and edited by Irma Richter, Oxford: Oxford University Press, p. 1 (1952; the original notes were taken by the artist throughout his lifetime: 1452–1519).

[15] Ibid., p. 5.

of Constantine. According to legend, the Emperor Constantine, on the fourth day after his baptism, purportedly conferred upon the Roman Pontiff almost unlimited sovereignty in matters temporal and spiritual. The document containing this alleged donation was enshrined by the popes in their constant struggle against the secular rulers of the lands of Christendom. As it turns out, the "donation" was a forgery. However, to speak up against its authenticity was not a trifling matter. Considering the risks of doing so, Valla wrote:

[S]hall I be deterred by the hazard of death? Away, then, with trepidation, let fears far remove, let doubts pass away. With a brave soul, with utter fidelity, with good hope, the cause of truth must be defended, the cause of justice, the cause of God.[16]

Valla first goes into a psychological foray of exploring the soul of Constantine. He addresses himself to an imaginary audience of temporal rulers and asks them whether they would consider it reasonable to donate the lion's share of their worldly possessions and then retreat to a backwater province like Byzantium. He appeals to their presumed appetite for further territorial acquisitions and, in a spirit presaging the modern insight about endowment effects,[17] adds:

But if domination is usually sought with such great resolution, how much greater must be the resolution to preserve it! For it is by no means so discreditable not to increase an empire as to impair it, nor is it so shameful not to annex another's kingdom to your own as for your own to be annexed to another's.[18]

Far more importantly, in the first scientifically informed *historical* inquiry of modernity, Valla shows that Constantine was a devout Christian from his boyhood. From this he infers that it was not reasonable to believe that he was swayed to donate his most precious possessions in recognition of some mysterious baptism in his later years. Finally, in the first *linguistic* exploration ever, Valla demonstrated that the vulgar Medieval Latin, in which the "donation" was composed, could not have possibly been employed in the fourth century A.D., when the document was supposedly drafted.[19]

---

[16] Lorenzo Valla, *The Treatise of Lorenzo Valla on the Donation of Constantine*, translated by Christopher Coleman, Toronto: University of Toronto Press, p. 23 (1993; the *Treatise* was first published in 1440, although the present translation uses a manuscript dated 1451).

[17] This modern observational insight reveals that most individuals ascribe a much greater value to items that they own than to items owned by others. For example, people normally demand a much higher price for parting with items belonging to them than the price they would have been willing to spend to acquire similar items if they hadn't had them in the first place. See Daniel Kahneman, Jack Knetsch, and Richard Thaler, "The Endowment Effect, Loss Aversion and Status Quo Bias," *Journal of Economoc Perspectives* 5:193 (1991).

[18] Valla, ibid., p. 31.

[19] Like Valla in his *Donation of Constantine*, many Renaissance humanists, including a number of jurists, called for an independent perusal of ancient texts in quest of their meaning, instead of relying on their glosses and interpolations. This too amounted, just as in the case of Valla, to an attempt to approach the truth by probing objective phenomena (texts) rather than by relying on the opinion of former venerated scholars (glosses and interpolations).

Perhaps the most notorious Renaissance champion of empirical observation as a method of truth revelation was the founding father of all political science, Niccolò Machiavelli. It has often been observed that Machiavelli was hardly a Machiavellian political theorist. His true normative preferences in the political sphere are spelled out in great detail in his longer work, the *Discourses on Livy*. This work is actually arranged as a commentary to Livy's first ten books on Roman history, but it uses this subject as a mere point of departure. The *Discourses* continues the tradition of essays on the Good Government.[20] It speaks of the superiority of democratic government, of the necessity of even despotic regimes to be based on popular consent, of the need of nations to stay united within a viable political entity, of the vital role of leadership, on the imperative to have secure boundaries, of the need to select a state religion such that it would best cement the sense of unity of purpose and social cohesiveness, and, in addition, on the necessity to use harsh measures when they are needed as the only means of survival.[21] Only this latter imperative is fleshed out in his more famous work, *The Prince*. But even there, it is rather clear that Machiavelli is merely pointing out, based on his acute observations of human nature, what might be the consequences of alternative political strategies, thereby laying the foundations for the work of all positive (as distinguished from normative) theorists in the modern era. Here is the master himself:

[I]t has appeared to me more fitting to go directly to the effectual truth of the thing than to the imagination of it. And many have imagined republics and principalities that have never been seen or known to exist in truth; for it is so far from how one lives to how one should live that he who lets go of what is done for what should be done learns his ruin rather than his preservation.[22]

Even if one wishes to manipulate the feelings and emotions of other people, one ought to understand what makes real people tick, how they might in fact react to the observer's strategies, rather than speculate about what they should have done, if they conformed to some normative *desiderata*:

[A] dispute arises whether it is better to be loved than feared, or the reverse. The answer is that one would want to be both the one and the other; but because it is difficult to put them together, it is much safer to be feared than loved, if one has to lack one of the two. For one can say this generally of men: that they are ungrateful, fickle, pretenders and dissemblers, evaders of danger, eager for gain. While you do them good, they are yours...when the need for them is far away; but, when it is close to you, they revolt.

---

[20] For a painterly analogy see Chapter 4, supra, discussing the *Allegory of Good Government* by the Sienese master Ambrogio Lorenzetti.

[21] For an excellent, albeit somewhat outdated outline of this opus, see Max Lerner's introduction to Niccolò Machiavelli, *The Prince and the Discourses*, New York: The Modern Library (1940).

[22] Niccolò Machiavelli, *The Prince*, translated by Harvey Mansfield, Chicago: University of Chicago Press, Chapter 15 (1985; the work was first published in 1532, almost 20 years after it had been composed, in 1513).

And the prince who has founded himself entirely on their words . . . is ruined . . . and men have less hesitation to offend one who makes himself loved than one who makes himself feared.[23]

The Prince follows a long tradition of both medieval and humanist essays on rulers and their callings. But whereas all his predecessors wrote in the idealistic and scholastic tradition of the Middle Ages, Machiavelli discarded all of this to make room for a *realistic* account of the actual demeanor of princes. By inventing the concept of empirical observation, Machiavelli managed to substitute facts for aspirations and science for metaphysics.

The substitution of science for metaphysics swept the minds of men and women across Europe and across all scientific disciplines known at that time.

Ancient knowledge was compounded in a small number of canonic volumes that held their sway on the human mind throughout the Middle Ages. I always thought that the most fascinating of them all (but there are several other strong contenders) is Pliny the Elder's *Natural History*. Pliny (Gaius Plinius Secundus) was a first-century A.D. soldier, sailor, diplomat, and, above all, a scholar of insatiable curiosity. His encyclopedic compendium spans nearly all accepted wisdom in the Early Imperial Period, from geography to astronomy to agriculture, from botany, medicine, and magic to minerals, painting, and architecture. Many of Pliny's observations are still considered valid today, but perhaps not all:

As an aphrodisiac, Salpe bids one plunge an ass's penis seven times in hot oil and then rub the appropriate part with this. Dalion prescribes the ash from it to be taken in drink . . .[24] if a horse casts his shoe . . . and someone retrieves it and puts it aside, it is a cure for hiccoughs for those who remember where they put it! . . . wolves will not enter a field, if a wolf has been caught, his legs broken, a knife driven into his body, the blood sprinkled a little at a time around the edges of the field and the body itself buried in the place from which it was first dragged.[25]

It was not until the end of the fifteenth century, however, that a Renaissance author dared to question Pliny's observations; but then it came with vengeance: In a book published in 1492–93, *Castigations of Pliny*, the author, Ermalao (or Ermolao) Barbaro, pointed out not less than 5,000 errors in Pliny's manuscript! For good measure he also published an indictment of Aristotelian scholarship, especially in the natural sciences, as well as a reexamination of other ancient luminaries.[26] Barbaro's work was typical of a great wave of similar pioneering

---

[23] Ibid., Chapter 16.
[24] Pliny the Elder, *Natural History*, translated by John Healy, New York: Penguin Books, materia medica Section 262 (1991).
[25] Ibid., Section 263.
[26] See, for instance, Ermalao Barbaro, *Scienti Naturalis Compendium* (1597). To the best of my knowledge, Barbaro's work was not translated into English. Interesting information about Barbaro's work in context can be found, e.g., in Nicholas Rubinstein, "Ermolao Barbaro and Late Quattrocento Venetian Humanism," in John Hale (ed.), *Renaissance Venice*, Totowa, NJ: Rowman and Littlefield (1973). See also, Eric Cochrane, "Science and Humanism in the Italian Renaissance," *American Historical Review* 81:1039 (1976).

manuscripts that sought to replace ancient authority with fresh insights based on observation and experience.[27] For example, the Jesuit José D'Acosta, who served as a senior missionary in Peru, wrote a book based on his actual travels and observation, giving account of the existence of other continents, a very unorthodox view.[28] To make things worse from a scriptural perspective, he also observed that those newly discovered lands were inhabited by people. He acknowledged that the authority of the ancients was fallible and stopped just short of admitting that it was acceptable to approach Biblical authority with a grain of salt. He tried to explain the inhabitants by suggesting their attribution to the ten lost tribes of Israel, but ended up rejecting that hypothesis because he did not observe any greedy tendencies amongst them. He concluded that they must have migrated from Asia on a land crossing.[29]

A similar transformation occurred in the field of human anatomy and physiology. All medical knowledge in this field was derived, for almost 1,500 years, from a single volume, Galen's *On Anatomical Procedures*.[30] Galen was a Greek physician who lived in Alexandria in the second century A.D. He dissected animals, especially Rhesus monkeys, but his followers were prepared to make the heroic assumption that human anatomy closely resembled the results of his observations. He also committed some major errors in his physiological understanding. His most notorious mistake was inherent in his belief that the blood moved between the coronary ventricles through invisible pores in the membrane separating them, an error that was not to be corrected until 1628, with William Harvey's pioneering discovery of the circulation of blood in the body.[31] The most interesting aspect of Galen's domination of medical wisdom for a millennium and a half was that, contrary to popular belief, late medieval and early Renaissance physicians (as well as artists) did perform numerous dissections of human cadavers. They could have seen for themselves, if they were so inclined, the clear evidence contradicting Galen's authority. Nevertheless, they chose to consult his book as a practical guide in treating their patients (or painting their pictures), thus giving precedence, as it were, to Galen's opinion over what they saw with their own eyes.[32] In Figure 43 we see an enigmatic depiction of a standing man with an X-ray view of several of his internal organs, his veins,

[27] For a breathtaking survey of this revolutionary period in the history of science, see Marie Boas, *The Scientific Renaissance 1450–1630*, London: Collins (1962).

[28] To be sure, D'Acosta's work was published a full century after Columbus' landing in America; nevertheless, the diehard myth of a Ptolemaic universe conforming in its physical contours to scriptural dogma still reigned supreme. See infra about the Copernican revolution.

[29] José D'Acosta, *The Natural and Moral History of the Indies* (translated by Edward Grimston in 1604 and edited by Clements Markham in 1880; the book was first published in 1590).

[30] The book was known in the Middle Ages in its Latin translation. The surviving parts of it (which are quite substantial) were recently translated to English and edited by Charles Singer for Oxford University Press (1988).

[31] William Harvey, *An Anatomical Dissertation Upon the Movement of the Heart and Blood in Animals*, printed for G. Moreton in 1894; the original work was published in 1628, and completely revolutionized the whole discipline of internal medicine.

[32] Marie Boas, ibid., pp. 120ff.

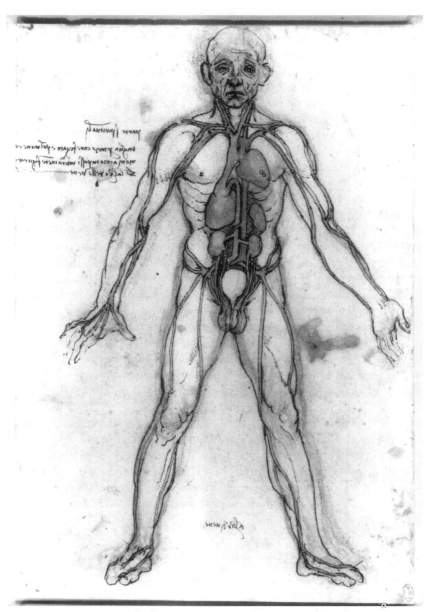

FIGURE 43. Leonardo da Vinci, *The Tree of Veins*, 1488–92.

and his arteries. It is a drawing by Leonardo, no less, called *The Tree of Veins*, executed sometime between 1488 and 1492.

The whole internal structure is portrayed in conformity with Galen's specifications. Consequently, it is anatomically absurd. The blood vessels, which are the named subject matter of this drawing, are shown exactly as Galen would have them, that is, there is no recognition of the interdependence of veins and arteries, or of the heart's function in regulating the circulation of blood. I find this whole drawing so puzzling, because we know of Leonardo's fascination with human dissection as well as of his strong contempt for naked authority when it conflicts with experience. He did not know about blood circulation, of course, but he did know a lot that was not revealed, or was incorrectly portrayed, in this drawing; indeed, in some of his later works his anatomy gets much closer to the truth. Perhaps he was simply attempting to render not the human body, but Galen's portrayal of our internal constitution, thus showing his skill in translating verbal communication to pictorial iconography.[33] Be it as it may, Galen's authority was not shattered until 1543, when Andreas Vesalius published his groundbreaking book, *On the Fabric of the Human Body*,[34] which revolutionized the field overnight, although it did commit some apparently unavoidable errors.[35] By drawing on his own direct experience, based on numerous human dissections, Vesalius not only laid the foundations for the modern science of anatomy, but he also gave an impetus to the development of other medical arts, including physiology, the elements of contagion, occupational disease, and some initial steps in pharmacology.[36] Without prejudice to Vesalius' anatomical breakthrough, his discovery was long in the air, as both scientists and persons of letters took a keen interest in the constitution of our bodies and in probing underneath the skin as a method of establishing a connection between internal anatomy and outer appearance. A famous Giorgione masterpiece seems to illustrate this Renaissance taste rather forcefully. In his luminous portrait, *Old Woman*, executed circa 1508 (Figure 44), the elderly sitter is holding a ribbon containing the inscription *col tempo* (in time), which records the inevitable decay of the flesh when time takes its toll. A popular story has it that the sitter, still deliciously attractive when Giorgione painted her, turned down his amatory advances. This prompted him to spitefully anticipate the effects of old age on her vein carnal splendor. The story, alas, seems to lack real historical support,[37] but nevertheless the portrait does record the effects of diseased and deteriorated internal tissue on the sitter's skin, eyelids, toothless mouth, and general wobbly appearance.

---

[33] See Carmen Bombach (ed.), *Leonardo da Vinci, Master Draftsman*, New Haven, CT: Yale University Press, pp. 25, 408ff (2003).

[34] Vesalius' book is now available in English in three volumes, translated between 1998 and 2003 for Norman Publishing, Novato, CA.

[35] As noted previously, the circulatory system was not properly understood until Harvey's discovery in 1628. Vesalius also treated anatomy and physiology as one subject, as he held the philosophical view that anatomy had to be interpreted teleologically.

[36] Marie Boas, ibid.

[37] Perhaps this otherwise false story has some psychoanalytic roots. There is some evidence that the sitter is Giorgione's own mother; the portrait can be read, then, as a lamentation for the downfall of a loved one, who may still linger in one's memory as an early object of adoration. See Ludwig Baldass, *Giorgione and Giorgionism*, New York: N. H. Abrams, p. 159 (1965). Baldass notes that Renaissance poets used the expression *col tempo* as a "stock phrase" to describe temporal corrosion.

FIGURE 44. Giorgione, *Old Woman* ("*Col Tempo*"), circa 1508.

In the very same year, 1543, when *On the Fabric of the Human Body* saw the light of day, a parallel revolution came to life with the publication of Copernicus' *Revolution of the Heavenly Spheres*. Just as Vesalius' book was aimed at shattering Galen's authority, so Copernicus' revelation started a long process of splitting apart Ptolemaic astronomy.[38] Interestingly, Copernicus led a peaceful life and returned his soul to his Creator without being so much as

[38] Ptolemaic astronomy, and the entire worldview that is supported by it, is contained in one canonic volume, *The Almagest*, written by Claudius Ptolemaeus, or Ptolemy, during the entire second quarter of the second century A.D. Very little is known of Ptolemy the man, except the approximate dates of his birth and death (c. 100–c. 178 A.D.) and his probable place of residence, Alexandria or its whereabouts. He was clearly a member of the Hellenistic oriental elite, and his fame was preserved in the annals of history thanks to his Arab disciples, who are also responsible for the title of his work as it is known today, which is made up of two words, "the greatest," the first (*al*) in Arabic and the second (*megiste*) in Greek.

summoned for questioning by the Inquisition. On the contrary, the Church welcomed his speculations because they proved useful in calendar calculations. The clear reason for this docile acceptance of heresy was that Copernicus did not prove anything at all. *Copernicus was a speculator, not an experimentalist.*[39] To use his own language:

Although there are so many authorities for saying that the Earth rests in the centre of the world that people think the contrary supposition inopinable and even ridiculous; if however we consider the thing attentively, we will see that the question has not yet been decided and accordingly is by no means to be scorned. For every apparent change in place occurs on account of the movement either of the thing seen or of the spectator, or on account of the necessarily unequal movement of both. For no movement is perceptible relative to things moved equally in the same direction.[40]

A major leap forward was attempted by Johannes Kepler more than half a century later.[41] Kepler did use in his work a series of empirical observations, especially those made and recorded by his one-time mentor, Tycho Brahe. But Kepler himself was not an experimentalist, or at least not mainly so, as his main ambition was focused on attempting to offer a mathematical formulation of the heavenly spheres. In one of his earlier works he mused, showing his fascination with the universe and his enthusiasm for his own work:

The sphere of the Earth is the measure of all. Circumscribe about it a Dodecahedron: its circumscribed sphere will be [that of] Mars: circumscribe a Tetrahedron about [the sphere of] Mars: its circumscribed sphere will be [that of] Jupiter. Circumscribe a Cube about [the sphere of] Jupiter: its circumscribed sphere will be [that of] Saturn. Now inscribe an Icosahedron within [the sphere of] Earth: its inscribed sphere will be [that of] Venus. Inscribe an Octahedron in [the sphere of] Venus: its inscribed sphere will be [that of] Mercury. Here you have the reason of the number of the planets.[42]

Like Copernicus before him, Kepler was not pestered by the Church (but he was badly tormented by his creditors), not only because as a Protestant he was not under the effective protection of the Holy Office, but also because the Vatican failed to see how mathematical ideas could seriously transform the human mind and cause otherwise pious souls to lose their faith in dogmatic truth.

---

[39] He speculated, for instance, that Earth could move, in spite of its great mass, because the alternative, namely that the greater firmament could move around us, was even harder to grasp. Whereas the hypothesis of the Earth's movement is expected to show "parallax," a small movement of the remote stars, he explained away our inability to observe this phenomenon by the great distance separating us from these stars.

[40] Copernicus, *Revolutions of Heavenly Spheres* 514–15, in *Great Books of the Western World*, Volume 16, translated by Glenn Wallis, Chicago: W. Benton/Encyclopedia Britannica (1938).

[41] Kepler's two most important publications are *The Harmonies of the World* of 1619 and his *Epitome of Astronomy* of 1618–21.

[42] This excerpt, cited at Marie Boas, ibid., p. 279, is taken from the preface of his early work, *Cosmographical Mystery*, which saw the light of day in 1596.

The Church grasped the severity of the situation and then panicked and fought back with all its might only when Galileo burst upon the scene,[43] armed with a telescope, which he himself perfected, and offered all and sundry an *observational* view of the universe. And lo and behold, what dangerous sights made their appearance on the other side of that enchanted lens! The viewers could verify, just as Galileo did, that the moon was built very much like our own planet, thereby destroying the Aristotelian dichotomy between bodies celestial and terrestrial. They could notice, by just looking through the telescope, that Jupiter had moons of its own, thereby falsifying the view that the universe was a hierarchical structure that was singly dominated by the Earth. They could observe spots on the surface of the sun, which Galileo interpreted as imperfections, in sharp contrast to the Aristotelian notion of celestial flawlessness. In short, the whole Ptolemaic worldview was plainly exposed as a myth. At a certain point they refused to look anymore, citing the well-known excuse of optical illusions. After all, if we all recognize that the senses are apt to deceive us, why should we form our opinion about God's creation by using these fallible means, if we have the scriptures to guide us in quest of the truth? But Galileo, the great experimentalist, did not rely in his investigations on the sensual stimuli alone. The signals transmitted by the senses needed interpretation, and Galileo was much too sophisticated to overlook this fact. As William Shea puts it, Galileo's main achievement was in providing mathematical proofs to the propositions suggested by experimental observation.[44] This too was an anti-Aristotelian (and hence anti-scholastic) stance,[45] which won him the following rebuke from one of his opponents, Lodovico delle Colombe: "In Aristotle's time this [mathematics] was considered a schoolboy's science ... and yet these modern mathematicians solemnly declare that Aristotle's divine mind failed to understand it, and that as a result he made ridiculous mistakes." To which Galileo retorted: "And they are right in saying so, for he committed many serious errors and mathematical blunders, though neither so many nor so silly as does this author every time he opens his mouth on the subject."[46] We shall return to this subject of wedding experience to rigorous reasoning later on in

---

[43] Galileo's main opus, the *Dialogo Sopra i Due Massimi Sistemi Del Mondo, Tolemaico e Copernicano*, was first published in 1629 with an express approval by the pope. The pope blundered, however, in granting his consent, because he erroneously believed that Galileo, like Copernicus before him, would just speculate rather than prove his hypothesis by experimental (and mathematical) means. Having realized his error he was quick to act. The rest of the story is too well known to be narrated here. The book is available in English under the title *The Two Chief World Systems, Ptolemaic and Copernican*, translated by Stillman Drake with a foreword by Albert Einstein, Berkeley: University of California Press (1953). It is interesting to note that Galileo's name was not cleared by the Catholic Church until 1992 (!) by Pope John Paul II.

[44] William Shea, *Galileo's Intellectual Revolution: Middle Period, 1610–1632*, New York: Science History Publications (1977).

[45] Ernst Cassirer, "Galileo's Platonism," in M. F. A. Montagu (ed.), *Studies and Essays in the History of Science and Learning*, New York: Henry Schuman, p. 279 (1944).

[46] This lovely exchange is cited in Gary Tomlinson, *Monteverdi and the End of the Renaissance*, Berkeley: University of California Press, pp. 12–13 (1987).

this chapter. Numerous modern scholars offered this two-pronged approach in quest of the truth, but it was Galileo who paved the way and laid the foundations for them all.

In this long (though incomplete) train of pioneering empiricists I saved the last word to an Englishman, the indomitable Francis Bacon (1561–1626). This choice was made not only because his voice is perhaps the clearest and most articulate, but also because Bacon was a leading jurist and an important judge. It is fascinating to observe how his philosophical ideas, some of which were articulated after he quit his position on the bench (in personal disgrace),[47] are reflected in his legal (i.e., nonphilosophical) work.

In his philosophy, Bacon was a great champion of empirical observation. In the very first aphorism, which opens his great book *Novum Organum*, Bacon proclaims:

Man, as the minister and interpreter of nature, does and understands as much as his observations on the order of nature, either with regard to things or the mind, permit him, and neither knows nor is capable of more.[48]

Bacon waged a major war against the method of syllogism as a scientific means of acquiring knowledge. In treading this path, Bacon challenged large parts of the ancient Aristotelian tradition,[49] and hence much of the scholastic method, which was largely based on this "logical" trope:

The syllogism consists of propositions, propositions of words; words are the signs of notions. If, therefore, the notions (which form the basis of the whole) be confused and carelessly abstracted from things, there is no solidity to the superstructure. Our only hope, then, is in genuine induction.[50]

Like all the truly great champions of empirical investigation, however, Bacon was acutely aware of the ambiguity of the phenomenal world and that our

---

[47] Bacon was impeached by Parliament for accepting bribe from a litigant. He confessed to the crime, was removed from the bench, and imprisoned in the Tower. He spent only four days there, as James I, who was well served by Bacon, both freed him and paid his fine. Relieved from the onerous office of the chancellorship, Bacon turned to philosophy and forever transformed the human mind.

[48] Francis Bacon, *Novum Organum or True Suggestions for the Interpretation of Nature*, revised edition of both *The Advancement of Learning* and *Novum Organum* by James Creighton, Colonial Press, p. 315 (1899; the original version of the *Novum Organum* was published in Latin in 1620).

[49] A good example of scholastic reasoning may be found in Aquinas' attitude to the concept of usury. Rather than pose the empirical question of how might lenders and borrowers react to a rule that does not allow one to charge interest on a loan, Aquinas reasoned that the use of money is not differentiable from the money so used itself, and hence it followed that one could justifiably expect the principal amount to be duly returned, but could not justifiably make a claim for the use. See A. W. B. Simpson, *A History of the Common Law of Contract*, pp. 510ff (1975).

[50] Ibid., aphorism 14, at page 316.

relentless efforts to decipher its secrets are more contingent than absolute.[51] This is perhaps why he phrased so many of his propositions as aphorisms rather than as statements of fact; he sensed that one needs to fend off all attempts to "cook the books" by spurious "certainties" and to always leave room for further speculation and improvement. In commenting on his own literary style he wrote:

Whereas I could have digested these rules into a certain method or order, which, I know, would have been more admired, as that which would have made every particular rule, through his coherence and relation unto other rules, seem more cunning and more deep; yet I have avoided so to do, because this delivering of knowledge in distinct and disjoined aphorisms doth leave the wit of man more free to turn and toss, and to make use of that which is so delivered to more several purposes and applications.[52]

In his *New Atlantis* (1624), a book that was clearly inspired by Thomas More's *Utopia*, the inhabitants of an ideal island are in constant quest of the truth by experimental means, but with constant recourse to reasoning;[53] even in his supposedly historical account of a former sovereign, *History of the Reign of Henry VII*, he idealizes the subject of his narrative by ascribing to him the "correct" methods of acquiring scientific enlightening.

How, then, did Francis Bacon the jurist implement his philosophy in his professional work? First of all, let us review the sources. Francis Bacon was made Solicitor General by James I in 1604, promoted to Attorney General in 1613, and to Lord Chancellor in 1618. He served in that capacity until 1621, when he was charged with accepting a litigant's bribe; he confessed to the crime, served a (very) short term in the Tower, and spent his years of retirement completing his philosophical *oeuvre*. Very little is known not only about his activities as a lawyer but even about his tenure on the bench. This surprising void has two reasons: the custom of the day to be very sparing in the writing and publication of law reports[54] and a deliberate move to obliterate Bacon's judicial output in retribution for his dishonorable fall from grace.[55] A first compilation

[51] See, for instance, Lisa Jardine, *Francis Bacon, Discovery and the Art of Discourse*, New York: Cambridge University Press, Chapter 4 (1974).

[52] This passage is contained in Bacon's *Maxims of the Law* (1597), cited in Brian Vickers' introduction to Francis Bacon, *The Essays or Counsels Civil and Moral*, New York: Oxford University Press (1999). See also, Brian Vickers, *Francis Bacon and Renaissance Prose*, Cambridge: Cambridge University Press, Chapter 3 (1968).

[53] The imaginary island of the New Atlantis is inhabited by peaceful and hospitable residents bent on the service of the larger community by the expansion of knowledge through experimental means. The State maintains and nourishes a scholarly institution known as "Salomon's House." Its main purpose is thus described: "The end of our foundation is the knowledge of causes, and secret motions of things; and the enlarging of the bounds of human empire, to the effecting of all things possible." For example: "We have also parks, and inclosures of all sorts, of beasts and birds; which we use not only for view or rareness, but likewise for dissections and trials, that thereby may take light what may be wrought upon the body of man."

[54] William Holdsworth, *Some Makers of the Common Law, The Tagore Lectures 1937–38*, Cambridge: Cambridge University Press, Lecture 5 at p. 106 (1966).

[55] See George Keeton, "Bacon as a Chancery Judge," *Iowa Law Review* 18:476 (1933).

of his rulings was published only as recently as 1932 in England, and even this important treasure does not contain the great jurist's actual words but only a summary of his pronouncements gleaned from the court records.[56] More than this thin record simply does not exist. On the other hand, Bacon's polemic writings are all well preserved. They reflect much more richly his ideas about the law, and it is to this source that I will return shortly. But let us first pause to consider Bacon's record, however scant, as a lawyer and a judge.

The record shows that Bacon was involved as an advocate in the *Slade Case*, representing the defendant-promisor (Morley) and doing his best to fend off the triumph of assumpsit. How could this great champion of law reform harness his talents to the "wrong" cause? To begin with, the plaintiff, Mr. Slade, was represented in this case by Bacon's archenemy, Sir Edward Coke, who later became the Chief Justice of England and who also reported the case. Coke's reporting was not entirely objective; he articulated his own arguments with great skill but did not dispense the same high standard of coverage to the pleadings of his adversary. Even if one takes Coke's narrative on face value, Bacon's role as counsel in this case can be explained away by the simple fact that he was acting for a private client and for a fee, and given his opportunistic character and the adversary nature of the Common Law, his labors did not necessarily reflect his own personal preferences. Other commentators offered the view that Bacon objected to the triumph of assumpsit because it was largely based on legal fiction (recall the momentous words, reported by Coke, that "every contract executory imports in itself an assumpsit"). Bacon is known to have abhorred legal fiction because he preferred to tackle difficult situations by the more direct means of either express legislation or by substitution of the harsh Common Law rules by the more charitable principles of Equity.[57]

Although very little is known about Bacon's judicial output, a leading English legal historian (William Holdsworth) expressed the view that he will always be remembered "as the fourth and the greatest of the founders of the English system of Equity."[58] This surprising statement requires a few words of explanation. First, a terminological clarification for nonlawyers (members of the legal profession will find this clarification unnecessary). "Equity" is a system of law that flourished in Elizabethan and Jacobean times side by side with the traditional Common Law. It was mainly informed by the need to mitigate some of the hardships of the latter and to pump new blood into the clogged arteries of the older system. Rules of Equity are still current in contemporary Anglo-American law as well as in the rest of the Common Law world. Bacon's predecessor as Lord Chancellor, Lord Ellesmere, who served *ex officio* as the formal head of

---

[56] This compilation was put together by John Ritchie as the *Reports of Cases Decided by Francis Bacon*, London: Sweet & Maswell (1932). I refer to Ritchie's compilation in this chapter as the *Reports*. The political reason for suppressing Bacon's opinions is shortly analyzed by W. S. Holdsworth in his note, "Francis Bacon's Decisions," *Law Quarterly Review* 49:61 (1933).

[57] See Daniel Coquillette, *Francis Bacon*, Stanford: Stanford University Press, pp. 136ff (1992).

[58] Holdsworth, ibid., p. 102.

the Courts of Equity, had a long feud of jurisdiction with Lord Coke, who headed the courts of the Common Law. Ellesmere was partially successful in his campaign to subordinate the scholastic rigidity of the Common Law to the more humanist principles of Equity. Bacon served as Ellesmere's immediate successor as Lord Chancellor. During his tenure Coke was dismissed from office by James I, largely for bad reasons (Coke led a spirited struggle to subordinate the prerogative of the crown to the Rule of Law). Regardless of the merits of Coke's removal from office, Bacon was able to take advantage of his adversary's downfall to consolidate the supremacy of the courts of Equity and to end the dispute.[59] This per se is sufficient to lend credence to Holdsworth's high esteem of Bacon's chancellorship. But that is not all. In those early heady days of Equity, almost every doctrine was breaking new ground.[60] A lot depended on the discretion of individual judges, and in particular on the discretion of the chief judge in Equity, the Lord Chancellor.[61] It was at this age that the devotees of the old system coined the plaintive phrase that redress in Equity was made to fit the "Chancellor's foot." What this adage actually meant was that the certainty of fixed dogma was replaced by the uncertainty of individual discretion, and discretion largely depended on the inquisitiveness of the individual judges and on the facts that they deemed crucial for an equitable adjudication of the dispute. It is easy, then, to take this derogatory term, the "chancellor foot," and by flipping it over admire its silver lining: Equity metamorphosed the legal system by replacing static dogma with dynamic empiricism; by increasing the sensitivity of judicial outcomes to the particularity of fact, it forced lawyers to do their job by looking at the world. Judges, in their turn, could no longer do justice by deductive scholastics and had to reason inductively, from fact to principle to outcome.

Numerous doctrines of Equity originated during Bacon's term, and given his universally recognized intellectual leadership, many must have been penned by him. For example, it appears that the doctrine of "equity of redemption"[62]

---

[59] The personal enmity between Bacon and Coke, however, never subsided. The deposed Coke was elected to Parliament and was instrumental in concocting ironclad impeachment proceedings against Bacon, which led to his final disgrace.

[60] It is customary to refer to the corpus of the Common Law as consisting of "rules" and to the system of Equity as consisting of "principles." Whereas rules are perceived as fixed injunctions grounded on authority, principles are more commonly conceived as grounded on reason, a much more elastic concept. See Gerald Postema, *Bentham and the Common Law Tradition*, Oxford: Clarendon Press, and New York: Oxford University Press, pp. 443 (1986).

[61] For Bacon's approach to the problem of judicial (or any other) innovation, see his essay *Of Innovations*, where he wrote: "He that will not apply new remedies must expect new evils: for time is the greatest innovator; and if time of course alter things to the worse, and wisdom and counsel shall not alter them to the better, what shall be the end?"

[62] If a debtor, D, borrows money form a creditor, C, and mortgages some real property as security for the debt, C had, under the old Common Law, full authority to forfeit the collateral in satisfaction of the debt. The so-called "equity of redemption" recognizes the special bond between a person and her land, and allows D to redeem the property by paying the debt even when it is overdue, and (subject to some limitations) after C's forfeiture proceedings had been lawfully concluded.

materialized in this period,[63] and it was he who first interpreted and enforced the law against fraudulent preferences.[64] His training and disposition as a devout humanist impelled him to fashion the entire court system under his tutelage to suit the real needs and comfort of the litigants and their counsel,[65] by both establishing a workable procedure for the Court of Chancery and by waging a war against the law's delay, thus clearing, for the first time in recent memory, an incredibly congested court docket.[66]

But all these important contributions are only obliquely related to the law of contract. More to the point, Bacon is reported to have expanded the reach of contract by making the remedy of specific performance more accessible to disappointed promisees.[67] Whereas the Common Law judges, with their obsession with the technicalities of the law (the writs of action) turned a blind eye toward the special circumstances of individual cases, Bacon, the great empiricist, made almost everything turn on the pertinent factual backdrop of individual cases. For him, the fact that the parties signed a written document or otherwise gave consent to be bound by contract, was only the beginning of the inquiry, not its end. He wanted to know if their consent, given all the circumstances of the case, reflected their true and autonomous intention. For this reason he refused to enforce obligations that were wrenched out of the promising party by oppressive means or by undue influence,[68] or were fraudulently obtained,[69] or were generated by a reasonable mistake of such a nature that performance could not be reconciled with the true intention of the parties.[70]

---

[63] J. H. Baker, *An Introduction to English Legal History*, 3rd ed., New York: Oxford University Press, p. 356 (1990).

[64] This doctrine holds that a donation made by potentially insolvent people can be set aside and used for the settlement of their legitimate debts. This general idea, that a person ought to be just before she is generous, has it roots in classical Roman Law (the *actio Pauliana*) and was consolidated in statutory form under Elizabeth; still the enforcement of this doctrine seems not to have been attempted before, and it took some judicial courage to undo perfectly valid donations in conformity with this new invention. See Alan Harding, *The Social History of English Law*, Magnolia, MA: Peter Smith, p. 148 (1966).

[65] Bacon's attitude to law in the service of society is reminiscent of Alberti's view that architecture was primarily a tool to make the lives of those who occupy dwellings more amenable. See Chapter 2, supra.

[66] Holdsworth, ibid., p. 106. Prior to Bacon's time, many instances were recorded in which cases languished within the court system for thirty years pending the final judgment.

[67] In one of these cases, *Eardley v. Sutton* (*Reports*, 19), a father promised to make a settlement in favor of his daughter subject to the condition that she should marry a certain man. The daughter kept her part of the deal and her husband was given specific performance of the father's promise.

[68] In *Joy v. Bannister*, a 1617 case reported in the *Reports*, at page 33, a woman applied undue influence over an 80-year-old person, induced him to make a will in her favor and by threats and cruelty prevented him from revoking it. Bacon ruled that the will was void. See George Keeton, "Bacon as a Chancery Judge," *Iowa Law Review* 18:476, 485 (1933). The 1932 compilation also reports another case, *Waller v. Waller*, in which a land conveyance was set aside when it was proven that the conveyance was fraudulently obtained from a person "weak in mind."

[69] *Hall v. Stanley*, ibid., p. 104 (1618).

[70] *Wyatt v. Wyatt*, *Reports*, p. 126 (1618–20).

This almost furtive inquiry of Bacon's judicial output is much enhanced by the reading of his papers. Before commenting on his direct contribution to contract doctrine it must be stressed that he was primarily, and perhaps above all, an advocate of law as order, or of transparency, of all legal norms. Whereas he halfheartedly endorsed Coke's lasting contribution of anchoring the Common Law to a system of precedents,[71] he was a pioneer in calling for codification of the law, an effort that was aimed at both pruning its undesirable excesses and simplifying the remaining legal rules and casting them in accessible language to all learned readers. About Coke's labors he grudgingly admitted:

> Though they may have errors ... the law by this time had almost been like a ship without ballast, for that the cases of modern experience are fled from them that adjudged and ruled in former times.[72]

Unlike Coke, however, who thought that the existing stock of precedents was both necessary and sufficient for ensuring satisfactory results in future cases,[73] Bacon wanted to facilitate the process by writing law digests, law dictionaries, and a variety of other legal publications (including materials for law teaching at the Inns of Court) – all in the service of a humanist administration of justice.[74]

Bacon's understanding of contract and contract interpretation is best illustrated in his legal work, *The Elements of the Common Lawes of England*.[75] The fountainhead of every obligation, he held, lies in its clarity. If promisors were allowed to plead in their defense that they intended to promise something different from what they actually stipulated, no one would be willing to rely on stipulations or give value in consideration for their fulfillment. In recognition of this simple insight Bacon championed a rule of interpretation, "*contra proferentem*," that is, favoring outcomes that are more beneficial to promisees.[76]

---

[71] For Coke's contribution see Hastings Lyon and Herman Block, *Edward Coke, Oracle of the Law*, Boston: Houghton Mifflin (1929). In this floridly written biography, the authors describe in great detail the story of the personal and ideological rivalry between these two great jurists of the Jacobean era, Coke and Bacon.

[72] Cited at Harding, ibid., p. 199.

[73] Old cases very seldom "rule" new situations, and thus Coke's position, that he was merely applying existing law rather than inventing new precedents, can no longer be viewed with much credulity. One wonders whether Coke himself believed in this rhetoric.

[74] On Bacon's place in history as a legal reformer, see Barbara Shapiro, "Sir Francis Bacon and the mid-17th Century Movement for Law Reform," *American Journal of Legal History* 24:331 (1980).

[75] The book was printed posthumously in 1630, four years after the author's death. It contains maxims of the law with explanations, commentary, and examples drawn by the author. The maxims are phrased in Latin and the English text is dotted with Latinisms and the customary Law French of the period.

[76] In regula 2 of the *Elements* he explains: "This rule that a mans deedes and his words shall be taken strongliest against himself, though it be one of the most common grounds of the law, it is notwithstanding a rule drawn out of the depth of reason; for first it is a Schoole-Master wisdome and diligence in making men watchful in their owne businesse, next it is author of much quiet and certainty ... for if the labour were onely to picke out the intention of the parties, every Judge would have a severall sense, whereas this rule doth give them a sway to take the law more certainly one way."

Similarly, since it is a policy of the law (he held) to enhance the freedom of every person to trade in his possessions, contractual terms must be interpreted strictly, giving effect only to what was *declared* to have been intended. Otherwise the freedom to contract would be impaired, because the parties could not be sure what might be either taken from them or granted to them as a result of their agreement.[77] There is, however, a small set of cases in which the parties' "true" intention, as distinguished from the words in which it was couched, ought to be given priority. These are the circumstances under which reason dictates that no other intention could be meditated, regardless of the words used in the contract. One such contingency exists in which the fulfillment of a promise is frustrated either by dire necessity or by an act of God.[78] More generally, where the true intention of the parties can be gathered from their agreement, the words can be ignored and the intention implemented.[79] Nor may words be allowed to restrain the will, and therefore a contractual stipulation intended to bar the parties from changing their minds and reaching an alternative stipulation is void.[80] Finally, no one is allowed to exercise his clout over other persons to induce consent, because consent must always emanate from free will.[81]

Bacon's empiricist posture shines through his entire legal output. A legal strategy is never "right" a priori;[82] its desirability is always derived from

---

[77] In regula 4 he states: "The Law permitteth every man to part with his owne interest, and to qualifie his owne graunt as it pleaseth himselfe, and therefore doth not admit any allowance or recompense if the thing be not taken as it is granted." And he exemplifies: "So if the kinde be specified, as if I let my Park reserving to myselfe all the Deere and sufficient pasture for them, if I do decay the game whereby there is no Deere, I shall not have quantitie of pasture answerable to the feed of so many Deere as were upon the ground when I let it, but am without any remedy except I replenish the ground againe with Deere."

[78] In regula 5 he writes: "The law charges on man with default where the act is complusorie, and not voluntary, and where there is not a consent and election; and therefore if either there bee an impossibility for a man to doe otherwise, or so great a perturbation of the judgement and reason as in presumption of law mans nature cannot overcome, such necessity carrieth a priviledge in it selfe."

[79] In the words of regula 13, "Though falsitie of addition or demonstration doth not hurt where you give a thing a proper name, yet neverthelesse if it stand doubtfull upon the words, whether they import a false reference and demonstration, or whether they be words of restraint that limit the generality of the former name, the law will never intend error or falsehood."

[80] Such a restraining language, called *clausula de non obstante de futuro*, is void, says regula 19, because "the law judgeth to be idle and of no force ... it doth deprive men of that which of all things is most incident to humane condition, and that is alteration or repentance."

[81] "If a party menace me," he illustrates in regula 22, "except I make unto him a bond of 40 l. and I tell him that I will not do it, but I will make unto him a bond of 20 l. the law shall not expound this bond to be voluntarie, but shall rather make construction that my mind and courage is not to enter into the greater bond for any menace, and yet I enter by compulsion, notwithstanding, into the lesser."

[82] In this respect Bacon takes a sharp turn from some of his recent illustrious predecessors in the realm of legal philosophy. A leading example is Abraham Fraunce, who published in 1588 a learned treatise entitled *The Lawiers Logike, Exemplifying the Praecepts of Logike by the Practise of the Common Lawe*. Fraunce's heroes are the pillars of scholastic thought, from Aristotle to Ramus. Shakespeare may have learned his law from this book, although Fraunce's

observation, from the expected outcome of its application in real life. Why must the law be redeemed from its obscurity and be recast in clearer, more accessible terms? Because its end users would better understand it and more fittingly internalize its injunctions, if they can learn the rules and plan their strategies in conformity with their spirit (hence his appeal to codify case law). We should expect, of course, that even educated legal consumers might encounter some difficulties in hard subjects. To mitigate this problem we must give them tools to overcome these difficulties (hence his proposals to compose legal dictionaries). One must ensure that the law is not ambiguous and does not impose on its users onerous obligations, which they did not anticipate in advance. If we are not sufficiently vigilant in this respect, people might shy away from the law's domain, which could, in turn, jeopardize some of its important policies; hence the need to give a lot of weight to objective appearance, even if it is not compatible with a hidden intent (this explains his inclination to construe language according to its normal dictionary meaning as well as to interpret terms *contra proferentem*). On the other hand, intent lies at the heart of all legal obligations, and therefore it must take precedence over its objective manifestations, if by observing all the circumstances of the case the real intention can be brought to light (his attitude to the law of frustration of purpose or of duress follows from this principle). If we observe common forms of legal abuse, a remedy must be found to fit the injury (fraudulent preferences). If we observe that certain players attach a greater subjective value to a certain object, their interests should receive an extra measure of protection (equity of redemption).

But observation is not everything. To better appreciate the history of axiomatic reasoning, we should turn to other great thinkers in the annals of modern Western history.

Modern philosophers almost take it for granted that rational belief must rest on both good reasons and empirically supportable data, thus echoing the Kantian motto that "intuitions without concepts are blind, whereas concepts without intuitions are vacuous."[83] But those moderns did not stumble upon this discovery on their own accord. Many refer to the seventeenth and eighteenth centuries as "the Age of Reason," precisely because, side by side with the

---

contrived hexameters (he often took flight in poetry) were ridiculed by Ben Jonson as "foolish." Fraunce's treatise exalts Aristotelian syllogisms and other a prioristic "logical" tropes and finds in them the main justification for legal rules. In the revealing dedication of his book to his benefactor, the Earl of Pembroke, Fraunce sets the motto of the entire opus: "If Lawes by reason framed were, and grounded on the same;/If Logike also reason bee, and thereof had this name;/I see no reason why that Law and Logike should not bee/The nearest and the dearest friends, and therefore best agree."

[83] E.g., Robert Nozick, *The Nature of Rationality*, Princeton, NJ: Princeton University Press, pp. 64ff (1993). The epistemic proposition that truth, or at least the quest thereof, is the combined product of empirically derived facts and normatively inspired principles of reason was fully developed by the philosopher Alvin Goldman in a series of publications. See, for instance, Alvin Goldman, *Epistemology and Cognition*, Cambridge, MA: Harvard University Press (1986), especially Chapter 7.

empiricists, a strong contingent of philosophers propounded the role of reason as the *primary* cause for the validity of propositions.[84]

First and foremost of them was, of course, René Descartes.[85] In his arguably most important philosophical work, *Discourse on Method*, Descartes launched his inquiry from the same starting point of the empiricists, the renunciation of authority as a definitive factor in accepting the validity of propositions. As his starting point, Descartes joined the mutiny against *ille philosophus*, Aristotle, and against the Thomistic authority of the Middle Ages. But rather than approach epistemic issues with an agnostic spirit, with an open mind to "believe" in what we gather through our senses, he announced his "principle of doubt." This principle stood, in effect, for the view that nothing could be relied on as "true," not even what we perceive with the senses, unless we have some *innate* "reasons" to accept its validity. The process of legitimizing propositions was thus reversed by discarding inductive learning based on "external" evidence and relying instead (mainly) on innate sources of intuitive reasoning. Those innate sources of knowledge were implanted in our minds by God, and thus the existence of God as the primary source of our innate knowledge must precede, in terms of causality, even our ability to think of our selves. Descartes' disdain for the phenomenal world as a source of epistemic perception led him to pioneer the field of analytic geometry. In this branch of mathematics, all geometric problems can be formulated in algebraic terms, thus liberating physical entities of their corporeal attributes. Physical phenomena are thus abstracted to sets of ordered numbers that, given the limitations of our senses, can often be unperceivable in tangible terms (e.g., a geometrical "form" with more than three dimensions). Before tackling the problem of validity, however, Descartes felt that he had to settle the problem of existence, because it does not make sense to ask the question if a given proposition is valid if we do not even know if it relates to an existing entity. Descartes sought some logical starting point, something about whose existence there are compelling reasons. That Cartesian starting point, as we all know, turned out to be someone's self. The primary existence of the self was justified by Descartes in the following manner. We normally cannot trust

---

[84] Interestingly, many of these scientists and philosophers, including Descartes and Leibniz, but also Newton, interpreted their own scientific projects in theological terms. There is certainly no equation between reason, or rationality, on the one hand and secularism on the other. Whether modern science can or cannot be reconciled with a theistic view of the universe is deliberately left outside the ambit of this book.

[85] Rational inference was widely practiced during the Western Middle Ages as well (the whole opus of Thomas Aquinas being a prime example). The scholastic method in general and its Aristotelian-Thomistic applications in the legal field in particular were highly polished methods of deductive reasoning. See, generally, Alexander Murray, *Reason and Society in the Middle Ages*, Oxford: Clarendon Press, and New York: Oxford University Press (1978). The champions of reason in the seventeenth and eighteenth centuries differed, however, from their medieval precursors primarily because they did not limit their claims to deductive reasoning and (what can really be reduced to the same proposition) did not necessarily anchor the source of their axiomatic knowledge to any kind of authority, sacred or profane. As I demonstrate infra even the medieval version of rationality never took root in Russian culture.

the senses, because we may suspect that there exists some cunning deceiver who distorts sensory stimuli and makes them appear different from what they really are. But for that deceiver to be successful, someone out there ought to be deceived, and the deceived entity is one's self. Thus even misinterpreting the deceiver's clues (which implies thought) indubitably proves the existence of the deceived, that is, of one's existent self. When a thinker thinks that he sees a widget, the thing observed may not truly be a widget, or, indeed, there may be nothing to be observed at all. But a deceiver cannot deprive the thinker of her belief that she sees a widget. The thinker may justifiably doubt whether what she sees is a widget, but even her doubt cannot be ascribed to a nonexistent entity. Some critics raised the point that Descartes may be convincing in his claim that the self thinks, but he is less convincing in his inference that the self exists as well (*cogito ergo sum* is not such an easy proposition, after all). To make that inference one has to make a further assumption, for example, that thinking objects necessarily exist. But one could claim in his defense that this further assumption is self-evident, because it is hard to conceive of a thinking entity that nonetheless does not exist.[86]

Descartes' method was taken one step further by Gottfried Wilhelm Leibniz, the ultimate rationalist ever. In a nutshell, Leibniz (unlike Descartes) held that the phenomenal world does not have an "independent" existence. It is not "real" but only a confused representation of an ideal reality; space is not a thing in itself, but merely a system of rules that is used by our cognition as a tool to set order to the sensory stimuli; the emphasis here is not on the perceived object but rather on the perceiving subject. There is no meaning to the external world without our perception of it. Our perception is thus a relationship of reflection. Human perception is flawed and therefore we are prone to misperceive everything. But in principle a flawless perception could exist (and does exist in God), whereby all objects retain their meaning through some thinking mechanisms without recourse to any external evidence. It is not surprising that it was he who invented (side by side with Newton) our modern calculus, complete with all its elusive concepts (e.g., infinity or infinitesimally small magnitudes), whose existence can only be *reasoned*, but not *perceived* by the senses.[87] His main philosophical achievement was in proposing the existence of an infinite number of "monads," thus laying the foundations for his system of "monadology." A "monad" is a wholly innate thinking object (the supreme monad being God). Monads are also embedded in the human mind and give us our sense of reality. Monads have "no windows," that is, they are blind to the phenomenal world, and all their reasoning functions are performed "internally."[88]

---

[86] For an easy introduction to Descartes' method of reasoning, see Margaret Wilson (ed.), *The Essential Descartes*, New York: Meridian (1976).

[87] For excellent introductory treatises on Leibniz see Nicholas Rescher, *Leibniz: An Introduction to His Philosophy*, Aldershot: Gregg Revivals (1979); C. Broad (with an introduction by C. Lewy), *Leibniz: An Introduction*, New York: Cambridge University Press (1975).

[88] To Locke's contention that our mind can comprehend only external signals he famously replied that this did not apply to the mind itself. This contention looms large in his dissertation, *New*

Leibniz's highly idealistic interpretation of our cognition was an important building block in Kant's *Critique of Pure Reason* (1781). Kant's original contribution, however, was in wedding the idealistic formulations of thinkers like Descartes and Leibniz with the empiricist beliefs of such philosophers as Bacon and his (mainly British) followers (notably John Locke, George Berkeley, and David Hume). Following the empiricists, Kant recognized the role of objects in the formations of our beliefs: Our perceptive faculties seem vacuous if there is nothing out there to be perceived. And yet he also followed the idealists in recognizing the role of innate reason in lending these objects their "meaning." There is no "objective" connotation, he held, to external objects without the defining effect of our internal thinking processes. It seems that after the *Critique of Pure Reason*, nothing much was left to say (at least not until post-modernism, psychoanalysis, and cognitive psychology) about the twin roles of observation and rationality in Western Man's beliefs concerning the validity of propositions. Can the same conclusion be drawn about Russia?

Observation and Reason in Pre-Revolutionary Russia

Recall the combined empiricist and rationalist assumption that lies at the base of Western contractual culture. Remember the image of its rational players who work hard to collect information about their own bundles of entitlements and about what is owned by others and then amicably exchange parts of their bundles in a mutually beneficial fashion. Now compare the image with the following rhymes, written by Simeon Polotsky, Russia's greatest poet of the Petrine era, describing, in downright brutal terms, the process of exchange in his own eyes. Whereas Western Man's faith in reason presupposes a domesticated world, based on experience, and amenable to beneficial human modification, and hence hospitable to contract, Polotsky's lyrics reflect a deep suspicion of the marketplace and a downright hostility to its practitioners. His lines may not impress one as particularly refined, but they excel in their sense of purpose and directness of expression: [89]

Essays on Human Understanding, edited by Peter Remnant and Jonathan Bennet, New York: Cambridge University Press (1966). The dissertation was first published posthumously in 1762 and designed as a detailed reply, chapter by chapter, to Locke's *An Essay Concerning Human Understanding*. Locke's treatise was published in 1689.

[89] Polotsky (1629–1680), a West Russian who settled in Moscow, became the most successful Russian poet of the seventeenth century. His poetry was mostly composed in a style that required that each line have eleven or thirteen syllables and be constrained by other formal requirements, which made it rather heavy and unnatural. In his mature years he wrote in Church Slavonic, which was largely archaic at this period. Nonetheless, he was the first to have been appointed a court poet, and the first poet to see his work in print. He was also appointed a tutor to Czar Alexis's children. See Serge Zenkovsky (editor and translator), *Medieval Russia's Epics, Chronicles and Tales*, revised and enlarged edition, New York: Plume, p. 517 (1963).

The merchant class can hardly keep from sinning.
The Evil Spirit to his ways is winning,
Great greed the merchant's soul is e'er infesting,
His entire life with gross misdeeds investing.
First, every merchant's greatest desire
Is to buy things for less and sell them higher...
The second sin of merchants is False Promise
Seduction of the buyer their sole premise...
The fourth sin on criminality verges
When, often, in weighing, the merchant perjures.
When purchasing their scale shows less than's in it,
Yet when they sell, their scale extends its limit...
Oh you sons of darkness in evil thus abiding...
Give up this black business, forsake these acts of thieving...[90]

Polotsky was giving vent to a common mind-set in casting the process of contracting in such derogatory terms. The same attitude lingered on for centuries. Even the Russian revolution, it seems, had its initial successes because, among other factors, its main protagonists harped on a popular chord when they challenged the commercial and mercantile underpinnings of bourgeois society.[91]

This contemptuous indictment of trade was nourished from many sources, some of which (e.g., belief in the redeeming value of *kenôsis* or the exaltation of authority) were discussed in previous chapters. It is hereby contended that it also drew its vigor from a long standing Russian tradition of viewing both observation and pure reason as foreign elements in the validation of contested propositions.

Western Christendom recognized, until the twilight of the Middle Ages, the revered figure of the "holy fool." A holy fool is a person who, though seemingly bereft of worldly reason and blind to his physical environment, is held to be clairvoyant with his or her "spiritual eyes" and is thus empowered, through divine grace, to guide his or her followers in quest of the Truth. The Franciscan order in the fourteenth century spawned such figures,[92] and even St. Francis himself, though certainly not demented in any form, underscores in his personality strong otherworldly traits that are unrelated to the faculties of the brain. This Western fascination with alternative means of cognition was not in the mainstream of medieval Christianity, and at any rate failed to survive

---

[90] Simeon Polotsky, "The Merchant Class," in Zenkovsky, ibid., p. 518.

[91] When the revolution was tempered by the practical necessities of commerce, diehard revolutionaries interpreted it as an act of treason. Trotsky's hostility to contract as a means of economic and social exchange is manifested in Leon Trotsky, *The Revolution Betrayed: What Is the Soviet Union and Where Is It Going?*, 5th ed., translated by Max Eastman, New York: Pathfinder Press (1996). See also Michael Head, "The Passionate Legal Debates of the Early Years of the Russian Revolution," *Canadian Journal of Law and Jurisprudence* 14:3 (2001).

[92] The life of a famous Western fool, a direct disciple of St. Francis, is narrated in Giorgio Petrocchi, *La Vita di Fra Ginepro*, Bologna: Commissione per i Testi di Lingua (1960).

the Middle Ages;[93] throughout the formative period of contract it was long forgotten.

Not so in Russia. Holy foolishness was a highly respected practice for centuries. Scores of such fools were formally canonized by the Church and thousands were active in almost very town and village. Most of them were believed to have feigned their imbecility as a means of imitating Christ's self-imposed humility and following in His footsteps. Conceivably, some actually did. Many were recognized as born idiots and yet believed to retain holy characteristics. This did not mean, of course, that every deranged individual automatically earned this special veneration, but the numbers of venerated, or at least greatly respected, fools was very significant.[94] A vivid, relatively modern firsthand account of such a fool was put together, about a hundred years ago, describing the life story of a certain woman, Pelagia Ivanovna Serebrenikova. I repeat the essentials of this tale because it is characteristic of many such biographies of a similar feather.[95] Pelagia was a normal country girl in her early youth, but due to undisclosed circumstances lost touch with reality and was pronounced an idiot. She was married off to the one and only suitor who consented to marry her, but having been beaten almost to death by her spouse for not fulfilling her marital obligations, she fled to the monastery of a famous ascetic saint, Saint Seraphim of Sarov, who once met Pelagia in her youth and was deeply moved by her "powers." When Pelagia was admitted to the monastery the old saint was no longer alive, but it was commonly believed that he took her under his tutelage as a beloved new recruit. Gradually, she built a reputation for herself by her powers of clairvoyance and ability to perform miracles. She became known as a fool for Christ's sake and was assigned the task of accepting pilgrims and offering them cure and solace. Her behavior was totally out of touch with her environment. For example, she used to address her fellow nuns and superiors in the male gender. She was ascetic and devout, praying and crying ceaselessly for several days and nights, without giving cause for her lamentations. She carried heavy stones and threw them into a well, which was interpreted as an act of carrying Christ's cross. There was none held in such high esteem in the whole neighboring country.

[93] In the late Middle Ages it was a common practice in France to crown fools and social outcasts as substitutes for clergy and noblemen for a brief period during carnivals. This practice is picturesquely drawn in the work of Rabelais and analyzed in a scholarly manner in Mikhail Bakhtin, *Rabelais and His World*, translated by Helene Islowsky, Indianapolis: Indiana University Press (1988). It can be inferred from the brief span of the fool's tenure in these carnivals that in the period described vocational fools as well as genuine halfwits idolized for their detachness from reality have already fallen out of vogue.

[94] See Harriet Murav, *Holy Foolishness, Dostoyevsky's Novels and the Poetics of Cultural Critique*, Stanford: Stanford University Press (1992).

[95] *Seraphim's Seraphim, the Life of Pelagia Ivanovna Serebrenikova, Fool for Christ's Sake of the Seraphim-Diveyevo Convent*, translated from the Russian text by the Holy Transfiguration Monastery, Brookline, MA, in 1979; the original account was written sometime in the fin de siècle "by the handmaiden of God, the nun Anna Gerasimovna, who tended to the holy fool, and also by others who knew her.

This kind of deep veneration of mystical powers and belief in their iron grip on natural phenomena was very widespread among the peasantry. It also left its mark, albeit in a much more subdued form, on the Russian intelligentsia.

The spiritual world of the peasantry is best captured by the plethora of country folk tales, "memorates,"[96] "fabulates,"[97] and legends, many of which were skillfully compounded in one fascinating volume by Linda Ivanits.[98] The peasant's life was dominated by a constant interaction between living persons, like herself, and a whole pantheon of canonized dead saints who observed her every step and were ready to respond in kind, with each saint according to his character and inclinations. The most important saint in Russia was St. Nicholas the Wonderworker. This early fourth-century bishop of Myra, the principal city of Lycia (now in Turkey), was a famous performer of miracles who was also known for his chastity and benevolent nature (very little is actually known about him as a historical figure). He was Russified by the peasants' belief that he was also an apostle, coming with Christ to Russia to baptize the heathen. One of his principal tasks was to mitigate the wrath of the more severe saints, such as Elijah the prophet (in Russia, probably a baptized heir of the early pagan deity Perun, the thunder god), not to mention the fearful Cassian. Cassian was an angry saint, stooped in heaven with his eyebrows cast down all the way to his knees. On February 29 of each leap year, he would lift his eyebrows and gain some view of earth. Whatever met his angry gaze withered away on the spot. The peasants chose to keep this day in pious veneration to appease the saint, and it was not even safe to leave home. Cassian did not curry much favor with God either because, unlike the beloved Nicholas, he never stooped so low as to perform charitable deeds. This is why God gave him only one saint-day every four years.[99] The devil was, and still is,[100] literally ubiquitous. He personified the "unclean" elements in the universe. While domestic spirits, often of mischievous nature, and notably the *domovoi*, which usually predate Christianity, it seems that the devil, as an entity that is exclusively bent on harming humankind and is universal in its nature, is basically a Christian formulation and closely follows Christian iconography. Folk belief had it that Satan multiplied into a variety of demons. Demons had the power to change form and appeared in black cats and dogs, as well as in a variety of other objects. Black cats and dogs

---

[96] 78 A "memorate" is a short anecdote relating a supernatural event as an actually transpired fact.

[97] A "fabulate" is some kind of a hybrid between a memorate and an artistic story, as it embellishes the dry narrative somewhat and may involve a report of more than a single event.

[98] Linda Ivanits, *Russian Folk Belief*, Armonk, NY: M. E. Sharpe (1992).

[99] Ivanits, ibid., pp. 24ff.

[100] I. G. Dubov, "Level of Religious Commitment and the Influence of Religious Precepts on Russian Citizens' Attitudes Toward Political Leaders," *Russian Politics and Law* 31 May–June: (2002). In this paper Dubov shows that a solid majority of contemporary Russians, including those who define themselves as "secular," believe that the kingdom of darkness, reigned by the devil and administered by his many ministers, defies every possible rational or scientific explanation.

had to be driven out of the house during thunderstorms, because at that time Elijah was targeting the unclean, and fire could break out. Demons married witches. They both had human traits and liked drinking and feasting. Some legends assign Satan a role in the creation of the world, alongside with God. They later quarreled, and Satan transformed himself into a variety of unclean entities that were ultimately driven out of heaven and cast to earth, as well as underneath it, by the archangel Michael. Since the devil is everywhere, one must always be on one's guard, the best method being making the sign of the cross. Some female devils, dressed as hags, were responsible for particular diseases, including smallpox. Cattle epidemics could be resisted by invoking the sacred power of the earth. This procedure, which persevered well into the twentieth century, could be performed only by widows and virgins, in the dead of night, unbeknown to the men, with the performers running around naked except for shifts and with loose hair, and plowing the ground.[101] Belief in sorcery was widespread well into Communist times. It has its origins in the pre-Christian era, with possible connections to Finnish shamanism. It pervaded all walks of society, even the family of the czars.[102] Sorcerers and witches were either born (being the offspring of three generations of illegitimate births) or gained this trait voluntarily (making a pact with the devil) or involuntarily (a contagious spell). Voluntary acceptance of sorcery powers forfeited salvation. Sometimes, but not always, involuntary assumption of sorcery could be fended off by seclusion in monasteries and other religious rites. Natural disasters, family discords, and other woes were attributed to sorcery. Sorcerers and witches had helpers from among the natural and other spirits. The helpers lived in barns, bathhouses, and other places but could not reside with their masters in a house that had an icon.[103] Sorcery was performed by an act called "spoiling." Spoiling was commissioned by private parties, with the most common motivation being envy. Sometimes practitioners acted on their own behalf to avenge an insult. This is why particular caution had to be taken not to incense a recognized practitioner. Spoiling could be countereffected by healing, done by either other practitioners or by specialized healers. There were some known remedies as well, for example, a special kind of milkweed harvested on May 9, St. Nicholas Day. The most prevalent affliction caused by spoiling was the shrieking illness, which affected mostly women. The sufferer would be possessed by howling, cursing, and convulsions (supposedly generated by demons), especially in the presence of religious objects such as icons. Sometimes the shrieking disease attacked in epidemics, especially at vulnerable venues such as weddings. Healing procedures were quite involved and depended on local practices. The fact

---

[101] Ivanits, ibid., pp. 38ff.

[102] Even the last Romanovs subscribed to these views. When the young czarevitch, sick with hemophilia, was in mortal danger, the only cure found for his recovery was in the magic powers of Rasputin, who restored him to life. See, for instance, Colin Wilson, *Rasputin and the Fall of the Romanovs*, New York: Farrar, Straus, Chapter 5 (1964).

[103] Ivanits, ibid., pp. 83ff.

that sometimes priests were handy in healing spoiling gives rise to the suspicion that priests also possess the power of sorcery. Not only priests, but certain other professionals, including herdsmen, millers, carpenters, blacksmiths, beekeepers, and stonemasons, were commonly assumed to possess sorcery powers of their own.[104]

Many observers make the point that very little can be learned from the behavior of the ignorant peasantry on the refined and sophisticated demeanor of the Russian intelligentsia.[105] According to this line of argument, it is grossly unfair to draw a comparison between such Western luminaries as Bacon, Leonardo da Vinci, or Leibniz and the overworked, badly exploited and poorly educated *mujik* of the remote backwaters of the Russian provinces. One observer muses:

Peter succeeded in forcing European civilization on the nobles, but the people remained unaffected. The nation was, as it were, cleft in two, and with each succeeding generation the cleft widened. Whilst the masses clung obstinately to their time-honored customs and beliefs, the nobles came to look on the objects of popular veneration as the relics of a barbarous past, of which a civilized nation ought to be ashamed.[106]

Part of the response to the unfairness allegation lies in a simple number count, as the Russian peasantry, or the "uneducated classes," far outnumbered their Western counterparts and thus had a greater weight in the overall characterization of the national Geist. But it is submitted that Peter's ambition to westernize his country had only a superficial effect on many members of the educated classes as well; underneath the educated classes' skin-deep occidental veneer it is easy to observe the underlying original traits.

Once again, Dostoyevsky is a good point of departure. Some of his attitudes to the "brainy" Western paradigm are explicitly hostile; more subtly, some are tragic and implicit. A clear example of his *explicit* hostility to the reign of reason may be found in his great novel *The Idiot* (1868). This tale unfolds the story of Prince Myshkin, a thoroughly charitable person who carries the cross of his benevolence in the midst of a society corrupted by the wily, self-seeking, materialistic, and rationalist values of occidental lineage. This Christ-like figure symbolizes the superiority of the traditional Christian values, even at the cost of some simple-mindedness, to the morally corrupt Rational Man of the West.

---

[104] Ibid., pp. 103ff.
[105] For example, Georg Brandes, *Impressions of Russia*, New York: Thomas Y. Crowell, Chapter 4 (1899; reprinted in 1966). Brandes was an illustrious Danish historian and literary critic who visited Russia in the fin de siècle and based his impressions on both direct observation and literary criticism, thus presaging the modern trend in cultural studies to integrate historical, political, and cultural insights in a unified vision. Brandes took the view that a deep ravine separated the Russian peasantry and the educated classes.
[106] Donald Mackenzie Wallace, *Russia on the Eve of War and Revolution*, Princeton, NJ: Princeton University Press, p. 221 (1984; first published in 1877, but revised by the author in 1905 and 1912). The author, a leading editor, journalist, and correspondent of *The London Times*, died in 1919.

Similar themes dominate many of Dostoyevsky's novels.[107] Dostoyevsky's *subtler* approach to this issue was recently explored by Liza Knapp in a fascinating volume about the complex relationship between the Russian mind and the laws of physics.[108] Knapp starts out by recording the cultural response within Russia, in the course of the nineteenth century, to the scientific innovations imported from Europe. Many educated Russians resisted the intrusion, and some were inclined to suggest alternative approaches to scientific problems based on mystical and unverifiable theories. One of these dissenters was a physicist called Pisarevsky, who was greatly admired by Dostoyevsky. Pisarevsky held that the Newtonian laws of gravity apply only to inanimate objects, but living organisms possess a "vital force" that enables them to halt movement or change its course at will. Pisarevsky did not attempt to provide a scientific explanation for this "vital force," and Dostoyevsky was apparently not eager to challenge this omission. But whereas for Pisarevsky the "denial of inertia" (to use Knapp's phrase) was presumably a law of nature, in Dostoyevsky's feverish mind it was transformed into a moral ideal, almost a watershed dividing the saved and the damned. This moral principle was apparently derived from the Patristic literature, which affirmed that Christ's incarnation and resurrection defied the laws of physics not only for Himself, but also for the entire human race.[109] Knapp discusses several stories revealing Dostoyevsky's interpretation of this principle. In *Notes from the Underground* (1864), the underground confessor narrates a tale of a ruined life. The source of his misery is caused by letting his destiny be governed by natural laws and swept by inertia. He realizes, for instance, that in his own life "two times two equals four is the beginning of death" and that "two times two equals five is sometimes a nice little thing." Letting oneself be run by inertia mechanizes existence, and although it may guarantee an effortless life, it trivializes free will and is tantamount to death. An opposite kind of human being is lovingly painted in a short story, "In the Hospital," which forms a part of his chain of sketches, *The House of the Dead* (1862), which illuminates anecdotes from the life of inmates in a Siberian penal colony. As one recalls, Dostoyevsky himself was such an inmate after the czar commuted his death sentence to a term of long imprisonment in Siberia. The protagonist of *In the Hospital*, Orlov, is a convicted felon sentenced to beatings

---

[107] See Harriet Murav, *Holy Foolishness, Dostoyevsky's Novels and the Poetics of Cultural Critique*, Stanford: Stanford University Press (1992).

[108] Liza Knapp, *The Annihilation of Inertia, Dostoyevsky and Metaphysics*, Evanston, IL: Northwestern University Press (1996).

[109] This Christological issue, of "Christ the universal man," is admirably discussed in Jaroslav Pelikan's book, *The Spirit of Eastern Christendom (600–1700)*, Chicago: University of Chicago Press, pp. 75ff (1974). A typical early text, composed by Athanasius (296–373) reads in part as follows: "And thus, taking body like to ours, because all men were liable to the corruption of death, he resurrected it to death instead of all, and offered it to the Father... that by all dying in him the law touching the corruption of mankind might be abolished." See the citation of this and similar texts in Henry Battenson and Chris Maundner (eds.), *Documents of the Christian Church*, 3rd ed., New York: Oxford University Press, p. 36 (1999).

and then to a long exile in Siberia. The number of blows prescribed for Orlov was so great, and their severity so exacting, that they were divided into two installments; even with this considerate method nobody believed that Orlov could come out alive after the first round. But he took his punishment bravely, maintained his human dignity to the end, and refused to succumb to the cruelty of his tormentors. He dreamed of surviving the second round and then managing an escape to the open meadows, to trees and forests, to life. He refused to be governed by the laws of inertia and thus earned spiritual salvation. Unfortunately his body did not prove equal to the task and he died under his tormentors' sticks.[110] Orlov's death, I submit, is essential for the integrity of the message. Had Orlov been successful in his attempt to defy his jailers and to dash for freedom, his plan could have been interpreted, by its very success, as "rational." Dostoyevsky's point, as I see it, is that the defiance of the mechanical laws of nature ought to be pursued in spite of their irrationality, and solely for the sake of gaining spiritual, not temporal, salvation. In this subtle sense Orlov is a "holy fool" as well, not for any deficiency in his cognitive faculties, but for his avowed determination to be governed by the transcendental forces of his spiritual calling, rather than by the voice of reason.

Dostoyevsky, of course, has always been an orthodox Slavophile and his notorious xenophobic inclinations were such[111] that one cannot use his example for more than what it is, a starting point. Dostoyevsky's nationalism, religiosity, and condescension of the other may not have been shared by some of the other members of the educated classes. His rejection of the "Western" scientific method, however, and his inclination to search for occult, or at least unobservable, causes for natural phenomena is deeply rooted in ancient Orthodox dogma, which predates the very inception of the Russian nation. A glaring example is the mysterious writings of the so-called pseudo-Dionysius, about whose life next to nothing is really known, except that he wrote in the fifth or sixth century in a semi-Christian, semi-Platonic tradition and had an immense influence on later theological developments, although the exact trail of his doctrinal penetration to Russian Orthodoxy is, to the best of my knowledge, not documented. A characteristic citation of his theology of "negative knowledge," or lack of our ability to grasp the ultimate causes of all phenomena, is appended in the footnote.[112] I also append a more modern example showing the current

---

[110] See Knapp, ibid., Chapter 2.

[111] Dostoyevsky hated almost anybody who was not an ethnic Russian and above all Germans, Poles, and particularly Jews. His unmitigated bigotry to the Hebrew race is best evidenced by his *Diary*. See Fyodor Dostoyevsky, *The Diary of a Writer*, translated and annotated by Boris Brasol, New York: George Braziller, pp. 637ff (1954). The particular entry in question was composed in 1877.

[112] In a short key chapter of his work *On Mystical Theology*, entitled "That the supreme Cause of every conceptual thing is not itself conceptual," the pseudo-Dionysius explains what might constitute the real cause of things (note the sublime lyricism of this otherwise analytical text): "It is not soul or mind, nor does it possess imagination, conviction, or understanding. Nor is it speech per se, understanding per se. It cannot be spoken of and it cannot be grasped

acceptance of the pseudo-Dionysian doctrine of "seeing with spiritual eyes," taken from the teachings of Saint Theophan the Recluse (1815–1894), a Russian bishop who sacrificed the glories of the material world to become a hermit and then was canonized by the Russian Church as recently as 1988.[113]

On a more general level, it seems that the occidental approach to truth described in the previous section did not take firm root on Russian soil. In a recent book, Martin Malia attempts to make some generalizations about this assertion. According to Malia, all the Western champions of both observation and reason – Hobbes, Locke, Newton, and Hume in England; Voltaire, Diderot, and the *philosophes* in France; and the idealists in Germany – advocated the Rule of Reason with an underlying commitment to republican ideas, which were floating in the air anyway as a result of a long historical and cultural evolution. In some form or another, this was true even of those philosophers who supported absolute monarchy and yet eroded it from within by subjecting everything to the overarching rationale of reasoned existence. In Russia, Reason was espoused not from the grassroots but from the autocracy, that wished to institutionalize Reason without its republican undertones. The European Enlightenment was a movement, according to Malia, that European nations grew with and could hardly be joined in midstream by other nations.[114] Although somewhat sweeping in his conclusions, it seems that Malia's general observations are well supported by historical fact, especially if we trace the fortunes of the Russian Enlightenment through the successive biographies of the Romanovs and their reigning spouses. Emperor after "enlightened" emperor, from Catherine the Great to Alexander I and then to Alexander II, not to mention the reactionary czars, they all reneged on their support for the Enlightenment

by understanding. It is not number or order, greatness or smallness, equality or inequality, similarity or dissimilarity. It is not immovable, moving or at rest. It has no power, it is not power, nor is it light. It does not live nor is it life. It is not a substance, nor is it eternity or time. It cannot be grasped by understanding since it is neither knowledge nor truth. It is not kingship. It is not wisdom. It is neither one nor oneness, divinity nor goodness. Nor is it a spirit. . . . It is not sonship or fatherhood and it is nothing known to us or to any other being. Existing beings do not know it as it actually is and it does not know them as they are. There is no speaking of it, nor name nor knowledge of it. Darkness and light, error and truth – it is none of these. It is beyond assertion and denial." See *Pseudo Dionysius, the Complete Works* translated by Colm Luibheid, Mahwah, NJ: Paulist Press, p. 141 (1987). The date of the original publication is not known.

[113] "You must reinterpret in a spiritual way all that you see around you. Then fight with all your forces to imprint that new interpretation on your mind. Then, when you look at something, while your eyes see a tangible object, your mind will be contemplating a spiritual one. . . . We will walk and act inside the field of senses and materiality, yet in reality we will move in the realm of the Spirit. Everything will unveil its divine dimension for us, and this will reinforce the power with which our attention turns towards Him." See *The Heart of Salvation, the Life and Teachings of Saint Theophan the Recluse*, translated by Esther Williams, Chicago: Praxis Institute Press, pp. 16–17. The publisher declined to specify the date of publication, but it must have been in the last year or two of the twentieth century. Nor is an exact date indicated relating to this specific sermon.

[114] Martin Malia, *Russia Under Western Eyes*, Cambridge, MA: Belknap Press, pp. 110ff (1999).

as soon as they sensed that Reason might not be as compatible with their auto-cratic ambitions as they previously anticipated. Reason was tolerated and even admired as long as it gave fodder to polite *salon* talks in the halls of royalty and in the noble *dvors* of St. Petersburg, but it was persecuted with the utmost cruelty when it started to spawn republican ideas.[115]

Why did the intelligentsia put up with this despotic strategy? Let us con-sider the case of the nobility first.[116] During the eighteenth century, Western ideas were assimilated by the entire Russian nobility. But they were, by the same token, assimilated in a manner idiosyncratic to Russia, which intro-duced important mutations into their very core. Largely speaking, the shell of Western ideas was taken up uncritically, without making an attempt to internal-ize their underlying rationales. For example, "Voltairianism" flourished among the nobility of this time. But whereas within the French context the holdings of Voltaire were directed at achieving greater social justice and were meant to espouse the separation of Church and State, in Russia it simply provided cheap fuel for "rationalist" social discourse. The deeper message got lost, because the Russian nobility was not preoccupied with excessive Church power (it was subordinated to the State anyway) and most boyars were not truly interested in implementing social justice in their own backyard.[117]

The Western notions of abstract rationality, the freedom of will, and human dignity were embraced with enthusiasm by the nobility, but it was done in a crude form. The nobility, uncritically believing in the rationality of man, thought that the Enlightenment could be brought to Russia overnight by means of a proper education. The resulting intellectual product was merely didactic and its practical results nil, given the autocratic nature of the regime and the underlying cultural background of the masses. Whereas in the West the ideas of the Enlightenment were designed to remove obstacles to the ongoing process of change, in Russia, having begun at a much more primitive stage, the same ideas were erroneously thought of as capable of initiating the change itself.

Natural law concepts were also naturalized in Russia. However, since most sponsors of this doctrine were of German descent, it is the Protestant version of natural law that was mainly circulated, complete with the Lutheran doctrine of the calling and the acceptance of the need for a strong central authority resulting in the obligation of the individual to submit oneself to autocratic order. There is little wonder that the pioneer propagator of natural law doc-trines in Russia was Peter the Great himself. For many intellectuals, however, notions of natural law formed the basis for a search for reform. A famous example is Radishchev's book, *A Journey from St. Petersburg to Moscow*,[118]

---

[115] See, for example, James Billington, *The Icon and the Axe*, London: Vintage, pp. 207ff (1970).

[116] A plethora of information about the Russian nobility and the ideas of the Enlightenment is provided in Marc Raeff's book, *Origins of the Russian Intelligentsia, the Eighteenth Century Nobility*, New York: Harcourt, Brace & World (1966).

[117] Raeff, ibid.

[118] A. N. Radishchev, *A Journey from St. Petersburg to Moscow*, translated by Leo Wiener, Cam-bridge, MA: Harvard University Press (1958; the original was published in 1790). In this

which earned the author a harsh sentence from the incensed Catherine the Great.[119] Natural law also propelled many initiatives to start a codification of the legal system, notably Catherine's *Nakaz*. The story of its resounding failure was already recorded in a previous chapter.[120] In this case like in other cases, the Russian intellectual appealed to his Western erudition as a source of understanding universal truths about human nature, overlooking the fact that the application of these insights had to bank on the local conditions about which, unlike his European counterpart, he was largely ignorant. This triggered, in response, a contrary movement, a nationalistic or "sentimentalist" one, stressing the importance of resuming the link with the peasantry and the simple folks. The Russian intellectual was driven to search for a unique mix of enlightened goals blended with sentimentalist feeling toward the large masses. An example of this concoction is evidenced, for instance, by the thriving of Freemasonry in the eighteenth century, which combined Western rationalism with social commitment to the rank-and-file of the entire Russian nation. Russian Freemasonry socialized the idea of the Good by coming to the rescue of the needy through an organization. Thus the giving individual did not have to "empty" himself, as in the traditional *kenôtic* practices, and his action had to have a real impact on the recipient. This emphasis on good works strengthened the "sentimentalist" elements of Freemasonry and restored to its arsenal of ideas, rather than the original notions of rationalism, a host of mystical holdings; the latter accounted for Freemasonic translations of works of Western Mysticism, Pietism, and Methodism. These translations, which were avidly read, prepared the ground for the explosion of mystical and religious fervor that swept Russia in the early nineteenth century, especially in the wake of the Napoleonic invasions.[121]

Another facet of the intellectual reception of Western ideas in Russia has to do with the history of science itself. There was hardly any science in Russia before Peter the Great. Peter devoted himself to advance science among his unscientific countrymen, but his interpretation of this endeavor was largely practical and was intended to foster useful skills in the service of his war machine, his diplomatic service, and his factories and shipyards.[122] The first periodical and

volume, Radishchev preached for the abolition of serfdom and for the institution of other political and civil rights like the freedom of expression, religious toleration, and procedural rights at trial. Many of his compatriots, including Pushkin, hailed Radishchev as the first harbinger of civil liberties in Russia.

[119] Radishchev was initially sentenced to death. In her magnanimity, the empress proclaimed that although she found him richly deserving of this sentence, she decided to commute it to a long term of imprisonment with hard labor in Siberia. This attitude was typical of this "enlightened" czarina in the wake of the French Revolution and, indeed, of every single "reforming" czar when the price tag of reform, a weakening of his or her autocratic rule, became self-evident.

[120] See Chapter 4, supra.

[121] Raeff, ibid.

[122] Arnold Toynbee takes the interesting position that the Russian interest in technology has always been, from its very inception, motivated by an existential need to defend their territory against the advancing Western aggressors – the Poles in the sixteenth century, the Swedes in the

the first secular book ever published in Russia appeared, under his reign, only in 1703 (a full century after Shakespeare), and even in the year following his death only seven books were published in Russia. When the Academy of Science was established in the eighteenth century, its eminent figures were all foreigners, for example, the famous biologist and mineralogist Peter Simon Pallas and the German mathematician Leonhard Euler.[123] The only towering figure of the Russian Enlightenment was Michael Lomonosov, a physical chemist of great distinction as well as Renaissance person in terms of his scope of interest.[124] Not until the end of the nineteenth century did the Academy dismantle its foreign cloth and became truly Russian.[125] For long periods in between, every stage of progress was succeeded by a phase of reaction, and the cause of science was carried forward sluggishly and haltingly. James Billington writes:

The material world, which was increasingly preoccupying a Western world in the throes of the Industrial Revolution, was simply not yet on the agenda of Russian thought. Occult spiritual forces were still thought to rule the world; and small circles of dedicated truth seekers were believed capable of understanding and serving these forces. As the optimism and reformist enthusiasm of the Alexandrian era waned, Russian thinkers turned from the outer to the inner world.[126]

Other commentators share a similar view, that the anti-rationalist intellectual environment of traditional Russia was an impediment to the development of Russian science.[127] To be sure, the long era of scientific backwardness no longer reflects the modern standing of Russian science. Judged by its results, it has certainly come of age.[128] But whereas in the West science emerged from a deep

seventeenth and eighteenth, the French in the nineteenth, and the Germans in the twentieth century. He also claims that the fact that Russians have always been ruled by despotic autocrats stems from the same existential need – to have a strong centralized power as a defense against foreign aggression. In this vein it is easy to comprehend why the Russian autocracy, starting with Peter himself but going on in an uninterrupted chain until Stalin (Toynbee's paper was written more than half a century ago), have always been the greatest champions of technological advances. See Arnold Toynbee, "Russia and the West," in *The World and the West*, New York: World Publishing, p. 235 (1948).

[123] Billington, *The Icon and the Axe*, London: Vintage, pp. 182ff, 214ff.

[124] See Boris Munshuktin, *Lomonosov: Chemist, Courtier, Physicist, Poet*, Princeton, NJ: Princeton University Press (1952).

[125] Nicholas DeWitt, "Scholarship in the Natural Sciences," in Cyril Black (ed.), *The Transformation of Russian Society, Aspects of Social Change Since 1861*, Cambridge, MA: Harvard University Press, p. 385 (1960). See also, Ludmilla Schulze, "The Russification of the St. Petersburg Academy of Sciences and Arts in the Eighteenth Century," *British Journal of the History of Science* 18:305 (1985).

[126] Billington, ibid., p. 307.

[127] Alexander Vucinich, *Science in Russian Culture: A History to 1860*, Stanford: Stanford University Press (1963).

[128] It is a hard philosophical question: When can a given scientific environment be considered "mature"? Without elaborating on this issue beyond the pale of this book, I propose the following Kuhnian definition: A scientific environment is not mature if its practitioners are normally associated with a skilled application of existing scientific insights and proceed in

layer of beliefs and aspirations grafted upon an underlying cultural substratum, the end result popped up in Russia, *deus ex machina*, without that supportive layer.[129] To say more about this fundamental cultural divide, I conclude this chapter with a brief comparison between the artistic styles of Russia and the West, with special emphasis on the elusive concept of "perspective."

Truth in Perspective

"Perspective" is nothing but a system of representing a three-dimensional space on a two-dimensional plane.[130] There are a variety of such methods, and none is more "correct" than the others a priori. For example, one could argue that representing more distant objects as if they were diminishing in size is a more "accurate" description of reality, because this is what we observe when we look at three-dimensional spaces. One could counter, on the other hand, that keeping the size constant regardless of distance is a better reflection of "reality" because objects do not in fact shrink as a function of their distance from the beholder. Again, it could be disputed that remote objects should look *larger* on the canvass, in acknowledgment of the limitation of our sensory perception and

their work "by accumulation" of data; Thomas Kuhn labeled this practice "normal science." See his pioneering book, *The Structure of Scientific Revolutions*, 2d ed., Chicago: University of Chicago Press (1970). A mature scientific environment spawns "extraordinary science," that is, major insights that repudiate large bodies of existing knowledge and replace them with alternative ways of looking at the world. Most scientists toil the fields of normal science. Examples of extraordinary visionaries include, e.g., such names as Copernicus and Einstein. The claim that modern Russian science came of age is tantamount, then, to an assertion that the Russian nation started to spawn extraordinary revolutionaries of the Kuhnian type. Examples may include Dmitry Mendeleev's publication of his "Periodic Table" (of chemical elements) in 1869 and Ivan Pavlov's path-breaking paper on conditioned reflexes, which he read in 1904.

[129] The often-extraordinary achievements of Russian and Soviet science are summarized in one volume in Loren Graham, *Science in Russia and the Soviet Union*, New York: Cambridge University Press (1993). As this thoroughly researched volume reveals, the Russian genius spawned world-class leaders in the theoretical sciences, such as mathematics and theoretical physics, but by and large lagged behind the West in the experimental sciences. As an example of the transformation of Western scientific ideas on Russian soil, Graham narrates the story of the acceptance of Darwinism in Russia during the nineteenth century. Superficially, the new theory was hailed with enthusiasm and without the kind of qualms that enveloped its acceptance in most Western nations. On the other hand, the Russians failed to distinguish between Darwinism and "evolutionism." The latter term simply implied that certain species evolved from earlier, supposedly more primitive ones. Darwin's main contribution was to provide an explanation, based on the idea of natural selection, for this observed evolution. During the nineteenth century, the enthusiastic Russians took Darwin as a simple "evolutionist" because this theory supported their aspirations for political and social change – "evolution" simply meant to them that primitive life forms are replaced by more sophisticated ones – and they paid no attention at all to the natural selection scientific explanation of the phenomena under observation. See ibid., pp. 56ff.

[130] Avigdor Posèk, *Perspective*, Tel Aviv: Tserikover (1982, reissued 1992, in Hebrew).

our recognition of the existence of a reality beyond reality. Or one could order the size of objects in proportion to their relative rank (e.g., saints should look larger and sponsors of the work of art smaller), to reflect by pictorial means their differential dignity.[131] Nor can we gain a better appreciation of the relative "accuracy" of the chosen approach by asking which method generates a greater "similarity" between objects and their representation, because the concept of similarity is contingent, just like the method of perspective, on the perceptual conditioning of the viewer.[132] Clearly then, in this matter, too, Truth is in the eye of the beholder.

Pre-Renaissance Europe was not familiar with the rigors of linear perspective. Figure 45 is a refined early thirteenth-century illuminated Psalter showing both the last supper and a scene representing Christ washing the feet of His apostles. This work of art is a wonder of blending figures with a circular, very well-balanced, composition and shimmering yet refined colors reflecting both the grandeur and the humility of the two scenes. The artist paid no heed, however, to the "correct" relative size of the apostles given their presumed distance from the viewer. The figure of Christ towers over the frames of His disciples, in recognition of His role as the principal protagonist in His own Passion. The natural world that consists of visual spaces is abstracted into sustained blots of color, as if the whole environment consisted only of the gospel characters and there was an ontological void between them. Sensory reality is thus reduced to a decorative role and it is wholly subservient to the didactic objective of the narrative. Nor does reason play any role in this representation, as the viewer is invited to accept reality on faith, rather than on observational or rational grounds.

All of this changed dramatically during the Quattrocento, as the principles of "linear perspective" were first formulated by Filippo Brunelleschi[133] (by actual demonstration) and by his friend and admirer Leon Battista Alberti (in a famous treatise on the subject),[134] and then executed, by progressive degrees of skill, by

---

[131] Ibid. The most influential study of this issue is the wonderful little treatise by Erwin Panofsky, *Perspective as a Symbolic Form*, translated by Christopher Wood, Zone Books (1997; originally published in 1924–25).

[132] E. H. Gombrich, "The Mask and the Face: The Perception of Physiognomic Likeness in Life and Art," in E. H. Gombrich, Julian Hochberg, and Max Black, *Art, Perception and Reality*, Baltimore, MD: Johns Hopkins University Press (1970). In this brilliant essay Gombrich discusses, for example, the "similarity" between a person and his or her caricature, showing that it is exactly the "unrealistic" features of a good caricature that evoke in the viewer a sense of verisimilitude. He goes on to ponder which objects look more "like" each other: Is a baby more "like" himself during adulthood, or is it more similar to all other babies? Is a photograph closer in appearance to its prototype, or is it more similar to all other photographs?

[133] Brunelleschi famously constructed a *camera obscura* equipped with a peephole and managed to harness the laws of optics such that a flat image of the Florence Baptistery within the darkened box would be viewed "in perspective" as if it had three dimensions.

[134] Leon Battista Alberti, *On Painting*, translated by John Spencer, New Haven, CT: Yale University Press (revised ed., 1966; originally published in 1434–36).

FIGURE 45. Illuminated Psalter, The Last Supper and Christ Washing the Feet of His Apostles, 1210.

the principal artists of the early Renaissance, like Paolo Uccello, Masaccio, and Piero della Francesca. It is submitted that linear perspective presages, by intuitive means and without rigorous articulation, the Settecento Kantian notion that Truth can be reached by the combined effect of empirical observation and innate reasoning.

The rhetoric of the Renaissance was quite simple. It held that Truth can be derived by observation[135] and that perspective was the principal method to faithfully represent reality.

Leonardo explains:[136]

"Now do you see that the eye embraces the beauty of the whole world? . . . It counsels and corrects all the arts of mankind . . . it is the prince of mathematics, and the sciences founded on it are absolutely certain. It has measured the distances and sizes of the stars; it has discovered the elements and their location . . . it has given birth to architecture and to perspective and to the divine art of painting. . . .[137] Painting is based upon perspective which is nothing else than a thorough knowledge of the function of the eye. And this function simply consists in receiving in a pyramid the forms and colors of all objects placed before it. . . . Therefore if you extend the lines from the edges of each body as they converge, you will bring them to a single point, and necessarily the said lines must form a pyramid. . . .[138] The body of the atmosphere is full of infinite radiating pyramids produced by the objects existing in it. These intersect and cross each other with independent convergence without interferences with each other and pass through all the surrounding atmosphere. . . .[139] Perspective . . . is to be preferred to all the discourses and systems of the schoolmen. In its province the beam of light is explained by methods of demonstration, wherein is found the glory not only of mathematical but also of physical science, adorned as it is with the flowers of both."[140]

"The function of the eye . . ." then "simply consists in receiving in a pyramid the forms and colors of all objects placed before it." This self-assured (but unfortunately wrong) assertion is directly derived from Alberti's *Della Pittura*, which posits a monocular vision, that is, a single eye "looking" at an object, and the existence of visual rays in the form of a pyramid between the eye and the object. These visual rays determine, by the application of rather complex

---

[135] About the style that originates with Brunelleschi, Uccello, and Masaccio, Vasari has this to say: "[T]he artists tried to reproduce neither more nor less than what they saw in nature; and as a result, their work began to show more careful observation and understanding. . . . They endeavored to compose their pictures with greater regard for real appearance." See Giorgio Vasari, *Lives of the Artists*, selection translated by George Bull, New York: Penguin Classics, p. 93 (1965; first published in 1568).

[136] In spite of the great importance that Leonardo assigned to the role of the senses in our understanding of the world, he was not oblivious to the role of reason. He thought that stimuli were processed by what he called the *sensus communis*, a central organ, as it were, responsible for the organized handling of stimuli and ultimately for their perception. See *The Notebooks of Leonardo da Vinci*, selected and edited by Irma Richter, Oxford: Oxford University Press, p. 108 (1952; the original notes were taken by the artist throughout his lifetime, 1452–1519).

[137] Ibid., p. 110.

[138] Ibid., p. 118.

[139] Ibid., p. 121.

[140] Ibid., p. 128.

geometrical rules, the size and brightness of all objects represented in the painting. A correct application of these mathematical rules generates the system
known as "linear" one-point perspective, where all diagonal lines within the
picture converge in a single "vanishing point."[141] A famous example of the
Albertian principles is Masaccio's *Holy Trinity* (Figure 46), which is commonly
believed to have been the very first "correct" application of these principles,
although it was executed in 1427–28, a few years before the publication of
Della Pittura. This flat mural definitely creates an illusion of depth, which is
mainly caused by the convergence of all diagonal lines to a single vanishing
point, located at the very center of the lower edge of the painting (just above
the triple-layered base). To identify that point, one has to continue the straight
lines formed by the barrel vaulted ceiling on the one hand and, this time from
the bottom up, by the diagonals of the base near the origin of the columns. This
is also the meeting point of the diagonal lines at the lower sides of the ceiling
on the one hand, and, more or less, of the imaginary lines between the donors'
heads and their outstretched hands on the other. Whether you look at this pictorial space from up above or from down below, from the majestic gaze of God
the Father or from the sides of the painting, everything leads to a single, cleverly chosen point. The entire image is admirably organized; nothing falls out
of line.

As it turns out, however, linear perspective is hardly what Alberti and his
cohorts imagined it to be, an impartial description of what the eye "sees." The
key element in understanding the Albertian fallacy is the simple fact that the eye
does not see anything at all. The retina of the eye, to be sure, becomes the repository of raw visual images, but the function of image *interpretation* is performed
by the brain, and there is a marked difference between the raw retinal reflection
and the "meaningful" image processed in our mind.[142] Whereas the anatomy
of the retina (more or less)[143] responds to the rules of linear perspective, the
brain "understands" that remote objects are not in fact diminished or more
faded. In recognition of this fact, it adds size and brightness to remote images,
thereby overriding, as it were, the raw retinal signals. For example, if a beholder
moves her hand away from her eyes, the hand is interpreted by the brain to be of

---

[141] The rules of linear perspective were first articulated in Alberti's book, *On Painting*, published
in 1435–36. Alberti's language in not always user friendly, and modern lay readers usually need
a good expository introduction to make heads or tails of it. See, for instance, John Spencer's
introduction to Alberti's book (revised ed. for Yale University Press, 1966).

[142] The first to insist on the primary role of the brain in perception were some of the early Gestalt
psychologists, e.g., Max Wertheimer, Kurt Koffka, and Wolfgang Köhler. See, for instance,
Wolfgang Köhler, *Gestalt Psychology: An Introduction to New Concepts in Modern Psychology*, New York: Mentor (1947; reissued 1992). Unsurprisingly, the same author saw the connection between issues of perception and the central question in this chapter, How does one
form an opinion about the validity of propositions? See, for example, his book *The Place of
Value in a World of Facts*, New York: Liveright (1966).

[143] Alberti's paradigm would have been registered on the retinal surface if it were flat; in fact, it
is concave, which makes straight lines appear curvilinear and curvilinear lines appear straight.
Of this more later.

FIGURE 46. Masaccio, *The Holy Trinity*, 1427–28.

constant size although its retinal image shifts rather dramatically. This property of our mind, called "perceptual constancy," in negating the optical illusion generated by our retinal anatomy, assists us in obtaining a more functional view of the world.[144] Albertian perspective, then, is not what we really see, if "seeing"

---

[144] There is a whole set of perceptual constancies along with the size and brightness constancies discussed in the text. For example, stationary objects appear to be what they really are, constant,

is the combined effect of our retinal signals and our perceptual interpretation. It is, rather, a geometrized organization of sight, a regimentation of our observational faculties by the orderly grammar of linear vision. This is, perhaps, what Erwin Panofsky meant when he wrote, three quarters of a century ago, that linear perspective was merely a "symbolic form," that is, a culture-based interpretation of reality embedded in the spirit of the Renaissance, and not necessarily an objective or more accurate pictorial representation of the "real" world.[145] The notion that geometry, especially straight lines, was "rational, was prevalent in Renaissance Europe.[146] Linearity was commonly believed to divide space into segments with ideal proportions, just as the Florentine urban architecture or agricultural fields had been.[147] As Edgerton points out, the idea that geometrical rules had to be applied to painting to make more "sense" of the scriptures was suggested, two centuries before Alberti, by the Franciscan monk

although the viewer might change her own location in relation to these objects. A recent compilation of materials on perceptual constancies is Vincent Walsh and Janusz Kulikowski (eds.), *Perceptual Constancy: Why Things Look as They Do*, New York: Cambridge University Press (1998).

[145] Erwin Panofsky, *Perspective as Symbolic Form*, translated by Christopher Wood, New York: Zone Books (1997; originally published in 1924–25). Panofsky brilliantly demonstrated how different cultures used alternative methods in their respective approaches to the problem of perspective. As is well known, Panofsky committed a technical error by addressing the issue of the concavity of the retina. He thought that since the retina is concave, we see objects accordingly, i.e., straight lines as curvilinear and curvilinear formations as straight. This is an error because we know that the brain corrects for the retina's anatomy and we actually perceive objects as they "really" are. Panofsky's critics thought that when he used the expression "symbolic form" he was alluding to this imagined difference between "reality" and linear perspective, resulting from the concavity of the retina. In fact, Panofsky was not explicit about this claim. The term "symbolic form" in art goes back at least to Hegel's *Lectures on Aesthetics* (delivered in Berlin in the 1820s) and it goes without saying that Hegel was not preoccupied by the verisimilitude of retinal images. The key for understanding Panofsky's intention must lie elsewhere. I am inclined to think that although Panofsky could not have been aware of the more recent literature in the field of perceptual constancies he sensed, with his acute art-historian's intuition, that something was fishy in the "realism" of linear perspective and made an enormous contribution by merely raising this issue to the surface. Another way of interpreting Panofsky's enigmatic term is by drawing on his famous distinction between iconography and iconology. Whereas the former is the study of the narrative attributes of objects, complete with their cultural connotations (for example, a saint pierced by numerous arrows bears the iconographic insignia of St. Sebastian), iconology implies a deeper understanding of the subject derived from the connoisseurship of style and a spiritual awareness of its development; Panofsky, following Ernst Cassirer, often referred to the latter as "symbolic form." See Erwin Panofsky, *Studies in Iconology, Humanistic Themes in the Art of the Renaissance*, New York: Harper & Row (1972; originally published in 1939).

[146] Samuel Edgerton, *The Renaissance Rediscovery of Linear Perspective*, New York: ACLS, Chapter 3 (1975). Edgerton's wonderful book seems to me the most thoughtful authority on Renaissance perspective. It is the only book one has to read on the subject if one is determined to read none other.

[147] Leonardo Bruni, *History of the Florentine People*, translated by James Hankins, Cambridge, MA: Harvard University Press (2001; originally published circa 1404). See also Edgerton, ibid.

Roger Bacon (1220–1292).[148] Alberti himself treated geometry as if it were the external manifestation of artistic Reason. This is particularly clear in his architectural achievements, of both the literary[149] and the practical[150] varieties. He was the first one to have challenged the medieval methods of town planning, where each person added to the existing urban landscape her own imprint as she saw fit, thus giving rise to typical medieval towns that were complete with a hodgepodge of crooked streets and alleys, towers and *palazzi*, dwellings, markets, and churches. Alberti, on the other hand, preached for straight and bright thoroughfares and centrally planned cities, such that the spillover effects of each structure upon the whole be taken into account in advance. By inventing our modern notion of zoning, Alberti coined the conjunction of geometry and artistic Reason.[151] This philosophy was evident in the work of many leading artists who sometimes were as interested in geometry as in aesthetics.[152]

The strong ties between the rule of Reason and linear perspective can be demonstrated by observing the collapse of perspective during periods of religious revival. These periods occurred, for instance, after great onslaughts of the Black Death, when men and women rediscovered the transcendental, the mystical, and the miraculous, as everything else failed them.[153] A similar effect occurred in Florence about a century later when Girolamo Savonarola (1452–1498) rose to power. This austere monk used his fiery speeches to denounce the humanist values of his time and called for spiritual revival, simplicity of manner, and, above all, axiomatic faith. It is a controversial question whether this wave of mysticism created a new art style, compatible with the spirit of Savonarola.[154] I submit, however, that it did. Figure 47, *The Entombment*, was painted by Fra Bartolomeo in 1515, some seventeen years after the burning of

---

[148] Roger Bacon, *Opus Majus*, translated by Robert Belle Burke, Philadelphia: University of Pennsylvania Press (2000; originally published in the late 1260s). See also Edgerton, ibid., Chapter 2.

[149] His treatise on architecture, *De re Aedificatoria*, was published in 1452.

[150] Alberti's signature architectural achievement seems to be the Florentine Palazzo Rucellai, which was already discussed in Chapter 2, supra.

[151] "Beauty," writes Alberti in his *De Re Aedificatoria* (Book 9, Chapter 5), "is a kind of harmony and concord of all the parts to form a whole which is constructed according to a fixed number, and a certain relation and order, as symmetry, the highest and most perfect law of nature, demands." See Anthony Blunt, *Artistic Theory in Italy 1450–1600*, New York: Oxford University Press, p. 15 (1962).

[152] Piero della Francesca is a good example. About Piero's geometrical writings and their intellectual pedigree see, for instance, Michael Baxandall, *Painting and Experience in Fifteenth Century Italy*, New York: Oxford University Press, pp. 86ff (1972).

[153] See, for instance, Milard Meiss, *Painting in Florence and Siena After the Black Death*, New York: Harper & Row (1951, reissued 1964). For example, Florentine painting was dominated around the middle of the fourteenth century by Andrea di Cione (better known as Orcagna) and his brother, Nardo di Cione. Both artists shied away from the innovations introduced by Giotto and his followers and reverted to a more inward-looking pictorial idiom reminiscent of Byzantine spirituality.

[154] One author, who devoted a small volume to this question, concludes that although Savonarola preached in his sermons for a "simple" art style, one that lays stress on the spiritual radiance of objects rather than on their bodily perfection, it is hard to detect a distinct art style that

FIGURE 47. Fra Bartolomeo, *The Entombment*, 1515.

Savonarola at the stake. Fra Bartolomeo, a Dominican monk, was a devout aficionado of Savonarola and actually followed him to the convent of St. Marco
to lead a life of austerity and devotion. *The Entombment*, executed during the
High Renaissance (Raphael, for instance, died in 1520!), exhibits clear signs
of regression in style, and especially in perspective. Note, for instance, that
the human figures at the remote background are considerably larger than the
grieving saints in the foreground, and that the body of the Redeemer lacks any
pretense of foreshortening.[155]

To conclude this point, it seems to me that linear perspective admirably
combines the light of Reason and the quest for Truth through observation and
experience, and none can be relied on as sufficient explanation of this cultural
construct without the other.

Several scholars identified the nature of the discrepancy between sight and
linear perspective, albeit in a somewhat fragmentary manner. William Ivins,
for example, writing in 1938, thought that perspective, being, as he phrased
it, "the most important event of the Renaissance," laid the foundations for all

---

mimicked these guidelines. See Ronald Steinberg, *Fra Girolamo Savonarola, Florentine Art and
Renaissance Historiography*, Athens: Ohio University Press (1977).

[155] Even the gracious Botticelli, in his later period, when he fell under the spell of Savonarola,
abandoned some of his earlier achievements in perspective. For example, in his celebrated *The
Mystic Nativity*, which belongs to this period, the shed of the nativity responds to the rigors of
linear perspective, but the other elements of the panel, including the relative size of the Virgin,
the admirers, and the angels, definitely do not.

subsequent scientific developments; it did so not only by reproducing the shape of objects as they "really" were, but also by introducing an "accepted grammar of representation." He held that the combined effect of these two factors introduced into Western culture a sense of "scientific awareness."[156] Ivins may have been wrong in assuming that perspective imitates reality (even in the subjective sense), but he did have the intuition that perspective was not only "discovered" but "invented" as well; the latter function, of inventing perspective, involved a process of "rationalizing sight," which is, indeed, the very title of Ivins' little book. Hubert Damisch attempted a heroic leap of faith by holding that perspective was entirely, or almost entirely, a cultural trope. For example, he showed that pictorial architecture preceded the actual construction of similar buildings and thus could only be interpreted as a catalyst for the formation of a new reality rather than as a reproduction of an existing reality. He also stressed the well-known point that perspective is entirely in the eye of the beholder (e.g., remote objects are not really smaller), and thus it is more a subjective account of reality than a detached objective report of what really is.[157] At a certain trivial level Damisch may have been justified in his claim that everything can be reduced to its cultural undergrowth. It is submitted, however, that Damisch failed to treat with sufficient respect the lust for knowledge, the eagerness to learn, that fired the imagination of the Renaissance artists. Piero or Uccello or Leonardo would have been surprised to be informed by Damisch that they were all trying to invent a new world from scratch, rather than devote their efforts to unveil the deep and exciting secrets of the existing universe. An important step forward was made by Michael Kubovy, a psychologist *cum* art historian, who demonstrated with admirable skill that in spite of all their geometric rhetoric, Renaissance artists found ways to set their *oeuvre* free from the technical and ultimately boring regimentation of linear perspective and paid a lot of attention to what we really perceive with our brain.[158] But perhaps he paid too little heed to the significance of the *opposite* contention – contrary to our holistic experience of seeing both with our retina and with our brain, linear perspective was invoked as an ideal in the first place (Leonardo called the "correct" use of linear perspective "*costruzione legittima*," thus delegitimizing, just like Vasari, the "naïve" Gothic or Byzantine traditions). I reiterate my basic contention that within the constraints of the Renaissance "symbolic form" linear perspective is not a mistake. It is an admirable blending of Reason and experience, the application of innate categorical imperatives and sensory *stimuli*, of empirical

---

[156] William Ivins, *On the Rationalization of Sight*, New York: Metropolitan Museum of Art (1938).

[157] Hubert Damisch, *The Origin of Perspective*, translated by John Goodman, Cambridge, MA: MIT Press (2000; originally published in 1987).

[158] Michael Kubovy, *The Psychology of Perspective and Renaissance Art*, New York: Cambridge University Press (1986). His main thesis is that "Renaissance painters deliberately induced a discrepancy between the spectator's actual point of view and the point of view from which the scene is felt to be viewed. The result is a spiritual experience that cannot be obtained by any other means." See ibid., p. 16.

FIGURE 48. Andrei Rublev, *The Holy Trinity*, 1425.

reality and its mathematical regimentation. How did the same symbolic form fare on Russian soil?

Figure 48, *The Holy Trinity*, was painted by the greatest of all icon painters in the history of Orthodoxy, the monk Andrei Rublev, in 1425. This panel is also the most celebrated of the great master's works, and along with the *Vladimirskaya*, which, one recalls, was not painted by a Russian, is considered to be "the icon of icons," one of a kind, sacred and glorious, venerated and loved by the entire Russian nation. About 150 years after its painting, The Council of 100 Chapters ordained that all Orthodox icon painters must mimic Rublev's masterpiece if they wish to represent the Holy Trinity and elevated it to the rank of a role model for Orthodox iconography in general.[159] Unlike its Masaccio counterpart, it has no trace of the Father, the Son, or the Holy Spirit. Three equally ranking angels are half-seated-half- floating around a table engulfed by a desert-like environment with a tree and a dwelling. These are the three angelic pilgrims sent by God to the elderly Abraham in the desert (Genesis, Chapter 18), announcing to him that his aging wife, Sarah, a barren woman, should expect a child soon, such that a great nation would flow forth from his offspring. A single goblet is situated right at the center of the table, suggesting the Holy Communion. The three pilgrims are exquisitely elongated; their bodies measure fourteen times the size of their heads, twice as long as a normal adult's. These proportions give them an airy, surreal appearance, accentuated by the fact that their feet barely touch their respective footrests at the bottom. Abraham's nomadic tent is transformed into a temple, and the biblical oaks of Mamre (in the plural) are transformed into the tree of life (in the singular). Whereas in Western painting "realism" is commonly invoked by the use of light and shadows, thereby deriving the painting's luminosity from external sources of radiance,[160] there are no shadows in Rublev's icon. His luminosity is entirely internal, because he views his subject with spiritual eyes, without paying any heed to external sensory stimuli. The absence of realistic properties is more than compensated in this icon by a plethora of symbolic and mystical elements. The obvious composition of the icon is circular, around the contours of the three pilgrims, with the Eucharistic cup at the center of the circle. In Orthodoxy, circles symbolize divine perfection and God's inexhaustible love for His creation. But there are at least two additional, subtler forms in this composition. The panel of the table facing the viewers contains a rectangular form, representing the canonic shape of the universe, as well as the more spiritual concept of the four corners of the earth. The tree of life is connected to the cup and to the rectangular form in a vertical line, which intersects with the horizontal line connecting the visitors' haloes to form a perfect cross. The circle, the rectangular form, and the cross are mystically conjoined to preach a gospel of salvation. The scepter of the right Person, assumed to be the Holy Spirit, points to the mountains on the right, which are God's creation. Thus, the universe is defined as what the message is all about. The middle figure, usually assumed to be the Father,[161] sits beneath the tree of life and

---

[159] See, for example, Paul Evdokimov, *The Art of the Icon: A Theology of Beauty*, translated by Fr. Steven Bigham, Princeton, NJ: Princeton University Press, p. 24 (1990; first published in French in 1972).

[160] The important subject of shadows, and what can be learned of the painter's perception of reality by watching his particular technique in this respect, was taken up by Michael Baxandall in one of his more recent books, *Shadows and Enlightenment*, New Haven, CT: Yale University Press (1995).

[161] The middle figure's robe is painted in deep purple, which is suggestive in Russian iconography to divine love, normally associated with the Father. In many other Old Testament trinities the middle figure is assumed to be the Second Person of the Trinity, perhaps because it is easier to associate Him with the Eucharistic cup. See Leonid Ouspensky, *Theology of the Icon*, Volume 2, translated by Anthony Gythiel, Crestwood, NY: St. Vladimir's Seminary Press, p. 292 (1992).

blesses the Eucharistic cup, which stands above the sign of the universe. The scepter of the Son, on the left-hand side, points to the temple, which symbolizes the New Jerusalem.[162] This "Old Testament Trinity" was crafted in this way, as a deliberate move to foil a straightforward portrayal of the "real" Trinity – the Father, the Son, and the Holy Spirit. Although there is nothing more "real" in Orthodox theology than the reality of the Trinitarian existence,[163] it is an existence that transcends sensory reality. To rely on the senses in quest of the ultimate Truth would be, for a Russian iconographer, a denial of the limits of human perception; it would be an impudent act of defiance, in direct violation of the Second Commandment.

To be sure, Western artists made deliberate use of symbols as well. Everybody knew, for instance, that the Three Persons of the Christian deity do not "really" look as Masaccio portrayed them. It was common knowledge that Masaccio merely used his imagination to invoke their hidden presence, much as any portraitist might invent the likeness of a person he never met or saw before (e.g., the likeness of a mythological hero). Nonetheless, Masaccio was banking on his senses to imagine how Truth *might* look, and on geometry to rationalize it and give it an orderly meaning. Rublev's semiotics was much more complicated. The use of symbols as a means to portray reality was considered too direct, so he used symbols (the pilgrims) as proxies for other symbols (the Three Persons) to suggest the presence of God, the One, and the Three, in itself totally incomprehensible from either a sensory or a logical point of view. The repudiation of either the sensory or the logical approach to the appreciation of ultimate reality, or Truth, is clearly manifested by Rublev's use of perspective. The table around which the pilgrims are suspended assumes *larger* proportions as it *recedes* into the distance, thus setting the standard for the famous "reverse perspective" style of the golden age of Muscovite painting.[164] In his revocation of perspective and commitment to two-dimensionality as the only proper method of representing three-dimensional space, the art of Rublev constitutes only a small link, albeit a splendid one, in a long chain of icon painters from the early Byzantine era to our day and age. This long-standing historical rupture between East and West is narrated by a modern Orthodox commentator as follows:

The sacred art of both East and West expressed the same realities up to the eleventh and twelfth centuries, with identical impetus that sought to reveal "things invisible." It was that marvelous period of Romanesque art which unveiled a world beyond the laws of

---

[162] Evdokimov, ibid., pp. 243ff.

[163] Evdokimov, ibid., writes: "Between being and nothingness, there is no other principle of existence than the Trinitarian principle. It is the unshakable foundation that unites the individual person and the community, giving final meaning to everything. Human thought receives the Revelation and crucifies itself in order to be reborn in the trisolar light of absolute truth."

[164] Reverse perspective was prevalent in non-Russian cultures as well, especially during the Middle Ages. See Samuel Edgerton, *The Renaissance Rediscovery of Linear Perspective*, New York: ACLS, Chapter 1 (1975). Edgerton shows that even Giotto used this style on occasion, although in some of his frescoes in Assisi's St. Francis he experimented with linear perspective.

gravity, and even showed us how stone could be spiritualized. . . . In Italy, however, we see Cimabue, Giotto and Duccio form a vanguard leading to progressive departure from the art of the Eastern Church. . . . The art of the transcendent fades with their introduction of such visuals a three-dimensional perspective, natural light and shadows, the return to realistic portrayal of people and use of the emotional.[165]

A resounding, and very clear, advocacy of the Orthodox point of view is offered by Pavel Florensky. He insists that Truth cannot be captured by the senses. Human faces, which Florensky treats as his paradigmatic case of "real" external objects, must be transformed "into a light bearing countenance by . . . revealing [the] under-revealed." Only this spiritual existence, which cannot be perceived with our carnal eyes, is fit to "bear witness and prove the truth of authentic reality."[166] Florensky goes on to suggest the implications of his epistemology within the domain of aesthetics and art theory. He describes all post-medieval Catholic art as three-dimensional (which he considered unduly sensuous) and all Protestant art, with its strong affinity to linear engravings, as one-dimensional (the cleanliness of the line suggested to him the dominance of reason over faith). Only Orthodoxy, especially of the Russian variety, maintained its allegiance to two-dimensionality. "Where the [three-dimensional] oil painting," he laments, "will express the world in sensuous images, and the Protestant engraving will give us the world in rational schemata, the icon makes visually manifest the metaphysical essence of the event or person it depicts." When Panofsky coined his enigmatic term "perspective as a symbolic form," his definition was warmly embraced by many modern painters,[167] among them numerous Russians, because it gave them a carte blanche license not to worry about perspective; they could, with a clear conscience, experiment with their various abstract idioms without feeling that they reneged on a commitment to seek, and then to find, the Truth. Several artists (Kazimir Malevitch appears to be their principal forbearer) rejected out of hand the meaningful possibility of all forms of perception that came through sensory intermediation. They advocated, instead, the representation of reality as it was perceived by an "inner eye," totally spiritual, and totally removed from both the domains of observation and reasoning. "There exists an internal eye," wrote one of Malevitch's followers, "analogous to the internal sense of hearing with which Beethoven worked without direct sense of hearing. . . . The figurative picture is a subordination of the internal eye to the direct vision."[168] A host of other stellar figures of modern Russian painters,

---

[165] Michel Quenot, *The Icon: Window on the Kingdom*, Crestwood, NY: St. Vladimir's Seminary Press, p. 72 (1996).

[166] Pavel Florensky, *Iconostasis*, translated by Donald Sheehan and Olga Andrejev, Crestwood, NY: St. Vladimir Seminary Press, p. 55 (1996; first published in 1922).

[167] Samuel Edgerton, *The Renaissance Rediscovery of Linear Perspective*, New York: ACLS, p. 153 (1975).

[168] These words, attributed to Boris Ender, writing in 1920, were cited by Charlotte Douglas in her essay "Beyond Reason: Malevitch, Matiushin, and their Circles," in Maurice Tuchman

including Vassily Kandinsky, Ivan Kliun, Pavel Mansurov, Liubov Popova, Alexander Rodchenko, and many others, in spite of the pronounced differences in their philosophical formulations, characterized the subject matter of their exploration by the umbrella term "nonobjective." This somewhat enigmatic term amounts to an assertion that external objects lack observable properties, and, in any event, their perceived "meaning" cannot be shared by more than one observer. Truth is not merely in the eye of the beholder; the eye of the beholder, to be truthful, must be of the "inner" or spiritual variety, which defies not only the comforts of falsifiable observation, but also the reign of reason itself.[169]

Does linear perspective have a musical equivalent? Let me speculate: If such an analogy can be conceptualized, then "musical perspective" would have to feature, at the very least, the following two properties. It would be attuned to sensory *stimuli*, and it would subordinate them to the principles of reason; it would be, in other words, an acoustic sounding of Masaccio's *Holy Trinity*. In this respect, Western medieval music, for instance, did not have musical perspective. Its aesthetic canons screened out all kinds of normatively unacceptable sensory stimuli, including female voices. The interplay of diverse voices, musically expressed by counterpoint and polyphony, was held to be sinful. *Crescendi* and *diminuendi*, echoing the sounds we actually hear from nature, were used very sparingly. And it objected, quite violently, as it turns out, to music that appealed to the senses, that was sensuously beautiful, rather than to the spiritual mind of the pious believer. When "modern" polyphony made its first tentative headway to lure the minds and hearts of late medieval audiences, a scandalized bishop wrote:

Bad taste has . . . degraded even religious worship, bringing into the presence of God . . . a kind of luxurious and lascivious singing, full of ostentation, which with female modulation astonishes and enervates the soul of the hearers. When you hear the soft harmonies of the various singers . . . you would think yourself listening to a concert of sirens rather than of men, and wonder at the powers of voices, which the nightingale, or the mockingbird, or whatever is most tuneful among birds, could not equal.[170]

The sense that pious devotion is jeopardized by polyphony, by sensuous beauty, and by the introduction of female voices was quite widespread on the threshold of the Renaissance. A Papal bull articulates this fear (and note the anxious plea to be careful with one's virility):

The mere number of the notes . . . conceal from us the plain-chant melody. . . . These musicians run without pausing, they intoxicate our ear without satisfying it . . . and instead of promoting devotion, they prevent it by creating a sensuous . . . atmosphere. Thus it

et al. (eds.), *The Spiritual in Art: Abstract Painting 1890–1985*, New York: Abbeville Press, pp. 185, 195 (1986).

[169] See generally John Bowlt, "Esoteric Culture in Russian Society," in Maurice Tuchman, ibid., p. 165.

[170] John of Salisbury, Bishop of Chartres, is cited by Robert Haybrun in his book, *Papal Legislation on Sacred Music*, Collegeville, MN: Liturgical Press, p. 18 (1979).

was not without good reason that Boethius said: "A person who is intrinsically sensuous will delight in hearing these indecent melodies, and one who listens to them frequently will be weakened thereby and lose his virility of soul."[171]

All of this changed, of course, in the late Renaissance; the conservative medieval theologians who bore down on Galileo the man, but who eventually had to yield the right of way to his rising method of inquiry, capitulated more easily (although not without a fight) to the music of such composers as Giovanni Pierluigi da Palestrina and then, after him, to Claudio Monteverdi. The latter put the seal on the old "flat" musical worldview and flung open the gate, with authority and finality, showing a brand new, and totally modern, musical landscape. Monteverdi's music had in it everything that is modern, humanist, and multifaceted: polyphony, sensuous beauty, female singers so sweet that even the "nightingale ... could not equal"; secular subjects, vernacular language, artistic emotion – and he even wrote the first real opera, *L'orfeo*, never equaled in its sensuous refinement by any music written before (or after).[172] In short, his music, in being all inclusive, curious to detail, and "scientific" in its receptivity, orderly, and reasoned in its structure, was fully three-dimensional – it had, in other words, linear perspective.[173]

If one accepts this definition of musical perspective, I would like to contrast it with what I consider the most Russian of all Russian modernist musical masterpieces, Modest Mussorgsky's opera, *Boris Godunov* (best known in the Rimsky-Korsakov arrangement). I leave it to the reader's judgment to decide to what extent this opera stands for the umbrella term of "modern Russian music." In this highly speculative domain, one thing is certain, that Mussorgsky himself was determined to fashion this opera, as well as his entire musical output, after totally Russian *leitmotifs*, thereby tossing off all the westernizing influences that crept into Russian composition in the wake of the corrupting Petrine revolution.[174] Together with Balakirev, Borodin, Rimsky-Korsakov, and Cui, Mussorgsky formed the St. Petersburg association known as the "Mighty Five," whose avowed purpose was to revive the old national style, deriving its

---

[171] Ibid. The bull was issued in the name of Pope John XXII, an able pontiff holding the Avignon Holy See in 1316–34.

[172] The Greek myth of Orpheus, revived in the Renaissance, reflected the supremacy of human aesthetics over the calamities of life, even unto death. The beauty of Orpheus' song and music demonstrated, as it were, how this beauty need stop at nothing, not even at the gates of Hades, and can even claim back lost souls, give them body, and instill in them their bygone spirit. It was only the temporary weakness of Orpheus' will that yielded his paramour back to the eternal shadows of nothingness. In the eighteenth century, the century of Kant and of the autonomy of the human will, this subject was picked up again by Christoph Willibald Gluck in his opera *Orpheus and Eurydice*, to revolutionize the "opera seria" style of Handel and his contemporaries, and discover new paths to modernity.

[173] Gary Tomlinson, *Monteverdi and the End of the Renaissance*, Berkeley: University of California Press (1987). The analogy between Galileo and Monteverdi is Tomlinson's. He also makes a similar comparison to the *oeuvre* of Giambattista Guarini, whose masterpiece, *Il Pastor Fido*, was criticized on similar grounds by the very same theologians who tormented Galileo.

[174] See Michel Calvocaressi, *Mussorgsky*, London: J. M. Dent & Sons (1974).

inspiration from popular melodies, country folk tales, and the deep secrets of the vast Russian forest.[175] He chose as his plot the tragic story of Boris Godunov, who ascended to the throne in 1598, following the mysterious death of Ivan the Terrible's son Dmitry, and, later, his other son (from a different marriage), Fyodor. Godunov was Fyodor's uncle, and, although suspected of instigating both the death of Dmitry and of Fyodor, he was crowned by popular acclamation. Godunov was haunted, however, both by a host of political enemies and by natural causes (one of the worst famine periods in Russian history) and could only preserve his reign by terror and murderous brutality. He was finally deposed by a false pretender, who impersonated the dead Dmitry and whose reign was as disastrous in its consequences as the deposed czar's. This period is known in the annals of Russian history as "The Time of Troubles," which still serves as the dreaded prototype for times of hardship and suffering throughout the long course of Russian history. Mussorgsky could not have selected a more Russian plot to accompany his music. The whole plot is dominated by dark, lustful ambition (of all the major protagonists), and it seems that the light of reason lost its grip on the course of human destiny. In this pit of lust, bloodshed, and despair, there is, however, one positive voice, honest, unassuming, totally committed to truth, to basic popular sentiment, and to goodness of character. This person is – how else? – a fool for Christ sake, whose superior moral standing earns him the privilege of uttering the concluding lyrics of the text:

Flow, flow, /bitter tears!/Weep, weep,/o soul of the Orthodox faithful./The enemy will soon be here, /darkness approaches, /with the impenetrable/blackness of the night. /Woe, woe to Russia, weep, /weep, ye Russian people, /ye starving people![176]

If Mussorgsky had it his way, the whole opera would have been sung without a major female participant. When he submitted the final version for the censor's approval in 1869, the permission to stage it was withheld exactly for that reason, and Mussorgsky was forced to rewrite the text to accommodate a couple of divas. Indeed, the 1872 version, which won the censor's approval, was corrected in this fashion. Today, of course, the two versions are commonly staged, and it is not easy to point out which is the more impressive. Both, however, including the corrected 1872 version, are deeply virile; the *Time of Troubles* is a men's inferno, dominated by basses, harsh, and resounding; there is very little hazard, in Western medieval terms, that the hearts of the listeners might be softened by the sweetness of female chant or that the audience's virility might be compromised on the altar of melodious loveliness. But this is not all. Mussorgsky was deeply contemptuous of musical "beauty," as he phrased it. His anathema was Tchaikovsky's adulation of the *joli*, the sensuous

---

[175] See Victor Seroff, *The Mighty Five – The Cradle of Russian National Music*, New York: Allen, Towne & Heath (1948).

[176] The libretto was written by Mussorgsky himself, after Pushkin. The English translation was prepared by Phillip Taylor in 1998 for a Phillips CD edition of the opera, produced at the Mariinsky Theatre in St. Petersburg, with Valery Gergiev conducting.

quest for melodious magnificence, which Mussorgsky (rightly) condemned as un-Russian. In the year of the second version of *Boris Godunov*, 1872, Mussorgsky reacted to the inclination of Tchaikovsky to appeal to the senses by writing acerbically that "the artistic representation only of beauty" is not manly; rather, it is "churlish childishness, art in its infancy."[177] Richard Taruskin sums it all up, as he characterizes Mussorgsky's music as totally Russian, to wit "the ideology of *yurodstvo*, Holy Foolery, a state of perfect freedom from cogitation (brains) and charm (beauty), a state of perfect authenticity."[178] Taruskin also points out that, contrary to popular belief that labels Mussorgsky, due to his country scenes and crude use of the vernacular, as a stark "realist" (in my terms, someone whose sense of the Truth is derived by observation), in actual fact he is not. His adulation of holy foolery, although triggered by what he actually experienced in his personal life, resulted in prototypical portrayals of the concept, rather than in a "realistic" execution of live characters. "Holy fool," he writes, "is the simpleton who speaks the truth. That was Mussorgsky among composers, and that was Russia among nations.... And so, whatever its anecdotal origins... it was no monument to realism.... Rather, it created and bequeathed an archetype, one that established a creative self-image and defined a Russia."[179]

[177] Mussorgsky's words are cited from Richard Taruskin, *Defining Russia Musically*, Princeton, NJ: Princeton University Press, p. 259 (1997).
[178] Ibid., p. 71.
[179] Ibid., p. 75.

7

The Icon and the Word

Polonius: What do you read, my lord?
Hamlet: Words, words, words.

—*Hamlet*, Act II, Scene II

Introduction

We think in words and images. When one thinks in images, one invokes pictorial representations of the external world to stimulate one's thought processes. When one thinks in words, one is using a plethora of verbal signs to figure out the world. Normal adults always use a medley of words and images to design their thought formations. Primitive thought is conceivable with images without words (consider the case of thinking animals or infants). It is not clear whether thought can be generated with words alone, but their combination with an active stock of images certainly facilitates abstract thinking. Let us denote an "image society" as a society that is heavily (although not exclusively) dependent on images in its approach to figuring out the world. Correspondingly, a "word society" implies a culture in which the relative weight of verbal signs is much more pronounced.[1]

---

[1] The assumption that words and images are the main vehicles for the formation of "thoughts" has been standard in the literature for many years. On the relative mix of words and images in the thinking process from a psychological and neurological point of view, see Rudolf Arnheim, *Visual Thinking*, Berkeley: University of California Press (1969). Arnheim suggests that it would be wrong to assume that scientific thinking is more verbal and creative (e.g., artistic) thinking is more image-oriented. To illustrate the indispensability of images in any verbal formulation, Arnheim cites (at page 232) a passage from Benjamin Whorf's book, *Language Thought and Reality*, Cambridge: Technology Press of Massachusetts Institute of Technology (1956). The citation indicates the rich imagery of verbal thought: "'Grasp' the 'thread' of another's argument, but if its 'level' is 'over my head', my attention may 'wander' and 'lose touch' with the 'drift' of it, so that when he 'comes' to his 'point' we differ 'widely', our 'views' being indeed so 'far apart' that the 'things' he says 'appear' much more arbitrary." Leonard Shlain, a brain surgeon cum amateur culture-studies aficionado, wrote a hugely successful popular study on the relationship between the naissance of the word, especially the written alphabet, and the rise of patriarchal

246

Medieval Europe was an image society in more than one sense. As long as it adhered to that tradition, the idea of contract lay dormant across the continent. It rose to prominence as this cultural orientation receded into the background and made room for a nascent verbal culture. The new lore made enormous headway with the spread of literacy, and especially since the fifteenth century, with the invention of the moveable type printing press. Russia, on the other hand, was slow to embrace the occidental culture of the word and sluggish in taking advantage of the printing press. For many long centuries, it has not only been an "image society" but an "icon society," in which an "icon" is the most transfixed, frozen, and immutable of all possible images. The central tenet in this chapter is that Russia's slow adaptation to the triumph of the word is a key element in understanding its stumbling contractual culture.

The linkage between a verbal culture and a flourishing contractual civilization is straightforward. Words, like contracts, have no shape. They are related to objects only by convention. Their abstract, incorporeal nature allows speakers to use them as proxies for any meaning they wish, depending only on the choice of the speaker and on her imaginative faculties. Words, like contracts, can be combined, separated, modified, and invented. They can be used in any conceivable context, in love and in war, in science and in art, in lyrics and in law. In the legal domain, words can be proclaimed, from the top down, in issuing decrees, writing law codes or pronouncing judgments, or painstakingly concocted by mutual consent, from the bottom up, for the drafting of agreements.

Images, on the other hand, have a definite form. Once crafted (if they are man-made) or otherwise fashioned (if they are not), they are immutable. An image culture is compatible with the recognition of off-the-rack agreements, like the medieval forms of action (debt, detinue, trespass, etc.) of the English medieval Common Law. For the medieval mind, these fixed "writs," or forms of action, could be conceived as external entities, just like so many heads of cattle or land for pasture; an image culture is also compatible with a barter economy or with instantaneous exchange, in which legal players can identify external entities as the icons of their desired objects. But an image culture cannot easily generate formless contracts (such as in *Slade's Case*), because the terms of a formless agreement exclusively draw on the verbal formulation

---

societies throughout the course of history. His main claim is that the verbal functions of the brain reside in its left lobe, which he claims is the "masculine" lobe, whereas the right side of the brain is the repository of images, which is more developed among women. Images are feminine, he claims, because they are holistic, simultaneous, synthetic, and concrete, which are all traits of women. Words are masculine because they are linear, sequential, reductionist, and abstract. The alphabet thus shifted the center of gravity to male territory. Unfortunately, some of Shlain's data require, I think, much further substantiation. See Leonard Shlain, *The Alphabet Versus the Goddess, the Conflict Between Word and Image*, New York: Viking (1998). Is it possible to think without either words or images? One should be careful with ruling out this possibility, especially when we consider thoughts about abstract entities (e.g., in mathematics). But even if this is possible, the role of words and images in the overall thinking process of normal adults cannot be doubted. Nor, perhaps, is it really crucial to assume that animals or infants "think" at all or that if they do their thought formations are similar to these of normal adults.

of the drafters rather than on the "real" presence of external objects. The power of the word to spawn contractual derivatives was further invigorated with the invention of the printing press. Print culture powered the individual, eroded central authority, and assisted in the triumph of the empirical approach to the solution of epistemic problems. It has already been demonstrated how individualism is an important element in a thriving contractual culture,[2] how central authority may dampen it almost out of existence,[3] and how contract depends for its vitality on empirical investigation.[4] These themes are further illuminated in this chapter. In this vein, I propose to record the metamorphosis of the occidental mind from image to word and from the spoken or inscribed word to the printed character, and in parallel lines to contrast it with the very different tale of the Russians.

Theology of Presence: Occidental Medieval Roots

In earlier stages of our civilization words were often conceived as independent entities, "things" that have a life of their own. They were believed to possess objective properties that do not depend on the context or on the circumstances of their use. When the elderly and blind patriarch Isaac was fraudulently led by Jacob to confuse him with his (Isaac's) favorite son Esau and consequently gave him (Jacob) a precious blessing that was actually intended for his better, it was commonly understood that as soon as the words were uttered and unleashed upon the world, Isaac had no authority to enfeeble their mission or to redirect the blessing to its intended beneficiary. The words had already performed their magical deed regardless of the intention of the speaker or of the foul play that induced their utterance.[5] This ancient conviction carried over, with some mutations, through the centuries and predominated much of the theological thinking in the Middle Ages. A fascinating example can be found in a famous twelfth-century allegory, *De Planctu Naturae*, penned by Alan of Lille some time between 1160 and 1170[6] and brilliantly commented on by Jan Ziolkowksi.[7] *De Planctu Naturae* is an allegorical *prosimetrum*, a hybrid between prose and poetry written in appropriate meters (like dactylic hexameters). The book starts by describing the glory of the natural world, governed, as it were, by natural law. A dreamer approaches Lady Nature who weeps profusely and laments her bitter fate. Her anguish triggers a dialogue between Lady Nature

---

[2] See Chapter 3, supra.

[3] See Chapter 4, supra.

[4] See Chapter 6, supra.

[5] When confronted with the fraud, old Isaac had only this to say: "Thy brother came with subtilty, and hath taken away thy blessing.... Behold, I have made him thy lord, and all his brethren have I given to him as servants." Genesis, 27, 35–37.

[6] Alan's masterpiece was republished as a double reader (Latin and English) under the English title *The Plaint of Nature*, Toronto: Canada Pontifical Institute of Medieval Studies (1980).

[7] Jan Ziolkowski, *Alan of Lille's Grammar of Sex, the Meaning of Grammar to a Twelfth Century Intellectual*, Cambridge, MA: Medieval Academy of America (1985).

and the dreamer. It transpires that God appointed Venus to assist Lady Nature to keep the good order by sexual reproduction. Lady Nature gave Venus her tools of trade: a *trivium*[8] of grammar, dialectic, and rhetoric, as well as a forge. Initially, Venus performed her obligations faithfully; this orderly economy was maintained as long as she was loyal to her husband Hymen and to her son Cupid. But then she committed adultery with one Antigamus and conceived a bastard son, Iocus. Her sexual transgression caused her to corrupt her grammar and mishandle her anvil, misdeeds that caused Lady Nature to suffer severe injuries. Lady Nature explains her woes by pointing to Man's sexual deviance. Finally the god Genius takes pity on the world and introduces a new pact: Those who perform unnatural acts will sever themselves from their link to God's grace. The new pact restores order to the universe and the dreamer collapses into the peaceful sleep of the just. Although the overt crime discussed in the allegory is Venus' adulterous flirtations, Alan's rage is covertly homophobic, as he describes instances of same-sex love as dual transgressions, against nature and against grammatical structures, thus:

The active sex shudders in disgrace as it sees itself degenerate into the passive sex. A man turned woman blackens the fair name of his sex. The witchcraft of Venus turns him into a hermaphrodite. He is subject and predicate: one and the same term is given a double application. Man here extends too far the laws of grammar.

There is a double innuendo here, of the most striking simplicity: Exactly as a predicate is meant to modify a subject, so is a stallion created to modify a mare, or a man to impregnate a woman; the pairs are intertwined: By mishandling one's grammar (say, letting a subject "modify" itself), one conspires in the corruption of the natural world, which depends on the proper use of words for its physical integrity. Likewise, by upsetting the natural course of things – in the writer's homophobic mind by engaging in same-sex love – one's grammar suffers some mortal injuries. It is not surprising, then, that in the Middle Ages the study of grammar was classified as an integral part of the discipline of morals. If words are "things," like people, animals, or the environment, the way one treats them carries obvious moral implications. Moreover, if the improper handling of verbal entities throws the entire universe into scandalous disarray, the moral implications of grammar assume a cardinal moral significance.

This intriguing equation, of the image and the word, is self-evident in many instances of medieval and Renaissance iconography, especially in the genre of illuminated manuscripts. Figure 49 is a delicate *Assumption of the Virgin* executed by an artist from the circle of Cosimo Tura sometime between 1470 and 1480, where the capital letter A, the initial letter of the word "assumption," constitutes the principal pictorial representation in this elaborate image. It is made of fantastic trees that lend support to an enormous green dragon.

---

[8] In the Middle Ages, the "trivium" was the lower division of the seven liberal arts, consisting of grammar, rhetoric, and logic, or dialectics.

FIGURE 49. Circle of Cosimo Tura, *The Assumption of the Virgin*, 1470–80.

The dragon shields under its protective wings ten kneeling saints raising their eyes in awe to the heavenly spheres, where the virgin is united with Her Son. The swirling, circular movement of the trees, dragon, saints, mother, and Son resonates in perfect harmony with the painted letters that the artist tossed about the page. Each letter and each stylized musical note has a body and a volume of its own; this is not a verbal account of the Assumption; it is its very image. According to Michel Foucault, this perception of the verbal sign did not change until the Reformation and the earliest buds of the

Enlightenment in the seventeenth century;[9] there is some evidence to support this view.[10]

The medieval roots of this perception are not entirely clear. Moshe Barasch seems to anchor these thoughts to an extant work of Dionysius Areopagita (the pseudo-Dionysius discussed in Chapter 6, supra), who claimed to have written a volume about symbols. According to secondary sources, Dionysius thought of signs in entirely reified terms. Barasch explains:

When we nowadays speak of "symbol" we tend to emphasize the gap between the object (or form) that serves as symbol and the idea (or other content) that is to be symbolized. In Dionysian thought, the *symbolon*, while never negating the difference between symbol and symbolized, represents mainly what they have in common. *Symbolon*, in his view, is not only a sign, but is actually the thing itself.[11]

This philosophy was basically motivated by a theological drive to understand the nature of the deity. The Dionysian symbol was intended to serve as a bridge between the descending movement of the transcendent to the world and the ascending attempts of material entities (including human beings) to the heavenly spheres. God is assumed to have a desire to reveal Himself to humanity, to practice theophany. In this revelation God must abandon His wholly transcendent nature, lest He remain hidden from human eyes. The revealed signs are part of His nature, which makes the sign "similar" to its prototype. By the same token, the Dionysian approach refused to acknowledge equivalence between sign and signified. Had there been such a perfect fit, nothing would be left of God's transcendence. This complex relationship of the sign and the signified led Dionysius to offer a concept of "dissimilar similarity." This is essentially a Platonic concept, as the idea is materialized in its concrete revelations, which are similar to it but do not fully duplicate its nature.[12]

Since images were thought of as embodying the presence of their prototype, they were believed to have objective properties corresponding to the properties

---

[9] See his path-breaking book, *The Order of Things, an Archeology of the Human Science*, New York: Routledge, pp. 34ff (translated to English by an undisclosed translator in 1971. The French original was published in 1966).

[10] Foucault, ibid., attributes the same proclivity to the great sixteenth-century French humanist, mathematician, logician, and grammarian Petrus Ramus (Pierre de la Ramée, 1515–1572), because the latter wrote about the "properties" of words and of sentence parts in the same vein that one could write about the physical properties of "things." One wonders if Foucault exercised enough caution in this interpretation, as it relates to a person who was also a Calvinist martyr who perished in the massacre of St. Bartholomew in 1572 (Calvinists were rarely "realists" in their epistemology) and who mainly spoke about the *rhetorical* properties of words, which he regarded as mere stylistic tropes. But the point seems to be well taken if it relates to the grammarians who immediately preceded Ramus, many of whom dealt with the so-called "speculative grammar" of the *modistae*, which bear this name because their works were often entitled *de modis significandi tractatus*, or treatises concerning the modes of signifying. The *modistae* sought to establish almost bi-unique pairings of words and things, viewing language as a *speculum*, or a mirror of the world.

[11] Moshe Barasch, *Icon*, New York: New York University Press, p. 167 (1992).

[12] Ibid.

of the prototype, which made it impossible, even heretic, to falsify their nature by the introduction of changes or alterations. Only one kind of symbol could legitimately represent the symbolized, simply because it consisted of the same essence as the symbolized itself, and the latter was perceived as having an "objective" or immutable nature. Emile Mâle describes the impact of this principle on medieval artistic iconography. All artistic symbols, says Mâle, had universal currency and were strictly adhered to by all artists across Europe. Deviation was heresy. For example, a nimbus above the head symbolized sanctity, but if a cross was included in the nimbus it was a sign of divinity. God the Father and Christ had to be barefooted, but the virgin and the other saints not. This fixity of style applied not only to the main characters but to iconographic details as well. For example, if Mary and the lance bearer were present at the crucifixion, they had to be at the right of the cross, St. John and the man with the sponge on the left. Nor was it possible to introduce fanciful ideas to church architecture. For example, the cold, northern side was used to depict scenes from the Old Testament, whereas the warm, south was used for the New. The west side, facing sunset, was used to depict the Last Judgment. The right side was considered a place of honor. Higher places are more distinguished than lower. For example, where Christ is depicted supported by the four beasts of the apocalypse, the upper right place is for the winged man, the upper left for the eagle, the lower right for the lion, and the lower left, the humblest, for the ox. The arrangement of human figures, too is not accidental and responds to canons of rank. Even minor figures are not unregimented. Large statutes are often supported by smaller crouching figures, which they trample. Thus, apostles tread underfoot the kings who persecuted them, Moses tramples the golden calf, and angels tread on the dragon of the abyss. Symmetry was very important. For example, the twelve apostles were positioned opposite the twelve minor prophets, the four major prophets faced the four evangelists, and so on. This quality was also reflected in the great deference given to numbers. Following a Pythagorean tradition embraced by St. Augustine, numbers were thought of as sacred, as the divine thoughts, and special attention had to be given to their interpretation and artistic representation. A special pride of place was given to the number 12, the number of the apostles. It is a product of 3, the number of the trinity, and hence of things spiritual, and 4, the number of the elements, and hence of things corporeal. The product symbolized the holy Church, which combines in its body all things spiritual and temporal. Likewise, the number 7 was imbued with mystic grandeur, as it is the sum of 3 and 4 and thus combines all there is in the world. Through his 7 ages, Man must attempt, with the aid of the 7 sacraments to achieve the 7 virtues and avoid the 7 deadly sins. His destiny was guarded by the 7 planets. The 7 tones of the Gregorian mode are nothing but a sensible reflection of this universal harmony.[13]

---

[13] Mâle's study emphasized French symbolism in the thirteenth century, but most of his claims are equally valid for broader national approaches to artistic iconography in the same period. See Emile Mâle, *The Gothic Image, Religious Art in France of the Thirteenth Century*, translated by Dora Nussey, New York: Harper and Row (1972; the French original was published in 1913).

Perhaps the ultimate manifestation of the epistemic unity of sign and object in the Middle Ages is embedded in the role of the human body itself, which was regularly used as an instrumentality in thinking about objects that are external to one's self. The human body is the first object identified by infants and it takes a while until they learn to differentiate between it and external objects.[14] By thinking about the world in terms of one's own body one is using, in one's method of perception, the image of the external world itself as a vehicle for its own awareness or comprehension. For a practitioner of this method of figuring out the world, the body is not a "sign" where the world is the "signified." By blurring the distinction between sign and signified, one relinquishes one's very ability to use signs. In Chapter 2, supra, I laid some stress on the so-called Burckhardt thesis and his nineteenth-century perception that the Renaissance "discovered" the individual person. Though I believe that the Burckhardt thesis is entirely correct, it does not follow that the kind of person "discovered" by the humanists of the Renaissance had a more flesh-and-blood countenance than the sort of person conceived in the medieval mind. On the contrary, medieval attitudes to the human body were radically down to earth. This red-blooded, carnal approach may not have registered in the high monastic culture of the *scriptoria*, but it may well have been hidden in subtextual disguise[15] and, without a

[14] Piaget spoke about the "adualistic" nature of infants, i.e., their inability to treat themselves and the universe as separate objects. Piaget's contention was recently challenged by some psychologists who documented some skills of differentiation among infants. See, for example, Philippe Rochat and Susan Hespos, "Differential Rooting Response by Neonates: Evidence for an Early Sense of Self," *Early Development and Parenting* 6:105 (1997) Nonetheless, the evidence suggests that these differentiation skills are very partial and come to maturity at a later stage of the infant's development. For example, if an infant's nose is smeared with lipstick and the infant is shown a mirror containing his own image, only by the middle of the second year of life do some infants recognize that the lipstick is painted on their own noses. See Michael Lewis and Jeanne Brooks-Gunn, *Social Cognition and the Acquisition of Self*, New York: Plenum Press (1979).

[15] Several commentators suggested a number of far-reaching and at times surprisingly physical interpretations of the seemingly chaste collection of medieval and Renaissance symbols. Leo Steinberg, for example, in his book, *The Sexuality of Christ in Renaissance Art and in Modern Oblivion*, New York: Pantheon Books (1983), suggested, to the horror of some critics and the admiration of others, that the focal point in Christ's iconography in the Renaissance was his penis. Steinberg attempts to substantiate his claim by showing how Christ, his mother, St. Anne, and a variety of saints repeatedly point to his genitals, and often touch or fondle them. He also seems to have claimed that Christ often had an erection under his loincloth. Steinberg also asserts that the fleshy attributes of Christ were theologically necessary as a vehicle for proving his humanity; by sharing with us our physical traits, the symbol of the Incarnation is complete. Caroline Walker Bynum, a leading feminist, does not endorse Steinberg's conclusions but suggests, in turn, that the medieval and Renaissance Christ was really female. In many texts and images, he was not only married to the Church, ecclesia, but ecclesia was really his body. He nourished the needy by his lactating breast. He was a life giver. Indeed, in many texts all bodily fluids are thought of as interchangeable, and blood is easily transformed to milk. Thus, the bleeding arch-sufferer is naturally transformed unto a great mother. Mothers breast-feeding their babies were thought of as offering them their very blood as nourishment, miraculously transformed into milk. Marian theology often treated Mary as the flesh of Christ, or He, offered in the Eucharist to humankind, as part and parcel of her body. Many witnesses testified to having seen the bread of the Eucharist drip blood, or even received the

doubt, burst into the open in more folkloristic events such as in times of carnival. All walks of life participated in carnivals, where the human body, especially its lower reaches, with its perennial functions of fecundity, mutilation, copulation, gluttony, drinking, defecation, pregnancy, and decay, follow each other in rapid succession. It is a well-known fact that medieval carnivals were frequent, lengthy, promiscuous, and lewd. The memory of this medieval carnival spirit was still fresh in the Renaissance and vividly reflected in some of its most brilliant literary achievements; it is sanguinely narrated in Rabelais' *Gargantua and Pantagruel*,[16] and it is strongly echoed in Shakespeare's bawdy and humoristic scenes, in other leading works of the English Renaissance,[17] as well as in the work of Miguel de Cervantes,[18] to name but a few notable examples. In the visual arts it quickens the imagery of such painters as Hieronymus Bosch and Pieter Brueghel. The latter's robust view of the body can be illustrated, for instance, in his famous canvass, *The Wedding Dance in the Open Air*, executed in 1566 (see Figure 50). There is nothing spiritual in the dancing characters' merriment. One feels as if they were all made of so many pounds of flesh, bent on their lovemaking, gluttony, and mirth. Nor is there anything apologetic about their lack of refinement. The body celebrates itself and is entirely self-sufficient.

Bakhtin illustrates the relationship between word and body in a famous medieval *commedia dell'arte* scene. A stutterer is hard at work trying to utter a word, but the word does not come out. He swirls and puffs, stumbles and suffocates, but the word remains obstinately locked in. His audience, Harlequin, gets tired of the long wait and rams his head right into the stutterer's belly. This abdominal shock, a clear act of midwifery, releases the word of its dungeon; it is delivered unto the world. In this anecdote the word (probably both in its literal meaning and in the meaning alluding to the Divinity) cannot be born by the upper strata of the body, the mind and soul; it takes the body, through

---

Stigmata. The majority of these witnesses were women. Iconographically, Mary is often seen as lactating, but what is more interesting is that she is often interpreted as offering humankind the Eucharistic food. Informed by the Eucharistic tradition, Christ is often depicted as food, just as is the case with Mary. The two figures often blend together. See Caroline Walker Bynum, *Fragmentation and Redemption, Essays on Gender and the Human Body in Medieval Religion*, New York: Zone Books, and Cambridge, MA: MIT Press, Chapter 3 (1992). Bynum developed similar themes in her book, *Jesus as Mother*, Berkeley: University of California Press (1982).

[16] The best analysis of Rabelais' attitude to the lower part of the body, its relationship to the carnival culture of the Middle Ages, and its significance as a cultural trope is Mikhail Bakhtin's famous book, *Rabelais and His World*, translated by Hélène Iskowsky, Indianapolis: Indiana University Press (1984; first published in 1965).

[17] A good example is Ben Jonson's *Bartholomew Fair*, which gives a very lively description of a sparkling marketplace. Indeed, markets and carnivals shared a lot in common, as they allowed for freer, more spontaneous modes of behavior that stood in sharp contrast to the high culture of the day.

[18] The main character in Don Quixote representing this healthy, down-to-earth attitude to the human body is obviously Sancho Panza. "Panza" in Spanish means "belly."

FIGURE 50. Pieter Brueghel the Elder, *The Wedding Dance in the Open Air*, 1566.

its lower reaches, to give birth to the word.[19] Another interesting contrast of body parts and the more spiritual world occurs in *Pantagruel* and narrates the story of Friar John warning the pilgrims that in their absence their wives might be impregnated by the local monks, thereby deriding asceticism and its self-righteousness. He then says, "The pox riddle me if you don't all find your wives pregnant on your return. The very shadow of an abbey spire is fecund." This is the ultimate fusion of the symbol of spirituality (the abbey spire) with a very concrete phallic symbol, frantically inseminating the pilgrims' wives. As Bakhtin explains, abstract ideas are merged into the physical world. This is typical, he says,[20] of medieval grotesque imagery, which turns everything upside down.[21] The top of the tower, supposedly thrusting to heaven, is actually transformed into a male sexual organ residing in the lower reaches of the body and longing to unite with a female sexual organ, *any* female sexual organ that might be available to accept its thrust.

Theology of Presence: The Eucharistic Debate and Beyond

This robust medieval economy, where even grammar is a thing, symbols are immutable, and the reigning image, at least in the lower spheres of folk culture is the human body itself, found its way to high theology as well and was securely encapsulated in the hallowed sacrament of the Eucharist. The eventual rise of

[19] Bakhtin, ibid., p. 304.
[20] Ibid., Chapter 5.
[21] On the reversal of roles, where holy is profane, flesh is spirit, lower and upper classes intermingle, and piety is love of the flesh in medieval carnivals see also Edward Muir, *Ritual in Early Modern Europe*, New York: Cambridge University Press, pp. 85ff (1997).

verbal culture in the West was closely associated with the first cracks in the citadel of this doctrine. As the cracks broadened and high waters started to gush in, a fertile environment was established for the emergence of contract. In Russia, on the other hand, the citadel of the Eucharist never gave way, and its continued stoutness still lends support to Russia's iconic resistance to things contractual.

In His last supper, Jesus pointed to the bread and said: "This is my body." He then held up a goblet of wine and said: "This is my blood."[22] What did He mean when He used the word "this"? Did He actually mean that His actual body, which was born, crucified, and resurrected, and the actual blood flowing in His veins were in fact "present" in the bread and wine? The only substance the sacramental bread and wine were made of? Or did He mean to imply only figuratively that the Eucharistic elements, although blessed in the sacramental rites, continue to contain (at least is some sense) their former material substance? Millions of lives were lost in a series of violent attempts to settle this controversy.

In the Middle Ages, the Eucharistic equation of the elements with the actual body and blood of Christ was taken quite literally. This strict hermeneutical approach – the so-called doctrine of transubstantiation – generated elaborate theological debates analyzing the risk that the holy matter might be contaminated when going through the lower parts of the digestive system. Some found solace in the thought that, unlike other foods, the Host was wholly absorbed into the blood in the stomach itself. Others fasted for long periods before Communion to ensure an empty stomach and a retardation of intestinal activity.[23] The "real" divine nature of the elements was revealed in many eyewitness accounts, narrating the actual bleeding of the wafer in response to theological doubt, violation of doctrine, or profanation by Jews.[24] The doctrine of transubstantiation was warmly embraced not only by ecclesiastical circles, but also by temporal power, as it assisted autocratic rulers to entrench their authority. The physical presence of Christ in the Eucharist served as the central element in bonding all the people under the auspices of their leadership. Secular rulers, especially in medieval France, instituted official Eucharistic parades (the famous Corpus Christi processions) where all and sundry were expected to join in one political communion, culminating in the person of their sovereign, exactly as the believers gathered to partake in the Host and unite in the kingdom of Christ.[25] Eventually, Eucharistic ideas spread to the core of secular authority, as kings claimed to have been transformed by their anointing and assumed the

---

[22] Matthew, 26, 26–27; Mark, 14, 22–23; Luke, 22, 19–20.

[23] Muir, ibid., pp. 155ff.

[24] Ibid.

[25] A theological foundation of this doctrine was found, *inter alia*, in the preaching of St. Paul (1 Corinthians, 10, 16–17), where the apostle says: "The cup of blessing which we bless, is it not the communion of the blood of Christ? The bread which we break, is it not the communion of the body of Christ? For we being many are one bread, and one body: for we are all partakers of that one bread."

properties of Christ. The only admitted difference was that whereas Christ was held to have obtained His divinity by nature, secular kingship followed in His wake by grace. As these practices were most prevalent in France, there is no wonder that French absolutism exceeded in its extremity other forms of divine kingship, a notion that served French monarchs to claim supremacy over other kings and over the Church.[26]

By a very slow process, the "realistic" interpretation of the sacrament, as expressed in the doctrine of transubstantiation, started to give way and be transformed to something entirely different. Even within the Catholic faith itself, where the doctrine is still held as dogmatic truth,[27] numerous voices have been raised that shook the foundations of its original meaning. Among the more important skeptics, the names of the Bohemian reforming theologian Jan Hus, the Englishman John Wyclif, and the Catholic humanist Nicholas of Cusa loom large. Erasmus, too, like many other humanists, mocked the old-style Eucharistic practice. Humanists were trained to employ hermeneutical methods to discern meaning in old texts and were thus conditioned to prefer the subtleties of interpreted meaning to the banality of the apparition that met the naked eye. Erasmus preached that the true imitation of Christ was in knowledge and prayer, both being totally internal processes, and therefore could not reside in the tangible elements.[28] Two stories from Vasari's *Lives* capture the changing mores regarding the relative dignity of word and image in the early modern Catholic world. In one of these stories, Vasari mockingly (and, in all likelihood, fictitiously)[29] narrates the tale of Giotto's contemporaries, Bruno, Buffalmacco, and Calandrino, who were "*goffi*," or clumsy, erratic, and inelegant, because their work was not "life-like." Bruno, for example, was supposed to paint a lady personifying the City of Pisa appealing to St. Ursula for help. Not knowing how to do this, he made a verbal inscription containing Pisa's request and another containing St. Ursula's response. Calling this a "*goffezza*" exemplifies Vasari's conviction that painting and literature were arts apart and could not be mixed with impunity. The text betrays a two-pronged proposition. On the one hand, Vasari's tale reflects his view that the external world, the state of being "life-like," cannot be represented by verbal signs, and the only appropriate way of expressing it is by crafting an accurate replica of the external object; on the other hand, he conceded a legitimate domain for verbal representation, as opposed to "real" presence, the domain of literature; for all its wordy materials, literature is not equivalent to "reality" but is merely "about reality." The second story apparently originates in Petrarch and is vividly

---

[26] Christopher Elwood, *The Body Broken, the Calvinist Doctrine of the Eucharist and Symbolization of Power in Sixteenth-Century France*, New York: Oxford University Press, Chapter 1 (1999).

[27] *The Catholic Encyclopedia*, which is available online, still defines all deviations from the doctrine of transubstantiation as "heresy."

[28] Muir, ibid.

[29] See Paul Barolsky, *Why Mona Lisa Smiles and Other Tales by Vasari*, University Park: Pennsylvania State University Press, pp. 14ff (1991).

elaborated by Rabelais. In his own version, Vasari attributes to Castiglione a story about some Lucca merchants traveling to old Muscovy with the hope of buying luxurious sables. Having reached the banks of the Dnieper they saw some Russian troops waging war against the Poles on the opposite bank. Loath to risk their own skin in the fierce battle, they shouted their offer across the river, and the Muscovites shouted back, but the weather was so foul that their words got frozen in midair and did not melt until the Poles lighted a fire on the icy river. Once unfrozen, the words became intelligible, but the counteroffer was not acceptable to the Lucchesi, who returned home without the merchandise. Castiglione's *"burla,"* or blatant lie, making fun of frozen words, can be linked to Vasari's own *burla* about Bruno's attempted use of verbal means to describe the emerging pact between Pisa and St. Ursula.[30] Clearly, Vasari was a few steps ahead in comparison to, say, Alan of Lille. For Alan, the real presence of verbal entities was serious business. Vasari treats the same subject frivolously,[31] its burlesque nature being common knowledge for the narrator and his audience alike. The Polish campfires melted forever the real essence of the word and made room for its new role, the role of *representation*.[32]

---

[30] Barolsky, ibid., p. 17.

[31] Barolsky, ibid., pp. 34ff, puts Vasari's equation of living organisms and their dead images in mythological terms. He shows how Vasari, following a well-known tradition in the Renaissance attributable to Petrarch and Boccaccio, makes repeated use of the Pygmalion and Medusa myths in his treatment of artistic critique. Reduced to their bare essentials, the Pygmalion myth describes how an artist can transform an inanimate object (a block of marble) into a living thing (the artist's loving bride). The very gaze of the Medusa, on the other hand, is sufficient to petrify the living. By thinking about art as a clever method to manipulate the Pygmalion-Medusa magic, one is breaking the sharp divide between the living thing (res) and its inanimate image (icon).

[32] Perhaps Vasari's sharp dichotomy of the image and the word was not shared by everyone during the High Renaissance, the example of Leonardo da Vinci being the most glaring and ostentatious of them all. Leonardo was much more prolific in writing than in painting. He would don special "ceremonial robes," seclude himself in his study, and engage in a verbal dialogue with imaginary contesters, e.g., the *auctores*, who represented the learned sages to whom he did not belong. He was ever attentive to the calligraphic quality of his characters, perhaps influenced by the notarial tradition of his father, Ser Piero da Vinci. Notarial writing recorded public facts and used to be embellished by calligraphic means. He was also aware of the fact, as is evident in his own writings, that writing and painting (especially drawing) share a common quality, the marking of white paper with lines emanating from the draftsman's pen. In his *Paragone*, Leonardo compares the arts of painting and poetry, emphasizing their similarity and calling poetry "a painting one hears rather than sees" as well as "blind painting." The fusion of verbal and visual signs is evident in many of his writings, where words take on painterly qualities without, however, losing their rhetorical oral characteristics. See Carlo Vecce, "Word and Image in Leonardo's Writings," in Carmen Bambach (ed.), *Leonardo da Vinci Master Draftsman*, New Haven, CT: Yale University Press, p. 59 (2003). Vecce cites, at page 65, the following description of a sea monster, penned by Leonardo and illustrating his treatment of pictorial and verbal signs as almost interchangeable: "Oh, how many times were you seen through the waves of the swelling and great ocean, with your bristles and black back, like a mountain, with your heavy and imposing carriage! And often you were seen through the waves of the swelling and great ocean, with imposing and heavy movements running in swirls in the waters of the sea, and with your bristles and black back, like a mountain that conquers and overwhelms. Oh, how many times were you seen through the waves of the swelling and great ocean, like a mountain that

But the greatest and most overt change came with the Reformation. The change started with Martin Luther and then among the French Huguenots, but it came to its most methodical formulation in the theology of Calvin. Calvin drew a sharp distinction between the visible sign and the invisible thing, which was signified by it. Whereas the sign was material, the thing was, in this case, spiritual. If the referent, that is, the signified, (Calvin held) were actually to be present in the sign, the sign, being thus transformed to spirituality, would lose its power of signification, which only resided, like in all other sacraments, in the material and visible. Calvin admitted God's spiritual immanence in the sacramental elements but denied His "local" presence therein, as he called it. He thus reduced the Divine presence in the elements to the level of mere signification.[33] Like Vasari and his *burle*, the theology of Calvin transformed, in this manner, *presence* into *representation*. Images lost their dominant grip on thought processes and were replaced by signs that merely suggested the existence of external entities. The artistic style of the Reformed Church clearly illustrates the new theology of presence. Following the violent Dutch iconoclastic outburst of 1566, many reformed artists started to paint clean interiors of churches, devoid of any decoration or visual embellishment. Some artists presaged in their imagery this iconoclastic mood. Figure 51, for example, was painted in 1635 by the great reformed artist Pieter Saenredam and shows parts of the empty ambulatory of the St. Bavo Church in Haarlem. This interior is totally devoid of any ornament. In some of Saenredam's other interiors the church organ is made visible, representing perhaps the primacy of imageless art (music), which was believed by some contemporary theologians to be instrumental in the processes of prayer and devotion (although some stricter theologians considered it too frivolous).[34]

According to Elwood, Calvin's novel method of interpreting reality had far-reaching political implications as well, mainly because it eroded the sacrosanct authority of kingship; this erosion was accomplished by splitting apart the unity of the material world and the divine immanence residing therein, thus disrupting the immanent grace of kingship and destroying the medieval notion of authority.

It is often said that the Eastern Orthodox Church in general and its Russian Patriarchate in particular, unlike the other branches of Christendom, has never gone through any fundamental doctrinal change.[35] The history of the

---

conquers and overwhelms, with your bristles and black back moving through the waters of the sea with your heavy and imposing carriage."

[33] Elwood, ibid., Chapter 3.

[34] Mariët Westermann, *A Worldly Art*, New York: Harry Abrams, p. 50 (1996).

[35] "We preserve the Doctrine of the Lord uncorrupted, and firmly adhere to the Faith He delivered to us, and keep it free from blemish and diminution, as a Royal Treasure, and a monument of great price *neither adding any thing, nor taking any thing from it*": Letter of the Eastern Patriarchs submitted in an inter-faith gathering to the other participants in 1718, cited in Timothy Ware (Bishop of Kallistos), *The Orthodox Church*, New York: Penguin Books, p. 196 (1997). The author singles out this statement as the most characteristic of the Orthodox faith. In fact, the great schism of the Church, finalized in 1472, although caused by complex historical

FIGURE 51. Pieter Saenredam, *View into the Ambulatory of the St. Bavo Church in Haarlem*, 1635.

processes, was dogmatically grounded on the pricipled refusal of the Eastern Church to introduce a one-word variation in its Creed. The theological question was whether the dogma of the double procession of the Holy Ghost from Father *and* Son as a *unitary* principle is correct. The Catholic Church ordained the correctness of this principle, and in evidence thereof, decided to include in the Creed the word "*Filioque*," or "and of the Son," after the words relating to the procession of the Third Person of the Trinity from the Father. The addition of the word *Filioque* was declared to be a dogma of the Catholic faith in the Fourth Lateran Council (1215), the Second Council of Lyons (1274), and the Council of Florence (1438–45). The Eastern Church opposed this meddling with the original wording of the Creed and made the addition of the word *Filioque* the official reason for the great schism, which changed the course of history.

FIGURE 52. *The Triumph of Orthodoxy*, Byzantine, circa 1400.

Eucharistic dogma is a perfect example of this assertion. Furthermore, the "real" presence of Christ in the Eucharistic elements accurately reflects both the ancient and the current Orthodox theology of presence in general, and not only in matters relating to the Holy Communion.

On March 11, 843 A.D., a celebration was held in the great Cathedral of Hagia Sophia in Constantinople; the second iconoclastic period in the history of the Church ended and the veneration of the holy icons was restored. This date is known in the annals of the Orthodox Church as the Triumph of Orthodoxy. The Triumph of Orthodoxy, the historical event, is in itself a famous icon (see Figure 52), painted circa 1400 and featuring a great icon of the Theotokos, the mother of God (of the Hodigitria type) flanked by the Empress Theodora, during whose regency the iconoclastic period ended, and by the patriarch Methodios, who played a major role in the event. The other figures in the icon are all iconodule saints, two of whom are also holding small icons of Christ.[36] The triumph of Orthodoxy, then, is an icon within an icon where the icons of the saints are also holding other icons in their hands.

The use of icons as the appropriate – the sole appropriate – method of making sense of the world *is* the triumph of Orthodoxy. St. Theophanes the Marked, a ninth-century theologian who fought the winning battle and served as the Metropolitan of Nicea (where the great Church Council was held) until his death in 847 A.D., composed a famous *kontakion*[37] that summarizes the very essence of the triumphant new Truth. The relevant part of the *kontakion* reads:

> No one could describe the Word of the Father;
> But when He took flesh from you, O Theotokos,
> He consented to be described, and resorted the fallen image to its former state
> By uniting it to divine beauty.
> We confess and proclaim our salvation in word and images.[38]

According to this view, the "real" nature of Christ in His image (not only in the Eucharistic elements) is a logical offshoot of the doctrine of the Incarnation. Christ had to be "really" present in His image, because side by side with His transcendent nature, He chose to practice *kenôsis* as a means of revealing Himself to humankind, as our human limitations enable us to perceive only with the eyes of the flesh. The corporeal nature of the Divinity is underscored by the fact that the *kontakion* is addressed to the Theotokos. The Incarnation was not possible without her and depended on her cooperation, as she said "let it be to me according to Thy Word" (Luke, 1: 38). The words in the *kontakion* about restoring to the fallen image its previous glory allude to the ultimate raison d'être of the Incarnation, the redemption of humankind of its sin. Unlike the original human form, which was corruptible by sin, the Incarnation bestows upon every one of us an incorruptible form, as the Passion of Christ sanctifies humankind for eternity.[39]

This Byzantine theological worldview, complete with its systematic theoretical foundations,[40] was incorporated without modifications in Russian

---

[36] Robin Cormack, *Painting the Soul*, London: Reaktion Books, p. 62 (1997).

[37] A "*kontakion*" is the first Byzantine poetic structure that was later replaced by the "*kanon*." Although meant for musical liturgical practice, the melodies of *kontakia* depended on oral tradition, because the text did not contain musical notes, at least not until the thirteenth century.

[38] The *kontakion* is translated and discussed in Leonid Ouspensky, *Theology of the Icon*, Crestwood, NY: St. Vladimir's Seminary Press, Volume 1, pp. 179ff (1978; name of translator not indicated; originally published in French in 1960).

[39] Ibid.

[40] The two most notable theologians who defined the centrality of the icon in the Orthodox faith are John of Damascus, in his famous book *On the Divine Images* (Crestwood, NY: St. Vladimir's Seminary Press, 1997) and Theodore of Studion, who wrote *On the Holy Icons* (Crestwood, NY: St. Vladimir's Seminary Press, 1997): "If He could not be represented by art," explained Theodore in his Third Refutation, "this would mean that He was not born of a representable mother, but that He was born only of the Father, and that He was not Incarnate. But this contradicts the whole divine *economy* of our salvation."

ecclesiastical practice; but whereas the Byzantines resorted to words for their theological discussions, the Russians reaffirmed the triumph of Orthodoxy with their icons;[41] words lost even their justificatory function and were entirely replaced by pictorial means. Moreover, this pictorial language was held to be dogmatically immutable, as evidenced by the following edict from 1551:

On icons of the Holy Trinity, some represent a cross in the nimbus of only the middle figure, others on all three. On ancient and on Greek icons, the words "Holy Trinity" are written at the top, but there is no cross in the nimbus of any of the three. At present, "ICXC" and "the Holy Trinity" are written next to the central figure. Consult the divine canons and tell us which practice one should follow. The Reply: painters must paint icons according to the ancient models, as the Greeks painted them, as Andrei Rublev and other renowned painters made them. The inscription should be: "the Holy Trinity." Painters are in no way to use their imagination.... In all towns and villages and monasteries of their diocese, the archbishops and bishops will inspect the icon painters and will personally examine their works.... The archbishops and bishops will personally assess the painters they have charged with supervising the others, and will control them rigorously.[42]

There can be absolutely no doubt that the resulting product, in this case the holy icons, was not made to *represent* anything at all. Rather, they were designed to *incorporate* the external entity itself. For the image-oriented mind, things can only be "present" in the extension of their own existence, rather than in something that is external to this existence and is crafted to serve as a mere sign. Paul Evdokimov explains:

In a nutshell, *the icon is a sacrament* for the Christian East; more precisely, it is the vehicle of a personal presence.... An image which has been verified for dogmatic correctness by a priest, which conforms to the Holy Tradition, and which attains a sufficient level of artistic expression becomes a "miraculous icon" by the divine response to the epiclesis in the rite. "Miraculous" here means exactly that the icon is *charged with a presence*.[43]

The Russian theology of presence, especially as it makes itself evident in the culture of icons, was not only rejected by the Reformed Church, but, in more recent times, regarded as sacrilegious in mainstream Catholic circles as well. Writing in 1981, Jacques Ellul, a renowned Catholic essayist, condemned the Russian doctrine in these words:

[T]his theology of the icon seems ... to correspond exactly to what we are prohibited biblically from doing: it is idolatrous. It rests on a certain conception of the Incarnation that utterly fails to take into account its unfulfilled aspects: the waiting and the hope.

---

[41] Leonid Ouspensky, *Theology of the Icon*, Volume 2, translated by Anthony Gythiel, Crestwood, NY: St. Vladimir's Seminary Press, pp. 253ff (1992; first published in 1980). (This volume must not be confused with the first volume of Ouspensky's work, which was cited previously.)

[42] See Chapter 41 of the Hundred Chapter Council (*Stroglav*) held in Moscow in 1551. The text is cited in Ouspensky, ibid., pp. 291ff.

[43] Paul Evdokimov, *The Art of the Icon: A Theology of Beauty*, translated by Fr. Steven Bigham, Torrance, CA: Oakwood Publications, p. 178 (1990; originally published in French in 1972).

"Having *reestablished* the sullied image in its former dignity, the Word unites it with divine Beauty." Everything is already accomplished.[44]

Ellul contrasts the Russian theology of presence with what he believes is the (true) Catholic doctrine; both the Creator and the creation can be conceptualized, he says, only by verbal means. Drawing on the gospel, Ellul reminds his readers that, "In the beginning was the Word, and the Word was with God, and the Word was God."[45] God can never be contemplated face to face, he explains. The only method to grasp Him is through the Word. God chooses His way of making Himself conceivable to human intelligence through the only vehicle that is entirely human, speech. For this reason, he concludes, there is no Christian faith outside the Word. "God creates through his Word; creation is an act of separation. The word is creator in that it names things, thus specifying them by differentiating them. . . . The word bestows being on each reality, attributing truth to it."[46] But Ellul was clearly mistaken on this score. The term "Word" as a signifier of the deity has more than one legitimate Christian construction, and Ellul appears to have focused on only one of its possible interpretations, his own. The Western term "Word" fails to capture the full richness of the original Greek term "Logos." "Word" and "Logos" are not good linguistic substitutes, because each plays a different role as a formative perceptive vehicle. As Evdokimov shrewdly points out,[47] the term "Word" alludes to what one hears, rather than to what one hears *and* sees *and* touches with one's own hands. The original "Logos," on the other hand, is not only about the subject's hearing faculties, as is evident from the first words of the epistle of John: "That which was from the beginning, which we have heard, which we have seen with our eyes, which we have looked upon, and our hands have handled, of the Word [Logos] of life."[48] It is this pictorial, material, tangible, carnal "Logos" that remained transfixed in the Eastern culture; it is the airy and abstract term "Word" that shaped the hermeneutics of representation in the proto-modern and modern occidental mind.

Whereas the Eastern theology of presence is pan-Orthodox in nature, its most robust manifestations developed on Russian soil. Most Russians think of themselves as "Orthodox" and often display hostile attitudes to Christians of other persuasions.[49] However, the pantheon of Russian saints, both those who were imported from Byzantium at the baptism of Rus' in the tenth century and

---

[44] Jacques Ellul, *The Humiliation of the Word*, translated by Joyce Main Hanks, Grand Rapids, MI: Eerdman Publishing, p. 104 (1985; the French original appeared in 1981).

[45] John 1, 1.

[46] Ellul, ibid., pp. 48ff.

[47] Evdokimov, ibid., p. 179.

[48] John 1, 1.

[49] Catherine the Great, for instance, a Lutheran princess by birth, had the political acumen to convert to Orthodoxy long before the beginning of her reign and thus to establish herself as a "real" Russian sovereign. Other sovereigns, e.g., her ill-fated husband, Peter III, who was also Peter the Great's grandson, was highly despised by his subjects for (among many other reasons) failing to embrace the Orthodox faith.

the new galleries of a more recent pedigree are by and large more pagan, and hence more corporeal, than their occidental counterparts. Many of them simply replaced the original endemic pagan gods, which were physical, concrete, and corporeal. For example, Elijah the prophet, an important presence in the Russian pantheon, is believed to have incorporated in his person the bad-tempered pagan god Perun, who roams the firmament in his fiery chariot and fires incendiary bolts to punish transgressions but is also capable of sparing some water of his flask to irrigate the arid land.[50] In addition to the familiar Perun, Russians venerated water, plant, stone, wind, and sun deities of various kinds. Many of them were associated with the exigencies of agricultural society, such as the ripening of the grain (sun deities and worship of the South) and the perennial need for timely irrigation (water). Similar pagan rites may have occurred in Europe as well, especially as part of the medieval carnival culture, which I discussed previously. But in Russia a lot of pagan practices survived almost to our own days. There is abundant evidence about the prevalence of Dionysian practices of debauchery, drunkenness, flogging to death, and promiscuity during supposedly Christian festivals, which were continuously practiced all the way up to the twentieth century.[51] The incorporation of the natural world into the worship of ordinary Russians from times immemorial may have been an additional factor in shaping a collective psyche of an image society, a society in which even abstract entities like the deity are commonly interpreted as embedded in material objects, and their presence cannot be easily conceived without them.

Of Literacy, Books, and the Printing Press

The printing revolution spread to Russia very late in history. Consequently, the literacy rate of the general population was extremely low until relatively recent times. It is both hard and unnecessary to determine whether the tardy appearance of literacy and print in Russia was the cause or the effect of the Russian proclivity to think in images. In all likelihood both of these explanations have some cogency and are mutually complementary; to wit, the absence of a flourishing word culture assisted in preserving the traditional image orientation in its dominant position, and the ingrained inclination to think in images retarded the emergence of a flourishing word culture. In the following pages I narrate some chapters of the history of literacy and print both in Russia and in the West, focusing on the presumed impact of this differential tale on the development of contract in the two cultures.

As soon as affordable texts became universally available, especially since the invention of the moveable type printing press, around the middle of the

---

[50] More details about this vengeful deity are narrated in the description of the icon of the Transfiguration of Christ in Chapter 2, supra.

[51] George Fedotov, *The Russian Religious Mind, Kievan Christianity*, New York: Harper, Volume 1, Chapter 12 (1946).

fifteenth century,[52] ordinary Europeans started to read. For obvious reasons, this movement picked up its momentum *in tandem* with the declining use of Latin and the rise of the vernacular. The frequent dialogue between reader and text further enhanced the dominance of the word in occidental lands, as people became used to following the verbal patterns laid out for their contemplation in written texts and to devising verbal patterns of their own in their turn. Perhaps the most famous literary example of this profound change is John Bunyan's inspired novel, *The Pilgrim's Progress*.[53] John Bunyan was the son of a maker and mender of pots and kettles. He also liked to read books. In 1644, at the age of 16, he enlisted in the Civil War, but history does not record on whose side. He married in 1648 a pious woman who inspired him to take interest in spiritual issues. A few years later, after having gone through immense spiritual struggles (perhaps of a psychotic nature), he started to exhort and soon became a regular Non-Conformist preacher. During the Restoration, Non-Conformist preaching was outlawed, and consequently, as Bunyan refused to abandon his calling he was incarcerated for a long period (about twelve years) wherefrom he started to write (although *The Pilgrim's Progress* was written after his release from prison). Apparently, the jail authorities were not very strict and allowed him to continue his reading and even to preach on occasion. He was released when the laws against Non-Conformist preaching were abolished.[54] During all this time Bunyan devoured books (and committed to paper his own thoughts in return). He read mostly everything, popular books of adventure, the Bible, and, significantly, the popular literature of the English Puritans,[55] which shaped his moral character as a devout Puritan and turned his masterpiece into one of the flagships of the Calvinist spirit, especially in its English-Puritan form. In turn, *The Pilgrim's Progress* was read by every man, woman, and child who

---

[52] Gutenberg put his famous gear in motion in 1452; he did not invent any new technology, but rather combined the well-known methods of paper production, the preparation of oil-based ink, and the handling of a wine press. The heart of the press was a type tray in which the letters, made of hard material and smeared with the ink, were prearranged for repeated printing. It is not clear how much credit for this combination is due to Gutenberg, especially since Dutch and other printers seem to have invented similar devices at approximately the same time, and other devices of a similar purpose were imported from the Far East in the thirteenth century. Whatever is the proper attribution of this invention, it is clear that before Gutenberg's machine was set in motion the "printing revolution" had not begun.

[53] Bunyan wrote his novel between 1678 and 1684. It is available in countless editions and inspired a large number of other artists in various artistic genres, notably Ralph Vaughan Williams' majestic opera bearing the same title.

[54] For a nutshell history of Bunyan's spiritual development, see the introductory note to *The Pilgrim's Progress*, edited by Charles Eliot, Cambridge, MA: Harvard University Press (1937).

[55] A notable example is John Foxe's important Protestant manifesto, *The Book of Martyrs*. The book was originally published in Latin in 1554 but was translated into English in 1563. It is now available in numerous editions, including the 1836 edition published by Hutchinson and Dwier. The book's subtitle, which speaks for itself, declares that it is a "History of the Lives, Sufferings, and Triumphant Deaths, of the Primitive as Well as Protestant Martyrs: From the Commencement of Christianity, to the Latest Periods of Pagan and Popish Persecution."

could master the art of reading, although not until the Romantic movement of the nineteenth century did it gain its current acclaim as a masterpiece of "high culture."

The Pilgrim's Progress is a Puritan tale of men and books. It tells the saga of a doomed person, called Christian, who slowly discovers the road to salvation. He is continuously confronted by sinful characters who attempt to lead him astray and guide him to sin. At a certain point Christian meets Mr. Worldly Wiseman, who observes the heavy burden on Christian's back and asks for an explanation. Christian explains that he is burdened by a book he is holding. And then Worldly Wiseman says:

I thought so; and it so happened unto thee as to other weak men, who meddling with things too high for them, do suddenly fall into thy distractions; which distractions do not only unman men . . . but they run them upon desperate ventures, to obtain they know not what.

Christian's soul was foully contaminated by what he read, suggests Worldly Wiseman, but the situation is not beyond repair; it is a blemish that the Law can ingeniously heal:

Why in yonder Village (the village is called Morality) there dwells a Gentleman whose name is Legality, a very judicious man . . . that has skill to help men off with such burdens as thine are from their shoulders.

Worldly Wiseman's advice is soon proved wrong, however, as Christian observes that Legality dwells on Mount Sinai, a clear allusion to the Mosaic Faith, and, I think, perpendicularly to the Anglican Church of Bunyan's own days. Christian's predicament is finally solved by the appearance of the Evangelist, whose true book assists Christian to find his way to salvation. All this is in the text itself. More subtextually one cannot help feeling that the forces of evil are guiding Christian from image to image, from swamp to mountain to meadows to water; he also encounters a set of human characters (like Worldly Wiseman) who are really stereotypical images of personality traits. This voyage is undertaken with the intent of trapping his soul in mortal sin, but the pilgrim realizes that none of these images, human or inanimate, holds for him the key to salvation. Salvation is in the Word, and the Word is in the words of the Evangelist's book. Word, words, and salvation are thus united. The Reformation spells the downfall of the image and the triumph of the word.

Side by side with Bunyan's celebrated pilgrim, thousands of ordinary Europeans started to read, and the immutable dogmas of previous generations, emblazoned, as it were, in the *biblia pauperum* of frescoes, pieces of statuary, and stained glass windows were shattered to pieces by the nascent culture of the word. Carlo Ginzburg did a pioneering job by unearthing the story of one such ordinary citizen, a sixteenth-century miller from the Friuli (a region in the vicinity of Venice) who suffered persecution from the Roman Holy Office and then burned at the stake in 1601, one year before the entirely unrelated

Slade's Case.[56] Ginzburg's accomplishment is particularly interesting, because until recently historians failed to take an interest in the lives of ordinary folks and no records were kept of their destinies. Ginzburg's protagonist, Domenico Scandella, called Mennochio, had a penchant for reading books, and although he lacked the means to buy a large number of them (the record shows that he bought with his own money just one book in a Venetian fair), he did borrow several from numerous acquaintances; what he read was undoubtedly tempered in his mind by his own baggage of peasant oral traditions and folk beliefs, but even with these modifications, some of the unorthodox publications that came to his attention (e.g., the Koran) revealed to him a totally new universe; it was not easy for him to reconcile this new *corpus* of knowledge with what he was expected to think and to believe by the ruling sacerdotal elite. Mennochio then started to develop, on the basis of his repeated perusal of the texts and of his own interpretation, a profound skepticism concerning such dogmas as the Three Persons of the Trinity, the divinity of Christ, the virginity of Mary, the superiority of Christianity to other religions, and most of the sacraments. His sense of discovery was such that he insisted on imparting his new knowledge to his friends and acquaintances, and it was this careless yearning to share his discovery that brought him to the attention of the Holy Office. The inquisitors fully understood what was at stake and reacted accordingly. Mennochio was not alone in threatening the monopoly of the Church on dogmatic teaching (Giordano Bruno was also interrogated at the same time and famously suffered the same consequences). To fend off this danger, the pope himself, Clement VIII, intervened in the proceedings and suggested the death penalty. Although the inquisitors were by no means bloodthirsty[57] (the Roman Holy Office must not be confused with the much sterner Spanish Inquisition), they accommodated their vicar and ended the life of this humble and valiant reader of the Friuli. But his words lived on.

The stories of Bunyan's pilgrim and Mennochio's struggle against the Holy Office illustrate how the written, and especially the printed, word can undermine political authority and give rise to a whole array of personal liberties. The first conscious articulation of this link can probably be attributed to John Milton in his famous pamphlet *Areopagitica.*[58] When Charles I convened the

---

[56] Carlo Ginzburg, *The Cheese and the Worms, the Cosmos of a Sixteenth Century Miller*, translated by John and Anne Tedeschi, Baltimore, MD: Johns Hopkins University Press (1980; the Italian original was published in 1976).

[57] Ginzburg was able to research the history of Mennochio because the Roman Holy Office kept minute records of the entire proceedings, which were ostensibly needed to ensure due process, subject, of course, to the overarching policy of defeating heresy and protecting the integrity of the Church.

[58] John Milton, *Areopagitica* (Liberty Fund edition, 1999; the pamphlet was originally crafted as an actual address to the Long Parliament, but the address was never delivered, nor intended to be delivered. The pamphlet was published in 1644). The name of this imaginary address is taken from the name of an old Athenian institution called the Areopagus, which was a large court elected by all free Athenian citizens.

Long Parliament out of financial necessity, it immediately abolished, in 1641, the dreaded institution of the Star Chamber;[59] this was done primarily to curb royal arbitrariness, but the abolished institution was also used as a censor of printed materials, and its abolishment made the printing of books free from regulation for a while. This increased the number of published pamphlets from 22 in 1640 to 1,966 in 1642. In 1642 the Civil War began as Charles gathered an army against the parliamentary forces. He had some initial successes and parliament became alarmed at its own disunity and the effectiveness of the king's propaganda. To check these dangers, a new censorship of print was reinstated and parliament exercised a monopoly over all printed matters. Milton abhorred this change and moved to address the Long Parliament with his celebrated essay. Milton was not successful in convincing the Long Parliament to restore uncensored publishing, but his essay continues to be a classic in the theory of free speech. His most celebrated reason for the abolishment of censorship concerns his deep conviction that false speech is bound to succumb to the more resilient properties of Truth, and thus suppressing it by arbitrary fiat apishly mimics the regressive institutions of Catholicism (the Inquisition, the Council of Trent, etc.) without accomplishing any redeeming social goal, thus:

And though all the winds of doctrine were let loose to play upon the earth, so Truth be in the field, we do injuriously by licensing and prohibiting, to misdoubt her strength. Let her and Falsehood grapple; who ever knew Truth put to the worse, in a free and open encounter?

As Vincent Blasi interestingly pointed out, one must resist the temptation to interpret this passage as a secularist advocacy of the "marketplace for ideas."[60] Milton was a deeply religious person, and his faith in the victory of worthy causes was grounded in his theology rather than in our own modern understanding of implicit markets.[61] No one can doubt, though, the far-reaching implications of his address or its ultimate political success in spite of its immediate failure. Milton's conviction, theological or otherwise, that the free use of words is closely associated with the other civil liberties, and its propagation is likely to spawn free human conduct overall, is clearly relevant to the rise of contract; this link becomes self-evident as we think of contract as a vehicle for the subordination of *centralized* legal ordering (the Star Chamber, the writs of

---

[59] The Star Chamber was an ancient political and judicial institution, but its bad reputation started under the tutelage of Chancellor Wolsey (1515–29). It became a symbol of the arbitrary exercise of the prerogative of the Crown as well as for its oppressive judicial procedures. Its abolishment by the Long Parliament was a triumph for the budding idea of the Rule of Law.

[60] This term posits the ahistorical notion of an invisible hand that weeds out individual aberrations in the service of the public welfare, a notion that was not developed until the end of the eighteenth century.

[61] Vincent Blasi, "Milton's Areopagitica and the Modern First Amendment," *Yale Law School Occasional Papers, Second Series*, Number 1 (2002).

action, and the entire array of image-oriented law) to the more finely attuned *private* ordering of individual pacts and agreements.

The most comprehensive treatment of the print revolution and its cultural and political implications was laid out, of course, in Elizabeth Eisenstein's pioneering study of this subject.[62] To give a sense of the proliferation of books after print, Eisenstein muses that their sheer number in the first half-century after Gutenberg's invention was substantially larger than the total number of books previously produced in more than a millennium. Since printers were commercial entrepreneurs, they could only function by relying on a broad readership that breached the traditional divide between patricians and plebs. In fact, many dignitaries of noble descent remained illiterate whereas thousands of commoners consumed the printed page in increasing numbers ever since the sixteenth century. Reading, holds Eisenstein, forever changed the thinking habits of the public. Before printing, she explains, the scarcity and cost of books made it necessary to commit information to memory. Memory had to rely on all kinds of mnemonic aids – the rhyme, the sign, and the image. Print rendered these devices redundant simply because not so much had to be committed to memory. The new freedom to dispense with mnemonic aids reinforced all sorts of iconoclastic tendencies, even if their initial drive was powered from other sources. Print, she continues the argument, destroyed the architecture of Gothic cathedrals, simply because their devotional function as the *biblia pauperum* could more reliably be replaced by the printed word. Even the pictorial properties of inscribed manuscripts (see Figure 49) had to be forever sacrificed, as the commercial exigencies of commercial print converged to standardized forms like Roman or Gothic characters, completely devoid of individual artistic imagery. Clearly, though, this efficient standardization in form made room for greater diversity in terms of substance. Literary works, like polemic speech, although printed in uniform characters, displayed, for the first time in many centuries, individual traits of the protagonists as well the personal, nonuniform touch of the speaker.[63] The speaker's audience, on the other hand, was better qualified to systematize the new form of printed information as well as to pass judgment on what they read, due to better tools (e.g., catalogs and indices, which were completely shunned by the scribal culture of the *scriptoria*).

It strikes me as a sensible hypothesis that this systematization of knowledge was partly responsible for the transformation of the law of *contracts*, numerous and yet finite, to the present doctrine of the law of *contract*, unitary and infinite in scope. To see how this process of unification and expansion of scope was

---

[62] Elizabeth Eisenstein, *The Printing Press as an Agent of Change*, New York: Cambridge University Press (1979). Eisenstein then moved on to abbreviate her scholarly two-volume set into a compact one-volume (highly readable) text entitled *The Printing Revolution in Early Modern Europe*, New York: Cambridge University Press (1983).

[63] A typical medieval literary character was a *commedia dell'arte* artist; all such characters were notorious for their uniformity. Eisenstein invokes the example of Montaigne as a hero for breaking these medieval stereotypes and introducing into his polemic discourse with his readers the unique and idiosyncratic (especially of himself).

facilitated by the invention of print, I would like to draw once again on an example discussed in Eisenstein's masterpiece. In the Middle Ages, the famous *Digesta* of Justinian, which purportedly served as the cornerstone of all European law, was kept behind bars in Pisa and could only be viewed through a system of grates. Print allowed for the first time physical access to this primary source of law, and indexed scientific editions, which soon proliferated, allowed legal scholars to systematize their otherwise fragmentary treatment of the law; had the former law of *contracts* remained in its diffuse form, rather than matured into an abstract *corpus* of unitary rules, it would have been very surprising indeed.

Whereas scribal culture protected knowledge by hiding perishable texts from the corrupting handling of the public, print culture protected knowledge by disseminating as many copies as possible to the largest number of users. The Common Law system as we know it today could not have moved forward in its historical course if precedents were either oral or inscribed on parchment, and for this reason alone it is hard to conceive how, and by what process, *Slade's Case* could have come to fruition in a scribal environment. Eisenstein contends that both the Renaissance and the Reformation could not have transpired without print. Her claim is reinforced when we examine a variety of other cultures that traditionally resisted print and compare their achievements to those of the various "print cultures."[64] In Europe, at any rate, the Quattrocento accomplished what former attempts of revival (the so-called "Carolingian Renaissance" and that of the twelfth century) failed to achieve, because antiquity, the fuel of Quattrocento humanism, was viewed "from a distance," a

---

[64] A prime example that comes to mind is Islamic culture, once the principal pillar of knowledge and scientific progress across the universe. But Islamic culture was not really oriented to the inscribed word, let alone to the printed word. The Koran, the "mother of books," was recited before it was written and continues to be recited even today, committed to memory, and its sound, rather than the shape of its letters (or even its ideas) has a profound influence on Islamic cultures. Oral traditions also played a major role in the teaching of Islamic philosophy or theoretical gnosis as teachers would impart to their disciples traditions that pass from generation to generation without ever being committed to writing ("the white parts" of the page). Some of the masters couched their writing in a deliberately difficult language to fend off uneducated challenges and imparted their full intentions by oral lessons only to those whom they judged to be worthy of their instruction. See Seyyed Hossein Nasr, "Oral Transmission and the Book in Islamic Education: The Spoken and the Written Word," in George Atiyeh (ed.), *The Book in the Islamic World*, Albany: State University of New York Press, p. 57 (1995). The history of printed books in the Islamic world is analyzed in admirable detail by Mushin Mahdi. Whereas copied manuscripts were held in high esteem in the medieval Islamic world and so were the scribes who toiled in these fields, the printing revolution, when it finally transpired, did not spread to this civilization until the second half of the nineteenth century and the beginning of the twentieth. Mahdi claims that the main reason for this attitude was the fear of the Islamic establishment that printers were taking liberties with texts that stood in sharp contrast to the loving care given to the same texts, primarily the Koran, by the scribes. European printers were also considered vulgar in their faulty sense of calligraphy and despised for their lack of discriminating taste with the language and some of its cultural undertones. See Muhsin Mahdi, "From the Manuscript Age to the Age of Printed Books," in George Atiyeh (ed.), *The Book in the Islamic World*, p. 1.

synoptic view that could not have relied on pictorial images alone. It needed mapping, documents, texts, and works of reference to gain a better view of the project. The case of Protestantism is even more obvious. Had it not been for printing, Luther's 95 "propositions" would have still been hung on his church doors, in Latin, and a cumbersome breed of Latin it was. The massive printing, translation, and dissemination of these propositions ended the hegemony of the priestly monopoly on Truth and opened the gate for individual lawmaking. By breaking the neck of a political structure that monopolized all lawmaking, the Reformation, assisted by print, made contract such an effective and attractive method of private ordering.

The Russian story followed an entirely different route. According to Bernard Pares, at the initiation of the October Revolution only 25 percent of the adult population in European Russia was literate, and the corresponding figures in Siberia and in the Russian territories in Central Asia were 15 percent and practically zero.[65] How could this come to pass?

We are used to thinking of Russian literature as one of the richest treasures of human civilization. It is also a fact, however, that this inexhaustible source of literary artistry is of a relatively recent lineage, and even as it finally came into full bloom, millions of Russians were not qualified to enjoy it, and even if they mustered some reading skills, they used them for the consumption of an entirely different kind of printed material. But let us start from the beginning. It all began even before the baptism of old Rus', when the two scholarly brothers Cyril (827–869) and Methodius (826–884) were sent from Thessalonica to Christianize the heathen Slavs and invented for their convenience an entirely novel set of characters that eventually developed into the Cyrillic alphabet. This alphabet became the building blocks for a liturgical language called Church Slavonic. Both the language and its alphabet were adopted in Russia. Cyrillic became the alphabet of the Russian vernacular. However, all written language was not only written with these characters, but actually phrased in Church Slavonic until late in the seventeenth century.[66] This made the liturgy more accessible to both the clergy and the laity, compared to the use of Latin in the West by members of the congregation who did not master that language. But both the Cyrillic script and Church Slavonic dealt a mortal blow to serious learning and, indeed, to the possibility of perusing a written text: Greek, Latin, and the European vernacular languages remained out of bounds even for Russians with scholarly inclinations, as virtually none of them could read another alphabet or understand another language. Robbed of the linguistic tools to dip into European written scholarship, early Russian literature remained in a humble state for many centuries. [67] D. S. Mirsky narrates the story from that point on.

---

[65] Bernard Pares, *A History of Russia*, New York: Knopf, p. 512 (1953).

[66] James Billington, *The Icon and the Axe*, London: Vintage, p. 5 (1970).

[67] D. S. Mirsky, *History of Russian Literature From Its Beginning to 1900*, edited by Francis Whitfield, adapting with a few changes a previous English version published in 1949, Chicago: Northwestern University Press (1958).

The written word, he says, was not familiar to ordinary Russians from firsthand sources, but only through the liturgy. Even the Bible, was not commonly known to the parishioners, with the possible exception of the Psalms, which were sung in the liturgy and memorized by rote. Next to the Bible the most authoritative texts were the Fathers, especially St. Chrysostom, and the most respected theologian was St. John of Damascus.[68] It is symptomatic that this primary theological authority, although inscribed in verbal signs, was obsessed with only one subject, the theological justification for the veneration of images. The old Russians derived from the Fathers not only their meager literary resources, but also their ideas about science and the shape of the natural world.

From the tenth century to the invasion of the Tartars in the middle of the thirteenth century, Kievan Rus' produced two, and only two, important literary works, *The Chronicles* and *The Campaigns of Igor*.[69] *The Chronicles* are annals of history, in all likelihood partly fact and partly unadulterated fiction, inscribed by bookmen and containing narratives varying in style and detail and spanning many generations. The original Kievan chronicles ceased to appear around 1200, but the tradition was continued in some other parts of the country, especially in the north. In Siberia it was carried on until the eighteenth century. Even more important is *The Word of the Campaign of Igor*. It was first discovered in manuscript form in 1795 (!), copied for Catherine the Great, but the original was later destroyed by fire. It is a unique genre of prose poetry, unconstrained by a line structure, and it is not clear whether it was originally sung or not. The work is a combination of a literary and patriotic-political oration, rather flamboyant in style, rich in imagery, and secular in approach. It is now (i.e., after its late discovery) familiar to every educated Russian. From the destruction of Kiev toward the middle of the thirteenth century to the unification of Russia under Ivan III, an austere literary silence fell on the whole of Russia. The first writer to have used the Russian tongue appeared on the scene in the last quarter of the seventeenth century. It was the autobiography of Avvakkum,[70] the famous Old Believer who resisted the liturgical reforms of the Orthodox Church[71] and was finally burned at the stake. In his account of his life struggle he employed a rich and colorful vernacular prose, which became a pillar of modern Russian literature. But this single volume was only

---

[68] The Saint's main book is *On the Divine Images*, translated by David Anderson, Crestwood, NY: St. Vladimir's Seminary Press (2000). Protected by an Islamic caliphate, St. John secluded himself from the world in a monastery in Palestine and wrote his polemic text in response to Emperor Leo III's iconoclastic policy. His main theological argument rests on the incarnation of Christ, which he interpreted as a mandate to use corporeal images as the icon of their prototype.

[69] Serge Zenkovsky edited and translated into English a convenient reader entitled *Medieval Russia's Epics, Chronicles and Tales*, New York: Penguin (1963), which includes the most important selections from *The Chronicles* and *The Campaign*.

[70] Archpriest Avvakkum, *The Life of the Archpriest Avvakkum by Himself*, translated by Jane Harrison and Hope Mirlees, London: L. and V. Woolf (1924; the Russian text was written in 1672–73).

[71] These reforms adopted the Greek liturgical model, e.g., by making the sign of the cross with three fingers rather than two and saying alleluia three times rather than only twice.

an early harbinger of things to come. The rich flow of literary works commonly thought of as "modern Russian literature" only started by the second half of the eighteenth century.[72] The recognized "founder" of modern Russian literature, Alexander Pushkin, was born in 1799; he and his great followers were all the children of the nineteenth century. The sheer paucity of literary materials in an accessible language and readable script throughout the formative period of contract law may have contributed to the fixation of the Russian mind on image-oriented thought formations[73] and retarded the development of commercial and contractual practices.

An additional, perhaps not less significant factor was the high illiteracy rate until recent times. This situation lingered on long after Russian literature became such a glaring example of literary excellence. To be sure, numerous Russian members of the nobility or intelligentsia were fluent in reading, often in several languages, for a couple of centuries before the Revolution. But the great bulk of the Russian nation was largely illiterate. The story of their gradual acquaintance with the written and then printed word started only in 1861, after the liberation of the serfs by Czar Alexander II.[74] During the five or six decades separating the liberation of the serfs and the October Revolution, primary schooling became accessible for the first time to the masses, and many common folks wished to take advantage of this opportunity, because they wanted to acquire some reading skills; however, most students did not stay in school for more than one or two years, which was deemed sufficient to give them the skills they wanted. In 1883, some 40 percent of primary schools were run and financed by the *zemstvos* (representative forms of local government, current between 1864 and 1917) although peasant communities assisted the enterprise by providing nonmonetary support, for example, by maintenance of school structures or paying instructors in kind. Elementary as this school system has been, it was by no means universal. As late as 1915, on the eve of the Revolution, only 58 percent of European Russian children and about 51 percent of all children throughout the empire ever attended school. Those who attended school learned rudimentary reading, but the traditional beliefs about the world that were instilled in them by their parents and associates were only minimally affected. Most schoolchildren, for instance, heard about the alleged existence of God but had only a fleeting sense of His noncorporeal attributes. Some thought that He was His image in icons, the local priest, or St. Nicholas the Wonderworker.[75]

Book printing was mainly undertaken by commercial, profit-seeking entrepreneurs who were keenly attuned to the mores of the time and to the

---

[72] For fuller details concerning the earlier literary sources in Russia, see Mirsky, ibid.

[73] Mirsky, ibid., p. 23, reports that one of the chief recorders of the so-called "times of trouble" (1604–13) (for a brief description of that historical period see Chapter 6, supra), Ivan Timofeyev, never called anything by its proper name, but only by its pictorial description. For instance, a river is "the element of watery nature" and the rich are "those who have large receptacles."

[74] Jeffrey Brooks, *When Russia Learned to Read*, Princeton, NJ: Princeton University Press (1985).

[75] Ibid., pp. 54ff.

leanings of their peasant and urban working-class clientele. The common folks were not interested in genuine nineteenth-century Russian *belles-lettres* (Chekhov, Tolstoy, etc.), although all these treasures were often available to them at subsidized rates (which were, however, more expensive than the cheap pamphlets of rudimentary fiction that were peddled to them on the street). The most popular form of folk literature of the period was called "*lubok,*" or "*lubki*" in the plural, meaning popular prints. Tracing the history of the *lubok* literature (as well as newspaper serials, women tales, and detective stories) is a good strategy (undertaken by Jeffrey Brooks) for detecting the changing mores among lower-class Russians – from undivided allegiance to the czar and the Orthodox church, imbued with traditional submissiveness, superstition, xenophobia and determinism, to more Western-like ideas such as individualism, faith in one's initiative, and a growing admiration of the foreigner.[76]

The image tradition dominated in many ways the *lubok* literature, especially in its earlier versions. It usually started with pictorial illustrations including a printed explanatory line. This line has in all likelihood been the first printed words ever to access many homes. Later the text expanded, giving room for lower-class authors to draw on their own life experiences and on popular culture, and finally to indulge in works of fiction of their own. *Lubok* fiction was usually told about a limited number of subjects, corresponding, as it were, to the stereotypic imagery of the readers about the possible range of possibilities. The most frequent examples drew on such images as folklore, chivalrous works, instructive literature, and tales about merchants. Banditry, science, crime and romance followed later on. Many such tales utilized familiar themes and modified them in conformity with popular taste. A typical modified folklore tale that was very favorably received by the public is *The Tale of Ivan the Knight, His Fair Spouse Svetlana and the Evil Wizard Karachun.* It recycles the story of a king who had three sons. He ordered them to shoot their arrows and marry the woman who captured them. Two sons aimed at women of the gentry, but the third son, Ivan, shot into a bog and the arrow was captured by an old hag. He did not wish to marry her but she threatened to inhale him in the quagmire if he should not. This convinced him to change his mind. She was then revealed to him as a beautiful princess enchanted by a wizard. She could only be delivered by lawful marriage to a prince. He took her home and had a hard time convincing his father to give his consent to the hag. Her secret was revealed prematurely, which made her disappear with the desperate lover in chase. He finally rescues her from a remote land. Many found fault with this corrupted version of a well-known lyrical fairy tale, but the public adored it and it was consequently printed in a large number of *lubok* publications.[77]

The constant interchange of ideas with the West during this period brought winds of change to Russia. Some were clearly reflected in the popular literature of the time, but always with a Russian twist. I will end this survey by mentioning

---

[76] Ibid., Introduction.
[77] Ibid., pp. 66ff.

one instructive example, the attitude to the concept of authority.[78] The erstwhile superstitious *muzhik*, prone to a life of submission and unquestioning allegiance to his superiors, was transformed to a more enlightened citizen of a more individualistic body politick. At the beginning of the twentieth century, freedom and rebellion emerged as the number one theme, reflecting the erosion of the concept of authority and the preparatory steps to the great Revolution. The new literature came in clusters devoted to stereotypical characters of this variety, the main one being the "bandit," a freedom-loving individual who rebels against authority and wishes to access the mainstream of society on his own terms. Akin to the character of the bandit, the *vor* (a general term for a thief or an outlaw), was also very popular. Bandits and *vors* were commonly associated with the supernatural, and wizards and witches often visited their carnal gatherings, not infrequently amidst thunderous storms and other manifestations of the supernatural forces that (as everyone believed) really dominate our lives. Bandits often feasted lavishly, and descriptions of these fierce and bawdy events abound. The interesting point to consider, however, is the marked difference between the emerging character of the popular Russian bandit and his literary counterpart in the West. Whereas the Robin Hoods of the West often engage in their unlawful occupations in vindication of some higher social cause, no such claim is made by the literary character of the Russian bandit, even if the corresponding historical characters that served as their prototypes (e.g., Stenka Razin)[79] could easily be identified with the great cause for which they fought and sacrificed their lives. By being assigned this self-regarding role, the literary Russian bandit became associated, in the eyes of his mesmerized public, with the devil himself, and the popular writers normally left him with only two options: either to repent for his wrongdoing, fight for the czar, and show his patriotism, or else be harshly punished for his revocation of authority and ultimately die in ignominy.[80] The public started to read but continued to be haunted, behind the transparent veil of words, by the ancient visions of yore.

I would like to end this chapter by adding a speculation about the reason (or at least an additional reason) for the retardation of meaningful print in Russia and for its failure to generate durable social effects as it did in the West. In the early years, the printing of books in Russia had been undertaken by the autocratic government, as part of the Petrine revolution of the eighteenth century. Its aim was not the dissemination of letters, and certainly not the propagation of dissent or free thinking. It was harnessed to the official goals of the government and was very harshly censored from the political point of view. As Gary Marker shows in an excellent book devoted to this subject, at a certain point the

---

[78] See Chapter 4, supra.

[79] Stenka Razin (1630–1671) was a Cossack leader who rebelled against the czarist government as a reaction to the heavy taxes and conscription duties imposed on the peasant population during the long and expensive war against Poland (1654–67). Although temporarily victorious, Razin was finally apprehended by the czarist army, tortured, and put to death. This lawless champion of the people was often immortalized in music, theatre, and literary tales.

[80] Brooks, ibid., pp. 166ff.

government decided to opt out of the book-printing business, largely because of its onerous financial consequences (it comes as no surprise that government publications are not an economically viable enterprise). The vacuum created by the exit of the government was filled by the intelligentsia, as far as "real" high-brow literature was concerned, and the government was content to recede to the role of an active, sometimes a hyperactive, censor. This active censorship created a barrier between the high-brow publishing sector, which was mainly designed to cater to a thin elitist group within the intelligentsia, and the broader walks of the general public; the publication of high-quality books did not spill over from the intellectual to the political arena.[81] What was left for the public to read was the pale concoction of the popular literature of the period, which was evidently too frail a catalyst to generate a meaningful social transformation. Not until the Communist rise to power, when the Gorkys or the Mayakovskys of the time served with their literary or poetic idiom the political goals of the regime, was the time ripe to allow the general public to consume some literary works of real enduring value.[82]

[81] Gary Marker, *Publishing, Printing, and the Origins of Intellectual Life in Russia, 1700–1800*, Princeton, NJ: Princeton University Press (1985).

[82] The consequences of this relative freedom, even if is dispensed to ostensible supporters of the regime, were not tardy in appearance. The early Stalinist *apparatchiks* did not plan on a Yevtushenko as a follower of Mayakovsky or on the transformation of the world musical scene by the genius of Shostakovitch. The free indulgence with the printed word was proven, once again, as an extremely perilous occupation.

Conclusions

The Russian nation has always borrowed large ideas from the West. The Ortho-dox faith came from Byzantium. Literature, drama, dance, architecture, cin-ematography, political thought, science, and technology were all stirred by foreign inspiration. Even the two greatest Russian revolutions, the Petrine upheaval and the October Revolution, drew on European sources for guidance and leadership. But none of these cultural achievements entirely mimicked their source of inspiration.[1] Russian devotional sentiment sharply swerved from its pan-Orthodox prototype. Russian literature is uniquely associated with the cultural environment that sprouted it. Russian icons sharply part with their severe Byzantine sources and borrow their unique coloration from their sur-rounding northern and often pagan imagery. Even when a deliberate attempt was undertaken to reflect, as if by a mirror, the European example (consider the architecture of St. Petersburg), the resulting outcome assumed pronounced local characteristics; Russia proved its originality in spite of herself.[2]

The reason is straightforward. When new ideas migrate to any foreign land they are not simply pumped into a vacuum. They always interact with the local conditions. The modified product is born of a mixed parentage and does not mimic any of its original ingredients. This universal phenomenon is particu-larly obvious in the case of the Russian culture, whose rich local hue almost instantly colors, for better or for worse, all the imported ideas. Writing in 1947, Arnold Toynbee had an inkling of what was afoot when he published his article, "Russia's Byzantine Heritage," in which he portrays Russia as the victim, rather than as the aggressor, in her history-long encounter with the

---

[1] The intricate interplay between Western ideas and the notion of "Russianness" runs like a red thread throughout Orlando Figes' thoughtful culture-historical study, *Natasha's Dance, a Cultural History of Russia*, New York: Metropolitan Books (2002).

[2] This perennial transformation of borrowed ideas to an original cultural idiom was stressed by James Billington in his two main popular books on Russian cultural history, *The Icon and the Axe* (1970) and *The Face of Russia* (1999).

West. According to Toynbee, what is called the "westernization" of Russia, and in particular the adoption of Western technology, was merely the adoption of the minimally indispensable measures that were necessary to fend off the aggressor. Thus, Russia's westernization ought to be interpreted, according to his line of reasoning, as a means to preserve her oriental heritage against the advancing Western foe, rather than as an independently chosen way of life.[3] For Toynbee, then, there is nothing genuinely occidental in Russian history, and the thin veneer of Western culture is nothing but a shield to protect the oriental core. One could take issue with Toynbee's historical outlook, which views the entire state of Russian culture from a victim's perspective. But he did correctly perceive the existence of an ingrained element in the Russian national character that metamorphoses imported models of thought into something of an entirely different ilk.

Half a century later, Oleg Kharkhordin offered another plausible explanation. The thesis of his book[4] is that the Communist regime prepared its subjects for a fierce and unique brand of individualism, which vigorously manifested itself after its collapse. The regime constantly demanded that people think about themselves, be "in touch" with their own lives, in order to steel their character for the purpose of becoming more self-conscious and loyal Soviet citizens. To facilitate this personal transformation, the regime sponsored countless party meetings and other public gatherings, where the participants were expected to prostrate themselves for public scrutiny, to become available for peer inspection, and to voluntarily adopt the necessary strategies for change and "amelioration." However, this brand of Soviet individualism lacked most of the characteristic features of its Western counterpart, such as the dignity of the person, the right of privacy, and a clearly demarcated public-private divide. These latter meanings of the term "individualism" are unique to the West and stem from old cultural practices, which have no parallel roots in Russian culture. I find Kharkhordin's analysis fascinating because he had the good sense to distinguish between what the Soviets called "individualism" and the meaning of this term in occidental lands. The word "individualism" itself is nothing but an empty cabinet, and it can assume the particular properties of a given cultural trope only in conjunction with its own holistic traditions. Kharkhordin's conclusion falls in line with the major tenet of this book that the failure of contract in modern Russia is occasioned by a deficiency in the cultural foundations that gave rise to it in the West, and that the importation to Russia of such superficial artifacts as contract legislation, contract vocabulary, or public declarations about the market economy, securitization or privatization, are not sufficient as a method of modifying the contractual culture itself.

---

[3] The article was originally published in a periodical called *The Atlantic Monthly* and later reissued in Arnold Toynbee, *Civilization on Trial* and *The World and the West* (bound together in one volume), Nashville, TN: World Publishing (1958).

[4] Oleg Kharkhordin, *The Collective and the Individual in Russia*, Berkeley: University of California Press (1999).

I find two faults with Kharkhordin's analysis, however, and this book seeks to fill its voids. His principal oversight lies in assigning such a major role in his theory to the conditioning effect of Soviet history. As this volume strives to demonstrate, the rift between Russia and the West is of a much older lineage, and the Soviet episode cannot be blamed for cultural characteristics that lingered on for a thousand years. If I am right in this observation, the downfall of Communism is not likely to cause a profound spiritual change in the destiny of the nation, unless it will be followed by a radical transformation of the underlying cultural substrata. The second problem with Kharkhordin's theory concerns his single-pronged analysis of the concept of individualism. In this volume I argue that the particular meaning assigned in a given culture to the concept of individualism has an important role to play in understanding the culture's overall characteristics, just as Kharkhordin professes. But individualism is not the *only* relevant variable. A full-blooded social configuration must be based on a much larger set of considerations. Besides the rich traditions that gave rise to an individualistic ethos in the West, I draw attention to at least five additional comparable traditions that revolutionized Western culture. Chapter 2 focuses on the humanist movement of the European Renaissance that created, or at least imagined to have created, an anthropocentric universe unparalleled in its intensity anywhere else in the world. Chapter 4 records the slow erosion of the concept of authority in Western culture and the resulting delegation of political power to individual actors. Chapter 5 highlights the Reformation's high esteem of personal and congregational wealth. Chapter 6, the penultimate, examines the empirical and rational revolution of the proto-modern West. The last chapter deals with the rise of the written and then the printed word in Western culture and the concomitant attrition of the former image culture. I argue that Western contract earned its high-profile status due to the integration of all these principles, deeply and securely, within the fabric of Western culture; by the same token, I show that the entire array of humanism, individualism, crumbling authority, the drive to accumulate worldly riches, epistemic beliefs based on science and rationality, and the triumphant rise of the word was not well received in Russia. When at long last all these cultural ideas started to move along the arduous migration path into Russian territory, the move may have been too tardy, too lily-livered, and altogether futile and wane.

This book does not make recommendations. If Russia wants Western contract, she must be "like" the West. She ought to renounce her own traditions and, for the first time in her history, import foreign ideas without tampering with them. If Russia should take this path, she might be successful in mimicking the West and instituting contract, and all the civic and commercial institutions that come in its wake; but in doing so she might cease to be attuned to her own historical definition. If Russia wishes to keep its allegiance to her own history and to forego contract, or else to become a contractual and corporate nation but sacrifice her traditional, and extremely spiritual, historical calling, is not for me to say.

List of Credits

Chapter 1

Figure 1: Evgeni Vuchetich, Pavel Fridman, Grigori Postnikov, and Pyotr Yatsyno, *We Swear to You, Comrade Lenin* (detail), photo by the author, taken from Matthew Cullerne Bown, *Art under Stalin*, Holmes & Meier, New York, 1949, location unknown.

Figure 2: Modern iconostasis, Greek Catholic Melkite Church of the Annunciation, Jerusalem, early twentieth century. Photo by the author.

Figure 3: Kazimir Malevitch, *White on White*, 1918, Museum of Modern Art, New York. Digital image © The Museum of Modern Art/Licensed by Scala/Art Resource, New York.

Figure 4: Kazimir Malevitch, *Black Square*, circa 1923–30, Musée National d'Art Moderne, Centre Georges Pompidou, Paris. Photo credit: CNAC/MNAM/Dist. Réunion de Musées Nationaux/Art Resource, New York.

Figure 5: *Man with a Mole* (a Fayyoum "portrait"), circa 130–50 A.D., The Metropolitan Museum of Art, New York. Photo credit: The Metropolitan Museum of Art, New York.

Figure 6: Theophanes the Greek, *Dormition of the Virgin*, late fourteenth century, Tretyakov Gallery, Moscow. Photo credit: Scala/Art Resource, New York.

Figure 7: *Boris and Gleb*, mid-fourteenth century, State Russian Museum, St. Petersburg. Photo credit: © The State Russian Museum/Corbis.

Figure 8: *St. George and the Dragon*, an early fifteenth-century icon from the Novgorod School, Tretyakov Gallery, Moscow. Photo credit: Bildarchiv Preussischer Kulturbesitz/Art Resource, New York.

Chapter 2

Figure 9: Leonardo da Vinci, *Vitruvian Man*, circa 1492, Accademia, Venice. Photo credit: Scala/Art Resource, New York.

Figure 10: *Last Supper* (with Judas depicted in profile). Monastery of Sts. Sergius and Bacchus, Malula, Syria. Photo credit: Liturgical Press, Collegeville, MN (from the book *The Icon* by Mahmoud Zibawi, 1993).

Figure 11: *Martyrs of Sebaste*, Church of the Forty Martyrs of Sebaste, Homs, Syria, seventeenth century. Photo credit: Liturgical Press, Collegeville, MN (from the book *The Icon* by Mahmoud Zibawi, 1993).

Figure 12: *Our Lady of Vladimir*, early twelfth century, Tretyakov Gallery, Moscow. Photo credit: Scala/Art Resource, New York.

Figure 13: Vladimir Grigorenko, *Our Lady of Vladimir*, a recent icon in the old tradition. Credit: © Vladimir Grigorenko.

Figure 14: Theophanes the Greek, *The Transfiguration of Christ*, early fifteenth century, Tretyakov Gallery, Moscow. Photo credit: Scala/Art Resource, New York.

Figure 15: Giovanni Bellini, *The Transfiguration of Christ*, 1460, Civico Museo Correr, Venice. Photo credit: Scala/Art Resource, New York.

Figure 16: Mikhail Cheremnykh and Victor Deni, Poster, "Comrade Lenin Cleanses the Earth of Scum," 1920, Russian State Library, Moscow. Credit: © Russian State Library.

Chapter 3

Figure 17: Filippo Lippi, *Annunciation*, circa 1442, San Lorenzo, Florence. Photo credit: Scala/Art Resource, New York.

Figure 18: Sandro Botticelli, *Annunciation*, 1489–90, Uffizi, Florence. Photo credit: Scala/Art Resource, New York.

Figure 19: Byzantine manuscript (*Sacra Parallela*) (ninth century) showing a monk in the act of copying icons. Bibliothèque Nationale de France, Paris. Credit: Bibliothéque Nationale de France.

Figure 20: El Greco, *St. Luke Painting the Virgin and Child from Life*, between 1560 and 1567, Benaki Museum, Athens. Credit: © 2003 by Benaki Museum, Athens.

Figure 21: Anonymous artist (claimed to be St. Luke), *The Virgin and Child Painted by St. Luke* (ostensibly an early twentieth-century canvass), Syriac Convent of St. Mark, Jerusalem, by permission of the Convent, photographed by the author.

Figure 22: Monk Gregory Kroug, *The Nativity of Christ*, twentieth century. Credit: St. Vladimir Seminary Press (from the book *The Icon* by Michel Quenot, 1996).

Figure 23: Georgii Kibardin, poster – "Lenin and the Airships," 1931, David King Collection, London. Credit: David King Collection, London.

Chapter 4

Figure 24: Cesare Ripa, *Spiritual Authority*, Hertel Edition, 1758–60. Credit: Dover Publications.

Figure 25: Duccio, *Presentation of Our Lord in the Temple*, 1311, Museo dell'Opera Metropolitana, Siena. Photo credit: Scala/Art Resource, New York.

Figure 26: Ambrogio Lorenzetti, *The Allegory of Good Government*, 1338–40, Siena, Palazzo Pubblico. Photo credit: Scala/Art Resource, New York.

Figure 27: Ambrogio Lorenzetti, *The Effects of Good Government in the City and in the Country*. Detail: *The Effects of Good Government in the City* (1338–40), Siena, Palazzo Pubblico. Photo credit: Scala/Art Resource, New York.

Figure 28: Ambrogio Lorenzetti, *The Effects of Good Government in the City* (detail: dancing citizens, 1338–40), Siena, Palazzo Pubblico. Photo credit: Scala/Art Resource, New York.

Figure 29: Ambrogio Lorenzetti, *The Effects of Good Government in the City* (detail: shops and commerce, 1338–40), Siena, Palazzo Pubblico. Photo credit: Scala/Art Resource, New York.

Figure 30: Ambrogio Lorenzetti, *The Effects of Good Government in the Country* (detail), 1338–40, Siena, Palazzo Pubblico. Photo credit: Erich Lessing/Art Resource, New York.

Figure 31: Sandro Botticelli, *The Calumny of Apelles*, 1495, Uffizi Gallery, Florence. Photo credit: Erich Lessing/Art Resource, New York.

Figure 32: Pietro da Cortona, *Ceiling Fresco with Divine Providence* (detail), 1633–39, Galleria Nazionale d'Arte Antica, Rome. Photo credit: Scala/Art Resource, New York.

Appendix to Chapter 4

Figure 33: The Fortress of Peter and Paul, St. Petersburg. Photo credit: Corbis.

Figure 34: The Hare Island Jail: Main corridor leading to inmates' cells (photography by the author).

Figure 35: Ivan Vladimirov, *Execution of Workers in Front of the Winter Palace in St. Petersburg, 9 January 1905*. Central Revolutionary Museum, Moscow. Photo credit: Snark/Art Resource, New York.

Chapter 5

Figure 36: Gerard Dou, *Old Woman Reading*, 1630–40, Rijksmuseum, Amsterdam. Credit: Rijksmuseum, Amsterdam.

Figure 37: Jan Van Eyck, *Giovanni Arnolfini and His Wife Giovanna Cenami*, 1434, National Gallery, London. Photo credit: National Gallery, London.

Figure 38: Adriaen Van Ostade, *The Alchemist's Shop*, 1661, National Gallery, London. Photo credit: National Gallery, London.

Figure 39: Gabriel Metsu, *Vegetable Market in Amsterdam*, early 1660s, Louvre, Paris. Photo credit: Réunion des Musées Nationaux/Art Resource, New York.

Figure 40: Jean-Honoré Fragonard, *The Swing*, 1766, Wallace Collection, London. Photo credit: Alinari/Art resource, New York.

Figure 41: Cesare Ripa, *Dolor*, Hertel Edition, 1758–60. Credit: Dover Publications.

Figure 42: *The Holy Face* icon, late twelfth century, Novgorod, Tretyakov Gallery, Moscow. Photo credit: Scala/Art Resource, New York.

Chapter 6

Figure 43: Leonardo da Vinci, *The Tree of Veins*, 1498–92, Windsor Castle, England. Copyright: The Royal Collection © HM Queen Elizabeth II.

Figure 44: Giorgione, *Old Woman ("Col Tempo")*, circa 1508, Accademia, Venice. Photo credit: Scala/Art Resource, New York.

Figure 45: Illuminated Psalter, The Last Supper and Christ Washing the Feet of His Apostles, 1210, Ms. 9/1695, fol. 23, French, 1210. Musée Condé, Chantilly, France. Photo credit: Giraudon/Art Resource, New York.

Figure 46: Masaccio, *The Holy Trinity*, 1427–28, Santa Maria Novella, Florence. Photo credit: Scala/Art Resource, New York.

Figure 47: Fra Bartolomeo, *The Entombment*, 1515, Galleria Palatina, Palazzo Pitti, Florence. Photo credit: Scala/Art Resource, New York.

Figure 48: Andrei Rublev, *The Holy Trinity*, 1425, Tretyakov Gallery, Moscow. Photo credit: Scala/Art Resource, New York.

Chapter 7

Figure 49: Circle of Cosimo Tura, *The Assumption of the Virgin*, 1470–80, Metropolitan Museum, New York. Photo credit: The Metropolitan Museum of Art, New York.

Figure 50: Pieter Brueghel the Elder, *The Wedding Dance in the Open Air*, 1566, The Detroit Institute of Art. Photo credit: The Detroit Institute of Art.

Figure 51: Pieter Saenredam, *View into the Ambulatory of the St. Bavo Church in Haarlem*, 1635, Gemaeldegalerie, Staatliche Museen, Berlin, Photo credit: Bildarchiv Preussischer Kulturbesitz/Art Resource, New York.

Figure 52: *The Triumph of Orthodoxy*, Byzantine, circa 1400, British Museum London. Photo credit: HIP/Art Resource, New York.

Index

1917 Revolution. *See* Russian Revolution